CIVIL DISOBEDIENCE
AND DEMOCRACY

ELLIOT M. ZASHIN

UNIVERSITY OF TEXAS, AUSTIN

Civil

Disobedience

and

Democracy

THE FREE PRESS, NEW YORK

COLLIER MACMILLAN LIMITED, LONDON

JC
328.3
.Z36

To my Father

Contents

PREFACE

My interest in civil disobedience was a product of the Berkeley milieu. I remember being exposed to this kind of protest for the first time when students from the University of California participated in civil rights sit-ins in San Francisco in the spring of 1964. Subsequently, I became involved in some of the activities generated by the civil rights, free speech, and antiwar movements on the campus. Gradually my interest focused on civil disobedience, and I discovered that, without being very conscious of it, I had begun to crystallize my views on the subject. I began researching and writing in 1965. Since then, radical activists have changed their orientation toward civil disobedience and nonviolent direct action, causing me to reconsider and revise some of my conclusions. As a result, I have had difficulty bringing this work to a close. While I do so now, I am not confident that events will not require further reconsideration of my views. Nonetheless, I hope that my analysis will help the reader place in context and evaluate any new developments in direct action tactics.

There are several people whose help I want to acknowledge. Foremost among them is John Schaar, who always gave me sound guidance and cheerful encouragement. The responsibility for the judgments made is, of course, mine, but this work owes much to his critical comments and suggestions. Thanks are also due to Michael Rogin and Hanna Pitkin, who read early drafts of several chapters, to Kenneth Dolbeare, for his valuable suggestions for revisions, to Jack Sando, who read some of the revised chapters, to James Rosenau for advice and encouragement on the final rewritings, and to Mmes. Tanquary, Woodlief, and McCann, who typed earlier drafts of the work. Finally, my wife Polly, who allowed herself to be coopted and then provided invaluable editorial assistance, deserves a special accolade.

Elliot M. Zashin
St. Paul, France

ACKNOWLEDGMENTS

Quotations from:

All About CORE (Pamphlet; Congress of Racial Equality, 1963). Reprinted with permission of CORE.

"Civil Disobedience," an Occasional Paper published by the Center for the Study of Democratic Institutions. Reprinted with their permission.

"Civil Disobedience in a Democracy," by Gene Sharp, in *Peace News* (February 22, 1963). Reprinted with permission of *Peace News*, 5 Caledonian Road, Kings Cross, London, N.1.

"Civil Disobedience: Philosophy and Tactics," Paper read at the Conference on Law Enforcement and Racial and Cultural Tensions, Berkeley, California, October 9, 1964, by Norman Jacobson. Reprinted by permission of the author.

"Civil Disobedience: Prerequisite for Democracy in Mass Society," Paper prepared for the 1966 Annual Meeting of the American Political Science Association, by Christian Bay. Reprinted by permission of the author.

"The Conditions of Direct Action in a Democratic Society," Paper prepared for the 1966 Annual Meeting of the American Political Science Association, by Donald Von Eschen, Jerome Kirk, and Maurice Pinard. Reprinted by permission of Donald Von Eschen.

"The Conditions of Direct Action in a Democratic Society," by Donald Von Eschen, Jerome Kirk, and Maurice Pinard, in *Western Political Quarterly*, Vol. XXII (June, 1969). Reprinted by permission of the University of Utah, copyright owners.

ACKNOWLEDGMENTS

"The Dangers of Mass Disobedience," by Charles E. Whittaker, in the *Kansas City Star* (July 25, 1965). Reprinted by permission of the Kansas City Star Co., copyright © 1965.

Democracy and Education, by John Dewey. Reprinted by permission of The Macmillan Company.

"The Essence and Ethics of Civil Disobedience," by Carl Cohen, in *The Nation* (March 16, 1964). Reprinted with their permission.

"Freedom as Politics," by Bernard Crick, in *Political Philosophy and Theory*, edited by Peter Laslett and W. G. Runciman. Reprinted with permission of the author and Basil Blackwell, Publisher.

The Ideology and Strategy of Direct Action: A Study of CORE, a Doctoral Dissertation submitted in the Department of Sociology, University of California, Berkeley, by Ingeborg Powell Bell. Reprinted by permission of the author.

Negroes and the New Southern Politics, by Donald R. Matthews and James W. Prothro, © 1966, by Harcourt, Brace & World, Inc. Reprinted with their permission.

The Negro Revolution in America, by William Brink and Louis Harris, Copyright © 1963 by Newsweek, Inc. and reprinted with the permission of Simon and Schuster, Inc.

Non-Violent Resistance, by Mohandas Gandhi, Copyright © 1951 by the Navajivan Trust and reprinted with their permission.

Obligation and the Body Politic, by Joseph Tussman. Reprinted with the permission of Oxford University Press.

Passive Resistance in South Africa, by Leo Kuper. Reprinted by permission of Yale University Press and Jonathan Cape Ltd.

Principles of Social and Political Theory, by Ernest Barker. Reprinted by permission of the Clarendon Press, Oxford.

"The Provocation of Violence: A Civil Rights Tactic?," by Jan Howard, in *Dissent*, Vol, 13 (January–February, 1966). Reprinted with permission of the author.

"The Psychosocial Meaning of Nonviolence in Student Civil Rights Activities," by Jacob R. Fishman and Frederic Solomon, in *Psychiatry*, 27:91–99 (1964). Reprinted by permission of The William Alanson White Psychiatric Foundation, copyright by The William Alanson White Psychiatric Foundation.

"Repressive Tolerance," by Herbert Marcuse, in *A Critique of Pure Tolerance*. Reprinted by permission of the Beacon Press, copyright © 1965 by Herbert Marcuse.

xii

ACKNOWLEDGMENTS

SNCC: The New Abolitionists, by Howard Zinn. Reprinted by permission of the Beacon Press, copyright © 1964, 1965 by Howard Zinn.

"Editor's Introduction," by Franz Neumann, in *The Spirit of the Laws* (pp. x, lxi), by Baron de Montesquieu. Reprinted by permission of the Hafner Publishing Company.

The Unexpected Revolution, by Paul Kecskemeti (Stanford: Stanford University Press, 1961) and reprinted with permission of the publisher.

Why We Can't Wait, by Martin Luther King, Jr. Reprinted by permission of Harper and Row, copyright © 1963, 1964 by Martin Luther King, Jr.

Acknowledgment is also made to T. M. Tomlinson for permission to quote from a personal communication.

CIVIL DISOBEDIENCE
AND DEMOCRACY

Introduction

When I first conceived the idea of this essay—over four years ago—civil disobedience[1] was still a relatively new phenomenon in this country. Civil rights demonstrators and student protesters were using it with some measure of success. The Automobile Row sit-ins in San Francisco in the spring of 1964, the Free Speech Movement sit-in at Berkeley in December of the same year, and the Selma civil rights march in the spring of 1965 were recent events. Although there were foreshadowings of more radical movements and tactics, these protest demonstrations seemed as radical as any that were attaining public visibility. Indeed, it was because civil disobedience appeared to have potential as an effective political technique that I became interested in studying it. What struck me was the possibility of legitimizing civil disobedience as a democratic tactic. Popular reactions to nonviolent direct action[2] were often negative. Yet civil disobedience seemed to be the answer to a recurrent political dilemma: minority groups with serious grievances were finding that conventional political techniques often were either not effective or not available. Civil disobedience enabled the basically *allegiant* citizen to continue his struggle for change where previously the failure of conventional techniques left him no alternative but begrudging acquiescence. Formerly, he appeared to have no choice but compliance with a law or policy he found objectionable—unless he dared question the basis of his allegiance to the polity.

Notes to this chapter will be found on page 6.

1

It seemed likely that conflicts between private convictions and political obligation were and would be common in our liberal-democratic polity for two reasons: because its ideals encouraged independent thought and freedom of conscience, and because the institutional bias of our politics seemed to favor those who opposed change. In other words, the system of separate but interacting levels of government and of branches within the federal government itself appeared to provide numerous points at which entrenched minorities could block change through the conventional channels. Moreover, radical dissenters and reformers have generally been isolated in America because the system has provided the majority of its citizens with considerable affluence. The groups which have had the greatest need for change generally have been relatively small minorities. Civil disobedience seemed to be a resolution of the conflicting tugs of private conviction and political obligation, a solution to the problem minority protesters faced when conventional channels afforded them no relief.

As I explored the ramifications of the relation between civil disobedience and liberal democracy, events in America raced on. Today the obituary of the "old" civil rights movement has been written; the assassination of Martin Luther King and the debacle of the Poor People's Campaign in the spring of 1968 impressed a sense of finality upon this stage of the "movement." Black Power advocates began to speak openly of using violence under certain conditions, and to recommend at least armed defense to ghetto dwellers. Riots in the ghettoes multiplied; while the majority of blacks still opposed violence, they also thought that riots had helped, that violence might be necessary to obtain improvements in their living conditions. As the student activists became more involved in anti-war protest and began to move off the campus, their tactics became more militant, more pugnacious. Direct action began to encompass violent tactics (usually not highly destructive). The outbreak of campus protests in the last three years has manifested much less of a nonviolent attitude than earlier student protest movements. Many members of the New Left see no point in accepting arrest and punishment for illegal acts of protest: why allow oneself to be penalized by a system which is rigged against those who dissent from it? Since radicals are already at a disadvantage, why compound it by playing the game according to the rules of non-violence? Such rules, they feel, only strengthen those in positions of power.

Perhaps the prevalence of protest during the heyday of the civil rights movement contributed nearly as much to the emergence of more radical movements as did the war, the virtual lack of progress in alleviating black poverty, and the slow pace of change in more traditional areas of civil rights activity, e.g., school desegregation, effective use of the franchise, and opportunities in white collar jobs and the professions. Perhaps the movements in which civil disobedience was an important weapon provided the impetus for more radical movements, mobilizing people who were then further radicalized by the course of events and by their experience in protest activity. Perhaps for a small minority, at least, civil disobedience made violent and obstructionist tactics thinkable, opening the way for their use. Or perhaps it was the failure of civil disobedience—as this minority saw things—that freed them from inhibitions on the use of violence.

For those who condemn civil disobedience, to suggest that it has somehow contributed to the kind of radical activity we are now witnessing is to blacken it even more. For those who looked to civil disobedience as a means of jogging a system worth saving into timely reform, its results are problematic: reform there has been, but concrete evidence of change in the lives of real people is not manifest. What the nonviolent protest movement did, in effect, was to create awareness of more intractable problems by its success in dealing with relatively superficial ones. The Supreme Court has handed down many liberal decisions in movement-related cases and there are more civil rights laws on the statute books; but almost 80 percent of southern black children still attend segregated schools (generally second-rate in quality), and *de facto* segregation is growing throughout the North. More black people than ever before are voting; but there is still a much higher incidence of poverty and unemployment among them, and the public has been treated to shocking revelations about the breakdown of learning in ghetto schools. Moreover, the politicians resist the evidence even when it is presented by the highly respectable Kerner Commission. Thus, the Poor People's Campaign created little response, the Freedom Budget remains stillborn, and despite Nixon's welfare innovations, many poor people, white and black, will not emerge from below the current poverty line. Even on the campus, where student protest movements have begun to have some impact on basic university policies (i.e., policies relating to student governance, admissions, and relations with government agencies and private enterprise), this has come about only after tactics were escalated, leaving strict nonviolence further and further behind. Thus, for those who do not think the system worth saving, civil disobedience has had its day; nonviolence is passé. Radical politics has reached beyond the philosophy of civil disobedience, and to many radical activists and student protesters the tactics of civil disobedience seem outmoded.

Despite the apparent rejection of civil disobedience and nonviolence by many members of the movements which feel the greatest need for unconventional political tactics, the justification of civil disobedience in a liberal-democratic framework has a rationale. The term is still being used a great deal—often without much precision—for example, to make invidious comparisons with the kind of protest tactics which are now being used. Some persons hold up a "pure" concept of civil disobedience—i.e., strictly nonviolent with no attempt to avoid the penalty—as the only tolerable form of "illegal" protest and even then consider it acceptable only when used under narrowly circumscribed conditions. While this view may make its holders comfortable, I find it highly inadequate: it fails to grasp the conditions which produced the nonviolent direct action movements of the late 1950s and early 1960s; its understanding of liberal-democratic principles seems simplistic; its awareness of the intensity of contemporary discontent and frustration appears limited; and its conception of what will solve our social problems superficial and unemphatic. If this "pure" concept is a representative view, and it seems quite possible that it is, I believe that the future will be even more punctuated by violent protest than we like to think.

There are two major audiences for the argument to be made here: (1) people who feel loyal and at home in this polity, for whom democracy as they understand and experience it—in thought and practice—retains meaning and viability; and (2) people who are troubled by contemporary trends in our democracy but are not ready to abandon our political institutions. The first group must be made to recognize that the disaffection and alienation of a significant number of Americans is a sign of malfunction in our political and social institutions. The fact that many other Americans do not feel the way they do about our society and our politics is a real matter for concern. It is hard to deny that American democracy is in trouble, even if one believes in its resiliency. The second group may find civil disobedience a partial solution to their dilemma— how to approach more closely to our social and political ideals without basically changing our institutions. A third audience I have *not* included are those persons who believe that radical change is the only way to save this nation from destroying itself. I am not confident that a liberal-democratic defense of civil disobedience speaks to them. For I seriously doubt whether liberal democracy is sufficiently viable in America to permit such change through nonviolent revolution. Civil disobedience does not appear to offer them a perspective or a tactic which is likely to achieve their goal. Greater popular acceptance of civil disobedience— its philosophy and its use—may help a little to bring the allegiant, the waverers, and even some of the disaffected closer together. Of course, such acceptance implies changes in existing attitudes: greater willingness to admit the seriousness of the current situation, less fear and condemnation of what is radical merely because it is labelled radical. Ultimately, acceptance of civil disobedience implies greater tolerance of overt social conflict, of change, of differences in attitudes and life styles, and a commitment to realizing liberal-democratic ideals, even if this means tangible personal sacrifices.

The chapters to come will explore a variety of questions about civil disobedience and nonviolent direct action. In Chapter I, I trace the historical development—in the realm of political ideas—which created the preconditions of modern civil disobedience. As further background, Chapter II contends that the defense of individual moral autonomy, a primary value of liberal-democratic theory, has manifested itself anew in civil disobedience. In Chapter III, I cull the writings of several political theorists—from Hobbes to the present—for the propositions which form the framework of the modern theory of civil disobedience. Chapter IV deals with the problems of defining civil disobedience, understanding how the tactic works, and justifying its exercise. I analyze and revise the definition and conception of civil disobedience formulated by various academic and legal commentators, which overemphasizes nonviolence and moral suasion. I try to support the contention that civil disobedience has often worked because it pressures, rather than converts, opponents. Finally, I attempt a rebuttal of many common criticisms of civil disobedience. Chapter V examines the theory and practice of contemporary civil disobedience and nonviolent direct action. Gandhi's ideas and his use of *satyagraha* are compared to the recent American experience in the civil rights movement and on college campuses. In Chapter VI, I continue the argument against the "appeal to the majority" view of civil disobedience, referring to the observations of social scientists and to public opinion polls. Chapter VII discusses the argument that civil disobedience is unjustified because conventional channels for political action are available to dissenters. I undertake to examine recent social science studies of political links between representatives and constituents and of grass-roots political action in order to question the validity of this argument. I then propose a role for civil disobedience and nonviolent direct action when conventional channels are not really available. In Chapter VIII, my concern is regime response in different political systems to civil disobedience (and more generally, to dissent and public protest). Are liberal democracies more tolerant of such action? Assuming they should be, can they afford to be more tolerant? In the final chapter, I assess the limits of civil disobedience and of political obligation within the American political system today. I examine the more extreme tactics which protesters are now employing and explore the implications which their demands hold for our society. Finally I ask whether liberal-democratic theory has anything to say in justification of these steps beyond civil disobedience.

Notes for Introduction

1. For the moment, it is sufficient to define civil disobedience as a non-violent violation of a public norm (generally regarded as legally binding) as a means of social or political protest. In Chapter V, I discuss the definition at some length.

2. The term refers generally to unconventional political tactics, some-times called "extra-parliamentary" to distinguish them from electoral competition, lobbying, and common techniques of influencing legislators or other public officials, e.g., letter-writing, propaganda. This broader category subsumes civil disobedience; it includes legal and illegal acts.

The Concept
of the
Democratic Citizen

ACTS OF CIVIL DISOBEDIENCE are not novel phenomena of the 19th and
20th centuries. They appear as far back in the history of western civiliza-
tion as the Greek legend of Antigone, immortalized by the playwright
Sophocles, and the early Christian martyrs. In the tragic dramas of
Thomas Becket and Thomas More, we again watch lonely individuals
defying the dictates of temporal rulers in order to remain true to the
dictates of a higher law. Yet these are isolated acts of heroic individuals.
Though their deeds are an inspiration even today, their relevance to
civil disobedience in liberal-democratic societies is questionable. Certainly, their disobedience raised important questions about the limits of
political obligation. Religious and political thinkers posed similar
questions to claims of absolute obedience during the Middle Ages and
the Reformation. What separates these heroic actions and this sometimes bold theorizing from the contemporary experience of civil disobedience is the context. Prior to our own times, such opposition often
drew its sustenance from a deeply rooted belief that man's spiritual
destiny should be immune from the claims of secular rulers. Although

Notes to this chapter will be found on pages 31–33.

the tradition of civil disobedience motivated by religious conscience has not altogether withered, it no longer is the primary source of energy and ideas. For religious justifications are not as persuasive as they once were, and the church-state controversy has been resolved, so that what remains is merely sporadic skirmishing along the boundaries of accepted constitutional principles. However, it is much more than secularization in this sense which is responsible for making early theory and practice of limited value to the student of civil disobedience. Rather, it is a profound change in the nature of the polity and the relation of the individual to political authority.

While civil disobedience remains an exceptional act, it no longer retains the rare, heroic quality it often had in ancient and medieval times. To practice it still requires courage and conviction, but one need not be extraordinary either in the strength of one's courage or the intensity of one's conviction. Because subjects often believed that rulers had divine sanction, defying secular authority was once virtually tantamount to defying God; few would run that risk unless extraordinarily sure of the overriding importance of their convictions. Today civil disobedience is the act of the citizen, or of the "subject" who projects himself empathically into the citizen's role. To transform civil disobedience from an extraordinary deed into the potential act of an ordinary citizen, it was necessary first to bring secular authority down from the heavens. But it appears that *much more was required*: that is, the emergence of the liberal-democratic polity, in which traditions of constitutionalism and of democracy were finally joined in a symbiotic relationship. Both streams of this ultimate confluence were essential: to oversimplify, liberal constitutionalism provided the notions of a government limited by law—by real regularized restraints—and of individual rights which government was established to protect; democracy contributed ideas of popular participation, popular sovereignty, and self-government.

Why are these conceptions the precondition for modern civil disobedience? Prior to the emergence of constitutional notions, only religious matters were asserted—by churchmen—to be beyond the state's purview. Liberal constitutionalism broadened the spectrum of human activity, thought, and belief which was properly outside the state's jurisdiction. Before democratic ideas were revived, the resistance of the religious believer had no connection with his being a member of the polity. While resistance had political implications—because it questioned the ruler's authority—it was not really a political act. The subject was not a legitimate political actor. The change in the nature of the polity made resistance a public act because the citizen, in resisting, made claims which were based on the nature of citizenship (or membership). In contrast, the resistance of religious believers was not potentially relevant to all members of the body politic. Typically, such resistance occurred when a religious minority was in conflict with a majority of different religious views.

The substantive concerns which motivate civil disobedience in modern times often arise within the sphere of individual autonomy, which liberal constitutionalism sought to protect from interference. Combining the basic constitutional notion—that government should be limited—with the basic premise of democracy—that the individual is a legitimate participant in governmental affairs—creates a legitimate role for the individual in checking government officials. Previously, subordinate magistrates were sometimes viewed as the proper defenders of laws and rights when the prince overstepped his authority; subjects had to hope that their magistrates would take the initiative. Liberal democracy not only makes the individual citizen a participant in this important function, it also permits him to initiate action. He can organize, assemble, petition, express his opinions, and make his recommendations. To be a participant, he must believe that it is his right to participate in government, that he has rights upon which it is not legitimate for government to infringe (at least, beyond certain limits), and that he is entitled to act in defense of those rights. Without these beliefs, civil disobedience is not really conceivable for the average citizen. Liberal democracy changed the subject's relation to authority, and it changed his perception of himself vis-à-vis government.

The development of liberal democracy is not a simple uniting of two bodies of political thought; at various points in history, we find different mixtures of the democratic and the liberal constitutional elements. For instance, constitutionalism originally contained no implications of self-government or popular participation; it meant the existence of a realm in which royal authority was not absolute, a distinction between *gubernaculum* and *jurisdictio*. Bracton, in the 13th century, asserted that in the former, the king had no peer: "his strictly governmental acts [were] beyond question."[1] The significance of *jurisdictio* was not so much what fell into this category as the notion that within this area, "there [were] bounds to the king's discretion established by a law that

[was] positive and coercive, and a royal act beyond these bounds [was] *ultra vires.*"[2] According to C. H. McIlwain, Sir John Fortescue's 15th century phrase "regimen politicum et regale," describing the English government, expressed the same distinction:

To Fortescue, as to Bracton, it means no more than a negative, legal limit to the king's government, formed by the rights of his subjects which the king has sworn to maintain, and which he cannot lawfully change or blemish or arbitrarily transfer from one to another.[3]

Thus, the realm of *jurisdictio* included the legal rights of English subjects; these evolved and accrued largely as part of the common law.

McIlwain traces the origins of constitutionalism even farther back in western history. It is sufficient here to note that, at least by the 15th century, the notion of limitations on political authority was linked to a concept of rights not subject to the ruler's absolute discretion. The problem was then, McIlwain says, to provide effective sanctions for these limitations on the royal will. It appears that the striving to secure rights provided the impetus which eventually linked constitutionalism with democracy. Although not so direct, the lines lead from the need for sanctions to protect rights to the demand for participation in governance—from private and civil rights to political rights. Then, via the extension, in theory, of rights to all men, they go from the liberal state of the middle classes to modern liberal democracy.

As McIlwain indicates, *gubernaculum* virtually absorbed *jurisdictio* in the early 16th century when "doctrines of almost unlimited obedience" prevailed: "Throughout the whole range of political literature there is probably no period in which obedience to kings is so stressed as [then]."[4] The 16th century was hardly devoid of a conception of disobedience; the early figures of the Reformation, including Luther and Calvin, rather uniformly asserted that when the secular ruler commanded anything inconsistent with God's law, the Christian was bound to disobey, for he must obey God rather than man. However, this was as far as they wished to qualify the duty to obey duly-constituted authority. Conscientious disobedience might be the Christian's highest obligation, but it could never justify armed resistance or rebellion. One had to endure punishment or, at most, seek refuge in flight,[5] for the duty to obey secular rulers was not a civil obligation but a religious one. Temporal authority was divinely ordained. However, the beleaguered minority position of the French Protestants engendered some rather different notions about authority. The Huguenot writers went beyond their Protestant forebears in espousing the right of forcible resistance, but their conception did not prevail. They derived temporal authority from God, but insisted that He conferred it only for the benefit of the people; thus, obedience was conditional upon its proper use. While not denying to any man the right to judge whether a ruler was a tyrant, they restricted the right to act on that judgment to the community, led by its official representatives. The private man was not to take action against the tyrant.

Nevertheless, perhaps because much of Europe was politically unsettled, the major concern of the thinkers of the 16th century was to shore up authority, not to justify disobedience to it:

In the first place was growing a sense of the need for recognition of a single will as supreme and endowed with power to make law absolutely: in the second the conception of this needed sovereign power as ordained and directly created by God as His agent for the welfare of society. The *princeps* in whom France was coming to believe . . . is not the *princeps* of Roman Law, a delegate with all the powers of the Sovereign people, but a King who owes his throne to God's arrangements and his powers to God's gift.[6]

In the latter part of the 16th century, this need for a strong central authority able to establish and maintain order in France was reflected in the writings of Jean Bodin. Bodin accepted the view that a tyrant by usurpation might always be legitimately resisted—a concession frequently made by medieval thinkers—but not so a legally constituted monarch who ruled tyrannically. Bodin apparently "wavered between the notion of legal sovereignty as complete and indivisible and the conception of sovereignty as necessarily limited by the nature and purposes of the state."[7] Nonetheless, logically the subject could not be conceived as having any jurisdiction over the sovereign. So while certain actions might not be rightfully done by the sovereign, there was no remedy for his subjects. Rebellion, Bodin thought, was never justified.

In England, the dominant tenor of thought showed the same thrust:

The strength of the English conviction of the wickedness of rebellion was not in the main derived from religion or from any theory of divine right. It was derived from the sense of the need of order, from the sense that the welfare and very existence of the commonwealth was bound up with obedience to authority.[8]

John W. Allen suggests that English writers of the 16th century generally insisted "that disobedience to the lawful magistrate or rebellion against the Prince [was] unlikely to produce anything but disorder and misery."[9] It was not considered the business of subjects to seek the reform of the commonwealth upon their own initiative. The right to decide when and whether rebellion was legitimate was not even conferred on the nobility or any class of officials.[10] Nor was such a right granted to the people as a body. What distinguished English thought "was the general refusal to admit that any case [could] be made for a right of rebellion."[11]

Some of the writers who deviated from the general trend of thought respecting political authority in the 16th century—for example, the unknown author of the *Vindicae* and John Ponet—reformulated the medieval view that authority is transmitted to rulers from God by way of the people. The works of both contain vague foreshadowings of constitutional limitations[12] and, more dimly, of self-government. The king, they asserted, derives his authority from the people; his guiding consideration must be their welfare and interest. He is limited by the law of the community, as well as by God's law and the law of nature. But neither the constitutional nor the democratic element shows signs of institutional development in these writings. The ruler is not considered absolute—his authority is limited by either human law or the ends for which authority is conferred—but real restraints exist only in the extreme case, when nobles, magistrates, or the common people rebel. The origin of political authority is attributed to the people, but again, only in the extreme case—when the grant is revoked—do they participate. Political authority is instituted for the benefit of the people, and its grant is made conditional upon serving the people's interest. As yet, however, the people play no part in defining their interest or in making the law which may restrain, *de jure* at least, the ruler from ignoring the conditions of the grant.

Doctrines of resistance to authority did not fare well in 16th-century England, but limits on the king's absolute discretion were preserved by "the unexampled toughness of the ancient, English common law."[13] Later in the century, the alliance of lawyers and Puritans began to encroach upon the power of the Crown. In impeaching Charles I, Parliament embarked on an unprecedented course of action; out of doctrines of religious conscience, natural law, and common law, a defense was constructed which placed this action within the framework of Parliament's role as defender of the law and rights of Englishmen. The king's parliamentary opponents claimed that Parliament had "supreme authority to determine the law of the land and anyone who disputed that authority or commanded that it be disobeyed was guilty of a high breach of the privilege of parliament."[14] They appealed to man's inherent duty of self-defense; the voice of reason and conscience which spoke to every man commanded that no man put himself under the domination of others. The principle was extended to apply to the people as a body; they, too, were to avoid oppression. "England [was] fortunate . . . in having found a means by which the people [might] give or withhold consent to the laws which rulers [sought] to impose upon them."[15] Parliament, the supreme law-declaring body in the realm, embodied and expressed the will of the people, which the king was bound to obey by conscience and the terms of his office, whatever might be the promptings of his private conscience or opinion.

The opponents of the king maintained an uneasy alliance while he yet posed a threat to their claims, but subsequently the Levellers turned the very claims that were made in Parliament's behalf back against it. They, particularly John Lilburne, questioned Parliament's right to be the final arbiter of the dictates of conscience and reason. In attacking Charles on the ground that he was threatening the safety of the people, Parliament had professed to speak in the name of the people, but now when Parliament denied men like Lilburne—a man of the people—his rights, was he not commanded by conscience and law to resist? And "were not the people required to protect themselves by whatever means they could against the renewal of oppression from any quarter,"[16] including Parliament?

Milton, who had written in defense of deposing the king, saw the Pandora's box that had been opened. During its struggles against the king, Parliament had encouraged at times, tolerated at others, that "disputing, reasoning, reading . . . discoursing" public which the preachers, the pamphleteers, and the press had created. "Liberty, which parliament had assured to the people, had 'enfranchised, enlarged and lifted up [their] apprehension'."[17] During the civil war, the men of Cromwell's army had been led to believe that they were fighting for their own liberty; now they demanded it as recompense for their sacrifices. Within the army, debates were held between the Leveller spokesmen of the rank-and-file and the leaders negotiating with Parliament. The Levellers issued a manifesto, the *Agreement of the People*, in which they demanded not only that limits be placed upon the powers of government but also that they be given the right to participate in the selection of their governors. All males of at least twenty-one years of age not servants[18] or almstakers (including those on relief) were to be granted suffrage; Parliament was to be prohibited from legislating in certain areas, such as religion. Also demanded were rights to counsel and speedy trial, protection against self-incrimination, equality before the law, and elimination of imprisonment for debt. The House of Commons was to be supreme, not subject to the veto of the king or lords, but at the same time, its powers were to be limited by specific prohibitions—including, in addition to those already mentioned, denial of the power to grant monopolies and to impress men for military service—and ultimately by the basic, inalienable rights of the people. Finally, the term of Parliament, as well as that of the elected representatives, was to be limited.

The Levellers believed "that liberty is a right demanded by the very nature of human beings: not merely a freedom from the restraint of others, but a conscientious and deliberate share in such arrangements as the community finds it necessary to make. From this right of the individual springs the sovereignty of the people."[19] The Levellers did not win all they desired; more conservative opinions—which feared an invasion of property should men who were not freeholders be granted the franchise—prevailed. Nonetheless, the Levellers represent an early recognition of the interdependency of rights against the state—which required constitutional limitations on government—and popular sovereignty—which entailed greater popular participation.

For [Lilburne] the people's own certain protection from the encroachments of rulers upon their rights was law, known law resting upon their consent and set down in English for everyone to read and obey. The only sure implement and guardian of liberty under law was a representative house of commons and always the recourse of free men against tyranny was the appeal to the judgment and conscience of their fellows.[20]

The Restoration of 1660 made manifest the exclusion of radical proposals of the Leveller variety, but the development of constitutionalism continued. The Glorious Revolution of 1688 and the resultant Bill of Rights, to which the new monarchs had to agree as a condition of their investment, was a significant advance, further limiting royal power and extending the sphere of individual rights. The details are well known. Similarly recognized as part of the development of modern liberalism are the writings of Hobbes and Locke.

Commentators have disagreed whether Hobbes may accurately be characterized as a proto-liberal, but there is more consensus in describing some of his notions about government as liberal. He does have a conception of rights preexistent to the institution of society and the state, although in covenanting with other men to institute the Leviathan, most of that natural liberty, or natural rights, is transferred; basically what remains—because, he says, it is inalienable—is the right of self-preservation. Despite the magnitude of the diminution and the virtual elimination of natural rights as a basis for limiting the power of the Leviathan, the subject within the state still enjoys certain protections which generally are included in liberal constitutional guarantees: the requirement that law be made known (a standing law); prohibition of *ex post facto* laws; the related freedom from arbitrary treatment where there is no law; protection against self-incrimination; equal justice before the law.[21]

It is a commonplace, I think, to point out that Hobbes's thought, especially his emphasis on submission to political authority, on order and security, was influenced by the disorder and civil war in England during his life. It may also be commonplace but more to the point here to note that his conception of the subject's place in the state may well be a reaction to the politicization of English society during the heyday of the Puritan preachers and pamphleteers. To his mind, the resultant disorder and overthrow of traditional political authority was quite threatening. For Hobbes, while conceding that the Leviathan can be an assembly of men, is not willing to allow the subject to be a political man at all. He should obey without judging the Leviathan's commands; he should not even entertain political opinions, much less act upon them publicly. He should substitute the public conscience, that is, the Leviathan's law, for private conscience. In a sense, the only time the individual acts politically is when he covenants to institute the Leviathan; thereafter, participation, for that brief moment virtually universal, vanishes.

Discussing the distinction between democracy and liberalism, Giovanni Sartori[22] points out that Hobbes realized the Athenians and the Romans were free only as commonwealths, not as individuals; "particular men had [not] the liberty to resist their own representative."[23] Hobbes goes on to declare that men have often been deceived in mistaking the liberty of the public, or commonwealth, "for their private inheritance." He suggests that men have acquired "a habit . . . of favoring tumults, and of licentious controlling the actions of their sovereigns, again of controlling those controllers" from reading the classical philosophers—Greeks and Romans who derived the rights of commonwealths "not from the principles of nature, but . . . out of the practice of their own commonwealths which were popular."[24] Then Hobbes distinguishes the liberty of the commonwealth, which resembles that of man in the state of nature, from the liberty of the subject. The subject's liberty has nothing to do with popular control over rulers. Thus, while Hobbes seems to understand that democratic participation is not a sufficient condition of individual liberty (rights against the state), he does not see that it may be a necessary condition. Perhaps, ironically, this results from the fact that the liberty he ascribes to the subject is already sufficiently circumscribed to make participation unnecessary for its defense. Nonetheless, even this reduced liberty lacks the kinds of defenses which liberals and constitutionalists espouse.

For Locke, the natural rights which men seek to preserve by founding a political community and government are broader than for Hobbes: life, natural liberties—as much as are compatible with "the good, prosperity, and safety of the society"—and property. Locke extended the meaning of property to include "the labor of [man's] body and the work of his hands" and whatever he had mixed his labor with. In order to protect these rights, government must be not only established but also limited:

> . . . though the [legislative] be the supreme power in every commonwealth, yet First, It is not, nor can possibly be, absolutely arbitrary over the lives and fortunes of the people. . . . [it] is bound to dispense justice and decide the rights of the subject by promulgated standing laws, and known authorized judges. . . . [It] cannot take from any man any part of his property without his own consent. . . . i.e., the consent of the majority, giving it either by themselves or their representatives chosen by them.[25]

Locke specifically declares that the prince's prerogative is a power to provide for the public good and is not something he possesses of right; rather, it was left with the crown by the community. The origin of political authority is popular, Locke asserts, and when the rulers alter the government and violate the purposes for which it was established, the people have a right to reassume their supreme power.

Locke goes well beyond Hobbes in specifying limitations upon the government and gives the people a larger role in maintaining the rights which government was originally established—and limited—to protect.

Nonetheless, both the democratic and the liberal aspects of his thought reveal an incomplete development. Apparently, Locke did not envisage anything resembling universal male suffrage; only men of property were to be full members of civil society. Therefore, his references to the consent of the people and to the liberty of the people to reconstitute their government do not imply the broad political participation which has become an element of liberal democracy.

Yet Locke was aware that the defense of men's liberty involves at least some participation, even if limited to a relatively small portion of the community, considerably less than the total adult population. The notion of government under law was rather ancient, but the idea of maintaining limits on government by popular participation was relatively new. Even as near to Locke's time as Coke's campaign to limit the king's prerogative, English lawyers relied primarily on the judges of the common law courts, instead of on any popular participation, to provide a limitation on the ruler's absolute discretion. As McIlwain points out, the problem was to develop regular and effective means of maintaining the distinction between *gubernaculum* and *jurisdictio*. In addition to his assertion of the supremacy of the common law, Coke also expressed a more modern view—that Parliament embodied and expressed the will of the people, though, of course, there was as yet no semblance of broad and equitable representation. Locke's ideas represent an advance in this direction. The English liberal development shows a tendency to ascribe rights against the state to all men and then to match this by gradually extending *political* rights, such as suffrage and office-holding, to a larger and larger portion of the adult population. At the same time, Locke's defense of individual rights falls short of the constitutional guarantees of individual rights and liberties which the modern liberal-democratic state maintains.

Locke did not think it desirable (whereas the Levellers in the *Agreement of the People* had thought it essential) to reserve some rights to the individual as against any parliament or government. No individual rights are directly protected in Locke's state. The only protection the individual has against arbitrary government is placed in the right of the majority of civil society to say when a government has broken its trust to act always in the public good and never arbitrarily.[26]

In France, the development of liberal-democratic thought begins with Montesquieu, who defines liberty as "a right of doing whatever the laws permit" and as consisting "only in the power of doing what we ought to will, and in not being constrained to do what we ought not to will."[27] Franz Neumann, in his introduction to *The Spirit of the Laws*, says:

> If we are to take Montesquieu at his word, the concept of liberty would either be meaningless or even quite dangerous. Who determines "what we ought to will" and "what we ought not to will"? It is, clearly, not the individual but the law, that is, the government. Consequently, my whole liberty would consist in doing what the law requires me to do and doing this not simply under compulsion, but with my full and hearty approval.[28]

Neumann thinks it is possible to reformulate Montesquieu's conception in a way that is congruent with the ideas he expresses in the books dealing with the protection of the individual and political liberty (XI and XII). He refers to the following statement—"A government may be so constituted, as no man shall be compelled to do things which the law does not oblige him, nor forced to abstain from things which the law permits."[29]—as "an approximation of the correct definition of constitutional liberty. . . . Liberty would then be the freedom to act unless the act is prohibited by law."[30] This is a minimal statement of the constitutional position—that is, that promulgated law is a restraint on governors' power—but Neumann suggests that Montesquieu also recognized the need for institutional checks:

> When the legislative and executive powers are united in the same person, or in the same body of magistrates, there can be no liberty. . . . Again, there is no liberty, if the judiciary power be not separated from the legislative and executive.[31]

Thus, Neumann argues, Montesquieu's definition of liberty under law refers to law enacted by a government embodying the separation of powers.

Montesquieu's work is not devoid of notions of self-government and democracy. He indicates that he thinks democracy has inconveniences, a major one being the fact that "the people collectively are extremely unfit" for discussing public affairs, but he does consider them well qualified to choose their representatives. Like later liberals, and somewhat reminiscent of Locke, Montesquieu sees dangers in a legislative body "always assembled": "When different legislative bodies succeed one another, the people who have a bad opinion of that which is actually sitting may reasonably entertain some hopes of the next."[32] This optimism is consistent with Montesquieu's belief in the people's ability to choose capable representatives and hints at a conjunction of constitutional limitations and popular participation. Both Locke and Montesquieu were concerned with the idea of a government under law and both saw a role for the people in governance—the choice of legislative representatives. Whereas Locke's suggestion that the representative assembly sit for limited periods was to ensure that the representatives themselves would be subject to the law they had made, Montesquieu's statement points toward the development of popular control over government and its responsibility to the electorate.

It is not clear how far Montesquieu's references to the people extend; for example, he says: "As in a country of liberty, every man *who is supposed a free agent* ought to be his own governor; the legislative power should reside in the whole body of the people."[33] He shows the concern of other liberals for checking the power of the people, while admitting them to a share in the governance of the state. For instance, Montesquieu recommends giving "persons distinguished by their birth, riches, or honors" a share in the legislature proportioned to these other advantages. If they were to be given equal votes with everyone else, this would mean their slavery; to "check the licentiousness of the people," nobles should be constituted as a separate legislative body.

Montesquieu realized that the people were not necessarily made free by possession of the supreme power itself: "Political liberty is to be found only in moderate governments. . . . It is there only when there is no abuse of power."[34] Neumann suggests that "Montesquieu's political conceptions had . . . the most direct effect on constitutionalism. . . . But he had practically no influence on democratic doctrines."[35] Montesquieu's doctrine of the separation of powers was taken up, Neumann asserts, in America, France, and Germany, because of its antidemocratic implications. Perhaps the application of his doctrine illustrates the real possibility of using constitutionalism against democracy, even though liberals like Montesquieu were cautiously receptive to democratic ideas. This serves to point up the fact that viable liberal-democratic governments have developed where liberals have been willing to accept an infusion of democratic ideas into liberal political institutions.

So far democracy has played a minor role in this discussion of the origins of the liberal-democratic polity. Rousseau is a striking contrast to those spokesmen for liberalism and constitutionalism who exhibit a wary attitude toward the *demos* and popular participation in government. Instead, he insists that democracy, rather than limitations on governmental power and restrictions on participation, is the only solution to the problem of freedom. No man can be free unless he participates in the determinations of the sovereign, i.e., the General Will, for freedom is obedience to the law one has made.[36] The People are the sovereign, and in this capacity, they can be represented by no one. All men equally bear the obligations of subjects and enjoy the rights of citizens.

In contrast to the natural rights of Lockean man, Rousseau's citizen does not reserve any rights upon which the state may not infringe. The General Will is the final judge of the extent to which the community may make claims on each member in his role as subject. There are no absolute guarantees of individual rights[37] because the sovereign cannot bind itself. Not only is it impossible for the sovereign to impose an inviolable law upon itself, it is also unnecessary. Rousseau, apparently with equanimity, banished the constitutional restraints and restrictions on participation which liberals relied upon to protect freedom—for some parts of the community, at least. For Rousseau was convinced that the nature and origin of the General Will compels it to be equitable. It applies to all subjects equally and therefore it is impossible for anyone to subject another to greater impositions than he will himself accept. All its determinations must be general as to their objects; specific individuals cannot be singled out for reward or penalty. It emanates from the expression of each citizen's individually deciding what constitutes the public advantage; moreover, the public advantage cannot be contradictory to the interests of the individual members of the community.

Rousseau insisted that the government he projects is a government under law, but he was referring to the compliance of the executive to the determinations of the sovereign people. He realized that the sovereign, as well as the government, may stray beyond its proper bounds—for example, it may legislate on particular matters for which it is not competent—but the government has no independent power to restrain it. If certain members of the community unite to oppress a minority, only the original liberty of the oppressed remains to them. Social bonds disintegrate, and men find themselves back in the state of war which Locke and Hobbes were anxious to avoid.

Commentators have often noticed the contrast between Rousseau's thinking and English liberal thought. Guido de Ruggiero says this of Rousseau's conception of the attributes of sovereignty:

These attributes are the exact opposite of the principles of guarantism as derived from the English Constitution. Indivisibility is the antithesis of the separation of powers and the system of balances; inalienability tends to destroy the prerogative of the Crown and turn the Monarch into a magistrate; the impossibility of representation tends to destroy the prerogative of parliament. But now that the opposition has been pushed to extremity, can we say that the rights of the individual are more effectively safeguarded? Can we say that freedom by means of the State, as Rousseau established it, is more secure then the traditional freedom from the State?[38]

Rousseau is often called the father of the French Revolution, and the excesses of that Revolution are sometimes ascribed to his ideas. Yet Ruggiero suggests that only a superficial examination of the *Declaration of the Rights of Man*, the opening manifesto of the Revolution, would lead one to believe that it expresses Rousseau's ideas alone. For Ruggiero, "the true immortality of the principles of 1789 lies in the fact that they express, even though in contingent and imperfect form, the inner conflict between the individual and the State."[39] Rousseau had attempted, by having the People "appropriate" (the term is Ruggiero's) the State, to make each individual dependent only upon the community and, therefore, not upon any individual or group. The Revolutionaries of 1789 also were concerned to free men from all the dependencies which traditionally had hampered and obstructed them. They apparently agreed with Rousseau that law, as an expression of the General Will (all citizens sharing in its formation), was the only proper definer of the limits within which liberty should exist. Nonetheless, as Ruggiero points out, the conception of liberty expressed in the *Declaration* seems to be torn between that of rights protected even from the state and that of rights protected by participation in formulating the law.

We find two elements . . . juxtaposed and to some extent confused: on the one hand, the freedom of a pre-political condition; on the other, the individual's participation in the formation of the State. . . . In Art. II we find a statement about the natural and imprescriptible rights of man, liberty, property, security, and resistance to oppression; in Art. III a statement of the principle of popular sovereignty . . . logically, [the two conceptions] are incompatible, because, once Rousseau had given currency to the principle of popular sovereignty, any idea of individual right as against the State, or of resistance to oppression, became impossible.[40]

To some extent, the framers of the *Declaration* may have shared Rousseau's optimism that the sovereign body of citizens (or their representatives), to whom the law was to apply equally as individuals, would make no oppressive laws. Ruggiero suggests that "the inexperience of the authors . . . left a loophole for experiments in various directions without overstepping the bounds of the constitution."[41] The course of the Revolution manifested the "danger of one-sided doctrinal formulae"; the conjunction of the two different conceptions of rights was not maintained. We will not examine the Revolution itself except to note again the problem which appeared in Rousseau's work: attempting to make the individual independent of every individual or group except the community may leave him without real protection against the community, should it fail to realize its ideal conception as the expression of his social being.

R. R. Palmer's description of the motivations of the French revolutionaries suggests that they failed to maintain the co-existence of liberty through limitations on government and freedom through political participation. The Revolution, he argues, "was a supreme attempt to realize the principle of individualism in the domain of actual institutions."[42]

[The liberty of the Revolution] is the liberty of the individual, equality the equality of individuals in possession of legal rights, fraternity a free, voluntary and enthusiastic coalescence of individuals into a body politic.[43]

This preoccupation with individualism was combined, in the minds of the revolutionaries, with an "exaltation of the civic spirit." They desired a community in which the common welfare was the supreme concern; "they held, in effect, that no merely private interest is legitimate at all."[44] Civic concern was not necessarily incompatible with individualism, for a citizen freed from all partial groups is free to consider the community welfare as paramount. Palmer says that the "exaltation of the civic spirit explains both the radical individualism and the glorification of the state and nation"[45] which the revolutionaries manifested. Yet such exaltation could not reconcile the two in actual practice. The subsequent course of the Revolution made that quite apparent. The freedom which individualism seems to require must be more than the freedom to participate in community affairs. The Revolution illustrates how men may define the general welfare as the only legitimate interest of individual members of the community; then not only is the self-interested man put beyond the pale, but the citizen whose definition of the general welfare is unorthodox may also be compelled to join him in the realm of unfreedom.

The thought of Benjamin Constant manifests the liberal reaction in France to that excessive power of government which was justified by appeal to popular sovereignty during the French Revolution and the Napoleonic period. Constant provides a clear statement of the distinction between liberalism and democracy:

> None the less one must not build upon an abstract idea, in the illusion that it can increase the sum of individual liberty; still less ascribe to it unlimited application. The citizen body is sovereign in the sense that no individual, no faction, no association can arrogate to itself a sovereignty not delegated to it by the people. But there is a part of human life which necessarily remains individual and independent, and has the right to stand outside all social control. Where the independent life of the individual begins, the jurisdiction of the sovereign ends. Rousseau failed to see this elementary truth and the result of his error is that the *Contrat Social*, so often invoked in favor of liberty, is the most formidable ally of all despotisms.[46]

> [Modern liberty] is every man's right to be subject to the law alone, the right of not being arrested, tried, put to death, or in any way molested, by the caprice of one or more individuals. It is every one's right to express his own opinion, to attend to his own art, to come and go, to associate with others. It is, lastly, everyone's right to influence the administration of the State, either by nominating all or some of its officers, or by his advice, demands and petitions, which the authorities are in a greater or less degree obliged to take into account.

> Let us compare this liberty with that of the ancients. That consisted in the collective but direct exercise of many privileges of sovereignty, deliberating upon the public welfare, upon war and peace, voting upon laws, pronouncing judgments, examining accounts, and so forth; but while the ancients regarded this as constituting liberty, they held that all this was compatible with the subjection of the individual to the power of the community. . . . Among the ancients the individual, a sovereign in public affairs, is a slave in all private relations. Among the moderns, on the contrary, the individual, independent in his private life, is even in the freest states a sovereign only in appearance. His sovereignty is restricted, and almost always suspended; and if now and again he exercises it, he only does so in order to renounce it.[47]

Whether Constant was historically accurate does not concern us here; only his sharp distinction between these two views of liberty is of interest. Constant's sympathies are apparent; he preferred protection against the state to direct participation in it. In theory, he was not willing to insist even upon limited participation in the selection of some or all of the governing officials as an essential part of a citizen's liberty. In practice, Constant opposed any broad extension of suffrage. Across the Channel, English liberals, who shared Constant's concern to protect the individual from the state, were coming to the different conclusion that political rights—primarily the right to participate in choosing one's representatives, at the least—were the best means of securing private rights and personal liberties.

The modern conception of the democratic citizen comes to fruition in the work of Alexis de Tocqueville and John Stuart Mill. Both may be characterized as liberals. They sought to protect the individual from the state and realized that participation in governance—the democratic infusion into the liberal system—was the most effective and perhaps the only means of achieving this goal, at least under conditions of increasing equality or, in Mill's view, of commercial progress and prosperity.

John Stuart Mill's views reflect the abstract and logical notions of Jeremy Bentham and his own father, James Mill. While Bentham devoted most of his life to the reform of law and legislation and not to political theory per se, his writings do contain ideas relevant to the developing conception of the democratic citizen. Bentham rejected the notion that obedience to law constitutes liberty. Every law is a restriction on freedom. Some restrictions, of course, are necessary to protect certain cherished values: "It is impossible to . . . protect the person, life, reputation, property, means of livelihood, nay, even liberty itself, save at the expense of liberty."[48] Nonetheless, restrictions should be minimized; unless the benefits of legislation outweigh the costs of coercion, it is unsound.

For Bentham, society was composed of atomistic individuals who pursued their own happiness by employing the hedonistic calculus. By reducing men to self-interest-seeking units, he placed them in a position of equality, where the claims of each to happiness merited equal attention from the legislator. The proper standard for the legislator to apply in evaluating proposed legislation was whether it favored the greatest number of interests. The legislator's adherence to this criterion would be assured by having the people elect their representatives, thereby taking advantage of the office-holder's desire to stay in office. While he occasionally expressed doubts about the people's ability to put their real interests before their immediate selfish interests, Bentham apparently believed that, in the long run, the majority principle would be consistent with social utility. In this qualified sense, he approved of the ballot as a means of defending the individual's happiness and interest.

All of Bentham's work was imbued with the principle that it was proper for government to be criticized and improved, so that liberty, as well as other values, would be enhanced. In a "liberal" system, he thought, this was the role of the good citizen: "Under a government of Laws, what is the motto of the good citizen? To obey punctually; to censure freely. Thus much is certain; that a system that is never to be censured, will never be improved."[49] This was consistent with Bentham's views of liberty and individual self-interest. The infringement which laws necessarily made on liberty could be minimized; the best judge, in effect, of how far the law interfered with the individual's happiness—his interest—was the individual himself. His criticisms could indicate where improvements were desirable, that is, useful. Of course, legislators might have to reconcile different criticisms, but without them, there would be little information or impetus to make changes.

Bentham's disciple, James Mill, carried the Utilitarian conception of government forward. While his mentor had been concerned primarily with specifying the principles of good legislation, Mill focused on the relation between good government and popular participation. He fully subscribed to the opinion that "upon the right constitution of checks all goodness of government depends."[50] And the solution to the problem of establishing checks was representative government. Even conceding that a popular electorate might make mistakes and act against its interest, Mill still thought it better to put checking powers in its hands rather than leave them to those whose interest did not correspond to that of the community as a whole. He felt confident enough to do this because the middle rank of society, which constituted a large proportion of the whole community, was the "most wise" and "most virtuous." If suffrage was "ever so far extended," he thought the opinion of the middle rank would prevail, for those beneath them—the majority—would, in large part, "be guided by their advice and example."[51]

Mill advocated liberty of the press because it made "known the conduct of the individuals who have been chosen [to wield the powers of government]."[52] Unless such knowledge was public, officials might serve their own, instead of the public, interest. Mill clearly favored public criticism of government; it was conducive to good government.

There can be nothing . . . in which [those who profit by the abuses of government] have a greater interest, than preventing the press from being employed in any such way as will lead the people to think that they have anything on the part of rulers of which to complain.[53]

Much more than earlier liberals, Mill emphasized the role of popular participation in maintaining limits on government. While exhibiting typical liberal caution about extending suffrage to the *demos*, Mill nevertheless made a strong case for institutionalizing restraints on government in the form of popular election of representatives, whose function is to watch over and control other public officials. The problem of whom is to control the governors may be solved this way: the representatives oversee the work of executive officials and the people oversee the work of the representatives. Recognizing the importance to good government of an intelligent and aware public, Mill insisted on the institutionalization of means to secure such a public, e.g., liberty of the press. Affairs of government were the people's affair; they had to have the opportunity to know what was going on in government.

James Mill's essay is but a step removed from the modern conception of liberal democracy. The final step was to make "the People," who participate in government, synonymous with the totality of adult citizens through the extension of the franchise. In theory at least, Mill's son, John Stuart, virtually completed the task in *Considerations on Representative Government*,[54] which has a close resemblance to the elder Mill's ideas.

Like Mill senior, John Stuart recognized that the people's role in ensuring good government was crucial:

If the checking functionaries are as corrupt or negligent as those whom they ought to check, and if the public, *the mainspring of the whole checking machinery*, are too ignorant, too passive, or too careless and inattentive to do their part, little benefit will be derived from the best administrative apparatus.[55]

James Mill had advocated some restrictions on suffrage; that his son moved a step beyond him is revealed by John Stuart's acceptance of broader citizen participation in the business of government:

There is no difficulty in showing that the ideally best form of government is that in which the sovereignty, or the supreme controlling power in the last resort, is vested in the *entire* aggregate of the community, every citizen not only having a voice in the exercise of that ultimate sovereignty, but being, at least occasionally, called to take an *actual* part in the government by the personal discharge of some public function, local or general.[56]

The primary reason, Mill emphasized, for extending political rights to the lower classes and involving them in governance was the protection of their own interests:

> The rights and interests of every or any person are only secure from being disregarded when the person interested is himself able, and habitually disposed, to stand up for them.[57]

Unless the lower classes were "present" to defend themselves, their interest was likely to be overlooked.

Mill was so impressed by the salutary effects of participation upon the individual that he espoused the "admission of all to a share in the sovereign power of the state" as the ultimately most desirable condition of popular government. Although he mentions the example of Athens, he probably had Tocqueville's *Democracy in America* in mind when he described the education provided by democratic institutions to lower-middle-class citizens—especially through their participation as jurors and parish officials:

> Still more salutary [than the elevation of his intellectual standards] is the moral part of the instruction afforded by the participation of the private citizen, if even so rarely, in public functions. He is called upon, while so engaged, to weigh interests not his own; to be guided, in case of conflicting claims, by another rule than his private partialities; to apply, at every turn, principles and maxims which have for their reason of existence the common good; and he usually finds associated with him in the same work minds more familiarized than his own with these ideas and operations, whose study it will be to supply reason to his understanding, and stimulation to his feeling for the general interest. He is made to feel himself one of the public, and whatever is for their benefit to be for his benefit.[58]

But liberal as he was, Mill was not so much of a democrat as to view the extension of the franchise to the lower classes as an unmitigated blessing. If upper-class voters did not consistently put the public interest before their own "immediate and apparent interest," why assume the laboring classes would be any different? Mill proposed various institutional mechanisms, such as proportional representation and plural voting, in order to insure "that no class, even the most numerous, shall be able to reduce all but itself to political insignificance and direct the course of legislation and administration by its exclusive class interest."[59]

At the same time, Mill believed that proper political principles—a "constitutional morality"—could, if "recognized and sustained by [public] opinion," play a crucial role in the functioning of restraints on government, even in a system which included constitutional checks and balances.[60] For, in the long run, a democratic government was only as good as the quality of its citizens. Basically, what concerned Mill was the education of men for participation as citizens in the liberal-democratic polity. Throughout the *Considerations* are to be found the component features of the ideal democratic citizen: he is well-informed, educated, and interested in political matters. He adheres to the general principles of constitutional morality, devotes himself to the welfare of the community, and makes independent, conscientious choices among political alternatives, guiding himself by a conception of the public interest.[61]

After discussion of Mill's views, the ideas of Tocqueville may seem anticlimactic, for many of his observations are similar to those of Mill. Yet Tocqueville's monumental work preceded Mill's *Considerations*, and it influenced Mill's thinking on the subject. In America, the limitations which Mill was inclined to place on the extension of democracy were not so necessary because the average citizen was more enlightened and class stratification was not significant. Tocqueville concluded from his observations

that universal suffrage is far from producing in America either all the good or all the evil consequences which may be expected from it in Europe and that its effects generally differ very much from those which are attributed to it.[62]

It is clear that Tocqueville was not ignorant of the dangers involved in the extension of democracy[63] and, as a liberal, he was vitally concerned about power without limitations.[64] What he feared in America were the "inadequate securities" against the power of the majority. The dominance of the majority was undermining independence of mind and freedom of discussion. Yet Tocqueville believed that more democracy was the antidote for the detrimental effects of democratic egalitarianism. Citizen participation, he concluded, was a key factor in the circumstances which contributed to the maintenance of democratic institutions in America. In the township, citizens participated in making decisions affecting their community and served as officers to execute those decisions. Township institutions imparted "to the people a taste for freedom and the art of being free."[65] The individual's attachment to his township made him jealous of its independence and sensitive to outside control. Participation in the minor, local affairs of government, Tocqueville argued, was essential to the proper exercise of power in more important matters. If centralized administration deprived the people of a role in local government, they would gradually become unfit to choose the representatives who exercised the centralized power of the national government.[66] As jurymen, citizens came under the salutary influence of the judges, imbibing their spirit and learning to judge matters from a viewpoint broader than their own predilections.

Under such institutions, men learn to respect the rights of others by being granted the same rights; they come to realize that rights depend on mutual recognition and that they can preserve their own by respecting those of others.

In America, the most democratic of nations, those complaints against property in general, which are so frequent in Europe, are never heard, because in America there are no paupers. As everyone has property of his own to defend, everyone recognizes the principle upon which he holds it. The same thing occurs in the political world. In America, the lowest classes have conceived a very high notion of political rights, because they exercise those rights; and they refrain from attacking the rights of others in order that their own may not be violated.[67]

As the exercise of rights teaches respect for the rights of others, participation in law-making helps to create respect for the law:

However irksome an enactment may be, the citizen of the United States complies with it, not only because it is the work of the majority, but because it is his own, and he regards it as a contract to which he is himself a party.[68]

One could continue to cite passages in which Tocqueville goes on drawing this picture of the democratic citizen.[69] He is the possessor of rights, particularly the right of political participation; he is attached to his community and to the broader welfare of the society; he respects law and the rights of others. He considers himself the equal of every other citizen; he is a man of independent convictions, considering his opinion no worse than that of any other individual. Yet at the same time, he recognizes the need to cooperate with others in order to achieve individual goals which others share. He has learned from political participation the value of association.

Yet Tocqueville was not sanguine about democratic man's ability to preserve freedom in an egalitarian society. Primarily he feared the privatization of democratic man: his withdrawal from public freedom into atomistic impotence; the loss of his ability to work with others for collective ends. He saw the individual slipping into subservience before public opinion, before the will of the majority. Retaining mastery over the art of association was the key to his remaining free. If government was not gradually to attain a position of benevolent omnipotence and omnipresence, democratic man had to act collectively. In democratic nations, Tocqueville asserted, associations ought to stand in lieu of those powerful private individuals whom the equality of conditions had swept away.

Tocqueville brought together the two strands of liberal-democratic thought to form a living amalgam, the democratic citizen; this was the culmination of a long development in political thought. However, even today, the two strands are sometimes distinguished as theorists continue to contrast positive freedom—freedom to achieve some good (attributed to Rousseau)—and negative freedom—freedom from restraint (attributed to Hobbes and Locke).[70] Recently, there have been attempts to restate the conception of freedom in such a way that a choice between public participation and private rights is not compulsory, at least not in a liberal democracy. For there, in many respects, the two are interdependent. In a state which excludes participation, private rights are precariously held; where private rights are denied, participation lacks roots in private activity which makes it both more secure and more meaningful. For example, Bernard R. Crick asserts:

Freedom depends on some distinction and *interplay* between both private and public actions and between the social and the political. For it is neither isolation from politics (as the liberal often wants to believe), nor is it loneliness (as following the concept of being an ' intellectual ' has often involved), nor yet again can it be any sense of total identification with the ' community ' (*some* degree of alienation is a condition of individuality). Freedom and privacy both thrive when government is conducted publically in the manner called political. Freedom, then, is neither isolation nor loneliness; it is activity of private men who help to maintain, even if not personally participating in, public politics. Privacy is itself a social relationship. Men who cease either to identify or to value politics usually lose and at best weaken freedom. Politics are the public actions of free men; free men are those who do, not merely can, live both publically and privately. Men who have lost the capacity for public action, who fear it or despise it, are not free, they are simply isolated and ineffectual.[71]

The free man of whom Crick speaks is much like the democratic citizen that Tocqueville described.

Notes for Chapter I

1. Charles Howard McIlwain, *Constitutionalism: Ancient and Modern* (Rev. ed.; Ithaca, New York: Cornell University Press, 1947), p. 78.

2. *Ibid.*, p. 85.

3. *Ibid.*, p. 88.

4. *Ibid.*, p. 94.

5. Cf. *Jean Bodin's Six Books of the Commonwealth*, trans. by M. J. Tooley (Oxford: Basil Blackwell, 1955), p. 68.

6. John W. Allen, *A History of Political Thought in the Sixteenth Century* (London: Methuen, 1957), pp. 273–274.

7. *Ibid.*, p. 425.

8. *Ibid.*, p. 135.

9. *Ibid.*, p. 129.

10. *Ibid.*, p. 130.

11. *Ibid.*, p. 131.

12. Michael Walzer, *The Revolution of the Saints* (Cambridge: Harvard University Press, 1965), pp. 81–82. Walzer says of the Protestant writers of this period: "they sharply insisted on the conventional nature of all human order . . . excluding the very possibility of both paternalism and charisma and opening the way for a straightforward constitutional politics."

13. McIlwain, p. 95.

14. William Haller, *Liberty and Reformation in the Puritan Revolution* (New York: Columbia University Press, 1955), p. 72.

15. *Ibid.*, p. 74.

16. *Ibid.*, p. 270.

17. *Ibid.*, p. 182. In addition to the quotations in this and the preceding paragraph, I have also paraphrased some of Haller's wording.

18. C. B. MacPherson, *The Political Theory of Possessive Individualism* (Oxford: Clarendon Press, 1962), pp. 107, 282–283. MacPherson maintains that the Levellers did not advocate manhood suffrage, for servants included wage-earners, and they constituted a large part of the adult male population.

19. George P. Gooch, *English Democratic Ideas in the Seventeenth Century* (Cambridge, England: Cambridge University Press, 1954), pp. 173–174.

20. Haller, p. 358. MacPherson, pp. 142–145, suggests that the Levellers considered the vote necessary only for certain economic rights not constitutionally guaranteed and that these could be best guarded by men directly interested; i.e., those who owned land or capital, or at least had not lost the property in their own labor.

21. These are principles included in liberal constitutional guarantees, but for the Leviathan, they would constitute merely a constitutional morality and not necessarily act as

restraints because there are no institutionalized powers of sanction behind them. Likewise, Hobbes makes several suggestions about what constitutes good laws, and these too are compatible with liberal notions. However, since the Leviathan, rather than the people, decides what is necessary and what is good for them, it might as well be said that they are compatible with benevolent despotism.

22. Giovanni Sartori, *Democratic Theory* (Detroit: Wayne State University Press, 1962), p. 260.

23. Thomas Hobbes, *Leviathan*, ed. by Michael Oakeshott (Oxford: Basil Blackwell, 1957), p. 140.

24. *Ibid.*, pp. 140–141.

25. John Locke, *Second Treatise on Civil Government*, Book XI, Secs. 135, 136, 138, 140, *in* Sir Ernest Barker, ed., *Social Contract: Essays by Locke, Hume and Rousseau* (New York: Oxford University Press, 1960). I have pieced on the last quotation, but I think it indicates what Locke means by consent. Also, I have cited the section numbers so that any edition of the *Second Treatise* may be consulted.

26. MacPherson, p. 257. I am not sure that Locke "did not think it desirable ... to reserve some rights ..."; it may be that he did not realize that institutional restraints were necessary —that is, something more than parliamentary representation.

27. Baron de Montesquieu, *The Spirit of the Laws*, trans. by Thomas Nugent, with an introduction by Franz Neumann (New York: Hafner Publishing, 1949), p. 150.

28. *Ibid.*, Editor's Introduction, p. L.

29. *Ibid.*, p. 150.

30. *Ibid.*, p. L.

31. *Ibid.*, pp. 151–152.

32. *Ibid.*, p. 145.

33. *Ibid.*, p. 154 (emphasis added).

34. *Ibid.*, p. 150.

35. *Ibid.*, Editor's Introduction, p. LXI.

36. The General Will is what men would will if they always followed their "real" will. Freedom is obedience to one's "real" will.

37. Jean-Jacques Rousseau, *The Social Contract*, Book IV, *in* Barker, p. 195. "It is agreed that what, as a result of the social contract, each man alienates of power, property, and liberty is only so much as concerns the well-being of the community. But further, it must be admitted that the sovereign alone can determine how much, precisely, that is." Thus, the alienation of all natural rights does not mean, in practice, that the individual, as citizen, retains no rights. Moreover, it appears that there is one right, the right to participate in determinations of the General Will, which is inalienable; however, it is not a natural right but a social one.

38. Guido de Ruggiero, *The History of European Liberalism*, trans. by R. G. Collingwood (Boston: Beacon Press, 1961), p. 62.

39. *Ibid.*, p. 70.

40. *Ibid.*

41. *Ibid.*, p. 71.

42. R. R. Palmer, "Man and Citizen: Applications of Individualism in the French Revolution," *in* Milton R. Konvitz and Arthur E. Murphy, eds., *Essays in Political Theory Presented*

to George H. *Sabine* (Ithaca: Cornell University Press, 1948), p. 131.

43. *Ibid.*, p. 132.

44. *Ibid.*, p. 151.

45. *Ibid.*

46. Quoted in Ruggiero, p. 161.

47. *Ibid.*, pp. 167–168.

48. Jeremy Bentham, *Theory of Legislation*, trans. from the French of Etienne Dumont and edited by Charles M. Atkinson (London: Oxford University Press, 1914), p. 120.

49. Jeremy Bentham, *A Fragment on Government*, ed. by Wilfred Harrison (Oxford: Basil Blackwell, 1948), p. 10.

50. James Mill, *An Essay on Government*, ed. by Currin V. Shields (New York: Liberal Arts Press, 1955), p. 66.

51. *Ibid.*, p. 90.

52. James Mill, "Liberty of the Press," *in* Philip Wheelwright, ed., *Works by Bentham, James Mill, and J. S. Mill* (Garden City, N.Y.: Doubleday, Doran, 1935), p. 264.

53. *Ibid.*, p. 259.

54. *Considerations on Representative Government* was published in 1861, some time after Tocqueville published *Democracy in America*. Mill was quite familiar with it since he wrote an extensive review of the English edition. Chronologically, Tocqueville should precede Mill, but in the theoretical development, Mill comes first.

55. John Stuart Mill, *Considerations on Representative Government*, ed. by Currin V. Shields (Indianapolis: Bobbs-Merrill, 1958), p. 27 (emphasis added).

56. *Ibid.*, p. 42 (emphasis added).

57. *Ibid.*, p. 43.

58. *Ibid.*, p. 54.

59. *Ibid.*, p. 128.

60. *Ibid.*, p. 176.

61. *Ibid.*, pp. 24–25, 156. While Mill apparently believed that men were capable of becoming such ideal citizens, he certainly did not think that all citizens in England were then approximating the ideal. This was the way he thought citizens *should* behave.

62. Alexis de Tocqueville, *Democracy in America*, ed. by Phillips Bradley (New York: Vintage Books, 1959), I, p. 206.

63. *Ibid.*, I, p. 256.

64. *Ibid.*, I, p. 270.

65. *Ibid.*, I, p. 310.

66. *Ibid.*, II, p. 339.

67. *Ibid.*, I, p. 254.

68. *Ibid.*, I, p. 257.

69. *Ibid.*, I, pp. 67, 73 (lower half). These pages are a good example.

70. A recent example is Isaiah Berlin's *Two Concepts of Liberty* (Oxford: Clarendon Press, 1958).

71. Bernard R. Crick, Inaugural Lecture, delivered at the University of Sheffield, January 12, 1966, p. 15. Crick says that Berlin's distinction between positive and negative liberty is all right "as far as it goes," but "the distinction is a dangerously incomplete account of what freedom has been and is" (p. 8).

II

Liberal Democracy and Moral Autonomy

LIBERAL-DEMOCRATIC THEORY gave rise to a conception of the citizen which made civil disobedience by real citizens conceivable. Moreover, the theory of civil disobedience represents a further extension of one of the most basic and enduring concerns found in both strands of liberal-democratic theory—the protection of the individual as an autonomous moral agent. This objective underlay the institutionalization of constitutional restraints, as well as the introduction of popular political participation. Locke's original conception of the proto-democratic body politic was partly motivated by this goal. While liberal-democratic theorists realized that some subordination to authority, some loss of individual autonomy, was required if the collective endeavor were to succeed, a recurrent intent of their thought has been to minimize the individual's subordination to purposes other than his own.

In his *Second Treatise on Civil Government,* John Locke suggested that the chief reason men established commonwealths was to preserve their property, for in the state of nature it was insecurely held. Most men, he said, were "no strict observers of equity and justice," and in the state of nature there was no commonly recognized law or judge to decide the disputes which arose among them.[1] This may seem a narrowly conceived justification for establishing a political community, but

Notes to this chapter will be found on pages 62-63.

Locke subsumed life, liberty, and estate in the property men sought to preserve. Thus, the preservation of liberty was a primary purpose for establishing a body politic. What kind of liberty did Locke have in mind? He may have been more concerned to justify rights of private property, yet he couched his language about liberty in terms broad enough to include individual moral autonomy.

Superficially, it might appear that freedom to do as one pleased would be the height of individual autonomy, but Locke recognized that man tended to be selfish and biased. Unless guided by some external direction, he would interfere with his fellow's pursuits, attempting to take his possessions or force him to carry out his orders. Despite his *capacity* for understanding the law of nature, man would not, in many instances, abide by it. Thus, in the state of nature men were not secure in their personal pursuits; they were subject to interference, to compulsion —their purposes and their choices were not securely their own, freely conceived and carried out. When the newly formed commonwealth consented to the delegation of legislative power to a number of individuals, its members thereby obliged themselves to obey the law promulgated. A common, standing law, enforceable by a superior power, meant restraints upon the liberty to do as one pleased—but it also meant freedom from the interference of others, freedom from the imposition of other wills. Laws were like "hedgerows," restricting men's liberty to do as they pleased in *all* things and protecting their liberty to do as they pleased in almost everything else—for example, where the law did not proscribe. Man, under law, was not "subject to the inconstant, uncertain, unknown, arbitrary will of another man."[2]

Although Locke does not specifically speak of the individual's use of property—his labor and external possessions—as an exercise of moral autonomy, I think it fair to characterize this pursuit as moral in the sense of good or right conduct. Industrious use of the goods of this world was, for Locke, an admirable activity. While the world was bountiful, it was only potentially so. Man's labor was necessary to make its fruits available for man's benefit and enjoyment. Unless some men had engaged in this activity, man's state would not have improved. Locke said that God "gave [the world] to the use of the industrious and rational . . . not to the fancy or covetousness of the quarrelsome and contentious."[3] In other words, the application of his reason and labor to developing the natural resources which God had provided was man's proper endeavor, and in that sense moral.

Locke's body politic, in which the people are sovereign and delegate the legislative power as a trust to those whom they think fit to exercise it, is essentially an attempt to conceive political power and authority in a way which would not destroy individual autonomy. It was obvious to Locke that man's life without political organization would be a rather insecure and unpleasant existence. Yet he was also aware that the institution of political power without limitations could recreate the insecurity of the precommonwealth state. Rulers had to be kept within due bounds or they, too, would interfere with the individual's autonomy—with his property, broadly interpreted.

It cannot be supposed that they should intend, had they a power to do so, to give to any one or more an absolute arbitrary power over their persons and estates, and put a force into the magistrate's hand to execute his unlimited will arbitrarily upon them; this were to put themselves into a worse condition than the state of nature.[4]

Locke's rudimentary formulation of constitutional restraints on government was early evidence of the concern in liberal-democratic theory for individual moral autonomy.

Locke probably was more concerned about the conditions under which his rational and industrious man could prosper than in defending the dictates of individual conscience. But the religious controversies which wracked English politics in the 17th century must have made him keenly aware that unless private judgments of the conscientious variety were protected from outside interference, the body politic would not be stable. His basic recommendation for avoiding clashes between governmental edicts and private conscience was a policy of toleration. If the legislative power were directed only toward "the temporal good and outward prosperity of society,"[5] leaving to the individual responsibility for his own salvation, it would be a rare occurrence when magistrates issued orders which appeared unlawful to the individual's conscience. Yet Locke must have felt it prudent to give private conscience its due: "the principal and chief care of everyone ought to be of his own soul first."[6] Nevertheless, he apparently thought that the private man should not follow his conscience to the point of disturbing the public peace. If reasonable men recognized the importance of stability, few *would* push doctrinal controversies to the point of upsetting social tranquillity. Moreover, there was a way of reconciling the conflicting claims of public peace and private conscience in a way which did not threaten public peace:

> Such a private person is to abstain from the action that he judges unlawful, and he is to undergo the punishment which it is not unlawful for him to bear. For the private judgment of any person concerning a law enacted in political matters, for the public good, does not take away the obligation of that law, nor deserve a dispensation.[7]

In addition, when the law extended to things beyond the magistrate's proper authority, it did not oblige the individual. In this way, Locke tried to strike a balance between the autonomy of the religious dissenter and the order of the polity.

Rousseau considered individual moral autonomy paramount, yet he too faced the problem of reconciling it with the social coordination necessary to a political community. The problem he set himself in *The Social Contract* was to define the conditions under which men could live in community, cooperating to achieve common purposes, and still remain autonomous individuals. To quote Rousseau's formulation:

> Some form of association must be found as a result of which the whole strength of the community will be enlisted for the protection of the person and property of each constituent member, in such a way that each, when united to his fellows, renders obedience to his own will, and remains as free as he was before.[8]

It was obvious that men had often obeyed wills other than their own, but it was not duty which had obliged them; rather, prudence or fear had often led men to obey. Rousseau did not think that man could fulfill his nature as a moral being unless he lived in community with his fellows, nor could he live a full, secure life without the protection of the community. Yet social organization historically had involved some form of subordination—one man or one group imposed its will on another group. Was there a will transcending men's immediate, personal preferences which they could follow and still be self-determining? Could the power exercised by those who governed be legitimated—that is, made consistent with individual autonomy? Legitimacy in this sense required agreement, but what kind of agreement? If every member of

the community had to agree to every decision, little could be accomplished even in a small community.

While Rousseau's General Will has been attacked as a conception which ultimately permits total domination of the individual, it is truer to Rousseau's intent to see the General Will as his groping for a solution to the conflict between the necessity for super- and subordination in social organization, and the individual's striving to be self-determining, obedient only to his own internally evolved choices. He considered the social contract the framework for a solution because dependence on other individuals was what Rousseau considered the major threat to freedom. By yielding up all his rights to the community, the individual, so Rousseau thought, escaped any personal dependence. The totality of the surrender was to ensure that no one had any claim against the community, and the equality of the surrender was to ensure that everyone gained the same rights over every other member as they gained over him. Rousseau did not see dependence upon the community as a threat to freedom because it was a supra-personal entity in which every member shared equally, and since all were equally subject to its claims, no one could have an interest in imposing any obligation on others which he would not himself accept. Being made up of all the individuals, the community could have no interest, no will, contrary to the individuals' wills—properly conceived. Rousseau believed that man was not fully human until his social faculties were developed, until he learned to view his own interest from a community perspective. To fulfill his potential, he had to transcend his idiosyncratic appetites and exercise his natural rights in ways which respected the rights of his fellows— something which man could only do when considerations broader and more comprehensive than the merely personal moved his judgment.[9]

Rousseau was not a constitutionalist and his conception of political authority has been criticized for its lack of constitutional restraints. Rousseau wanted to prevent any delegation of political authority; in contrast, liberals like Locke had placed limits on delegated authority. Yet Rousseau realized that political authority could not be based on the unanimity of transient individual preferences; some delegation was inevitable, and it may be that he wanted to avoid open admission of that fact. This may explain his conceiving a virtually metaphysical General Will. While the problem could not really be over-leaped by thinking of man as having two selves, one higher, more altruistic, and truer to man's real nature, a General Will representing man's higher self was not the totality of Rousseau's answer. Rousseau recognized that men were more apt to find themselves carrying out other's decisions, other's objectives, when they thought political participation was not worth their time and effort. The one right the individual in Rousseau's community could not cede without negating the social contract was the right to participate in the determination of the General Will. Rousseau also hoped that by making the community the focal point of the individual member's life, he might foster, not domination, but a spirit of mutuality which would inhibit any desire to exploit or oppress other members. If men did not consider their public liberty sufficiently important to exercise it, they would lose their private liberty in the long run. Autonomy was an indivisible condition; it could not be confined to the private sphere alone and survive.

Critics have suggested that there is a contradiction between Rousseau's conception of education for the individual and his conception of education for the citizen. They contend that his emphasis on individuality and autonomy in educating the male child, Emile, would have made him a poor citizen in the political community described in *The Social Contract*. Emile's sense of individuality would be too heightened. The community would have to re-educate him, to teach him to orient his actions by a concern for the consequences to the community. The ideal citizen is an individual whose satisfaction comes from willing in conformity with the General Will, from sharing in communal activities. In *The Social Contract*, seemingly harsh judgments are meted out to dissenters: "Whoever shall refuse to obey the general will must be constrained by the whole body of his fellow citizens to do so; which is no more than to say that it may be necessary to compel a man to be free."[10] Moreover, Rousseau suggests that the opinion of a citizen who finds himself in the minority—after the General Will has been determined by popular vote—is not merely unpopular; it is wrong. Had it won majority support, the citizen would "have done something quite other than [he] wished to do, and in that case [he] should not have been free."[11] Rousseau seems to be equating normative judgments—matters of value and opinion—with matters of truth and falsity. He seems to be suggesting that disagreements over normative matters constitute error and must be corrected. Rousseau goes even further: He says that the Sovereign can legitimately banish anyone who does not believe in the dogmas of the civic religion as "lacking in social sense, and being incapable of sincerely loving the laws and justice, or of sacrificing, should the need arise, their lives to their duty."[12] Anyone who acknowledges the principles of the creed and then acts contrary to them is deserving of death. Although the prohibition of intolerance is one of these dogmas, Rousseau's civic code seems intolerant of individual judgment and autonomy.

In apparent contrast, Rousseau spoke rather reverently of individual conscience in *Emile*: "Divine instinct, immortal voice from heaven; sure guide for a creature ignorant and finite indeed, yet intelligent and free; infallible judge of good and evil, making man like to God!"[13] Without conscience, Rousseau thought, man was an animal; true, he had reason, but he would wander "from one error to another" because his understanding was "unbridled." But *Emile* and *The Social Contract* can be reconciled: *Emile* was written for educating an individual who would have to live in society as it was then constituted, while *The Social Contract* represents Rousseau's view of men in a *properly* constituted political society. While it might seem that his concern with individual autonomy evaporates when he theorizes about "healthy" political relationships, this apparently was not what Rousseau thought. The education of Emile was designed so that he would grow up free of all dependencies; likewise, Rousseau wrote *The Social Contract* to elucidate the principles by which men could live *in community* without servitude, without dependence. Rousseau hoped to prevent Emile from becoming subservient to passions, to prejudices and social conventions which would bind him to views not his own, and to other people for his livelihood and self-esteem. He was to grow up a man whose judgment, whose conscience and actions, were thoroughly self-determined, so far as that was possible. "For his own part, he has all he wants within his reach. How should he be dependent on any one when he is self-sufficing and free of prejudice? . . . He has been brought up in complete liberty and servitude is the greatest ill he understands."[14] Inexorable necessities he would recognize as such and would not, therefore, see them as obstacles to his freedom. Nor would men in the just political community see the necessity for some restrictions, for some responsibilities in order to reap the benefits of living in community—security, comradeship, liberty—as a restriction on freedom. When placed in this context of fundamental requisites for a just community, even Rousseau's remark about compelling men to be free appears less foreboding.

Rousseau did not wish to suppress individual judgment; indeed, he asserted that community decisions would be good ones if citizens could, after being adequately informed, vote *without* consulting each other. "If . . . the general will is to be truly expressed, it is essential that there be no subsidiary groups within the State, and that each citizen voice his own opinion and nothing but his own opinion."[15] When Rousseau says that the minority's decision is wrong, he implies that the minority probably are putting their own personal interests first; as a result, their assessment of the broader community interest is mistaken. He said that they would have been acting against their "true" wishes, but he added, "This assumes that all the characteristics of the general will are still in the majority. When that ceases to be the case, no matter what side we are on, liberty has ceased to exist."[16] The whole structure of the community and the civic code are intended not to suppress individual conscience and judgment, but to inhibit personal preferences and prejudices from intervening in those matters which concern the citizens collectively.

In the healthy community, the exercise of conscience is fostered and reinforced. That men's thinking is swayed by social institutions to thoughts of common weal is, to Rousseau's way of thinking about morality, no impediment to moral autonomy. Conscience does not mean acting upon certain rules because the community approves them; it means following certain rules of conduct even—particularly—when no one else is present. This is what Rousseau wanted to inculcate in the citizen: a conscience which would not let him violate the rights of his fellows nor seek to shirk his communal responsibilities, even if he might do so with impunity—for example, by forming a majority to exploit the minority.

In the modern American view of moral autonomy, freedom of conscience is perhaps the most prominent aspect. To a considerable degree, Thomas Jefferson is responsible for this. Freedom of conscience is a recurrent theme in his writings. In the Act for Establishing Religious Freedom (1779), Jefferson proposed "that all men shall be free to profess, and by argument to maintain, their opinions in matters of religion, and that the same shall in nowise diminish, enlarge, or affect their civil capacities."[17] While his immediate object was to have the General Assembly of Virginia go on record in support of religious liberty and separation of church and state, Jefferson's conception of freedom of conscience was broader than the freedom to hold whatever beliefs one chose about religious matters, narrowly defined. He recognized the dangers in compelling men to profess any principles which they would not accept by the free use of their own minds. The natural freedom which men had been endowed with by their Creator included the freedom of the mind—to follow truth wherever it might lead. Jefferson believed that there was a truth about matters of right and wrong; and he was confident that men, if sufficiently educated and informed, would eventually find that truth. The way to combat mistaken opinion was not suppression but education and information. For error, even moral error, was a product of ignorance, and could be tolerated as long as the natural correctives were allowed to work; the mind, reason, had to be left free and provided with the means of attaining truth. Since truth had its normative aspect, Jefferson's endeavors to keep individual reason unfettered were directed toward preserving the autonomy of man as a moral agent. It was this conception of man which motivated Jefferson's attempts to have protections of individual rights written into the new constitution. Government had to be prevented from interfering with basic freedoms:

There are rights which it is useless to surrender to the government, and which governments have yet always been found to invade. These are the rights of thinking, and publishing our thoughts by speaking or writing; the right of free commerce; the right of personal freedom.[18]

Jefferson was always on guard against suppression of individual thought and opinion. He feared governments as the chief offenders, but he learned that public opinion and the press, if their preeminence were abused, could also inhibit independence of mind and conscientious judgment. While President, he refused requests that he communicate his religious beliefs to the public. This would, he thought, "seduce public opinion to erect itself into that inquisition over the rights of conscience, which the laws have so justly proscribed."[19] It was the duty of "every man who values the liberty of conscience for himself " to defend others from such invasions, because their case could become his own, and "to give no example of concession" when his own opinions were in question.[20] Yet ultimately Jefferson had faith in the judgment of the people and in freedom of the press. He saw America as an experiment which he hoped would demonstrate "that man may be governed by reason and truth:"

Our first object should therefore be, to leave open to him all the avenues of truth. The most effectual hitherto found, is the freedom of the press. It is, therefore, the first shut up by those who fear the investigation of their actions. The firmness with which the people have withstood the late abuses of the press, the discernment they have manifested between truth and falsehood, show that they may safely be trusted to hear everything true or false, and to form a correct judgment between them.

I hold it, therefore, certain, that to open the doors of truth, and to fortify the habit of testing everything by reason, are the most effectual manacles we can rivet on the hands of our successors to prevent their manacling the people with their own consent.[21]

Jefferson realized that ultimately the surest defense against oppressive government was to cultivate independence of mind, moral autonomy, and conscientious judgment in the people. Free minds could be developed, he thought, and his life work was filled with testaments to that belief: the Declaration of Independence, the Act Establishing Religious Freedom, his support for the Bill of Rights, his plans for public education and a state university in Virginia. The purpose of all these endeavors was to create an environment in which a free mind could grow.

Alexis de Tocqueville put his sociological insight in the service of his prime concern, preserving liberty in a world increasingly democratic and egalitarian. He saw the democratic revolution spreading throughout the West. Democracy was a "providential fact"—universal, durable, eluding all human interference, its progress furthered by all events. But the future, he thought, was not totally determined. In America, that revolution had proceeded farthest because the obstacles were fewest. By studying democracy in America, Tocqueville hoped to understand the general tendencies, the natural consequences—good and evil—which it would produce in other societies. With this knowledge, democracy could be channeled so that its detriments would not destroy its benefits.

In aristocratic society, the unique freedom of the nobles to act without constraint had barred the tyranny of princes. Yet the nobles had used their power with a sense of restraint. Tocqueville thought such freedom both admirable and functional, but he recognized that in a democratic age freedom had to be defined in broader terms:

According to the modern, the democratic, and, we may venture to say, the only just notion of liberty, every man, being presumed to have received from nature the intelligence necessary for his own general guidance, is inherently entitled to be uncontrolled by his fellows in all that only concerns himself, and to regulate at his own will his own destiny.[22]

Liberty was, for Tocqueville, freedom to choose and to act upon one's choices, and virtue was the exercise of freedom to choose rightly. According to Jack Lively:

[Liberty's] final justification in his eyes was that without the possession of uncoerced choices of action men could not express themselves as moral agents and that their stature as moral beings was cut down to the degree that their individual liberty was curtailed in extent or consequence. For him, the value of liberty was not so much that it allowed each individual to develop in his own way and toward self-imposed ends his personal potentialities, or that it created the intellectual dialectic without which there could be no progress, but that it allowed the individual the possibility of moral action. . . . Freedom no longer existed if men were coerced into actions decided upon by others to be objectively virtuous, but action was no longer virtuous if men did not make the free and voluntary choice of the good.[23]

Only a select few had enjoyed freedom in aristocratic society; in democracy political power was shared by many, but liberty was not thereby secured. Tocqueville could conceive of an egalitarian society in which men might act freely and yet without license, recognizing and respecting governmental authority as necessary, secure in their possession of rights, manifesting in their social relations a "manly confidence and reciprocal courtesy." Here liberty might flourish, for none would fear to exercise it nor would any seek to use it to the detriment of others. However, as Tocqueville examined American social and political institutions, he concluded that the confident exercise of rights in a democracy was threatened by certain consequences of the equality of conditions. Democratic man, despite his share in political sovereignty, tended to withdraw from freedom. Equality had contradictory effects:

When the inhabitant of a democratic country compares himself individually with all those about him, he feels with pride that he is the equal of any of them; but when he comes to survey the totality of his fellows and to place himself in contrast with so huge a body, he is instantly overwhelmed by the sense of his own insignificance and weakness. The same equality that renders him independent of each of his fellow citizens, taken severally, exposes him alone and unprotected to the influence of the greater number. The public, therefore, among a democratic people, has a singular power . . . for it does not persuade others to its beliefs, but imposes them and makes them permeate the thinking of everyone by a sort of enormous pressure of the mind of all upon the individual intelligence.[24]

Equality also fostered a kind of isolation: Each man strove to make his way independently and withdrew into the circle of his immediate family. Impotent in his isolation, he was nonetheless afraid to ask for help because he himself had not offered it. Equality made men jealous and suspicious of any kind of superiority or preeminence. The only superiority they would recognize was the superiority of numbers, inherent in equality; in politics, the majority was considered preeminent, based on the notion that where men are presumed equal, the predominance of intelligence rests with the greater number, as does the predominance of interest. In the face of the omnipotent majority and its embodiment, the government, Tocqueville had a troubling vision of democratic man being reduced to an enervated, passive subject.

After having ... successively taken each member of the community in its powerful grasp and fashioned him at will, the supreme power then extends its arm over the whole community. It covers the surface of society with a network of small complicated rules, minute and uniform, through which the most original minds and the most energetic characters cannot penetrate, to rise above the crowd. The will of man is not shattered, but softened, bent and guided; men are seldom forced by it to act, but they are constantly restrained from acting. Such a power does not destroy, but it prevents existence; it does not tyrannize, but it compresses, enervates, extinguishes, and stupefies a people, till each nation is reduced to nothing better than a flock of timid and industrious animals, of which the government is the shepherd.[25]

What Tocqueville especially objected to was the notion that the people had a right to do anything they desired. Unlimited power, wherever lodged, was a threat to freedom:

Social power superior to all others must always be placed somewhere; but I think that liberty is endangered when this power finds no obstacle which can retard its course and give it time to moderate its own vehemence. Unlimited power is in itself a bad and dangerous thing. Human beings are not competent to exercise it with discretion.[26]

The fact that the majority, representing the people, had passed a law was no guarantee of its justness:

A majority taken collectively is only an individual, whose opinions, and frequently whose interests, are opposed to those of another individual, who is styled a minority. If it be admitted that a man possessing absolute power may misuse that power by wronging his adversaries, why should not a majority be liable to the same reproach?[27]

It is interesting that Tocqueville's writing contains a reference to individual disobedience, as does the work of other democratic theorists. Locke, perhaps *pro forma*, asserted that the individual might disobey the law for reasons of religious conscience. Jefferson thought occasional popular uprisings of a moderate nature justifiable because they kept governors responsive. Tocqueville suggested that disobedience is justifiable when a nation's laws exceed the limits of what is just. He believed that there is a "general law"—that is, justice—which "has been made and sanctioned, not only by a majority of this or that people, but by a majority of mankind:"

When I refuse to obey an unjust law, I do not contest the right of the majority to command, but I simply appeal from the sovereignty of the people to the sovereignty of mankind. Some have not feared to assert that a people can never outstep the boundaries of justice and reason in those affairs which are peculiarly their own; and that consequently full power may be given to the majority by which it is represented. But this is the language of a slave.[28]

In general, the majority does have the authority to command citizens, but its authority is limited by certain universal principles of justice.

As Tocqueville perceived the Americans, their obedience to government was based on a sound appreciation of its utility. Such an obedience was bounded by the purposes for which it was required; it was not an abdication of one's individual autonomy. In describing the Americans' doctrine of the sovereignty of the people, Tocqueville used language similar to that John Stuart Mill would soon use in his essay, *On Liberty.* Wrote Tocqueville:

In the nations by which the sovereignty of the people is recognized, every individual has an equal share of power and participates equally in the government of the state. Why, then, does he obey society, and what are the natural limits of this obedience? Every individual is always supposed to be as well informed, as virtuous, and as strong as any of his fellow citizens. He obeys society, not because he is inferior to those who conduct it or because he is less capable than any other of governing himself, but because he acknowledges the utility of an association with his fellow men and he knows that no such association can exist without a regulating force. He is a subject in all that concerns the duties of citizens to each other; *he is free,* and responsible to God alone, *for all that concerns himself.* Hence arises the maxim, that everyone is the best and sole judge of his own private interest, and that *society has no right to control a man's actions unless they are prejudicial to the common weal or unless the common weal demands his help.*[29]

Tocqueville thought that Americans were fortunate, for there were at work many countervailing tendencies to the atomistic, impotent individualism that equality engendered: a free press, vigorous private associations, both political and nonpolitical, a strong, independent judiciary, a decentralized system of government administration, a conservative bar which was held in high regard by the general population. Nonetheless the dangers were real, and in Europe the countervailing tendencies were weaker or nonexistent. Tocqueville saw his mission as finding a "means to sustain in men an appreciation of liberty as a political value."[30] "The justification [for freedom] lay in the individual's needs as a moral agent, his need to bear the responsibility of active decision and to be recognized as being capable of bearing this responsibility."[31] "Men's needs as moral agents . . . justified individual liberty whether or not individuals desired that personal liberty,"[32] but men had to be convinced to desire freedom or they would withdraw from it, yielding up their autonomy to external authorities. He echoed Rousseau's warning to his contemporaries: Unless they considered participation in community affairs worth the sacrifice of time from private affairs, their commonwealth and their liberty would be short-lived.

John Stuart Mill's solicitude for individual freedom needs no extensive rehearsal. His essay, *On Liberty*, clearly demonstrates that Mill considered individual autonomy one of the most fundamental aspects of human existence. Basically he was attempting to define the proper limits of social control over the individual:

The object of this Essay is to assert one very simple principle, as entitled to govern absolutely the dealings of society with the individual in the way of compulsion and control . . . that the sole end for which mankind are warranted, individually or collectively, in interfering with the liberty of action of any of their number, is self-protection. . . . To justify [compelling him, or visiting him with any evil in case he do otherwise], the conduct from which it is desired to deter him must be calculated to produce evil to someone else. The only part of the conduct of anyone, for which he is amenable to society, is that which concerns others. In the part which merely concerns himself, his independence is, of right, absolute. Over himself, over his own body and mind, the individual is sovereign.[33]

For Mill, individual autonomy was necessary for the progress of the human race; only by exercising their faculties could men develop as human beings.

The human faculties of perception, judgment, discriminative feeling, mental activity, and even moral preference, are exercised only in making a choice. He who does anything because it is the custom makes no choice. He gains no practice either in discerning or in desiring what is best. The mental and moral, like the muscular powers, are improved only by being used. The faculties are called into no exercise by doing a thing merely because others believe it. If the grounds of an opinion are not conclusive to the person's own reason, his reason cannot be strengthened, but is likely to be weakened, by his adopting it: and if the inducements to an act are not such as are consentaneous to his own feelings and character (where affection, or the rights of others, are not concerned) it is so much done toward rendering his feelings and character inert and torpid, instead of active and energetic.[34]

Mill not only sought to throw a protective principle around individual liberty; he also defined that liberty broadly:

The appropriate region of human liberty comprises, first, the inward domain of consciousness; demanding liberty of conscience in the most comprehensive sense; liberty of thought and feeling; absolute freedom of opinion and sentiment on all subjects, practical or speculative, scientific, moral, or theological. The liberty of expressing and publishing opinions may seem to fall under a different principle, since it belongs to that part of the conduct of an individual which concerns other people: but, being almost of as much importance as the liberty of thought itself, and resting in great part on the same reasons, is practically inseparable from it. Secondly, the principle requires liberty of tastes and pursuits: of framing the plan of our life to suit our own character; of doing as we like, subject to such consequences as may follow: without impediment from our fellow-creatures, so long as what we do does not harm them, even though they should think our conduct foolish, perverse, or wrong. Thirdly, from this liberty of each individual, follows the liberty, within the same limits, of combination among individuals; freedom to unite, for any purpose not involving harm to others.[35]

Mill's attempt to protect the individual's private relationships (and some public ones) from unwarranted or unwise intrusions of social and political compulsion did not imply a lack of concern for social obligations. Mill wanted to hold the individual to a high standard of responsibility to his fellow men. When there were good reasons for not socially enforcing the individual's responsibility, he thought that:

The conscience of the agent himself should step into the vacant judgment seat, and protect those interests of others who have no external protection; judging himself all the more rigidly, because the case does not admit of his being made accountable to the judgment of his fellow-creatures.[36]

Mill and Tocqueville recognized that it was precisely where men had more freedom that a well-developed conscience and a sense of social responsibility were necessary. In contrast to liberal constitutionalists who tended to focus on the problem of controlling the governors, Mill and Tocqueville manifested a concern for the problem of self-government—that is, individual rather than collective self-government. A free society, they thought, should put few restrictions on its members' behavior; much of men's activity should be unencumbered, even activities which were social or public. This meant that democratic citizens had to develop a sense of social responsibility if their relationships with each other were to remain equitable and stable. Since they were to be granted a significant role in the governing of their society, responsible political action also was required. For this, too, individual conscience had to be developed.

Liberal-democratic theorists never thought that to preserve individual moral autonomy, it was necessary or wise to eliminate all law. Laws might restrict absolutely free choice, but such freedom was license and ultimately would lead to un-freedom for all but the most powerful. These thinkers always recognized that some laws were necessary to ensure freedom within society. Although they tended to define liberty as freedom from interference and viewed law as a public interference with individual desire and action, they also thought that some law was necessary to prevent interference from other sources—for example, from private individuals. Nonetheless, liberals such as Locke and Bentham thought that men would go about their private affairs with relatively little friction, and thus only a limited amount of governmental regulation would be required. The extent of government jurisdiction had to be limited; otherwise the government would become much more of a threat to individual freedom than the actions of private men. These predecessors having established the notion of constitutional limits, later liberals—especially John Stuart Mill and Tocqueville—turned their attention from government as the chief danger to individual freedom, to certain general social conditions and social patterns of thought. They warned of the tyranny of public opinion and of social convention. Although both Mill and Tocqueville stressed the importance of a strong (if pragmatic) sense of attachment to the public interest, there was in their views a tendency to see the individual confronting society as a whole. They thought that men should feel attached to the community because, ideally, individual goals and public goals were congruent—

but in the real world, this harmony could hardly be assumed. The views of the people, reified as public opinion or social convention, might press upon the individual in a more subtle way than government, not merely blocking the expression of individuality and autonomy, but eroding the will to act with independence.

Tocqueville and Mill had clearly emphasized the obligation of the individual citizen to the community, but the impact of individuals' using their private rights in such a way as to injure other citizens and community interests had not really begun to make itself felt in English and American society at the time they were writing. The liberal conception of freedom always drew the boundary of its exercise at the personal rights of other individuals: Each individual was free to exercise his rights up to the point of interfering with other people's rights. Events were making this conception less and less related to reality—that is, the individualistic idea of freedom was not as applicable to a society which was increasingly dominated by the large-scale organizations and social and economic institutions of a modern industrial order. A few decades later, liberal democratic theorists began redefining the relation of the state or government to individual freedom. What is important to note is that the goals did not change but that these theorists saw the need to redefine the means—the conditions under which individual autonomy could be preserved.

In his *Lectures on the Principles of Political Obligation*, T. H. Green attempted to reformulate the rights of the individual in relation to the state. He rejected the notion of natural rights as a misunderstanding of the way rights are created. To suppose that men had rights in a presocial condition was, to him, both illogical and ahistorical. At the same time, Green observed what use was being made of claims to absolute freedom of contract in England. Those who opposed reform in the land laws, in working conditions, in public health, defended the *status quo* by appeals to individual liberty. Some were merely interested in preserving their privileged position; others, he said, "do not sufficiently consider the conditions of its [i.e., freedom's] maintenance in such a society as ours."[37] Green saw a need for specifying the conditions for maintaining freedom in the society of his time. Rights were important to him because they were linked to the development of moral autonomy: The possession of rights was the condition of man's realizing his moral capacity.[38] For Green, moral autonomy meant "the capacity on the part of an individual for making a common good his own."[39]

Although rights were the preconditions of individual freedom, rights were not individual in their origin. Rights were "the recognition by members of a society of powers in each other contributory to a common good, and the regulation of those powers by that recognition."[40] In other words, there could be no rights which were opposed to a conception of ideal ends shared by members of a society. It was their recognition of powers which created rights.

[Rights] attach to the individual, but only as a member of a society of free agents, as recognising himself and recognised by others to be such a member, as doing and done by accordingly. A right, then, to act unsocially,—to act otherwise than as belonging to a society of which each member keeps the exercise of his powers within the limits necessary to the like exercise by all the other members—is a contradiction.[41]

While moral autonomy was ultimately social in its ends, it was individual in its development. The individual had to adopt, as his own, a conception of ideal ends; if he merely conformed to external rules, which might have been the product of the reason of autonomous individuals in the past, there was no real moral freedom. Reason and will had to operate in the same person, or there was "no real determination of the will by reason."

The determination of will by reason . . . which constitutes moral freedom or autonomy, must mean its determination by an object which a person willing, in virtue of his reason, presents to himself, that object consisting in the realisation of an idea of perfection in and by himself.[42]

Reflecting on past history in England, Green argued that laws had often been made which checked the "development of moral disposition" by attempting to promote directly a certain standard of morality. Some of these laws had been abrogated on the theory that the only purpose of law was to prevent interference with the individual's liberty. Green felt that this "laissez faire" view had now become a hindrance to "reforms which involve an action of the state in the way of promoting conditions favorable to the moral life."

It is one thing to say that the state in promoting these conditions must take care not to defeat its true end by narrowing the region within which the spontaneity and disinterestedness of true morality can have play, another thing to say that it has no moral end to serve at all, and that it goes beyond its province when it seeks to do more than secure that individual from violent interference by other individuals. The true ground of objection to "paternal government" is not that it violates the "laissez faire" principle and conceives that its office is to make people good, to promote morality, but that it rests on a misconception of morality. *The real function of government being to maintain conditions of life in which morality shall be possible, and morality consisting in the disinterested performance of self-imposed duties*, "paternal government" does its best to make it impossible by narrowing the room for the self-imposition of duties and for the play of disinterested motives.[43]

Green rejected the idea that political obligation is based on the individual's consenting to be bound by certain limits on his powers, that sovereignty is based on consent. He saw that consent could be interpreted in an anti-social way—that the individual could put his own good above that of the community—yet he recognized that in a free society the basis of obedience to law could not be fear of punishment. Political obligation could not be based on force because this would undermine the development of individual moral autonomy. Green tried to avoid the dilemma of having to choose between consent and force by basing political obligation on the individual's acceptance of a common good which the institutions constituting the state seek to realize. The conception of a common good has a constraining power over him, leading him to do certain things "because there is a law that he should," even though it is not his inclination to do so. "The consciousness that the constraint is for a common good . . . must always be an element in that obedience which is properly called obedience to law, or civil or political obedience."[44]

Like other liberal-democratic thinkers, Green posed the problem of legitimate disobedience to the laws. Because they were concerned with moral autonomy and viewed the state or government as a means to this end, theorists such as Green could not accept the state or government as the absolutely authoritative determinant of what action is permissible and what proscribable. While Green was reluctant to sanction disobedience, he was not satisfied with the position that disobedience is never justified.

But it may be asked, Must not the individual judge for himself whether a law is for the common good? and if he decides that it is not, is he not entitled to resist it? Otherwise, not only will laws passed in the interest of individuals or classes and against the public good, have a claim to our absolute and permanent submission, but a government systematically carried on for the benefit of a few against the many can never be rightfully resisted.[45]

There can be no rights against the common interest, but by the same token, the common interest is not always necessarily fostered by the state or government. There may be times when the state and the law work against the conditions of the moral life. Green permitted the individual to judge whether a law is for the common good, but he hedged on the right to resist. His "resolution" of the difficulties will be discussed later. What is of interest here is the recurrence of this problem. It becomes perhaps even more pressing when liberal democrats decided that a positive role for the state must be reconsidered. When governmental authority was being limited, the constitutionalist might have thought that the structure of limitations was sufficiently well-devised to make government intrusion on or inhibition of moral autonomy rare. But when theorists recognize the necessity for conferring on the state a considerable responsibility for creating the conditions of the moral life, the possibility of such interference through error, or even intentional perversion of governmental authority, increases. The nightwatchman state can be relatively amoral, but how keep the interventionist state moral in its goals and methods?

Among the theorists of democracy, the liberals tended to view the problem of autonomy in individualistic, or atomistic, terms: How set the individual free from interference by other individuals, groups, or representatives of society (official and unofficial), so that he could be self-determining? Other thinkers rejected this perspective, although they too wanted to preserve individual autonomy. T. H. Green firmly tied individual autonomy to a social milieu with his concept of rights as powers of the individual recognized by other members of society. Without rights, the individual could not realize his moral nature. While Green did define autonomy in individual terms,[46] when he spoke of political obligation, he defined it as the individual's capacity for making a common good his own. In a political, if not philosophic, sense, individual autonomy was social; it meant a capacity for participating in enduring social relationships.[47]

From Green to John Dewey is not a great step. Dewey considered the individual-society distinction a false dualism. The individual grew up in and was shaped by a social milieu; unless his associative character was recognized, the nature of a human individual could not be accurately grasped.

As a matter of fact every individual has grown up, and always must grow up, in a social medium. His responses grow intelligent, or gain meaning, simply because he lives and acts in a medium of accepted meanings and values. Through social intercourse, through sharing in the activities embodying beliefs, he gradually acquires a mind of his own. The conception of mind as a purely isolated possession of the self is at the very antipodes of the truth. The self *achieves* mind in the degree in which knowledge of things is incarnate in the life about him; the self is not a separate mind building up knowledge anew on its own account.[48]

Much of Dewey's writing was devoted to counteracting what he considered the detrimental effects of viewing man in terms of this dualism. Because of his view that man is a thoroughly social animal, we might think that there would be little room for individual moral autonomy in Dewey's conception of democracy. But this is not the case. In an early essay Dewey manifested the concern for individual autonomy that absorbed other liberal-democratic thinkers:

In one word, democracy means that *personality* is the first and final reality. It admits . . . that the chief stimuli and encouragements to the realization of personality cannot be procured for anyone, however degraded and feeble, by anyone else, however wise and strong. It holds that the spirit of personality indwells in every individual and that the choice to develop it must proceed from that individual. From this central position of personality result the other notes of democracy, liberty, equality, fraternity . . . from the democratic standpoint, it must be remembered that the individual is something more than the individual, namely, a personality. His freedom is not mere self-assertion, nor unregulated desire. You cannot say that he knows no law; you must say that he knows no law but his own, the law of personality; no law, in other words, externally imposed, however splendid the authority, and undoubtedly the goodness of those that impose it. . . . The democratic ideal includes liberty, because democracy without initiation from within, without an ideal chosen from within and freely followed from within, is nothing.[49]

While Dewey's later work drew out the social meanings of democracy, he apparently did not see in this a rejection of individual autonomy as an ideal. By his emphasis on the social, Dewey did interpret democracy in a unique way:

A democracy is more than a form of government; it is primarily a mode of associated living, of conjoint communicated experience. The extension in space of the number of individuals who participate in an interest so that each has to refer his own action to that of others, and to consider the action of others to give point and direction to his own, is equivalent to the breaking down of those barriers of class, race, and national territory which kept men from perceiving the full import of their activity.[50]

But the intent was not to submerge the individual; as Dewey continued:

These more numerous and more varied points of contact denote a greater diversity of stimuli to which an individual has to respond; they consequently put a premium on variation in his action. They secure a liberation of powers which remain suppressed as long as the incitations to action are partial, as they must be in a group which in its exclusiveness shuts out many interests.[51]

What is happening here is a reinterpretation of the role of autonomy, so that its orientation is basically social. This seems quite like Green's definition of moral autonomy as self-determination by a concept of a common good. For Dewey, "The moral and the social quality of conduct are, in the last analysis, identical with each other."[52]

It is precisely because of his realization that the individual bears great responsibilities in a democracy that Dewey was so concerned to inculcate in him a recognition of his social nature. "A [democratic] society must have a type of education which gives individuals a personal interest in social relationships and control."[53]

When the social quality of individualized mental operations is denied, it becomes a problem to find connections which will unite an individual with his fellows. Moral individualism is set up by the conscious separation of different centers of life. It has its roots in the notion that the consciousness of each person is wholly private, a self-inclosed continent, intrinsically independent of the ideas, wishes, purposes of everybody else. But when men act, they act in a common and public world. This is the problem to which the theory of isolated and independent conscious minds gave rise: Given feelings, ideas, desires, which have nothing to do with one another, how can actions proceeding from them be controlled in a social or public interest? Given an egoistic consciousness, how can action which has regard for others take place?[54]

But the essence of the demand for freedom is the need of conditions which will enable an individual to make his own special contribution to a group interest, and to partake of its activities in such ways that social guidance shall be a matter of his own mental attitude, and not a mere authoritative dictation of his acts.[55]

What Dewey wants is not a subordination of individual will and reason to the will of society: This is to think in terms of dualism. Even when socially beneficial objectives are imposed on the individual, the resultant conformity is undesirable if the objectives are external to him. For Dewey does not want to destroy individual autonomy; he wants to instill it with a thoroughly social perspective. This does not mean cultivation of unthinking obedience or mindless subordination to rules and regulations that others, as representatives of society, have promulgated. It does not mean an authoritative definition of the ends and means which are to be considered social. Rather, it means seeing with a social eye, experiencing virtually everything in terms of its myriad connections with the experience of other persons, present and past. When Dewey speaks of thinking, he indicates clearly that it is an individual activity where there is room for individuality. Thinking cannot be done collectively, but it can be stimulated and oriented by a social milieu.

Freedom means essentially the part played by thinking—which is personal—in learning:—it means intellectual initiative, independence in observation, judicious invention, foresight of consequences, and ingenuity of adaptation to them.[56]

As Dewey points out, an individual whose purposes, whose questions, are not his own will not be motivated to inquire and search. If the individual is to contribute as much to living with others as he gets from it, he must have something unique, some experience which will enlarge their experience.

A condition of intellectual subjection is needed for fitting the masses into a society where the many are not expected to have aims or ideas of their own, but to take orders from the few set in authority. It is not adapted to a society which intends to be democratic.[57]

A progressive society counts individual variations as precious since it finds in them the means of its own growth. Hence a democratic society must, in consistency with its ideal, allow for intellectual freedom and the play of diverse gifts and interests in its educational measures.[58]

Far from the individualism of Locke and the other liberal-democratic thinkers who accepted his premises, we still find in Dewey the concern for individual moral autonomy. Recognizing the inescapably social character of human existence, he attempted to formulate a concept of democracy in which the individual could act autonomously and yet fulfill his nature as a social being.

Thus, we can see that preservation of individual moral autonomy has been a primary concern throughout the course of liberal-democratic thought. While freedom may have undergone some redefinition in the process, there has been a persistent core of meaning: the ability of the individual freely to have opinions, to make choices and act upon them; the continued opportunity to determine his own purposes and actions so far as is compatible with like self-determination by other members of society. Explanations of the genesis of such freedom changed from the state of nature to participation in social relations, governed by a conception of the common interest; the main modes of expressing freedom—economic activity, communal participation, forms of personal behavior, political and religious opinions—have varied. Threats to autonomy and the means of protecting and enhancing it have been viewed differently from one generation of liberal-democratic thought to another. Early thinkers feared government encroachment and formulated constitutional limitations. Later liberal democrats encouraged feelings of political and social efficacy and self-determination to counteract the tyranny of the majority and of public opinion. They emphasized political participation and recognition of the value of political freedom because democratic man seemed to be withdrawing from politics and community. In more recent times, abusive use of individual rights to the detriment of other individuals and the community as a whole has been considered the threat, and state intervention the remedy. Throughout these modifications, there persists a perception of man as a moral being, needing autonomy to express his nature, needing freedom to develop his moral potential.

It was the same solicitude for individual moral autonomy that inspired Henry David Thoreau to write the most well-known piece on the subject, *Civil Disobedience*. Thoreau spoke, not as a theorist of liberal democracy, but as a member of a nation which happened to be democratic. He even wished to put aside the implications of his being a citizen, but he realized that he could not quite do this. He was not concerned to consider the compatibility of disobedience and political allegiance. Rather, he wrote and spoke (the essay was originally a lecture) as an individual trying to decide how to act morally in a situation where his government was acting immorally.

Thoreau virtually proclaims himself an anarchist— "That government is best which governs not at all"[59]—at the beginning of his essay. As far as he is concerned, most governments, his own included, "are usually inexpedient." Politics does not interest him, he does not see himself as responsible "for the successful working of the machinery of society."[60] "It is not my business to be petitioning the Governor or the

Legislature any more than it is theirs to petition me."[61] Thoreau prefers to support those activities of government which are useful to him or which he thinks valuable; when government is inexpedient, he prefers to ignore it.

Despite his desire to shed the role of citizen, Thoreau found that he could not "opt out" mentally. He had this allegiance, or at least, the government thought he had it and it expected him to meet certain minimal responsibilities—for example, to pay his taxes. This did not especially upset Thoreau when it was merely a matter of the government's acting inexpediently, but when the government of which he was a reluctant citizen was organized to uphold a system of oppression, then he felt he was implicated in a way which made him uncomfortable. Since he could not easily discard this allegiance, was he not responsible for the way he used it? This was the way he saw the problem; for him, it was not a question of whether or not disobedience is ever legitimate in a democracy. He felt that governments rarely promoted worthwhile objectives except by stepping aside, and they had often "suborned" men to engage in immoral acts: "Law never made men a whit more just; and, by means of their respect for it, even the well disposed are daily made the agents of injustice."[62] This was so even in a democracy; majority rule possesses no inherent morality—it is based on superior power. Majorities are not always morally right. Conscience was man's distinctive possession; why should he yield it to the legislator? Thoreau would have been happy to let the government go its own way if it would let him do so, but he realized that his unwanted political allegiance made him a tool of the government, a condition he could not accept when it acted immorally. "When a sixth of the population of a nation which has undertaken to be the refuge of liberty are slaves . . . I think it is not too soon for honest men to rebel and revolutionize."[63]

Some commentators have debated whether Thoreau really meant to disavow his allegiance to the government by such statements. If he did, so Carl Cohen argues, then he "did not engage in civil disobedience in the strict sense."[64] In response, Norman Jacobson asserts that Thoreau's intent was political education:

Thoreau's essay is as instructive for citizenship as his refusal to pay his tax in protest; and . . . his raising the question of the obligations of citizenship is at least as much of a contribution to the enlightenment of the political community as his moral arguments against the institution of slavery. In other words, he shaped both his act *and* the words explaining and justifying that act, to the instruction of his fellow citizens. To me that is the true, in political terms, the only spirit in which an act of civil disobedience assumes grandeur.[65]

It is true that Thoreau's language, and even some of his arguments, appear to go beyond the bounds of political allegiance to the government. He rejected the idea of obeying the law while trying to change it because, morally, this was an unsatisfactory position and because, tactically, it was not effective. The only way for the minority which opposed slavery to make its view felt was by noncooperation.

A minority is powerless while it conforms to the majority; it is not even a minority then; but it is irresistible when it clogs by its whole weight. If the alternative is to keep all just men in prison, or give up war and slavery, the State will not hesitate which to choose.[66]

Thoreau's choice of tactics implies a recognition that democracy may well be different from other governments: In a democracy, citizens can effect political changes by peaceful means, by acting morally. When the individual citizen refuses to comply, he confronts those who act as the government's agents with the meaning of their position: Can they remain in this service when it means treating a moral man as a criminal? Thoreau apparently had faith that the example of a few men acting morally would have a tremendous impact, first on other citizens, who would be moved to emulate it, and then on those citizens who serve the government with their bodies: They too would feel compelled to question whether they could continue doing what they have done. If enough just men were willing to go to jail, the government would find it inexpedient not to change its policy. Thoreau may have meant that it would be too costly in physical terms to keep so many citizens locked up; he implied that civil disobedience can severely hamper a government. But in what kind of system could a relatively small minority be expected to have so great an impact on their fellow citizens? In other words, a democratic government might find it impractical to put large numbers of moral men in jail because that would be politically costly. While Thoreau suggested that politicians and officials look at what government does from too narrow a perspective, ignoring the morality of their acts, he must have thought they could be moved by such considerations. Yet nondemocratic governments might not consider it inexpedient to keep just men in prison.

Thoreau admitted that democracy is an improvement over other forms of government, such as limited monarchy, and his appeal to American citizens fits well within the traditions of liberal democracy. His ideal conception of government, considering the problem from the citizen's vantage point, reflects the ideals of liberal-democratic theory.

The authority of government, even such as I am willing to submit to ... is still an impure one: to be strictly just, it must have the sanction and consent of the governed. It can have no pure right over my person and property but what I concede to it. The progress from an absolute to a limited monarchy, from a limited monarchy to a democracy, is a progress toward a true respect for the individual.... Is a democracy, such as we know it, the last improvement possible in government? Is it not possible to take a step further towards recognizing and organizing the rights of man?[67]

Ultimately, Thoreau's choice of tactics—if advising men to act morally can be called "tactics"—is based on a conception of democratic government that transcended the government of his day and ours:

There will never be a really free and enlightened state until the State comes to recognize the individual as a higher and independent power, from which all its own power and authority are derived, and treats him accordingly.[68]

Despite his urge to be a "no-government man," Thoreau called for civil disobedience as a challenge to democratic government: Can such a government recognize the moral nature of men, its citizens, and treat them accordingly? Thus, when Thoreau spoke as a citizen, he was imbued with the same basic concern as the liberal-democratic theorists: "What is the value of any political freedom, but as a means to moral freedom?"[69]

One of the objectives of this essay will be to assert that civil disobedience, in theory and practice, is part of this basic tendency of liberal-democratic thought. Liberal-democratic politics represents an attempt to exclude violence from the coordination of social relationships. It is a way of arriving at collective decisions while attempting not to impose upon the individual ends and means with which he cannot feel "any spontaneous interest" in complying—ends and means which are external to him because they do not present themselves as "the condition of the maintenance of those rights and interests, common to himself with his neighbors, which he understands."[70] The intent of democracy is also the intent of civil disobedience. Recognizing that the democratic process requires law and order for healthy functioning, theorists of civil disobedience have developed the notion of self-imposed limitations. The theory of civil disobedience is an attempt to mediate between the conflicting pulls of political allegiance and private conscience. Implicit in liberal-democratic theory is the faith that men can cooperate for social ends without yielding up their consciences, without feeling that to obey is to act immorally. Yet its theorists have perceived that sometimes this appears impossible for the individual or the minority. This is why the concern with legitimate disobedience is a recurrent one. The emergence of the theory of civil disobedience is another manifestation of that concern, of that solicitude for individual moral autonomy, which lies at the core of liberal democracy.

Notes for Chapter II

1. John Locke, *Second Treatise on Civil Government*, §§ 123–125, *in* Sir Ernest Barker, ed., *Social Contract: Essays by Locke, Hume and Rousseau* (New York: Oxford University Press, 1960). I have cited the section numbers so that any edition of the *Second Treatise* may be consulted.

2. *Ibid.*, § 22.

3. *Ibid.*, § 34.

4. *Ibid.*, § 137.

5. John Locke, *A Letter Concerning Toleration* (Indianapolis: Bobbs-Merrill, 1950), p. 48.

6. *Ibid.*, p. 49.

7. *Ibid.*, p. 48.

8. Jean-Jacques Rousseau, *The Social Contract,* Book I, Chapter VI, *in* Barker, p. 180.

9. *Ibid.*, Book I, Chapter VIII, pp. 185–186.

10. *Ibid.*, Book I, Chapter VII, p.184.

11. *Ibid.*, Book IV, Chapter II, p. 273.

12. *Ibid.*, Book IV, Chapter VIII, p. 306.

13. Jean-Jacques Rousseau, *Emile,* trans. by Barbara Foxley (New York: Dutton, 1963), p. 254.

14. *Ibid.*, p. 206.

15. Rousseau, *The Social Contract*, Book II, Chapter III, p. 194.

16. *Ibid.*, Book IV, Chapter II, p. 273.

17. *The Life and Selected Writings of Thomas Jefferson*, ed. by Adrienne Koch and William Peden (New York: The Modern Library, 1944), p. 313.

18. *Ibid.*, p. 466.

19. *Ibid.*, p. 567.

20. *Ibid.*, p. 568.

21. *Ibid.*, p. 576.

22. Alexis de Tocqueville, quoted in Jack Lively, *The Social and Political Thought of Alexis de Tocqueville* (Oxford: Clarendon Press, 1962), p. 12.

23. *Ibid.*, p. 13.

24. Alexis de Tocqueville, *Democracy in America,* ed. by Phillips Bradley (New York: Vintage Books, 1959), II, p. 11.

25. *Ibid.*, II, p. 337.

26. *Ibid.*, I, p. 270.

27. *Ibid.*, I, p. 269.

28. *Ibid.*

29. *Ibid.*, I, p. 67 (emphasis added).

30. Lively, p. 18.

31. *Ibid.*, p. 17.

32. *Ibid.*, p. 18.

33. John Stuart Mill, *On Liberty*, with an introduction by Russell Kirk (Chicago: Gateway Editions, n. d.), pp. 11–12.

34. *Ibid.*, p. 73.

35. *Ibid.*, p. 15.

36. *Ibid.*, p. 14.

37. Thomas Hill Green, "Lecture on Liberal Legislation and Freedom of Contract," *in* R. L. Nettleship, ed., *Works of Thomas Hill Green*, Vol. III (London: Longmans, Green, 1888), p. 367.

38. Thomas Hill Green, *Lectures on the Principles of Political Obligation*, reprinted from Green's *Works*, Vol. II (London: Longmans, 1941), p. 45.

39. *Ibid.*

40. *Ibid.*

41. *Ibid.*, p. 144.

42. *Ibid.*, p. 27.

43. *Ibid.*, pp. 39–40 (emphasis added).

44. *Ibid.*, p. 125.

45. *Ibid.*, p. 110.

46. Thomas Hill Green, "On the Different Senses of 'Freedom' as Applied to Will and to the Moral Progress of Man," *in* R. L. Nettleship, ed., *Works of Thomas Hill Green*, Vol. II (London: Longmans, Green, 1886), pp. 308–333.

47. Green seems to reflect a strong Rousseauean infusion into the liberal tradition.

48. John Dewey, *Democracy and Education* (New York: Free Press, 1966), p. 295.

49. John Dewey, *The Ethics of Democracy*, University of Michigan Philosophical Papers, 2nd series, no. 1 (Ann Arbor: Andrews, 1888), pp. 22–24.

50. Dewey, *Democracy and Education*, p. 87.

51. *Ibid.*

52. *Ibid.*, p. 358.

53. *Ibid.*, p. 99.

54. *Ibid.*, p. 297.

55. *Ibid.*, p. 301.

56. *Ibid.*, p. 302.

57. *Ibid.*, p. 305.

58. *Ibid.*

59. Henry David Thoreau, "Civil Disobedience," *in* Milton Meltzer, ed., *Thoreau: People, Principles, and Politics* (New York: Hill and Wang, 1963), p. 36.

60. *Ibid.*, p. 51.

61. *Ibid.*, p. 45.

62. *Ibid.*, p. 38.

63. *Ibid.*, p. 40.

64. Carl Cohen, "Essence and Ethics of Civil Disobedience," *The Nation,* 198 (March 16, 1964), 258.

65. Norman Jacobson, "Civil Disobedience: Philosophy and Tactics," paper presented at the Conference on Law Enforcement and Racial and Cultural Tensions, Berkeley, California, October 9, 1964, p. 8.

66. Thoreau, p. 47.

67. *Ibid.*, p. 58.

68. *Ibid.*

69. *Journal,* February 16, 1851, quoted in Meltzer, p. 62.

70. Green, *Lectures on the Principles of Political Obligation*, p. 129.

Toward a Theory
of Civil Disobedience

1. JUSTIFYING DISOBEDIENCE:
HOBBES, LOCKE, AND JEFFERSON

AT FIRST GLANCE, it would not appear that Hobbes's political theory would provide any basis for legitimizing civil disobedience. To do so requires two admissions: (1) that there are certain standards, however nebulous, by which governments may be judged; and (2) that it is permissible for the subject or citizen to make such judgments. True, Hobbes asserts that certain behavior is proper for the sovereign, for example, imposition of equal taxes, passage of "good" (i.e., necessary, beneficial to the people, unambiguous) laws, provision of public charity, application of rewards and punishments so as to benefit the commonwealth. Yet Hobbes does not intend that these "duties" be considered standards for judging the legitimacy of the sovereign's actions. The sovereign is the sole legislator (he decides what is legal and illegal), and the civil law is the only measure of good and evil. Thus, only he may judge of good and evil. By implication, no private man has the right to express opinions in these matters. The doctrine "that every private man is judge of good and evil actions" is a disease of a commonwealth:

Notes to this chapter will be found on pages 102–104.

From this false doctrine, men are disposed to debate with themselves, and dispute the commands of the commonwealth; and afterwards to obey, or disobey them, as in their private judgments they shall think fit; whereby the commonwealth is distracted and weakened.[1]

As a consequence, the people should be taught through public instruction:

how great a fault it is, to speak evil of the sovereign representative . . . or to argue and dispute his power; or any way to use his name irreverently, whereby he may be brought into contempt with his people, and their obedience, in which the safety of the commonwealth consisteth, slackened.[2]

The fact that the sovereign represents the members of the body politic could imply a limitation upon the sovereign—that is, that he should not act against the people's will. But, as Hanna Pitkin points out, Hobbes had a curious notion of representation. The subjects authorize *in advance* all the actions of the sovereign, who thus may bind them. "Authorization is a source of obligation to the sovereign. Through it, the sovereign is empowered to commit his subjects as if his will were theirs."[3] Except in extraordinary circumstances, the sovereign's will is to be taken for the subject's will. The subjects' will cannot then be taken as a criterion by which to judge the sovereign in his representative capacity.

Clearly, Hobbes provides no basis for private judgments that acts of the sovereign are illegal or improper. In other words, the grounds for justifying civilly disobedient acts are not to be found in his theory of civil society. Nonetheless a civilly disobedient act does not violate the premises of Hobbes's theory of political obligation; the formal characteristics of civil disobedience can be fitted into the interstices. Hobbes admits that breaking the law, while generally meriting punishment, is not always unjust. He defines injustice as "the not performance of covenant," but not all crimes constitute nonperformance.[4] Under the topic heading "Subjects are not bound to hurt themselves," Hobbes qualifies the subjects' obligation to obey the sovereign's command to perform some dangerous or dishonorable mission:

When therefore our refusal to obey, frustrates the end for which sovereignty was ordained; then there is no liberty to refuse: otherwise there is. Upon this ground, a man that is commanded as a soldier to fight against the enemy, *though his sovereign have right enough to punish his refusal with death,* may nevertheless in many cases refuse, without injustice.[5]

The elements of civil disobedience are here: (1) an act of disobedience, i.e., violation of a law or refusal to comply with an authoritative command, which (2) neither denies the sovereign power (the civil disobedient acknowledges the legitimacy of the sovereign), nor frustrates the end—protection—for which the sovereign was established, and which (3) may be punished legitimately by the sovereign and (4) is yet not unjust.[6] Apparently Hobbes's covenant does not demand obedience in all cases. The subject is explicitly absolved from obedience in a limited number of cases, e.g., self-harm. Pushing the above line of reasoning beyond Hobbes, one can argue that, in cases to which the obligation of obedience would, in Hobbes's view, normally extend, the subject may disobey without *necessarily* breaking the covenant. In other words, Hobbes's admission that not all disobedience constitutes nonperformance of the covenant permits a further examination of the bounds of justifiable disobedience. Disobedience which takes a "civil" form may fit within this category.

Although Hobbes does not favor permitting the subject to judge the sovereign, he adumbrated a principle which was later to become part of the justification for civil disobedience: individual consent is the basis of political obligation. The subject, Hobbes asserts, consents to be bound by the sovereign's action when he authorizes the sovereign as his representative. He agrees that the sovereign's will be taken for his own. To disobey the sovereign's will is to contradict his previous consent. Obligation is created by consent, not directly however, but rather through the creation of an authority with power to enforce covenants, including the original one. A covenant is not binding unless each party has assurance of its being fulfilled by the other parties. The existence of the sovereign provides this assurance. It seems that Hobbes is trying to confer upon consent the ability to create obligation, for he says there is "no obligation on any man, which ariseth not from some act of his own, for all men equally, are by nature free."[7] Although he is well aware that power or fear can "oblige," he seems reluctant to reduce obligation to this source alone. If obligation means merely that the sovereign's superior power "obliges" the subject to obey the original covenant, then the moral aspect of obligation is eliminated. But the original agreement to found a civil society was made in a body of men, each covenanting with the others, and Hobbes seems to recognize that personal commitments to others which are voluntarily undertaken have an element of moral compulsion. Having thus related consent to the origin of the body politic, Hobbes suppresses the democratic implications of consent by viewing it solely as an initial authorization which cannot be withdrawn unless the condition which makes it morally binding—the power of the sovereign to enforce it—is not present.

Locke also tried to relate consent and political obligation. Like Hobbes, he argued that the original basis of political society was voluntaristic—the covenant or social contract theory of political authority. Both men apparently recognized that "consent" had powerful appeal in rationalizing political authority; they wished to capitalize on the plausibility of feeling obliged because one had agreed. Yet neither wished to make consent an active principle in governance, nor were they proposing referenda on the contemporary form of government in England. Obviously, this meant that there were many persons in England in whom a sense of political obligation was desirable (or, perhaps more accurately—in terms of Locke's intent—whom others could look upon as obliged) but who had not explicitly consented to be ruled by the government. Locke tried to deal with this problem by expanding the notion of consent to include tacit consent and then interpreting the latter rather broadly:

The difficulty is, what ought to be looked upon as tacit consent, and how far it binds, i.e., how far anyone *shall be looked on* to have consented, and thereby submitted to any government, where he has made no expressions of it at all. And to this I say, that every man that hath any possession or enjoyment of any part of the dominions of any government doth thereby give his tacit consent, and is as far forth obliged to obedience to the laws of that government, during such enjoyment, as anyone under it, whether this his possession be of land to him and his heirs forever, or a lodging only for a week; or whether it be barely travelling freely on the highway; and, in effect, it reaches as far as the very being of anyone within the territories of that government.[8]

Few theorists have drawn out the radical implications of the consent principle—that the individual has the right to decide whether he is bound to obey any particular law; that his consent is conditional; that it may be temporarily revoked. Nonetheless, modern democratic theorists tend to accept Hobbes and Locke's insight that there is some connection between consent and a quasi-moral obligation to obey the law in a political society. The problem they encounter is the difficulty of defining consent. It is possible to interpret consent in such a way as to support the view that civil disobedience is a legitimate form of political participation.

In his *Second Treatise on Civil Government*, John Locke provides the substantive basis for justifying popular resistance which is lacking in Hobbes's *Leviathan*. Rulers, Locke asserts, are given authority as a trust by the people, and when this trust is violated, the people have the power to reconstitute the organs of government. Locke suggests that the trust may be violated "when either the legislative is changed, or the legislators act contrary to the end for which they were constituted."[9] For example, rulers may usurp formal powers not legitimately theirs or legislators may pass laws which invade the rights government was originally established to defend. By establishing standards for judging the legitimacy of the rulers' actions, Locke provides a justification for resistance. If the rulers act so as to subvert the ends for which government was erected—"if a long train of abuses, prevarications, and artifices, all tending the same way, make the design [of the rulers] visible to the people"[10]—then they have the right to revolt. By a long series of abuses, the rulers have made manifest an evil intent to subvert the commonwealth. The rulers are the rebels.

[T]hose . . . who by force break through, and by force justify their violation of [the constitutions and laws of the government], are truly and properly rebels . . . those who set up force again in opposition to the laws do *rebellare* —that is, bring back again the state of war.[11]

Logically, one may conceive of a resistance to the rulers' subversion of the commonwealth which does not entail force. However, Locke's critique of Barclay's *Contra Monarchum* indicates that he did not envision this possibility. Barclay asserts that the people may resist the tyranny of a prince, but they must not attack him; they must not "exceed the bounds of due reverence and respect." Locke answers by suggesting that it will take some skill to explain "how to resist force without striking again."

He . . . who may resist must be allowed to strike. . . . He that can reconcile blows and reverence may, for aught I know, deserve for his pains a civil, respectful cudgelling wherever he can meet with it.[12]

According to Locke, only a situation in which force has already been re-introduced justifies popular resistance. By performing illegitimate actions, the rulers have put themselves into a state of war with the members of the commonwealth where each group must look to its own defense, where the readiness to defend oneself by force is necessary for survival. In this case, the very framework which civil disobedience assumes, the stability and legitimacy of political organs, is undermined. Although Locke is quite aware of the possibility of rulers' committing less serious misdeeds, he does not envisage a response by individuals or the people graduated to the severity of the evil.

Of the three theorists being considered here, Jefferson comes closest to envisaging actual civil disobedience, as well as providing some rationale for it. In "A Summary View of the Rights of British America, 1774," he describes the Boston Tea Party in these terms:

There are extraordinary situations which require extraordinary interposition. An exasperated people, who feel that they possess power, are not easily restrained within limits strictly regular. A number of them assembled in the town of Boston, threw the tea into the ocean, and dispersed without doing any other act of violence. If in this they did wrong, they were known, and were amenable to the laws of the land; against which, it could not be objected, that they had ever, in any instance, been obstructed or diverted from the regular course, in favor of popular offenders. They should, therefore, have not been distrusted on this occasion.[13]

Jefferson's main concern here was to condemn Parliament's subsequent act, which discontinued shipping in the Boston harbor, as an unwarranted punishment for this defiance of the tea duties. Nonetheless, it may be inferred that he thought this defiance was, in a sense, both justifiable and punishable. Apparently, conceding the legitimacy of punishment through ordinary legal processes was not inconsistent, to him, with suggesting that the act was justifiable. That Jefferson was not disposed to look unfavorably upon resistance to British authority, especially resistance as restrained as this, is evident. He was contesting the authority of Parliament over the colonies. Yet it would appear that this was not crucial to his evaluation of the Boston Tea Party. Had it been the colonists' own elected representatives who had imposed some unjust exaction, the nature of the situation in question might still have warranted disobedience of this kind. This inference seems justified, for in a letter to Madison (1/30/1787), Jefferson, referring to "governments, wherein the will of everyone has a just influence," says:

Even this evil [popular turbulence] is productive of good. It prevents the degeneracy of government, and nourishes a general attention to the public affairs. I hold it, that a little rebellion, now and then, is a good thing, and as necessary in the political world as storms in the physical. Unsuccessful rebellions, indeed, generally establish the encroachments on the rights of the people, who have produced them. An observation of this truth should render honest republican governors so mild in their punishment of rebellions, as not to discourage them too much. It is a medicine necessary for the sound health of government.[14]

Jefferson feared the tendency of government to extend its sphere of concern beyond legitimate bounds, to encroach, for example, upon the rights of conscience. He was not comfortable with the idea of an energetic government because of its potential oppressiveness. To keep government within its proper sphere and governors responsive to the will of the people, Jefferson was willing to condone a little rebellion. This was not enough of a threat to the stability of society to make it intolerable; indeed, a certain amount of agitation could be functional in maintaining just government. Jefferson's remarks on Shay's Rebellion (in another letter to Madison, 1/20/1787) bear this out:

The late rebellion in Massachusetts has given more alarm, than I think it should have done. Calculate that one rebellion in thirteen states in the course of eleven years, is but one for each state in a century and a half. No country should be so long without one. Nor will any degree of power in the hands of government, prevent insurrections. In England, where the hand of power is heavier than with us, there are seldom half a dozen years without an insurrection. In France, where it is still heavier, but less despotic . . . than in some other countries, and where there are always two or three hundred thousand men ready to crush insurrections, there have been three in the course of the three years I have been here, in every one of which greater numbers were engaged than in Massachusetts, and a great deal more blood spilt. In Turkey, where the sole nod of the despot is death, insurrections are the events of every day. Compare again the ferocious depredations of their insurgents, with the order, moderation and the almost self-extinguishment of ours.[15]

He continues in this vein, in a letter of July 2, 1787:

And can history produce an instance of a rebellion so honorably conducted? I say nothing of its motives. They were founded in ignorance, not wickedness. The people cannot be all, and always, well informed. The part which is wrong will be discontented, in proportion to the importance of the facts they misconceive. If they remain quiet under such misconceptions, it is a lethargy, the forerunner of death to the public liberty. . . . What country before, ever existed a century and a half without a rebellion? And what country can preserve its liberties, if its rulers are not warned from time to time, that this people preserve the spirit of resistance? Let them take to arms. The remedy is to set them right as to facts, pardon and pacify them. What signify a few lives lost in a century or two? The tree of liberty must be refreshed from time to time, with the blood of patriots and tyrants. It is its natural manure.[16]

In condoning limited rebellion of this sort, Jefferson was even willing to admit that the cause itself might be a mistaken one, that it might not be real tyranny which brought it on. Even in this case, extreme measures ought not to be taken to prevent these outbursts, especially because such "rebels" are rather easily pacified. Apparently, they are not really mounting an attack on the whole institutional framework; they are not seeking a radical change in existing conditions. In order for them to be persuaded of their error in taking up arms, adequate information about the true situation will suffice. From this we might infer that the goals of the rebels are rather limited and that they adhere to the same basic view of the proper arrangement of society as do their governors. While Jefferson's optimism about the effect of education upon men is probably reflected here, what is also reflected is his reliance upon American conditions of relative equality and of broad value consensus. With occasional small jolts, the American republic would not degenerate into a tyranny.

In all probability, the use of civil disobedience to resist the encroachments of government upon, for example, rights of conscience, would have been acceptable to Jefferson. It would be clear evidence that the people still "preserve the spirit of resistance." In delimiting the proper sphere of government, setting apart certain special realms of human activity, Jefferson provided some basis by which people could judge the propriety of their rulers' actions. And he would have not denied the people the right to make such judgments and to act upon them, although he was well aware that they might be mistaken.

There are several useful propositions to be culled from the work of these three theorists: (1) a social contract theory of the state does not preclude legitimate disobedience to political authority—that is, not all acts of disobedience are inconsistent with the idea of a government established voluntarily by a body of men to protect their liberties; (2)

the consent of the individual is the source of the obligation to obey constituted political authority; (3) when governors commit acts which subvert the ends for which government was established, popular resistance is justified; and (4) popular willingness to resist can serve to keep governors responsive and less likely to infringe on the people's liberties. These are the basic components for constructing a full-blown justification of civil disobedience within the liberal-democratic polity. The first proposition provides the basis for a distinction between that disobedience which is not inconsistent with the maintenance of stable, legitimate political institutions and that disobedience which threatens to undermine the preconditions for maintaining such institutions. The principle which links consent and political obligation suggests that the citizen in a liberal-democratic polity must, in some meaningful way, be consulted by his governors in order for him to be considered obliged to obey them. There must be some means by which he can retain his autonomy, a form of participation which will help make government responsive. The third proposition asserts that the ends for which government was established are to be considered limits on the authority of governors. The government's fulfillment of these ends is the ultimate reason for allegiance and obedience to law. Assuming that legitimate disobedience is conceivable, what are the conditions which justify an act of disobedience or resistance? When officials violate the basic principles of the polity they have been empowered to govern, then citizens have the right to resist. While Locke conceived the right of resistance in terms of revolution, he formulated some general criteria for exercising that right. These criteria may, by extrapolation, help in the formulation of criteria for engaging in civil disobedience. For example, when the institutions of government are no longer open to the influence of certain groups, when they no longer serve their needs and meet their aspirations, it may be legitimate for them to engage in activities which will help reopen the conventional channels of political influence. Finally, proposition four represents Jefferson's functional argument for resistance. If responsiveness of governors to governed is an important part of liberal democracy, then it may be necessary to encourage, or at least tolerate, certain unconventional means of making governors responsive when conventional methods are not effective. Later theorists carried some of these insights closer to the formulation of an explicit concept of civil disobedience and a specific justification to legitimize it.

2. *FROM JUSTIFIED DISOBEDIENCE TO CIVIL DISOBEDIENCE: GREEN AND BARKER*

T. H. Green, in his *Lectures on the Principles of Political Obligation*, explicitly establishes the notion of certain transcendent purposes as the ideal criterion by which actual exercise of authority is to be judged. He links the obligation to obey government to the fulfillment of its ideal function; and he poses the question of whether and when government is to be obeyed from the individual's point of view. The function of government is to maintain "those conditions of freedom which are conditions of the moral life. . . . If it ceases to serve this function, it loses its claim on our obedience."[17] Green is willing to confer the right to make this judgment upon the individual; he may judge when the government has lost its claim to his obedience and may rightly be resisted. But Green hedges this concession in several ways. While the individual may decide that a certain law is against the common good, he should, if he is a member of a "popular government" with "settled methods of enacting and repealing laws," obey it until he can obtain its repeal by legal methods. "It is . . . the social duty of the individual to conform"[18] because the common good will be harmed more by resistance to a law or lawful authority than by conformity to a bad law until it can be repealed. However, Green suggests that in certain other cases, the matter is not so easily settled. The case most germane to this discussion is that "when the authority from which the objectionable command proceeds is so easily separable from that on which the maintenance of social order and the fabric of settled rights depends, that it can be resisted without serious detriment to this order and fabric."[19]

Green asks whether there may be, in such cases, "a right of resistance based on a 'higher law' than the command of the ostensible sovereign."[20] His answer, if answer it be, is somewhat confusing, based as it is on his concept of a right. He dismisses the idea that there can be some natural right of resistance separable from society, for "it is on the relation to a society, to other men recognizing a common good that the individual's rights depend."[21] While there can be no right against society, there can be a "social duty to resist" which, under certain conditions—general recognition that such resistance is for the public good—may become a right. This general recognition, "through which the power of resistance becomes a right, must be something more habitual and sustained and penetrating than any vote of a majority can convey."[22] Nor does mere approval by a majority *necessarily* make the act of resistance a duty, but it can be a duty "before a majority of the citizens approve it." Green thinks that rights are founded on general recognition; this notion apparently leads him to deny the possibility of a right of resistance without some kind of sustained public consensus. Nonetheless he realizes that it may be precisely in those cases where resistance is most important—that is, under the worst governments— that the likelihood of public recognition is smallest. For a solution to the dilemma, he develops the notion of a social duty, for example, to resist an unjust law—based on a conception of public interest. However, it is not fully clear what the public interest comprises. Green suggests that, as a general rule, "the public interest . . . is more concerned in the general obedience to law than in the exercise of those powers by individuals or classes which the objectionable laws unfairly withhold."[23] However, in certain circumstances, a social duty to resist may be counterposed to the general duty to obey the law. What these circumstances might be is revealed by implication. Green suggests that the duty to obey is sometimes paramount, for instance, where the violation is liable "to result in general anarchy, not merely in the sense of the dissolution of this or that form of civil combination, but of disappearance of the conditions under which any civil combination is possible. . . ."[24] Therefore, when a law violation will *not* produce such dire consequences, a social duty to resist, if it exists, would seem to be the superior obligation, even though there is no general consensus supporting a *right* to resist. This leaves considerable leeway for justifying civil disobedience because, if practiced by a minority, it probably would not cause the rather total breakdown of law and order of which Green speaks. He does not deal with the question whether or not the violator should resist enforcement of the law he breaks. Only in the case of forcible resistance, which is tantamount to rebellion, would such anarchy be a real possibility. Certainly it is difficult to see how peaceful resistance could bring about the calamity Green describes, unless a rather large part of the population were involved and their allegiance to the government were rather attenuated.

Thus, although Green denies the existence of a general right of resistance, he does admit the possibility of a more urgent imperative, i.e., a social duty to disobey under certain limited conditions. These conditions include the state of the public mind; that is, it must be considered in calculating the likelihood of a breakdown of the system of law and order.[25] Nonetheless, the duty to disobey apparently arises from something which cannot be negated by positive law or by public nonrecognition, whereas the *right* to disobey requires public consensus. Perhaps Green is reacting to pragmatic considerations. For men to risk disobeying their government when no public recognition of their cause exists, they may need something more than the sense of possessing a right. Under these circumstances, a sense of duty is more compelling. Obviously, if that duty had to be grounded in public consensus, the cause would be lost by default. On the other hand, if the consensus exists, much of the poignancy of the resister's dilemma evaporates. To base the right of specific disobedience on the existence of public consensus makes the right almost superfluous. The task of bringing the public's view around to that of the dissenter is virtually accomplished.

The doctrine Green was expounding had explosive implications. Having given the citizen the right to judge whether his government is fulfilling its ideal purposes, he apparently realized that granting a general *right* of resistance as well might mean that the largely habitual obedience upon which the fabric of society rests would be replaced by a great deal of dissent and disobedience. Therefore, Green repeatedly sounds the theme of the primacy of order; yet, simultaneously, he is not content that the claims of social order should always override the claims of justice. His specific remarks suggest that in a democracy, resistance would generally be more detrimental to the common good than conformity to a bad law, yet his discussion of the conditions under which there may be a social duty to disobey can be applied— without distortion, I think—to a democratic polity. The specific case he mentions—"when the authority from which the objectionable command proceeds is so easily separable from that on which the maintenance of the social order . . . depends"—seems readily applicable to a liberal democracy. The idea of constitutional restraints, an integral part of liberal democracy, is premised on the possibility of separating the authority to issue specific commands (or to legislate specific laws) from the authority to issue commands in general. For instance, the Supreme Court can overturn a federal law without impugning the legitimacy of Congress. In a political system without constitutional limitations, to say that a specific exercise of authority is illegitimate is to suggest that authority in general may be illegitimate. Because there are no clear boundaries, the attempt to draw a line over which the authorities should not step threatens to change the system fundamentally. Civil disobedience makes use of the possibility of separating the legitimacy of specific governmental acts from the general legitimacy of government, in order to claim that civil disobedience is not subversive of the fabric of law and order.[26]

In sum, Green develops the notion that disobedience to established law is legitimate under certain circumstances. He hints at the crucial distinction that the theory of civil disobedience makes between the legitimacy of specific acts of authority and the legitimacy of political authority itself. Green clearly gives the individual the right to judge the propriety of government actions, based on the principles of an ideal justice which government was established to foster. While recognizing the importance of order, Green also realizes that the public interest may sometimes (though not often) be better served by violating an objectionable law than be obeying it—for instance, when the violation represents "the general sense of right on which the general observance of law depends."[27] Here he foreshadows the argument of some modern commentators that civil disobedience is legitimately used to appeal to the sense of justice of the majority. Moreover, he suggests that resistance may be justifiable even when no such public support exists—as long as the violation is not likely to produce "general anarchy."

In *Principles of Social and Political Theory,* Ernest Barker develops some of Green's premises into a fairly definite conception of civil disobedience. Both connect the obligation to obey the government (or "State," in Barker's terminology) with the fulfillment of its ideal purposes. For Barker, it is the general idea of justice and the system of political values which that idea controls and coordinates that ultimately claims our obedience; insofar as the State represents and realizes those conceptions, it has a valid claim to our obedience. He suggests that this duality creates a dilemma: Which obligation is paramount—that to the "State-expression of justice" or that to a transcendent justice which the State fails to express (or to express fully)? Yet Barker's initial formulation suggests that there is no dilemma: The obligation to transcendent justice would seem to be higher. Apparently, Barker was not satisfied with this conclusion. It makes political obligation conditional: Only insofar as the State conforms to a transcendent standard can it legitimately expect the citizen to obey its commands.[28] Yet Barker believes that the political community *per se* has value and that a sense of political obligation is necessary to its survival. If political obligation is regarded as conditional, the existence of the political community may be threatened. If political obligation "is regarded as simply a matter of contract," then members may renege when they are personally dissatisfied.[29] Or the contract may be regarded as committing the member to obey the will of the community (or its majority), whatever this may be. Since justice and individual autonomy are important to him, Barker is not happy with this interpretation either. He needs a formula which will serve justice and protect individual autonomy while maintaining the stability of the political community.

First, he suggests that these competing claims might be reconciled if the process of State activity is analogous to the "process of social thought" by which the transcendent ideal of justice is formed and expressed:

The State should itself correspond, in its own nature and operation, to the process of social thought which it mediates, and should thus be a broad open channel for the flow of the product it expresses. The process of social thought is a process in which all members of Society can freely share, and to which they can all contribute freely.[30]

It begins with the production of ideas by individuals, followed by discussion, and results in the composition of a number of new and different ideas. "Each individual and each group, has something to throw into the pool of discussion in order to stir the waters."[31] Likewise, all members of the State should be able to share freely in and contribute to the process of its activity. While assuming that the democratic state alone permits this, Barker realizes that, even so, its law may not "square" with the ideal justice. If duly enacted, he says, this law "is legally valid and finally conclusive" in the State's sphere, but if it is not just, it would appear to lack moral obligation.[32]

Although he has spent many words trying to determine which was the superior obligation, Barker must have realized from the beginning that both political and supra-political obligations had to be satisfied. At this point, civil disobedience is brought in as the *deus ex machina*; it resolves the dilemma by giving both God and Caesar their due:

Because political obligation . . . remains, as such, absolute and unconditional, we may lay it down that in any case of disobedience or resistance to law, based on the idea of social justice and social obligation, it is the clear duty of the judge, in his capacity of judge, and of all the organs of government, in their capacity of organs, to enforce the established law . . . and it is equally the clear duty of the disobeying or resisting citizen to obey, as a citizen, the established law, by accepting the legal consequences involved in his disobedience or resistance. But because social obligation is also a fact, and because, to the "protestant" penetrated by a conviction of its sovereign nature, it is the highest fact, it is also his duty to accept its demand and offer his testimony to its sovereignty.

A group which feels its idea to be a vital element in any just order of relations will feel bound to stake itself upon that idea: it will seek, by *the visible testimony of its disobedience and its acceptance of the legal consequences to impress the value of its idea on others*, to get it incorporated in social thought, to make it part of common conviction, and ultimately to secure its adoption as part of the law of the State. . . . It is at once *a rejection and an acceptance of political obligation*: a rejection, so far as it denies that obligation on a particular issue: an acceptance, so far as it affirms it in general and on the whole, and so far as it attests its affirmation by facing and accepting the legal consequences of the partial denial.[33]

Barker adds that civil disobedience is virtually within the process of social thought; it "is a method of persuasion rather than a recourse to force."[34]

While civil disobedience appears to give both political and suprapolitical obligations their due, Barker apparently decided that the individual's own idea of justice was not sufficient reason for him to disobey the law. If the demands of political obligation were to be reduced to less than absolute and unconditional obedience, then there had to be a stronger competing obligation. Barker found this in the process of social thought, which produces the socially created and developed ideas, e.g., justice, of which he speaks. The process is paramount to these ideals because it is their *sine qua non*. In recognizing the obligation of the ideal (which is based on consensus), one recognizes the obligation of the process which makes that consensus possible. From this line of reasoning Barker concludes that there can be a social obligation binding the individual despite the absence of public support for his conception of justice. Barker realizes that some contributions to the process of social thought will not be painless, if they are to have impact. Such a situation occurs when an individual's or group's notion of justice comes into conflict with the State-expression of justice. This is the occasion of civil disobedience, for which the penalties may be high. But despite the civil disobedient's willingness to pay the price, Barker asserts, he still cannot escape the dilemma that seeking justice in this manner conflicts with the stability of the political community. For Barker, like Green, contends that such resistance disturbs "the *general* scheme of law and order, and the *general* validity of obligation."[35] He also remarks, as have other commentators, the incidental encouragement given to less scrupulous and more self-interested persons to disturb that system. Thus the resister must put his potential contribution to the social conception of justice into the scales against the possible costs of disturbing the scheme of law and order. Barker indicates that where there is a stable system of law, due to such factors as the "common love of use and wont, the strength of convention, the habit of tradition," the introduction of a new idea through the act of resistance may well be functional for the system—it corrects the tendency for custom to grow hard and inflexible.

Barker does not contend that the conflict of obligations exists only when the citizen considers the government legitimate and/or when the government is based on the principle of popular consent. Yet the dilemma seems most germane to the case of a democrat in a liberal democracy. True, the conflict of obligations can arise in other situations; in fact, it may be more likely to arise elsewhere because a government whose institutional form is rejected by the citizen probably is more likely to take actions that violate his conceptions of justice; it may offend merely in the way it makes and implements decisions. The superiority of the individual's ideal conceptions of justice *vis-à-vis* the State-expression will be quite clear, at least for the dissident citizen. He may, nonetheless, be well aware of the benefits of law and order and loath to disturb it by following his principles to the point of resistance. But would one say that he has the same sense of political obligation as the citizen who considers his government legitimate according to his principles? To imply, as Barker does, that the nature of political obligation is the same regardless of the citizen-state relationship, and/or of the type of political institutions, severs any connection with the idea of legitimacy, much less with consent. With regard to some polities, political obligation may thus be reduced to Hobbesian premises: One obeys because the order of the state is better than no order at all. If this can be the sole basis of political obligation, then it does not seem to have any real moral component. Yet democratic theorists have tried to suggest that obedience to law is a *moral* obligation because of the citizen's relation to the liberal-democratic state, because of the particular institutions of liberal democracy. Barker seemed to recognize this when he tried to analogize the democratic state to the process of social thought, when he argued that only the democratic state corresponded to that process. Since the democratic state apparently is unique in this respect, one would think that political obligation to it would in some way differ from political obligation to other polities.

If Barker gives no indication that the nature of the polity affects the sense of political obligation, it does appear that his solution to the problem of conflicting obligations, i.e., civil disobedience, is most relevant to a democracy. One might contend that even in some undemocratic states, there is a process of social thought to which the individual can contribute. However, if what he wants to contribute deviates considerably from the State-expression of justice, the costs of making his contribution may well be considerably higher than in a democracy. To make such a contribution in a democracy may entail the pain of engaging in civil disobedience, but the same act in another political system may have a very different meaning for the governors, and thus, it may have very different consequences. Barker sees civil disobedience as virtually within the area of debate; in conjunction with his notion of the process of social thought, it is a legitimate, if not legal, way of contributing. Now the civil disobedient in a nondemocratic system may have the same intention, but his rulers may not consider such an act virtually within the area of debate. The area of debate may be rather limited, both in terms of who may participate and what kinds of issues are open for discussion. One may retort that it will still be possible to contribute by breaking the law, and as Barker says, since the social obligation is higher, one must follow its demands and offer testimony to its primacy. Yet, for the civil disobedient to engage in this limited form of resistance, his rejection-acceptance of political obligation must be understood by the political officials he confronts. They may be unwilling to acknowledge his point that limited rejection of authority is compatible with general acceptance. To argue that the greater the pain suffered, the greater is the impact of civil disobedience seems unduly optimistic in light of the capacity of certain nonliberal, nondemocratic states to smother and conceal dissent. It is possible that mass civil disobedience can prevent an authoritarian regime from continuing a repressive policy, by making the costs unacceptably high, e.g., forcing the regime to intern and perhaps ultimately kill a large percentage of the population—perhaps more persons than the regime has the capacity, in terms of sheer physical resources, to cope with. However, this is not quite the same phenomenon as using civil disobedience to express a dissident point of view to the political community, and to convince both governors and citizens to change the community's laws or policies. Such a process requires a relatively open political arena. Thus, while civil disobedience certainly is possible in other regimes, its feasibility, in terms of the objectives Barker has set for it, is less than in a democratic political system.

Barker crystallizes the idea of civil disobedience as rejecting a specific act of authority while accepting the legitimacy of political authority in general. He sees civil disobedience as a way in which an individual or group can be loyal to a justice which transcends established law and yet not undermine the scheme of law and order. It is virtually a part of the democratic process; Barker "can almost say that resistance of this order is still in the arena of debate," that it is a "method of persuasion," not of force. Civil disobedience, in his view, is a form of moral testimony by which a group can seek to make its idea of justice part of the social consensus and ultimately part of the law. Here Barker adumbrates the contemporary view of civil disobedience as an extension of conventional methods of appealing to the majority.

Green and Barker developed certain ideas of the early liberal-democratic theorists into components of the definition and justification of civil disobedience. However, one concept which neither dealt with specifically is consent. This is an important concept in liberal-democratic theory upon which the justification of civil disobedience can draw. More recently, a number of theorists have explored this concept and its implications for the theory of political obligation in a liberal democracy. I will examine their work in the next section.

3. *CONSENT, OBLIGATION,*
AND CIVIL DISOBEDIENCE

Although today the social contract is, at best, viewed as a useful construct for examining the nature of political obligation in a democracy, the notion that the governors in a democracy rule with the "consent of the governed" is widely held. In some way, not clearly indicated, the citizen in a democracy has consented, or at least, has been given the opportunity to consent, to the existence and maintenance of certain institutions and/or to specific individuals' occupying certain institutional positions. By thus consenting, or perhaps failing to dissent—how he might *not* consent is not clear—the citizen puts himself under an obligation to obey the products of those institutions, e.g., laws and judicial decisions and/or the orders of the officeholders. It is for this reason that the conflict between political obligation—or more simply, the obligation to obey the law—and commitments to supra-political ideals is the most poignant in a democratic polity, specifically in the case of a citizen who adheres to democracy and considers his polity legitimate. The sense of obligation to obey the law seems stronger because citizens have somehow consented to be governed. However, it is not to be assumed that the consent principle undermines the possibility of a justification for civil disobedience. Rather, this concept has implications which can be worked into a theory of civil disobedience. The problem—first revealed in the work of Hobbes and Locke —has been to develop an unambiguous meaning of consent, and this has not proved easy. Liberal-democratic theorists have generally linked consent to political obligation, but the problems of defining consent have inhibited clarification of the relationship.

J. P. Plamenatz, in his short but provocative book, *Consent, Freedom and Political Obligation*, has grappled with the problems of definition. He defines consent as including several elements: (1) an act which expresses a desire that another person act in a certain way, made with (2) the knowledge that it is this expression of desire which creates or increases the other's right to do so, and with (3) the intention that the expression do this. Plamenatz says that this is the only definition of consent "which makes government by consent equivalent to responsible government."[36] This does not mean that the governed who consent are directly responsible for their governors' actions—apparently because one can be directly responsible only for what one does oneself—but that the governed are directly responsible for *enabling* their governors to act in a certain way. Consent implies indirect responsibility, i.e., such responsibility as is involved when one acts so as to grant another person a power (in the sense of making something possible) or a right to act in a particular way. However, the converse is not true. In other words, a person may be indirectly responsible for another's acting in a particular way without having consented, i.e., either without knowing what the effect of his act will be or without intending that it have this effect. This distinction is important because of the implications of consent for political obligation.

While Plamenatz is not very explicit about the relationship between consent and obligation, by inference it would seem inconsistent to act so as to resist those persons authorized by oneself to perform certain acts when they do perform them. But as Plamenatz more or less admits, it is obvious under his definition of consent that no unanimous consent to the acts of officials in a representative government exists. Many citizens probably have not fulfilled the three conditions involved in consent. Moreover, as Plamenatz implies, if voting means consent to the making of laws by certain people, even the majority of *eligible* voters may not have consented.[37] One can argue, like Locke, that in a liberal democracy, citizens have as least tacitly agreed to the principle of majority rule; that is, there is unanimous agreement that the majority's decision shall be binding on everyone, and the majority's right to make laws rests on this agreement, or consent. Although Plamenatz says that the actual form in which consent is given is not important, such tacit consent does not qualify as a proper case of consent unless "it . . . be made with the intention of informing another or others that they have been endowed with the right to perform a certain action."[38] Thus, we still lack a basis for considering that those who have not consented (in Plamenatz's sense) are obliged to obey.

Are those citizens obliged to obey who have not consented but who might be considered indirectly responsible for enabling their governors to act in a certain way? It does not appear so. One could contend that even the large majority of citizens who probably have not consented in any way may, by their repeated acts of obedience, make it possible for their governors to obtain, or coerce, the acquiescence of those predisposed to disobey and thus to carry out the general functions of government. They make it possible for the regime to act effectively, and, in the long run, to act at all. Indirect responsibility cannot, however, be imputed to them unless they are aware or intend that they thereby facilitate the government's functioning. Assuming at least some of them are aware of this, it would seem odd to suggest that an obligation to obey in the future can arise from such habitual obedience and the indirect responsibility which results from it. Therefore, indirect responsibility, which does not imply consent, does not appear to imply obligation.

Plamenatz is compelled to conclude that consent cannot be considered the only basis (or perhaps even the most important one) of political obligation, though consent to a law may impose a special obligation to obey it. The nonexistence of consent, he says, cannot be the basis of an inference that there is no obligation. Thus, accepting the protection of a government does not constitute consent but it creates an obligation to obey.[39] Rather than take Locke's way out, i.e., that acceptance constitutes tacit consent, Plamenatz prefers to be rigorous about following his definitions. This entails recognition that, while consent is the basis of representative, responsible government, it cannot be said meaningfully that all or even perhaps the majority of the governed have consented.

By implication, Plamenatz suggests another way in which to relate the obligation of non-consenting citizens to the concept of a government whose basis is consent. He does this by introducing the notion of representative government—that government whose legislators (and those officials who administer and adjudicate the law) "can be said to represent the governed in so far as their right to make laws depends upon consent."[40] There are certain goods "which every rational being is obliged to promote,"[41] such as minimization of coercion, and "that good which is the usual accompaniment of actions from desired motives."[42] A government based on consent is the precondition of these goods, and thus if a rational being is obliged to seek them, he is also obliged to accept the means—representative government—of achieving them. For those who have *not* expressed a wish that their governors should act in a particular way, these goods may be only potential because they have not authorized their governors and cannot be said to be submitting—when they obey—to the foreseeable consequences of their own acts. Nonetheless, it would appear that they have the right (opportunity) to express such authorization. In other words, they are members of a polity in which they *can* act to authorize certain persons to govern them (and presumably they can also revoke their authorization). Those citizens who take an interest can—in a representative government—specifically enable certain persons to govern them.

Nothing in Plamenatz's definition of consent seems incompatible and inconsistent with the theory of civil disobedience. If his definition implies that resisting officials one has authorized is a contradition of one's consent, one can respond that the civil disobedient is not attempting by his act to revoke his "authorization" of his governors. He demonstrates this by his willingness to suffer arrest (and possibly punishment if found guilty). He realizes how important respect for law is in a democracy. Unless most citizens generally obey the law without having to be impressed with the likelihood and severity of sanctions, presumably the government would have to employ considerably more coercion to gain compliance. Most civil disobedients probably would not welcome such an outcome.

Since civil disobedience does not appear antithetical to Plamenatz's view of consent and its implications, it would seem that the imputed obligations of those who have not consented also do not rule out civil disobedience. For, presumably, these are weaker obligations than that entailed by consent. Accepting the protection of a government does not seem to imply that one must submit to it unconditionyall. It might be ethically contradictory to accept the government's protections while undermining its ability to provide them, but the limitations of civil disobedience serve to minimize this possibility. Neither is the obligation to pursue the rational goals of which Plamenatz speaks repudiated by civil disobedience. Surely such goods are among the objectives of civil disobedients. They wish to minimize the psychological coercion resulting from the authorities' insistence that citizens participate—even if indirectly—in actions and policies which they personally consider unjust. Civil disobedients also claim that voluntary acceptance of arrest and of the risk of punishment negates coercion, or at least minimizes it; so does their practice of nonviolence. Civil disobedience also appears to promote that good which accompanies acting from desired motives. In cases of civil disobedience, the participants, at least, do not consider conforming to the rules to be "acting freely" (in the immediate sense), even though they may have "consented" to certain persons making such rules. For them, following the dictates of conscience is acting from desired motives. Thus, if Plamenatz is right that pursuit of the goods he mentions is an obligation of the rational being, civil disobedients do not by their acts disavow this obligation. A critic might respond that surely Plamenatz does not mean to suggest that, when there is a conflict between actions from desired motives and obeying the law, pursuit of the good which comes of acting from desired motives is an obligation stronger than the citizen's obligation to obey. If it were, that justification might well be given by anyone who prefers following his desires, thereby breaking the law, to obeying. Assuming that he is willing to accept the consequences, it might well seem that his claim was as valid or as invalid as the civil disobedient's. The proviso that he accept the consequences surely is significant, but not sufficient to overcome the unacceptability of such a position, i.e., that it is permissible to break the law, regardless of motive (even a mere whim will suffice) as long as one accepts the punishment. The condition of nonviolence is another important limitation, but this line of discussion need not be pursued at length here since the issue of generalizability will be dealt with elsewhere.

Thus, although Plamenatz's analysis of consent and obligation does not eliminate the *possibility* of justifying civil disobedience in a government based on consent, it does not by itself provide any justification for civil disobedience. However, I think the concept of consent can be interpreted in such a way as to provide support. An obvious argument would be that an individual is not obliged to obey if he has not consented; for him, civil disobedience would be legitimate. This argument again raises the question: What is to be taken for consent? If consent is interpreted as a concrete, personal, and conscious expression of allegiance, most commentators probably would retort that few citizens in a democracy give consent in that manner. Even if consent were defined less stringently, this argument would not be satisfactory, since I want to develop a justification for the civil disobedient who is allegiant, who feels some political obligation because he adheres to democratic principles and because he has not decided that the polity and its representatives have lost all legitimacy for him. Moreover, if we define consent in such a way that a large number of citizens cannot be considered to have consented, we lose a principle which is supposed to be basic to liberal democracy and which has generally been used to justify political obligation.

Plamenatz views consent as an initial act (an authorization), but in a sense, a liberal democracy requires a *recurring* authorization, for example, through elections. What lies behind this notion? Not, I think, the intent to make the governed responsible *for* the acts of their governors, but rather to make governors responsible *to*, i.e., accountable to, the governed. Why make authorization periodic if not to ensure that representatives are responsive? This is to interpret consent as a continuing act. It also suggests that consent may be viewed as a form of continuing participation rather than an initially required but subsequently unnecessary act which sets the process of governance in motion. This also points us toward a consideration of participation in the context of institutions which embody the notion of consent and its related concepts, accountability and responsiveness.

In a general way, this is the direction of Joseph Tussman's *Obligation and the Body Politic*. The main concept for which he seeks a meaning is membership in a democratic polity. Tussman asserts that if we consider all citizens members of the body politic (which he does not), "consent cannot be taken as a necessary condition of membership."[43] This parallels Plamenatz's finding that consent could not be taken as the necessary condition of political obligation. It is obvious that "many native 'citizens' have in no meaningful sense agreed to anything"[44] that could allow them to be called parties to a social compact, and yet we apparently consider such persons to be members. But, as Plamenatz refused to accept the notion of tacit consent, Tussman refuses to eliminate the voluntary character of membership; consent is a prerequisite, he argues. Unless a citizen has consented to something, he cannot be considered fully a member. We have to face the fact that the number of citizens in a democracy who lack full status, or who are in a prolonged period of tutelage and dependence, similar to minors, is larger than we think.

Having concluded that some "shrinkage" in membership must be accepted, Tussman puts aside the question of how many actually consent. His concern is with those who can reasonably be considered voluntary members. Tussman begins his discussion of membership by asserting, as a basic empirical proposition, that in order for any group to make decisions, some subordination of personal decision-making must occur. If unanimity were required at all times, the group could not long function as a decision-making entity. Thus, to be a member implies a certain degree of subordination, a certain degree of abdicating one's autonomy. Tussman then suggests that the principle of majority rule may have been the "crucial invention of the political mind."[45] "The unanimous agreement to transcend the demand for unanimity"[46] (i.e., the unanimous agreement to the "bindingness of subsequent non-unanimous decisions") was the solution to the problem of decision-making in a group where members possessed the right or power to participate in that process. It was the solution which best balanced the demands of acting with a single mind and according each member a vote. Because majority rule has this democratic aspect, Tussman contends, people tend to forget that some abdication of autonomy is nonetheless taking place. Majority rule itself is not intrinsically authoritative; it must arise from the consent of each party in order to gain that quality. Secondly, it must be remembered that even with that unanimous consent by each individual, the rule of the majority does not mean an unbounded subordination of private decision, for the subordination involved in accepting majority rule is a "purposive act." The individual who accepts majority rule accepts subordination only to achieve certain generally specified purposes.

The mere fact of being a voluntary member does not solve the problem of reconciling freedom and collective decision-making. First, Tussman implies that majority rule was the best method of "reconciling membership [or better, the implications of membership, i.e., some subordination of private decision] and freedom,"[47] but now he recognizes that this is not an adequate description of the modern body politic. What we really consent to is not to making group decisions by majority rule but "being governed without our further consent."[48] He asks, "Can the voluntary acceptance of membership be regarded as sufficient, by itself, to make the system of law and authority self-imposed?"[49] Clearly, even more than in the simple case of participation with majority rule, there is some abdication of autonomy in making decisions. Is the abdication which is involved when membership "does not carry with it the right of further participation in the public decision-making process"[50] the best way of reconciling membership with freedom? Even with the condition that the individual retains the option of withdrawing under some circumstances, Tussman's answer is no. But, although he is opposed to abdication, he thinks that some subordination (as a result of delegation) will be necessary, even in the best solution. Seeing the problem in terms of an antithesis between abdication and participation is not, Tussman argues, the most accurate way of looking at it. The alternatives are really delegation and abdication. "The necessary subordination of private to public decision which inescapably confronts the member of the body politic with the obligation to acknowledge the authority of a decision with which he may disagree appears at best as 'delegation'."[51] At worst, it is abdication. In other words, some subordination is inevitable in the situation, but that does not require the member to renounce his decision-making autonomy altogether where governing is concerned. The member may participate; although Tussman does not elucidate, he implies that this participation prevents delegation from becoming abdication. While the member may be obliged to "acknowledge the authority of a decision with which he may disagree," he apparently is free to judge whether the purposes for which he has subordinated himself are being served. For example, Tussman says that democratic procedure, like other forms of political process, "is not an end in itself;"[52] rather, it must always be judged by the ends one wishes to fulfill. This, in itself, constitutes no more than conceding the freedom of individual conscience and judgment which a liberal democracy presumably protects. However, Tussman goes further. He appears to justify disobedience when "the general structure of authority is unimpaired."[53] In our political system, this structure includes democratic procedures, and presumably they would be available to the dissenter. Yet disobedience is legitimate because it "is usually the initiation of an appeal."[54]

Tussman's notion of disobedience as appeal certainly fits in with the theory of civil disobedience. He says that disobedience has a role even when a society has decided the question "who is to judge whether an act of government is 'constitutional'?" by putting the highest court in that position; disobedience can still be a means of *initiating* an appeal. Tussman does not say whether he thinks that in a liberal democracy such as ours, the Supreme Court should be the final arbiter. He suggests that "acceptance of its authority involves, for the individual, the abdication of the final authority of his own judgment—and conscience."[55] But other possible final arbiters are also not fully satisfying; thus, "the right to disobey and to revolt seems . . . to get lost in the question 'who is to judge'?"[56]

Tussman uses the notion of a "healthy tribunal" in specifying the condition under which disobedience as appeal is justified. How widely, or narrowly, one defines "tribunal" sets the limits to justified disobedience; if one defines it in a nonlegal sense, the termination of an appeal, for instance, in an adverse decision certainly is less determinate than in the case of a Supreme Court decision. Therefore, disobedience might be justified as a way of initiating and continuing the appeal because, outside the adjudicatory process, the "processing" of an appeal, e.g., to public opinion, would not constitute any precise sequence of procedural steps.

Tussman's discussion of disobedience takes place in the context of distinguishing situations in which disobedience is justified from ones in which revolt is justified. It should be pointed out that he does not specify the conditions of justified revolution in unambiguous fashion; in one place, he says "a situation in which the bonds of authority and obligation are dissolved"[57]—which seems to mean that there is a general breakdown of legitimacy and law and order. Shortly thereafter he says that revolt "marks the abandonment of hope in tribunal remedies"[58]—which clearly implies an attitude in the minds of the rebels.

Although actual dissolution of authority may have occurred, it is not necessarily a precondition for this attitude. Thus, he may mean that revolution is justified when either or both of these conditions occur. From this it might be inferred that disobedience, but not revolt, can be justified even when these conditions do not exist, i.e., when the dissident still respects authority and feels a sense of obligation. The dissenter, in contrast to the rebel, hopes that the political system will respond to his appeal; he has not lost faith in its institutions. The rebel, in contrast, has lost it; the institutions no longer hold his respect; he does not feel obliged. Thus, one could argue that, if disobedience is not motivated merely by the consideration that revolt is not feasible, the dissenter by choosing disobedience rather than rebellion indicates that he maintains a commitment to the general structure of authority.

The grounds for disobedience derive from the notion that "authority . . . is limited; it is possible that it may be abused or exceeded by its wielders." Tussman continues:

The claim that authority has been exceeded usually takes one of three familiar forms.

First, it may be held that the wielder of authority is frustrating or ignoring the purpose for which the authority has been granted. This is seldom a clear or easy matter, but the distinction between proper and improper purpose is built into the conception of a purposive delegation of authority and provides a basis for challenge.

Second, an act may be challenged on grounds of arbitrariness, as lacking in procedural propriety, or even as so failing in wisdom as to fall outside the range of permissible folly. This, too, is vague; but authority is limited by such considerations.

And third, "higher law" doctrines confront the exercise of authority with the assertion that there are rules or principles or "rights" which are impervious to the demands of political authority and which mark its limits.

I take it as beyond argument that, in principle, the member has an obligation to obey only the "authorized" actions of public authority.[60]

Although he is vague, Tussman has attempted to indicate the limits on political obligation which can be derived from the view that voluntary acceptance of membership in the body politic is a purposive act—as it was in social contract theory.

In the theory of the body politic which Tussman originally developed, consent implied continuing participation—i.e., in majority decision-making—but when he revises this theory to make it more descriptive of the contemporary situation, he faces the fact that consent, in the sense of voluntary acceptance of membership, does not imply continued participation. But without continued participation, delegation becomes abdication. Thus, Tussman argues for participation and implies that disobedience is one form it could take; it would be a means of preventing delegation from degenerating into abdication.

So far, the analysis of the concept of consent has revealed certain dilemmas. First, if consent is interpreted as a personal, conscious expression, then it is clear that many citizens in liberal democracies probably have not consented.[61] But the consent of the governed is generally considered to be one major aspect which makes a polity liberal-democratic. Second, if consent is interpreted as an initial act, for example, as authorization, then it does not seem to prevent the necessary subordination of individual preferences to decision-making by governors from becoming a significant loss of individual autonomy. It appears that the concept was originally conceived out of recognition that membership in a polity meant some loss of personal autonomy (though it is not clear that Hobbes and Locke were more concerned to prevent that loss than to conceal it).[62]

The first dilemma cannot be avoided; if one is concerned about political obligation, it is a problem. Plamenatz tried to bridge the gap here by finding alternative sources of obligation. Tussman views nonmembers as in a state of tutelage, and since he is more concerned with freedom than obligation, he does not focus on those citizens who would not be conscious of a conflict between membership and autonomy. It is possible that Tussman's nonmembers are, for the most part, apolitical and not likely to break laws for political reasons—a situation in which the question of political obligation might be considered crucial. If, instead, their apathy represents alienation, then on becoming politically conscious they might not feel a sense of political obligation. This would depend on whether the representatives and institutions of the polity convinced them of its legitimacy.

To the second dilemma, Tussman suggests participation as an answer. It must continue beyond the point at which the participation involved in delegation ends. What he is doing, in a sense, is interpreting consent as a continuing act—participation—instead of an initial one; at times, participation may legitimately take the form of disobedience. For example, when his governors overstep the bounds of legitimate authority, the citizen may disobey. In other words, if consent is to be meaningful for the individual, he must have the moral right to refuse his consent to certain acts of government.

Several other contributors to the contemporary discussion of political obligation, consent, and democracy reflect these problems and responses. John H. Schaar sees consent as a basic principle of democracy: "political authority must rest on consent."[63] It is the source of the moral obligation to obey the law. What consent apparently means for Schaar is that, if a man considers himself a democrat and allegiant to a polity he considers democratic, then he has consented to be bound by the acts of the political authorities of that polity. Consent involves adherence to democratic principles and belief that a particular set of political institutions conforms to them. This is clear because Schaar specifies two types of individuals who would not be obligated to obey in a political system generally considered democratic: (1) the person "who refuses to subscribe to democracy itself or to the particular institutional form democracy may take" and (2) the person who "may subscribe to democracy itself but insists that the political arrangements of a particular system which calls itself democratic are in fact something quite different."[64] Apparently, neither has consented. In effect, consent appears to be an initial act, even though Schaar does not say that it is a conscious, explicit decision made at a determinate point in time. Just how it is expressed is not clear. But it is an initial act in that, once the attitude and the belief are embraced by the citizen, he is bound by the acts of political authorities.

The difficulties with this conception of consent soon become apparent. A democrat (one who subscribes to the principles of democracy) "who does not argue that the methods by which the law in question was passed were undemocratic, can [not] claim personal exemption from it just because he thinks it destructive of democracy."[65] To allow such an exemption would contradict the principle of majority rule, to which the democrat also subscribes. The majority must remain as the "final judge of what is right and good in a democratic polity."[66] Schaar suggests that constitutional limits on majority rule do not provide a justification for disobedience which the democrat can employ with logical consistency. What limitations on majority rule there are exist by the consent of the majority; they are not a basis for moral disobedience to the will of the majority by a minority.

In Schaar's view, the obligations implied by consent reduce to a kind of implicit logical consistency between beliefs and behavior.

Adherence to democracy includes acceptance of majority rule. This implies a willingness to accept the results of majority rule as long as the preconditions are fulfilled; that is, as long as political institutions are democratic—establishing mass suffrage on a basis of legal equality, permitting citizens to express opinions and attempt to persuade others, and the like. When majority rule functions unimpaired, the individual may disagree but not disobey. He has no grounds consistent with his adherence to democracy which would justify obeying his conscience instead of the law. Even though he may find particular laws morally repugnant, his only morally permissible recourse is to obey the law while trying to reverse the result of majority rule. Thus, Schaar's conception of political obligation involves a significant loss of moral autonomy, despite his assertion that the democratic theory of political obligation rests in part on the principle that "the citizen is presumed endowed with reason and conscience."[67]

Only where the particular institutions are undemocratic and alteration by democratic methods is impossible will Schaar allow the democrat the right to engage in civil disobedience. If "possible" here means the *availability* of democratic channels, rather than the likelihood of success through employing them (Schaar's precise meaning is not clear),[68] then the democrat who employs these channels and fails has no moral claim to exemption from obedience, i.e., no right to engage in civil disobedience. Since this may well be the case, particularly in the short run, of the minority dissenter, the result is that civil disobedience is morally consistent with adherence to democratic principles only where particular institutions are undemocratic and democratic techniques unavailable. This seems to assimilate the right of civil disobedience to the right of revolution. As Tussman points out, the exercise of the right of revolution presumes the dissolution of political authority; it presumes the loss of legitimacy by the existing political authorities. If democratic means of change are not available to him, the democrat is likely to deny the legitimacy of the governing institutions; he would then feel no political obligation to obey; he might even become a rebel. Yet the purpose of civil disobedience is to avoid getting into this situation, to find an alternative to both rebellion and acquiescence (where either conventional democratic techniques have failed to produce change or present no likelihood of success). The dissenter needs an alternative to rebellion because he does not think the system is totally devoid of democratic legitimacy, and an alternative to acquiescence because his conscience will not permit his giving in.

According to Norman Jacobson's definition of civil disobedience[69] —in which the actor acknowledges the legitimacy of the political authorities—Schaar has eliminated civil disobedience from the democratic state. There is no acute *moral* dilemma for the democrat where the political institutions lack legitimacy for him, i.e., where institutions operate undemocratically and democratic channels are unavailable. It is primarily a question of expediency whether he will obey or disobey the law. Moreover, if democratic channels of change are totally unavailable, this implies that the individual is denied access to the political realm, e.g., that he lacks the right to vote or to seek redress in the courts. A democrat would be unlikely to consider a polity democratic if he were denied democratic rights within it. Thus, by Schaar's definition, his consent could not be considered as granted. Nor could it be said that he consented in some other way to the practices and institutions of the government, particularly because his specific consent has not even been solicited. The only real difference between this situation and the one in which democratic techniques are available but of very doubtful efficacy is the opportunity to make use of such techniques. If, as Schaar implies, civil disobedience is legitimate only when democratic techniques are not available, the key to political consent must be the opportunity to use them, regardless of the likelihood of success. If one adheres to democratic principles and has the opportunity to employ democratic methods, one has, in effect, consented to obey the majority's decision. Strictly interpreted, Schaar's view would rule out even one important means of employing democratic techniques, i.e., violation of a law in order to test its constitutionality. The Supreme Court has recognized that, where compliance would effectively negate their rights, individuals need not comply with a statute before contesting its validity. Moreover, civil disobedience can be seen as a means of opening up conventional political channels, making the effective use of more acceptable methods possible.

There is a real conflict between majority rule and individual conscience. How far do the claims of each justifiably extend? Can the majority morally oblige the individual? Do the dictates of individual conscience supersede the majority's decision? David Spitz attempts to deal with the problem of reconciling the two in an article entitled "Democracy and the Problem of Civil Disobedience." He argues that insistence on obedience to the command of the state, even when the act commanded conflicts with the individual's conscience, is an insistence that the individual act immorally. Unless it is willing to admit the immorality of its command, the state must vindicate its claim to obedience by insisting that its moral judgment is the true one and that the individual is wrong. Now, Spitz suggests, the essence of democracy is "a method whereby men can resolve peacefully which of competing moralities shall temporarily prevail. It cannot—if it is to remain a democracy—maintain that it has discovered the true morality which shall henceforth bind all men."[70] Seemingly, Spitz is implying that the democratic state can insist that the individual violate his conscience only at the price of denying democracy. In other words, since democracy is a way of peacefully making *temporary* determinations of what is right, a democracy cannot require absolute obedience to its laws. However, contrary to Spitz's argument, insistence by the state on obedience to the majority decision does not appear to compel the state to insist also that the majority's moral judgment is absolute; majority rule is precisely the method by which men may resolve which morality shall *temporarily* prevail, and Spitz seems to concede the legitimacy of determining temporary dominance. The person whose conscience prompts him to disobey will have to choose between violating his conscientious scruples and going to jail, but he is not asked to affirm the moral superiority of the majority's decision.

Perhaps this may seem a quibbling way of reconciling the conflict between political obligation and individual conscience, but I think this is, in effect, the way civil disobedience attempts to resolve the conflict and preserve the individual's autonomy. It recognizes the right of the majority to create a *legal* obligation binding on the individual's actions, to decide matters of general concern, and to punish those who violate its decisions. This is what individual consent implies. It does not imply an abdication of the individual's moral autonomy. Only if the civil disobedient contested the legal right of the majority to punish him for not obeying would he be contradicting his "consent"[71] to the democratic system. What civil disobedience does not recognize is the right of the majority to establish a standard of moral judgment for the individual; the majority cannot morally oblige the individual. To concede the former would be to concede the latter.

The principle of majority rule becomes a stumbling block because, although it is a necessary element in democracy, it also allows the possibility that individual moral autonomy will be eclipsed. This is more likely in a system with complex representative institutions—it is not the majority rule of the town meeting or the city-state. However, the principle of majority rule does not necessarily preclude the possibility of justified disobedience. It is an important aspect of liberal democracy but only one aspect. The protection of individual autonomy—the free use of reason and conscience—is another. Indeed, majority rule, as Tussman suggested, is a means of balancing the value of individual autonomy against the necessity of collective action. Yet this is to say that the justification for majority rule is partly based on expediency; in a sense, it is a device of convenience, which presumably serves the interests of all because a government paralyzed by the requirement of unanimity would not be in anyone's interest.

A justification of disobedience based on the individual's convenience certainly would not be considered sufficient to override the convenience of all. But civil disobedience does not claim to be based on considerations of convenience. It asserts that it is based on conscientious judgment that the object of the protest is a serious injustice, that more acceptable alternative means of opposing it are either not promising or not available (based on previous experience, direct or indirect). Its very form—risking arrest, violence, and conviction—is designed to make disobedience a matter of inconvenience to the dissenter in order to limit or balance the inconvenience to the majority. By accepting penalties, civil disobedients attempt to demonstrate that their act is not taken in disregard of the majority.

Viewing the question of justified disobedience in this way assumes that the individual has consented to abide by majority decisions and thus, if he is to disobey one of them, he must justify his disobedience. He must reconcile his disobedience with his earlier consent; some principle must be found which could justify overriding the majority principle. However, the assumption of individual consent to majority decisions is shaky, as an examination of consent theory indicates. While Locke said that the parties to the original contract agreed "to submit to the determination of the majority,"[72] he had to blur the concept of consent so that it could be applied to subsequent generations. While later generations might be looked upon as tacitly consenting to the terms of the original contract—and self-consciously a democrat in our day might be looked upon as doing this, too—this perspective still raises a lot of questions. As was already suggested, it is not clear that majority rule is the paramount principle of liberal democracy. Assuming that the self-conscious democrat accepts it as one of his principles, what does agreeing "to submit to the determination of the majority" mean in the context of complex representative institutions? If it is difficult to speak of an actual majority of the citizens as responsible for any specific determination, what should be taken in lieu of a majority? And what of those who are not self-conscious democrats—are they bound by majority rule?

Spitz's discussion of the conflict between majority rule and individual conscience seemed to make the conflict turn on the question of whether or not democracy means that the state or the majority can create a moral obligation binding upon the individual. From Schaar's position, it can be argued that the obligation to obey is not created by the state (or the majority) but by the consent of the individual to majority rule. The state (or majority) merely insists that the individual not renounce the obligation under which he put himself, that he be consistent. In effect, the controversy returns to the interpretation of consent: What does it mean? Under what circumstances can consent be taken as given? Who is to decide the extent of that obligation?

In his answers, Schaar tries to balance competing claims of order and autonomy. He gives both the individual and the majority a part to play. Individual consent is operative initially. The citizen who subscribes to democracy has the right to determine whether democratic conditions prevail within his political system. But once he has made that determination positively, he conveys consent and is not thereafter morally justified in disobeying specific laws or orders of that system. In contrast, Spitz implies that consent is *always* conditional upon the specific determination of individual conscience. In effect, consent is a continuing act of the individual; he continues to consult his conscience to decide whether he will obey the laws of the polity.

Hanna Pitkin attempts a reinterpretation of consent which seems more consistent with certain developments in the theory of the liberal-democratic state. The original notion of a personal, conscious expression of consent really was attenuated even in Locke's theory. His notion of tacit consent weakens the relation between consent and political obligation; one is expected to obey without having consented. Thus, notions of representation, accountability, and responsiveness have superseded consent. Pitkin argues that the basis of obligation is the government's possession of certain characteristics, e.g., acting within the bounds of its trusteeship. The obligation to obey depends on the nature of government: "a legitimate government [is] . . . one to which [the subjects] *ought to consent.*"[73] If one assumes this position, then "majority consent may be relevant as a way of assessing" the nature of the government. "Roughly speaking, a government is likely to seem to us deserving if it is open to the governed."[74]

In other words, the characteristics which make a government legitimate in liberal-democratic theory include procedures for soliciting the opinions of the citizens which provide some sanctions so that the consultation is not merely advisory. They also include procedures for assuring (or attempting to) that all citizens may participate on the basis of a minimim equality in those consultative procedures. In more familiar language, a legitimate government for liberal democracy must be one in which there are free elections which determine who will actually govern, as well as other means of communicating with government officials; moreover, there must be equal protection of legal rights for all to participate, which are defended by an independent judicial system.

It has been pointed out that taking consent in a tangible sense raises a large number of questions: What forms does consent take? Whose consent—the individual's, the majority's, the people's—is binding upon the individual? To what must they consent—the general form of the political system, the governing officials, specific laws and policies —for there to be an obligation to obey the law? Viewing the consent principle as being satisfied by the existence of institutions which solicit the citizens' opinions (e.g., free elections) may avoid these questions, but it does not solve the problem of what obligation is entailed for those whose government has these institutions. Does their mere existence bind the individual in some way? Must he actually make use of them, e.g., vote, before he can be considered bound to acquiesce in the political outcomes which emerge from these institutions? Or is it sufficient that he have the opportunity to participate, whether he does so or not? What does having the opportunity mean? That he is legally able to register and vote, that he can register and vote without fear of extra-legal sanctions? Must his electoral participation have certain characteristics—choice between competing alternatives, between competing and differentiated alternatives, and so forth? It is apparent that this approach to the problem also raises a considerable number of probably unanswerable questions, without even beginning to consider whether and when the obligation entailed in this way may be overriden. It is doubtful that some general principle will answer them. Even guidelines—the criteria that might be relevant to the judgment that obligation exists or does not, or if it does exist, is outweighed by other considerations—leave play for subjective evaluation.

As Pitkin points out, these questions of obligation can be viewed internally and externally—whether the individual feels obliged or unobliged may not be congruent with whether others think he is fulfilling or avoiding his public obligations. The individual may feel free of obligation because he may not consider the government (which is issuing orders) legitimate, while those observing him may think he *is* obliged because of the effects of his obeying or disobeying upon others; or they may feel themselves obliged and cannot see how his situation differs sufficiently from their own to void his obligation. To suggest that the inner perspective is the only valid one implies that, unless the individual feels he has agreed to accept the system (or its products) in some way, he is not obliged. To suggest that the only valid perspective is the external one creates the possibility that the extent of the individual's obligation will be determined by those who are the cause of his wanting to throw it off. In terms of the requisites for a "healthy" polity, the problem is one of bringing these two perspectives into congruence, or at least, preventing their being antithetical. The difficulty is heightened, on the level of concrete action, by the fact that consciousness of the two perspectives is likely to be greatest when they point in different directions. In a revolutionary situation, congruence may not be achievable because the authorities of the majority who decide the question of obligation—from the external perspective—may be the very ones challenged by those who have decided they are not obliged—from the internal perspective. This is another way of describing the situation where, for Locke, there was no appeal possible to a mundane authority.

Traditionally, we have accepted implicitly the existence of "consent" institutions as the reason for the obligation to obey. Recently, the public view has been modified to mean the legal opportunity to use these institutions. This may be satisfactory for the majority of politically aware citizens, but it will not necessarily satisfy those who find that legal rights to vote, campaign, hold office, and communicate freely with the public promise little hope even in the long run (much less the short) of basically changing policies which they consider objectionable and even seriously detrimental to their lives. In other words, the legal opportunity to participate does not appear sufficient to keep the two perspectives together.

In times of social conflict, such as today, we face this problem in a heightened form, though less than in Locke's type of revolutionary situation. If institutional political channels are to be open and political officials responsive to all members of the polity, then some means consistent with democratic values is necessary to give politically ineffective groups a real chance to exert influence. Recently, there have been attempts to reconcile minority disobedience and democratic notions of political obligation within a context of wide acceptance of the legitimacy of the legally constituted government. For instance, it has been proposed that those who are prevented from using conventional political channels for protest may have less obligation to obey the law in attempting to communicate with the community and the authorities. Similarly, it has been suggested that the constitutional rights of assembly and petition of those subjected to illegal and extra-legal harassment and repression by private and public persons may be greater than those of the ordinary citizen.[75] The theory of civil disobedience which I have extracted from the works of traditional and recent liberal-democratic theorists is another attempt to reconcile disobedience with accepted notions of political obligation in a democracy. Rather than imply that the political obligation of citizens in certain circumstances is attenuated, it attempts more explicitly to give both civic obligation and individual autonomy their due. The theory tries to reconcile the internal view of consent, that the individual's guide to political obligation must be his own conscience and judgment, with the external—what duties others think the individual should perform as a citizen. Civil disobedience does this by its self-imposed limitations; it recognizes that a citizen has some obligation to be "civil" even when he cannot, according to the dictates of his conscience, fulfill *all* the public obligations that others may expect of him. According to the theory, the individual can insist on the inner perspective but he must pay a ransom for it, particularly if his judgment is "wrong," i.e., if the authorities, and/or the majority, do not think that his view of his obligations is correct. As we shall see, my justification for the civil disobedience which took place in the 1960's combines these two kinds of arguments: (1) for citizens in certain circumstances, civil disobedience is functional and necessary if they are to enjoy the benefits of liberal democracy; and (2) civil disobedience is consistent with the kind of behavior a liberal democracy may legitimately expect of its citizens.

Notes for Chapter III

1. Thomas Hobbes, *Leviathan,* ed. by Michael Oakeshott (Oxford: Basil Blackwell, 1957), p. 211.

2. *Ibid.,* p. 222.

3. Hanna Pitkin, "Hobbes's Concept of Representation," *American Political Science Review*, 58 (December, 1964), 916.

4. Hobbes, p. 94. For example, Hobbes suggests that being misled by an evil teacher "*in all crimes that contain not in them a denial of the sovereign power*, nor are against an evident law, excuseth totally." Hobbes, p. 198 (emphasis added). Also see Thomas Hobbes, *De Cive, or The Citizen*, ed. by Sterling Lamprecht (New York: Appleton-Century-Crofts, 1949), Ch. IV, § 13.

5. Hobbes, *Leviathan,* p. 142 (emphasis added).

6. In a sense, point (4) is a statement of (2), because justice for Hobbes meant the keeping of valid covenants. In other words, an act of disobedience which meets these conditions does not violate the obligation of the citizen. Although Hobbes saw this obligation as arising from an original covenant, his idea of a disobedience which does not violate the *moral* obligations (however incurred) of a citizen to civil society is important.

7. Hobbes, *Leviathan,* p. 141.

8. John Locke, *Second Treatise on Civil Government*, § 119 (emphasis added), *in* Sir Ernest Barker, ed., *Social Contract: Essays by Locke, Hume and Rousseau* (New York: Oxford University Press, 1960).

9. *Ibid.,* § 227.

10. *Ibid.,* § 225.

11. *Ibid.,* § 226.

12. *Ibid.,* § § 233–235.

13. *The Life and Selected Writings of Thomas Jefferson*, ed. by Adrienne Koch and William Peden (New York: Modern Library, 1949), p. 301.

14. *Ibid.,* p. 413.

15. *Ibid.,* p. 440.

16. *The Living Thoughts of Thomas Jefferson*, presented by John Dewey (New York: Fawcett World Library, 1957), p. 301.

17. Thomas Hill Green, *Lectures on the Principles of Political Obligation*, reprinted from Green's *Works*, Vol. II (London: Longmans, 1941), p. 78.

18. *Ibid.,* p. 111.

19. *Ibid.*

20. *Ibid.*

21. *Ibid.,* p. 110.

22. *Ibid.,* p. 117.

23. *Ibid.,* p. 150.

24. *Ibid.,* p. 153.

25. Green does not address himself to the question: Who is to judge the state of the public mind and the strength of the social fabric? Presumably, the individual may judge, since he is allowed to judge the justice of the government. To allow him to make the latter judgment and deny him the right to decide when to act upon it would largely negate the first concession. Specifying the proper conditions for dutiful disobedience puts the burden of careful deliberation and judicious decision on the resister. This is quite compatible with the theory of civil disobedience.

26. In a sense, its contention goes

even further, making a distinction between moral and legal authority, i.e., admitting that a specific exercise of authority is legally binding but denying that it necessarily binds morally. This distinction may seem overly subtle; insisting on the separation of law and morality may seem to undermine the law's legitimacy in the average citizen's mind. Nonetheless, the civil disobedient in a liberal democracy insists on the right to make that distinction; however, he is far from contending that the government—its institutions and practices—lacks any moral legitimacy. Indeed, it is his purpose to insure that there be a closer congruity between laws and ethical principles.

27. Green, p. 150.

28. Moreover, it raises new problems: Who is to say what the political values "controlled" by the idea of justice concretely mean, and who is to judge whether the state is realizing these values?

29. Sir Ernest Barker, *Principles of Social and Political Theory* (Oxford: Clarendon Press, 1951), p. 195.

30. *Ibid.*, pp. 203–204.

31. *Ibid.*, p. 223.

32. *Ibid.*, p. 216.

33. *Ibid.*, pp. 222–223 (emphasis added).

34. *Ibid.*, p. 224.

35. *Ibid.*

36. J. P. Plamenatz, *Consent, Freedom and Political Obligation* (London: Oxford University Press, 1938), p. 18. Plamenatz formulates the logical relation between consent and indirect responsibility so as to link "government by consent" with both "self-government" and "responsible gov-

ernment." What is to be noted is his definition of responsible government. He suggests that it is a government in which the governed are "indirectly responsible" for the acts of their governors because of their consent. The authorizing act (consent) is the people's own act (suggesting self-government). Another definition of responsible government is that it is a government in which the governors are responsible to, i.e., accountable to, the governed for their actions. This is the general thrust of constitutional thought, and the more usual definition. If the emphasis is placed on this definition instead of on Plamenatz's, then consent as a personal authorization diminishes in importance; what becomes more important is the possibility of checking the governors, rather than authorizing their actions.

37. There are elections in which less than a majority of the eligible voters go to the polls.

38. Plamenatz, p. 9.

39. *Ibid.*, p. 24. Plamenatz says it is "a special case of the general obligation to help persons who benefit us."

40. *Ibid.*, p. 19.

41. *Ibid.*, p. 25.

42. *Ibid.*, p. 146.

43. Joseph Tussman, *Obligation and the Body Politic* (New York: Oxford University Press, 1960), p. 37.

44. *Ibid.*, p. 36.

45. *Ibid.*, p. 27.

46. *Ibid.*, p. 26.

47. *Ibid.*, p. 53.

48. *Ibid.*

49. *Ibid.*

50. *Ibid.*

51. *Ibid.*, p. 55.

52. *Ibid.*, p. 74.

53. *Ibid.*, p. 43.

54. *Ibid.*, p. 44.

55. *Ibid.*, p. 45.

56. *Ibid.*, p. 46.

57. *Ibid.*, p. 43.

58. *Ibid.*, p. 44.

59. This, Tussman says, "is intrinsic to the concept . . . . 'Absolute' authority . . . is complete license." Authority implies responsibility. *Ibid.*, pp. 42–43.

60. *Ibid.*, p. 43.

61. Even Locke faced more or less the same problem.

62. Rousseau conceived the social contract as a means of protecting individual moral autonomy, but he saw the need for continued participation after the initial agreement to form a body politic.

63. John H. Schaar, *Loyalty in America* (Berkeley: University of California Press, 1957), p. 48.

64. *Ibid.*, pp. 48–49.

65. *Ibid.*, p. 51.

66. *Ibid.*

67. *Ibid.*, p. 48.

68. Schaar says that no citizen who subscribes to democracy can claim exemption from a law if he does not argue that it was passed by undemocratic methods. If he does not make such an argument, it implies that democratic methods (of opposing the law's passage) were available to him. Thus, the possibility of morally justifying disobedience appears to turn on the availability of democratic methods.

69. Norman Jacobson, "Civil Disobedience: Philosophy and Tactics," paper presented at the Conference on Law Enforcement and Racial and Cultural Tensions, Berkeley, California, October 9, 1964, p. 2.

70. David Spitz, "Democracy and the Problem of Civil Disobedience," *American Political Science Review*, 48 (June, 1954), 400.

71. As defined by Schaar (see above).

72. Locke, § 97.

73. Hanna Pitkin, "Obligation and Consent," Part I, *American Political Science Review*, 59 (December, 1965), 999.

74. Hanna Pitkin, "Obligation and Consent," Part II, *American Political Science Review*, 60 (March, 1966), 43.

75. *Williams v. Wallace*, 240 F. Supp. 100, 104 (M. D. Ala. 1965).

IV

Civil Disobedience— Definition, Explanation, and Justification: The Modern Statement

THE CONFUSION OF CONTEMPORARY REACTIONS to civil disobedience suggests a need for greater clarity in three areas: defining the concept, understanding how the tactic works, and justifying its use. It is obvious that many persons have applied the label indiscriminately to many kinds of unconventional political tactics. They have not distinguished between protests in which laws are deliberately but civilly disobeyed, protests which are quite legal and unexceptional exercises of constitutional rights, and protests which involve violence and unwillingness to submit to arrest. They have failed to distinguish nonviolent tactics from violent actions, or protesters' violence from spectator and police violence. They have not recognized the self-limitations often observed by civil disobedients, (such as not resisting arrest, informing local authorities of demonstration plans beforehand, and refusing to respond violently to physical attacks.) It is not surprising that many people fail

Notes to this chapter will be found on pages 145-148.

105

to make such distinctions. Apparently, a common reaction to unconventional political action is to feel threatened, and direct action seems especially provocative. Since many protests have been attended by violence from one quarter or another, those who feel threatened might well perceive the demonstrators to be initiating the violence.

Even some presumably more sophisticated commentators have been careless in their characterizations of civil disobedience. Perhaps the most distressing aspect of the more critical comments—especially by legal writers—is their linking of civil disobedience with violence, and this is an important source of misunderstandings about civil disobedience. Despite the fact that there is and has been considerable violence—private as well as officially sanctioned—in our society, the American "ideology" is very negative towards violence when it is not sanctioned by the authorities. It is undeniable that civil disobedience (and nonviolent direct action generally) has on many occasions been connected with violence, and the American public—watching TV and listening to radio news broadcasts—has been an audience to some of it. Yet one must recognize that the great majority of those who have consciously practiced civil disobedience have not attempted to achieve their objectives by taking violent action themselves, that it has frequently been local officials, police, and hostile spectators who were violent. In some other cases, persons perhaps sympathetic to but not involved in protest demonstrations have committed violent acts. At times, such incidents may well represent a failure on the part of protest leadership to take adequate precautions. Some demonstrations have included persons inadequately prepared for nonviolent action. For example, in the Memphis march which Martin Luther King led before his assassination, a band of youths allegedly broke from the march and smashed store windows. March organizers claimed that they were not really participants, and it probably would have been difficult to prevent them from joining the march. This is not to deny that nonviolent demonstrators have sometimes benefited—and been aware that they were benefiting—from the violence used against them (or the possibility of such violence). Nevertheless, those commentators who fail to distinguish civil disobedience from violence may inhibit the development of the popular tolerance necessary to permit it to function effectively as a form of political communication and political pressure.

Closely related to misconceptions about the nature of civil disobedience are misperceptions of the way it operates. Since it tends to be conceived as violent, lawless, unrestrained, and beyond the bounds of acceptable methods, civil disobedience is generally seen as coercive: it succeeds by compelling opponents through the use of force to accede to demonstrators' demands. Finally, civil disobedience is usually condemned as illegitimate and unjustifiable, precisely because of these definitions and perceptions of its workings. Violence, coercion, deviation from legitimate methods cannot be justified, particularly in a democracy. Violence disrupts and lawless behavior destroys the basic requisite of any society—order. Coercion negates the possibility of voluntary consensus and violates the basic premise of democracy—the agreement to disagree peaceably, to eschew the use of force in politics. When institutional channels are available which permit peaceful pursuit of political demands, then violence, coercion, and unconventional tactics are all the more unacceptable.

These kinds of arguments are made by the more vehement legal critics of civil disobedience. For example, Morris L. Ernst[1] characterizes tactics commonly used by civil disobedients, e.g., sit-ins, sit-downs, and "going limp," as violent, and he strongly suggests that they are coercive in nature. He says that the intent of such tactics is "to persuade by a show of force." In his view, protest of this variety is premised on what he calls the anti-law mandate: "You will gain your goal by mass pressure provided only that you get enough publicity for your mass discontent." Morris I. Leibman,[2] chairman of the American Bar Associations' Standing Committee on Education Against Communism, implies that civil disobedience is lawless behavior. Intentional disobedience, the specific intent to disobey, he says, "is ordinarily treated as the essence of criminality."[3] Moreover, it is not acceptable in a society which "more than any other" provides means for orderly development and change and protection for every minority. "I cannot accept the right to disobey where, as here, law is not static and where, if it is claimed to be oppressive or coercive, many effective channels for change are constantly available."[4] Another example of the lack of definitional clarity is found in Judge Frank Johnson's condemnation of civil disobedience:

The philosophy that a person may—if his cause is labeled "civil rights" or "states rights"—determine for himself what laws and court decisions are morally right or wrong and either obey or refuse to obey them according to his own determination is a philosophy that is foreign to our "rule of law" theory of government. Those who resort to civil disobedience such as the petitioners were engaged in prior to and at the time they were arrested cannot and should not escape arrest and prosecution. . . .

Demonstrations and protests in a disorderly and unpeaceful and unlawful manner are not sanctioned by the law as this court understands it. There is a place in our system for citizens, both Negro and white, who wish to protest civil wrongs or present grievances against violations of their rights, to do so provided they act in a peaceful and orderly manner and provided they resort to the courts and not to the streets when they are thwarted in the exercise of this privilege by authorities acting under color of the law.[5]

Johnson ignores the possibility that civil disobedience involves important self-limitations and that the philosophy of civil disobedience does not justify the individual's deciding whether to obey or disobey the law without further conditions. Former Supreme Court Justice Whittaker expresses a more extreme view in his description of civil disobedience. His language strongly suggests violence:

Some . . . leaders have *incited* their followers to assemble in large groups, which at least resemble *mobs*, to wage "demonstrations" to demand their "rights" without recourse to legal processes.

In the beginning, those "demonstrations" consisted of episodic group *invasions* and temporary *appropriations* of private stores. . . .[6]

He contends that such conduct, while parading under "the banner of peaceable civil disobedience . . . is neither 'peaceable' nor 'civil'." In addition, Whittaker implies that civil disobedience means violating laws one does not like or, "in other words, the taking of the law into [one's] own hands."[7] He says:

The avowed purpose of such demonstrations is to force direct action outside the law and hence is lawless, and of course, inherently disturbing to the peace of others. The pattern of forcing demands by mass or mob actions, outside the law and the courts, has proved—as certainly we should have expected—to be tailor-made for infiltration, use and takeover by rabble-rousers and communists who are avowedly bent on the breakdown of law, order and morality in our society, and hence, on its destruction.[8]

Moreover, this conduct cannot be called civil "for the simple reason that willful conduct violative of criminal laws is not 'civil' but is 'criminal' disobedience."[9] There is no mention of what the term "civil" in civil disobedience means to those who have developed the concept. And Whittaker plays the familiar refrain that the existence of legal processes of redress means that no other methods are legitimate: "There is no other orderly way to decide peaceably and fairly the issues that arise among us, and to have an ordered liberty."[10] These excerpts illustrate the basic confusions and misrepresentations which are permitted and even encouraged when the meaning of civil disobedience is not clearly articulated.

I

It is somewhat difficult to deal separately with the problems of definition, explanation, and justification in civil disobedience because they are so often connected in discussions about the subject; nevertheless, I will try to do so for the sake of clarity. The first task, then, is to define civil disobedience in an unambiguous manner.[11] Immediately, two criteria present themselves for consideration—distinctiveness in relation to other forms of direct action and applicability to real phenomena. Both are important in making the concept useful to the social scientist. Unless civil disobedience can be distinguished by observable characteristics from other forms of direct action, then the category is superfluous; but on the other hand, if civil disobedience is defined in a way that excludes most occurrences generally referred to as civil disobedience, it will not provide much matter for study. Some academic commentators whose definitions are too restrictive may find that civil disobedience, as they define it, rarely occurs. For a political scientist, it is more useful to begin with a definition which encompasses a sizable number of actual cases. These cases might then be examined carefully to determine the relevance of more rigorous criteria.

The distinctiveness and applicability of the definition also help provide a foundation for justification. Distinctiveness is crucial here, because proponents of civil disobedience contend that its claim to legitimacy is partly based on its differences from violent tactics, lawlessness, and revolution. At the same time, its efficacy within the bounds of democratic processes depends on its distinctiveness from conventional methods. The criterion of applicability is also important to justification, because a defense of a civil disobedience which is not often practiced will not take us very far toward justifying certain unconventional tactics used by political dissenters. If one believes that the viability of such tactics is important for preserving liberal-democratic values and the possibilities of social reform in our system, then one does not want a definition which makes such rigorous demands on practitioners that their actions will be severely inhibited. On the other hand, there is a danger that defining civil disobedience operationally and then undertaking a legitimation of it within the context of liberal-democratic theory (as I do) might be taken to imply agreement with the tactics or aims of all civilly disobedient acts. While I wish to show that civil disobedience (broadly defined) is a political tactic compatible and consistent with liberal democracy, this is not to say that all uses of it are well-thought-out or appropriate. I advocate the legitimacy of such tactics *not* because I think they are always employed responsibly, but rather because I believe that our society suffers from serious social defects which do not seem remediable by conventional political tactics.

A study of recent academic writing on civil disobedience, beginning with Hugo A. Bedau's article of 1961,[12] yields a rough consensus on the following definition: it is (1) a deliberate violation of a valid law or, at least, of a public norm generally considered binding; (2) committed as a form of protest, which is (3) nonrevolutionary, (4) public, (5) nonviolent (entailing at a minimum nonresistance to arrest and refusal to respond with violence to provocations from any source), and (6) done with intent primarily to educate or persuade the majority. I do not believe this definition is completely adequate and I will indicate my disagreements as I take up each characteristic.

1. The first characteristic, that civil disobedience involves violation of a valid law *or* a public norm generally considered binding, is really a combination of two competing views. One view is that the demonstrator must break a legally valid law to commit civil disobedience; the other view does not require the law to be legally valid as long as it is generally thought to be. The debate between the two positions has focused on cases of testing—individuals who violate a law which they claim is unconstitutional. Some commentators consider testing to be civil disobedience and they attempt to define civil disobedience to make it include such acts. For instance, Bedau does not consider the civil disobedient's attitude toward the law the crucial factor in the disobedience involved in the act; rather, it is the "authorities at hand" whose attitude is important: Do they consider the act illegal? Christian Bay[13] makes a similar point: The civil disobedients can consider their act legal; the

characterization of an act as civil disobedience depends on the fact that "powerful adversaries deem it illegal" and that the actor knows this. A few commentators completely exclude "testing" from the purview of civil disobedience. Richard Wasserstrom asserts:

If an act is performed under a claim of ultimately legal, that is, constitutional right, it is simply not an act of civil disobedience, although it may be a protest against a serious wrong and may be conducted in a fashion otherwise identical to that of an act of civil disobedience.[14]

Other commentators accept testing only if the claim of constitutionality fails and the violated law is upheld in the courts. Carl Cohen[51] argues that when a claim of constitutionality is made by civil disobedients, there is no civil disobedience if the claim is vindicated in the courts. He says there can be no *legal* justification of civil disobedience. Those who reject the possibility that an act of civil disobedience can ultimately be found legal in the courts tend to take this position because they consider the admission of illegality (and acceptance of punishment) a crucial aspect of civil disobedience—it is one of the characteristics which justifies committing a violation of the law. According to Cohen, the actor's admission that he has broken the law demonstrates his recognition that he is "rightly subject to the legal system and he acts—even when he breaks the law—within the frame of constitutional authority." Similarly, accepting the legal consequences of the act is "public proof of his deep concern over the issue." "Undergoing punishment . . . helps establish the seriousness of the demonstrator."[16] Wasserstrom argues that civil disobedience must be considered lawbreaking without justification by a claim of constitutionality, because this impresses the seriousness of the act upon the dissenter:

It forces the proponent of civil disobedience to take account of the fact that the act is illegal, and that the burden of proof rests on him to show the justifiability of his action. It makes every proponent of civil disobedience confront the moral issues surrounding the contemplated action.[17]

Accepting the punishment plays a similar role:

The fact that a person who engages in civil disobedience is willing to suffer the legal punishment of his illegal conduct helps to guarantee that motives of self-interest will not lead him to make faulty calculations of the rightness of his actions.[18]

Such commentators fear that civil disobedience may bring disrespect for the law in its train unless this criterion is met. They are concerned that the motivation of the act not be misinterpreted.

While this concern for justifying civil disobedience is legitimate, there are good reasons why it should not color the process of definition too much. If illegality is a required characteristic, then certain acts which on their face appear similar or even identical to civil disobedience as so defined will have to be distinguished from it—for example, disobedience which is made either under a claim of the law's unconstitutionality (e.g., the law against draft-card burning), or under a closely related claim that the act is protected by constitutional principles even though it might involve technical violation of a law (e.g., certain forms of trespass alleged to be "symbolic speech" protected by the First Amendment). It seems sufficient for purposes of definition that the public authorities immediately involved consider the act illegal. Excluding acts a demonstrator considers legal excludes testing, and yet the only difference between civil disobedience so defined and testing may be the demonstrator's attitude toward his act: whether he thinks it ultimately legal or illegal. The way the authorities and the public will view his act and deal with him will generally be very similar. In both cases, the intent is to convince the authorities to alter a law or a policy (which enforcement of the law may represent). In the case of testing, the authority directly appealed to is the judiciary; where the violated law is admittedly valid, the protest is directed ultimately at influencing legislative or administrative officials. This difference does not seem to be a decisive reason for excluding testing from the purview of civil disobedience.

Moreover, while it is important to distinguish civil disobedience from other forms of protest, especially more extreme ones, this need for definition does not justify insisting on the requirement of ultimate illegality. Even though it appears to separate civil disobedience clearly from other methods, this requirement is really a demand that civil disobedients themselves consider their act illegal, regardless of what the authorities and the courts think. Thus, in actual practice, the illegality requirement makes the distinction depend on the attitudes of the actor. While attitudes may have a lot to do with the philosophy of civil disobedience—particularly its moral justification—they are difficult to determine at the time of the act or even afterwards (they may change). As between the case where the illegality of demonstrators' acts is legally questionable and they intend to defend themselves in court, and the case where their acts are unquestionably a violation of the law and they do not deny it, there is no great *external* difference. In both cases, demonstrators may risk arrest and accept it without resistance. Some persons may think a decision by demonstrators to defend themselves against legal charges reflects poorly on their motives. But the demonstrators' conduct after arrest does not seem necessary to differentiate civil disobedience from other forms of protest. The decision to undertake a legal defense is more relevant to the tactics of civil disobedience than to its definition.

Thus a definition including illegality could exclude acts from the category without providing an easy way of determining at the time the acts were committed, or even afterwards, whether they were or were not civil disobedience. From the political scientist's vantage point, such a definition suffers from the defect of being hard to operationalize. It seems that the writers who insist on the illegality criterion are basically concerned that civil disobedients be serious in purpose and carefully weigh the likely consequences—good and bad—of their act. If the actor's attitude is an important way of differentiating civil disobedience from more extreme forms of protest, some manifestation of the appropriate attitude should be included in the definition. But the idea that every act of civil disobedience should be a "hard case" in the actor's mind does not seem to require that he also admit that his act is necessarily a crime. To be sufficiently impressed with the seriousness of his act, the civil disobedient does not have to concede that it lacks any possible legal justification, especially before adjudication takes place.

In addition, most writers define civil disobedience as involving a *deliberate* act of violation. Bay, for example, calls the act premeditated. None of these writers thinks civil disobedience should be employed without considerable thought and conviction. However, if "deliberate" violation is interpreted to mean more than "knowing" violation, then conscientiously premeditated acts of civil disobedience will be difficult to distinguish from other apparent acts of civil disobedience. Again, the problem is one of operationalizing the definition. When civil disobedients are in the act, how can one tell whether they have been conscientious about their decision to commit civil disobedience? The most visible indicator of their motivation is their outward deportment: Are they relatively orderly and nonviolent? Do they resist arrest or seek to escape it? Presumably, "civil" behavior indicates a willingness to bear at least some consequences of violating a public norm. In judging whether an act of civil disobedience is responsible, it is legitimate to demand that civil disobedients be conscientious, but this is an internal attitude, hard to detect in actual exercises of civil disobedience. For purposes of definition, I would agree with Stuart M. Brown.[19] He says that civil disobedience need not be planned. Thus, if police say that an assembly is illegal and order the area cleared, demonstrators who stay after hearing this order are committing civil disobedience.

It is important that civil disobedience be regarded as defying a norm generally considered binding[20] for otherwise it loses its distinctiveness from other forms of direct action, e.g., uncontestably legal picketing and marches. There is little point in differentiating civil disobedience from actions most people agree are legal unless civil disobedience involves a more serious commitment, i.e., willingness to risk arrest, prosecution, and conviction for what will be regarded as a law violation. In sum, civil disobedience involves a knowing but not necessarily planned violation of a norm considered binding by local authorities but subject to invalidation in the courts.

2. The next characteristic is obvious: Unless civil disobedience constitutes a protest against what is perceived as an injustice, then it cannot be distinguished from certain kinds of public law-breaking of a minor nature. For example, the cases of the illegal parker who prefers to pay for the ticket or the businessman who would rather pay a penalty fine than comply with a particular law might seem analogous to civil disobedience. In the parker's case, the objection to obeying probably would be mere inconvenience, as he might well accept the policy of rationing parking space. In the latter instance, the objection might be principled, that is, the businessman might think the law is unconstitutional, and this could be a case of civil disobedience—if the other requirements were met. However, the element of protest should be relatively clearcut; it is important that civil disobedience not be thought of as mere law-breaking.

3. Most of these writers define civil disobedience as nonrevolutionary; they clearly differentiate it from rebellion or subversion. Cohen, for example, says that "rebellion seeks the overthrow of constituted authority, or at least repudiates that authority in some sphere; civil disobedience does neither."[21] This does not mean that civil disobedients cannot

legitimately condemn various practices of the system or acts of its officials. But practitioners of civil disobedience maintain an allegiant perspective at least to the extent of not repudiating totally the authority of political officials, or of the regime and its self-proclaimed values. According to these writers, this aspect of civil disobedience is crucial to its viability. However, like conscientiousness, this is an internal attitude and subject to the same criticism that it is not easily operationalized. In order to avoid making the definition turn on an internal attitude, it is necessary to look to the implications of the outward form of civil disobedience. Civil disobedience may appear threatening, but its practitioners, *by their self-limitations*, attempt to communicate to authorities and public that they ought not to be regarded as revolutionaries. They are not acting in ways which compel a liberal-democratic regime to defend itself by means which violate its own norms. Generally, civil disobedience has been used to remedy injustices by going outside established mechanisms yet without seeking to overthrow or subvert those mechanisms. It has sought to supplement them when they failed to meet the needs of aggrieved groups. It is through their self-restraint that civil disobedients have manifested an ultimately allegiant attitude. It is possible that the limitations of civil disobedience might not be joined with an allegiant perspective; persons dedicated to the overthrow of a regime might engage in civil disobedience. Nonetheless, as long as they observe the limitations of civil disobedience, they indicate to the regime their willingness to carry on the conflict in a fashion which presumably permits the regime to respond in an equally civil manner.[22]

4. The concern to distinguish civil disobedience from revolution largely explains other characteristics which most commentators include in the definition. Defiance must be open or public to demonstrate that there is no intent to subvert. Civil disobedients are not covert plotters trying to bring down the system. They make their defiance known to the authorities (often in advance—partly to minimize disorder). Moreover, civil disobedience must be public for other reasons as well. Unless it is visible to the public, there is little chance that enough people will be persuaded by the demonstrators' appeal to influence the outcome. Even when conversion of the public fails or is not part of the demonstrators' intent, the visibility of protest is important because it can produce detrimental consequences for the target (this will be discussed in the next section and in Chapter VI).

5. Virtually all academic commentators consider nonviolence an essential characteristic of civil disobedience. Without it, disobedience cannot merit the qualifier "civil"; moreover, the self-imposed restrictions of nonviolence and nonresistance to arrest are intended to differentiate civil disobedience from rebellion and subversion. Among those who specify what nonviolence means, there seems to be agreement that civil disobedients may not use violence under any circumstances. Cohen writes:

The deliberate injury of persons, damage of property, riot, sabotage—these I would not classify as civil disobedience. Of course, civil protest may be greeted most uncivilly, but so long as the protester does not respond in kind, his conduct may remain civil. This means that he must be prepared to meet violence with nonviolence, and suffer the consequences—which may range from assorted indignities to physical beatings. In some communities the civil disobedient risks being jailed indefinitely on trumped-up charges; he may even risk being shot. It is surely clear that civil disobedience is not child's play. One might argue that if the act of protest is violent, it might still be an act of civil disobedience, although very likely an unjustifiable one. This, I believe, is wrong; deliberate public riot, with the rioters resisting arrest, I would not think is widely considered disobedience at all.[23]

Christian Bay is perhaps the only commentator who takes exception to the criterion of absolute nonviolence. "Civil," to him, connotes "carefully chosen and limited means"; civilly disobedient acts must be designed to maximize efficiency in achieving their limited ends and in minimizing the costs of the struggle, e.g., suffering and deprivation. Rational calculation to this end will mean, in practice, vigorous efforts to avoid or reduce violence; but Bay suggests that the question of whether violence is to be employed is a pragmatic one. At the same time, he rules out physical or moral destruction of one's adversaries as a legitimate aim of civil disobedience, but "at times a calculable risk of casualties may be tolerated."[24]

While Bay opens up the possibility of confusing civil disobedience with violent forms of direct action, there is some reason for not going as far as Cohen in defining nonviolence. As in the case of accepting legal punishment, an insistence on rigorous nonviolence puts the civil disobedient in a vulnerable position. Not resisting arrest—if properly made and without undue force—and not *initiating* violence either toward police, public, or property *must* be included in the definition, because without these limitations, civil disobedience is not sufficiently differentiated from violent direct action (e.g., from obstructionist activities like overturning vehicles, actively blocking streets or buildings, throwing objects at police or other officials, setting fires or destroying property—all of which might be done for limited aims and do not seek to destroy the adversary). However, violence in self-defense, seeking only to protect oneself from physical harm by police or spectators, not to escape arrest, should not exclude an initially nonviolent disobedience from the category. While it is sometimes difficult to determine whether police used excessive force, the rigorous definition of nonviolence puts civil disobedients in the position of having to suffer whatever brutality might be vented upon them; otherwise, some commentators say, they undermine the credibility of their sincerity and conviction. This concern for credibility seems to relate more properly to the question of tactics—what works most effectively in achieving one's goals within this form of self-limited protest action?—or to the question of justification—does absolute nonviolence make violation of the law more legitimate morally?—than it does to the question of definition. For purposes of definition, a qualified nonviolence seems sufficient; i.e., practitioners do not initiate violence, use it only in response to violence, in self-defense, and do not resist or seek to avoid arrest.

6. The last characteristic—that civil disobedience is practiced with the intent primarily to educate or persuade the majority—is really an explanation of how civil disobedience does or should work, even though it is framed in terms of the practitioners' intent. As I have said before, motivation is difficult to determine; while the intent of demonstrators can sometimes be expressed by their actions, there are considerable possibilities for subjective interpretation. If demonstrators protest on a scale that makes them visible but does not lead to disruption, one might assume that their intent was to educate, to make people aware of their grievances. This might be the difference between a sit-in in a restaurant by a small number of persons and a sit-in by a number sufficient to bring the normal operations of a restaurant to a halt. However, the difference in effect might not be due to a difference in intent; it is possible that the intent might be virtually the same in both cases. In the first instance, the protesting group might not be numerous enough to stage a mass sit-in, or they might fear the personal repercussions of protest on a larger scale. Thus, they seek merely to make their protest visible and appeal to the

restaurant's owners and patrons. In the second instance, the intent might also be an appeal, but it might have been the protesters' experience that small sit-ins were totally ignored and gave them no real visibility. In other words, the physical appearance of the demonstration might not indicate unambiguously the participants' intent. The criterion of intent to appeal to or educate the majority is a difficult one to apply. Moreover, it seems unnecessary because civil disobedience already is differentiated from other forms of protest by its self-limitations.

Thus, I would modify the definition originally given accordingly: Civil disobedience is a knowing violation of a public norm (considered binding by local authorities but which may ultimately be invalidated by the courts) as a form of protest; it is nonrevolutionary, public, and nonviolent (i.e., there is no use of physical violence except self-defensively when participants are physically attacked, and no resistance to arrest if made properly and without undue force). This definition takes into consideration important realities of contemporary protest action without sacrificing the distinctiveness of civil disobedience. In later chapters, we shall see that the actual use of civil disobedience has often been closer to this definition than to the more rigorous one suggested by academic commentators.

II

Explanation of the way civil disobedience works is the second aspect which needs to be clarified. The main emphasis among the academic writers is on the educational and conventionally democratic aspects of civil disobedience. Virtually all consider civil disobedience compatible with democratic political processes because it is closely analogous to other methods generally considered the essence of democracy—for example, written and verbal communication with the public in an attempt to sway the majority to particular views. Cohen, for example, tends to view civil disobedience as a technique of publicity and persuasion; it achieves its goals primarily by making others aware of a problem and, to be effective, it presumably must convince them of the desirability of change. Among the "factual questions" which, he says, must be answered in judging any specific case of civil disobedience, are the following:

How intensely will it focus public attention upon a community injustice long in need of remedy? If public attention is so directed, is that likely to increase the pressure upon the lawmakers? Or might misunderstanding of the demonstrators and resentment of them do their cause more harm than good?[25]

Even Bay, who tries to put the least restriction on civil disobedience while still defining it as a form of self-limited protest, says that "educational objectives prompt most civil disobedience campaigns and are never wholly absent."[26]

Acts of civil disobedience seek . . . to call public attention to the view that a principle of moral importance is held to be violated by a law or policy sanctioned by public authorities.[27]

Above all, the proclaimed ends of civil disobedience, as the concept is understood here, must be formulated with a view to making them appear morally legitimate to onlookers and to the public.[28]

The ends of civil disobedience must be potentially acceptable to those in the *role* of adversaries even if they to current adversaries may be anathema on psychological grounds.[29]

Norman Jacobson is perhaps the most explicit in his insistence that civil disobedience is a form of political communication. He does not think it can be considered genuinely civil unless it "contribute[s] to the extension of relevant speech rather than to its contraction."[30] Violence must be rejected as a possible element in civil disobedience because it is "dumb"; "it contributes nothing whatever to the idea or substance of citizenship."[31]

To qualify as civil disobedience an act must by the means at its disposal either maintain the political dialogue, or, in its absence, strive to re-establish it. For the most valuable contribution of which civil disobedience is capable in a democratic republic is that of political education.[32]

In addition, when civil disobedience is viewed as an appeal to the law (i.e., as testing), it is also considered compatible with democratic processes. Employing litigation to settle a conflict through judicial processes is a characteristic American response to political problems. Alexander Bickel sees testing as very much within the boundaries of acceptable protest:

In our federal system, however, the appeal to a higher law is not a call for revolutionary change to be imposed on the legal order by forces operating from outside, but an appeal—almost in the technical legal sense—to higher lawmaking institutions, which the system provides. In such a system some flouting of the local law, aimed at provoking action by the higher sovereignty, is virtually invited.[33]

Despite the heavy emphasis which these writers place on civil disobedience as a kind of democratic pedagogy, they nevertheless exhibit some awareness of other facets of civil disobedience. Bedau's definition[34] of civil disobedience intimates that, although civil disobedience is a "civic act" and an attempt to make the community aware of an injustice, it might not always achieve its aims through what would generally be called persuasion. Carried out on a large scale, civil disobedience—in the sense of obstructing the enforcement of a law—might pressure the authorities into altering the objectionable law or policy. Harrop A. Freeman asserts that civil disobedience "is grounded in a theory similar to non-violent coercion."[35] As he describes the latter, it works not by appeal to conscience alone but by compulsion as well.

Under modern conditions the "power structure" against which the resistance is directed must have the cooperation of the resistance group to survive. The non-cooperation compels power (which thought it had such absolute control as to prevent effective dissent) to make concessions, *even against its will.*[36]

Bay seems to recognize that civil disobedience *might* work, under some conditions, such as widespread use, by frustrating attempts at enforcement of a particular policy or law, thereby convincing the authorities to change it. Gene Sharp[37] is also aware that civil disobedience (and other forms of nonviolent direct action) can be used obstructively, and he thinks it might even be possible to overthrow a government in that fashion. However, this alone would not be, in his view, a way of achieving stable change.

If a policy is to be permanently secured by non-violent means it can only be done by building up conviction of its rightness among the population to the point where it has majority support and strength to carry through its policy and to defend it non-violently against minority attempts to impose the old policy.[38]

A minority which came to power via coercion (even if nonviolent), rather than persuasion, might engender a violent counterattack by a minority within the disaffected majority. This could put the new government in the position of having to use repression in order to survive.

If, therefore, non-violent action in general, and civil disobedience in particular, is to advance the minority dissenters' cause, it must conform to certain standards which not only make it effective in the long run but also simultaneously make it compatible with democracy.[39]

At the same time, Sharp suggests that civil disobedience (and other forms of nonviolent direct action) could be used to bring down a government which refused to accept the fact of a changed majority view or prevented dissenters from using constitutional means to change governments. Thus, while civil disobedience must be ultimately persuasive to be effective in the long run, it need not always achieve proximate goals by persuasion. By a mass civil disobedience campaign, a recalcitrant government conceivably could be convinced that it could not hold power without considerable difficulty. Charles Frankel suggests that civil disobedience can be a form of pressure: "[It] is an effort to change the law by making it impossible to enforce the law, or by making the price of such enforcement extremely high. It is a case, as it were, of holding the legal system to ransom."[40] In *The Paradoxes of Freedom*, Sidney Hook seems to admit that civil disobedience may—even though intended as a means of "re-educating" the community in democratic ways— work because the "targets" yield for reasons of convenience or business consideration.[41]

Thus, to see civil disobedience primarily as a tactic which demonstrators use to appeal to and persuade the majority of the justice of their cause is not an adequate explanation of the way civil disobedience works. It is not clear that persuasion, in the sense of conversion to the civil disobedients' views, has often occurred among opponents in cases of civilly disobedient protest. Such protest may, however, mobilize latent supportive attitudes among the public or among key decision-makers in the national government and thus may produce a response which pressures those who are the immediate targets of the protest. We will explore this idea in detail later.

I have already suggested that many persons associate civil disobedience with coercion. This is natural for those who consider it physically violent, but even commentators who recognize its nonviolence sometimes see civil disobedience as working by the use of force. Harry Prosch asserts that when civil disobedience becomes action, its practitioners have not opened a dialogue but have initiated a state of war, for the opponent has "only the same sort of choice that an army has": to capitulate by failing to uphold the law, thereby permitting the law, or laws, to become inoperative, or to uphold the law, necessitating a resort to violent force.[42] The civil disobedients have forced their opponents into a situaation where "moral persuasion of the argumentative type" and "political maneuvering" are not available as alternative forms of contention. "It is a contest of force, even though the only force [the civil disobedients] may be resorting to is that of the inertia" of their own bodies.[43]

Thus, Prosch characterizes civil disobedients as compelling their opponents to choose between violent counterforce and capitulation. Presumably neither alternative is palatable to them. Several objections to Prosch's characterization should be registered. We have already seen that most commentators insist that civil disobedience requires no resistance to arrest. If this is so, the opponents in most cases can utilize police forces to arrest civil disobedients without using violent (in the sense of destructive, injurious, severe) force, or at least without using illegitimate force. Civil disobedients will not resist such arrest, even though—or because they may—be trying to illustrate the immorality of enforcing unjust laws. Sometimes they may even consider arrest necessary in order to present to their audience the hopefully edifying spectacle of normally law-abiding citizens going to jail because they cannot, in good conscience, abide an unjust law or practice. Thus, the alternatives are not as stark as Prosch suggests, for urging police to arrest civil disobedients is not necessarily distasteful for the opponents,[44] and obviously, if the police are antipathetic to the protesters, as they often are, their opponents will not even have to do that. The possibility of the opponent's reexamining his values as a result of seeing morally conscientious persons going to jail to protest an alleged injustice is not ruled out. At the same time, the act of civil disobedience may introduce the issue into the courts or the policy-making branches of government, opening acceptable (to Prosch) processes of changing opinions. Moreover, civil disobedience does not necessarily render the law, or laws, inoperative if the opponent fails to uphold it. It does, of course, in the specific case, and "success" may encourage further attempts; but usually acts of civil disobedience are rather isolated and engaged in by small numbers. Unless the protesters can win a legislative or court victory, it is unlikely they can render a law inoperative. Thus, the southern sit-ins did gain a certain amount of voluntary "submission," but probably the greatest impetus to rendering segregation in public accommodations inoperative came from Supreme Court decisions reversing state convictions of sit-in demonstrators, and from the Federal Civil Rights Act of 1964.

In what other sense might civil disobedients apply force or coercion? Prosch implies physical coercion, but at most only self-defensive physical force is compatible with civil disobedience. Proponents of civil disobedience probably would not deny that there are elements of psychological constraint in the use of the tactic. In other words, civilly disobedient acts sometimes put opponents in the position of having to make (occasionally inconvenient) either-or choices—for example, either stop the activity the protesters consider objectionable or call police to remove the demonstrators. Sometimes neutral persons into whose activity demonstrators interpose themselves are given the choice of foregoing some desired activity or compelling demonstrators forcibly or through police action to leave. Thus, while civil disobedience *may* work strictly as a form of persuasion through symbolic speech, it often seems to fall in a middle ground between rational, ethical conversion and physical compulsion—a process of influence where settlements are based on calculations of benefits and costs, and inducements and constraints are employed.[45]

For example, a common criticism of civil disobedients is that they "coerce" opponents to yield by creating fear of disorder. If so, how does the decision process differ from what Prosch calls a moral resolution of a moral controversy? Prosch indicates that in the latter situation, there is a preexisting agreement on the hierarchy of basic values (though not necessarily awareness of this fact); it is a question of determining what values are at stake in the competing claims, and once the situation is perceived in a common way and the fundamental consensus revealed, the solution begins to emerge. For instance, if there is consensus (immediately apparent or subsequently emergent) upon the priority of equality as a value among the disputants, then it is a matter of gaining agreement whether a real inequality of a remediable kind exists, and if this can be achieved, the debate will then center on the appropriate means to an agreed end. The schema is more or less static. Some change in the value hierarchy might occur, assuming agreement on fundamental values, if one side convinced the other that, in terms of the basic values, one ordering of subordinate values had more logical consistency than another. Conceivably, where values of roughly equal importance (both sides agree on the approximate equivalence) are in conflict, a compromise may be worked out, so that each is maximized so far as is possible. But the values that are considered relevant are the same ones throughout the controversy.

Where civil disobedience is employed, the situation does not remain static. Take, for example, the case where staunch segregationists are the opponents of civilly disobedient civil rights workers. The former do not agree with the latter about the importance or paramountcy of equality. They do not find equality a particularly compelling value, for they do not feel the disadvantages of inequality and they probably reap some of its "benefits". On the other hand, the value of order may be very important to them, whereas it probably ranks lower for the civil rights workers who may have grown somewhat accustomed to operating in an environment of antagonism and insecurity. In the initial situation, i.e., before the civil rights workers commit civil disobedience, the value of order is not, at least directly, involved in the situation. Therefore, there is little or no motivation for the segregationists to change their policies or laws. If the activists then threaten to commit civil disobedience, the segregationists might realize that the value of order is, in the long run, at stake. In other words, a new perception of the situation might occur. An implicit appeal to their self-interest is being made because, obviously, order is of more than theoretic importance to them. The segregationists might decide that some concession to equality is necessary to preserve the order which they value so highly. Though far from Prosch's conception of moral persuasion (because agreement *based on value consensus* is not being sought), the appeal to self-interested considerations and the introduction of other values is well within the arena of legitimate political and economic bargaining.

The resort to civil disobedience is closely analogous not to force as Prosch says, but to the utilization of certain other methods in economic and political bargaining. For example, the strike is considered, in a large number of cases, a legitimate and legal tactic in labor-management conflict, and the threat of a strike, while often condemned as coercive, is an accepted counter in economic bargaining. The same is true of the boycott, which is legal and legitimate in many cases. Formerly, such tactics were not widely accepted and sometimes were subject to stringent legal penalties. It might be argued that while the strike and the boycott may be legal in most cases, civil disobedience cannot be; that is, public nonviolent violation of a law for conscientious reasons cannot be made sufficient grounds for legally absolving the violator from the penalty. Thus a basic difference between such techniques, or tactics, remains. If one views lawbreaking of this, or any, variety as virtually always more detrimental than beneficial in its effects, one may consider the difference crucial. If not, one may view civil disobedience as legitimately playing the same role in social and political conflict that the strike does in economic bargaining or that certain attempts to exert influence do in political bargaining. Such tactics attempt to introduce new considerations into the "debate," considerations which may lack impact unless they are made tangible in action. Bickel recognizes this aspect of civil disobedience:

> The movement has come into the streets, not in violation of a law it deems unjust and wishes to have changed, but often in violation of laws irrelevant to its ends; not in any sort of appeal to higher legal authority, but simply to bear witness to its own purposes and to show its force—peaceable force, but force; not to demand the intervention of a higher authority, but to bend local institutions to its will; not to activate legal processes of change, but to impress on the legal and social order the necessity of change, and if possible to impose change, all in ways altogether external to the legal and even the political process. . . .
> The ordered processes of litigation and legislation have never been the only legitimate ones in our system for the solution of social and economic problems. Another traditional—if extralegal and sometimes illegal—process is the peaceful trial of strength between contending forces; the trial of numerical, economic, and moral strength, which agitates public opinion until from it rises . . . a generally acceptable concept of mutual "duty to the community."[46]

Undeniably, such constraint or "peaceable force" is an important aspect of the way civil disobedience operates. This is not to deny that pedagogy is important, too; however, we shall see that civil disobedience has often been effective because of the pressure it can generate. In any case, an explanation which is relevant to contemporary political protest cannot exclude this aspect of civil disobedience.

III

It is obvious why those who perceive civil disobedience as a form of coercion condemn it as morally illegitimate, and why those who see it solely as an appeal to public opinion approve it; likewise, why those who define it as being violent and lawless reject it, while those who define it exclusively as involving absolute nonviolence and acceptance of legal guilt favor it. Rejecting these perceptions and definitions leaves us with a difficult problem of justification.

One of the common criticisms of civil disobedience is that it contributes to a breakdown of law and order; it encourages disrespect for law by its example of private men setting themselves up as judges and deciding that a law is not deserving of their obedience. Even granting that civil disobedients constrain themselves with certain self-imposed restrictions, one cannot ignore the fact that the public mind is not subtle enough to grasp the meaning of such limitations. The public has seen men deliberately and openly defying the law, marching despite court injunctions, sitting-in in public and private buildings, laying their bodies down in front of vehicles, going limp when the police come to take them in. Those who follow their example and begin to substitute their personal judgment of right and wrong for their obligation to obey the law may not be concerned with the niceties of civil disobedience. Similarly, some people object to civil disobedience because of the possibility that civil disobedience will provoke violent responses from the audience toward which it is directed. Even if the civil disobedients do not waver in their nonviolent stance, disturbances will occur that strain the capacities of police forces to maintain order; perhaps offended spectators will lose self-control and struggle with police, as well as with unresisting demonstrators. Persons, innocent and otherwise, will be injured. Again the bad example of disrespect for law will be on display as the public watches via the mass media. It has also been argued that civil disobedients, even those motivated by the most just of causes, will be encouraging others with less moral justification to employ the same tactic. Presumably this will cause the same detrimental effects, perhaps in greater degree, thereby permitting the more just cause to be condemned in the same breath with its imitators. Thus, to borrow an example cited by Sidney Hook, the disobedience of the Free Speech Movement is followed by the disobedience of the Filthy Speech Movement.[47]

Not only may civil disobedience subvert law and order by encouraging disrespectful attitudes; but, when employed on a mass basis, it may directly hamper the normal functioning of law enforcement and law adjudication agencies. For example, civil disobedience may require inordinate numbers of police to be deployed to protect demonstrators or arrest them. Arrested civil disobedients may swamp the court dockets with cases. Whether or not this is the intended effect, civil disobedients thereby deny to their fellow citizens basic rights and protections that they themselves demand.

For the most part, these objections assume that law and order is a basic requisite for any society, particularly a complex one. Civil disobedience, so the argument goes, cannot be justified because it threatens those conditions upon which the realization of *any* societal values and ideals rests, even though it may be motivated by commitment to the highest ideals of a society. But although public disturbances have occurred occasionally when civil disobedience has been used, there does not seem to be any clear and cogent evidence that civil disobedience has actually encouraged widespread or significant disrespect for the law. The question for empirical study is whether the civil disobedient's law-breaking has planted the notion in spectators' minds that disobedience is legitimate and/or feasible. Moreover, only the criticism that civil disobedience encourages disrespect for law apparently precludes civil disobedience entirely; criticisms that it can cause violent responses or hamper law enforcement merely imply that, under certain conditions, it ought not to be employed.

The critics, seeing that order is the basic prerequisite for society, tend to make it an absolute: order always takes priority. This is to assume the "indivisibility of order"; the disruption of any particular manifestation of legal and ordered relationships undermines the entire framework of law and order which makes society possible. To accept this assumption is to concede the argument. But order is not indivisible, and obviously, total obedience to law is not necessary to the maintenance of sufficient order and social peace for the large majority of people to live tolerably secure lives.[48] In a democratic society which espouses other values besides order, a monolithic sense of undeviating obedience to law would hinder the realization of these other values, such as equality and the various "freedoms to." As Thomas Jefferson suggested, we do not really want a nation of men who unquestioningly and docilely do exactly what their governors tell them. While civil disobedience *may* "encourage" an unthinking disrespect for law because of the public's lack of sophistication or self-control, it may also encourage a deeper realization of the values which law must embody in a democracy if it is to maintain a durable legitimacy in the minds of the large majority of its citizens.

Many civil disobedients are, in fact, sincerely seeking to bring law and morality into closer congruence, even if this requires breaking a few laws. For ultimately it is this congruence which underlies respect for law. Many members of the public may not be able to recognize that civil disobedience places a higher value on an ideal justice; instead, they may see only that it shows disrespect for the law. Proponents of civil disobedience cannot ignore the very real dilemmas that public lack of understanding about the nature of civil disobedience creates, but the fact that the public does not immediately grasp their intent is not a conclusive argument against civil disobedience. For civil disobedience, by its very nature, is directed toward making practitioners, adversaries, and bystanders more aware of and sensitive to transcendent ideals and present injustices. Civil disobedients try to communicate that they place a higher value on an ideal justice and that ultimately their acts may lead to greater respect for law by bringing law and justice closer together. This objective is hardly repugnant to the (at least) ideal commitment of our democracy to creating a political community of independent-minded, aware, and conscientious citizens. Moreover, liberal-democratic theory does not legitimate *any* kind of order; it does not approve an order imposed on unwilling subjects. At times, citizens may have to go along with policies and rules they do not approve, but in the long run, to warrant the description liberal-democratic, a polity must have for its basic institutions and fundamental policies the support of its members. In a nation whose citizens have been educated to understand the meaning of freedom, a system of law is most stable when the populace actively affirms its legitimacy.

But civil disobedience involves more than the intent to bring mundane law and ideal justice into closer congruence. The specific limits placed on its use express a commitment to preserving a framework of law and order. One way civil disobedients affirm this commitment is by limiting the act to a last resort (taken in a loose sense). In other words, civil disobedience should not be employed in most cases until the conventional political and legal channels have been utilized. The burden of proof that he has made sincere and strenuous efforts to obtain a remedy in these ways rests with the civil disobedient. Since civil disobedience is an extraordinary means, he should not consider its use until "normal" methods have failed.[49] What constitutes a good case will vary from situation to situation; where the evil or injustice is so immediate that delay will make its effects irrevocable, there may be grounds for moving to civil disobedience more quickly than usual. When the injustice is, for instance, some long-persisting condition of inequality, damaging but not destroying its victims, a more thorough utilization and exhaustion of the more conventional methods (such as litigation) may be appropriate. By limiting civil disobedience to a last resort, its practitioners attempt to minimize the disorder which civil disobedience may produce. They do not *want* to risk weakening the structure of order and respect for law unless there are strong reasons for doing so. Thus, they generally are willing to postpone civil disobedience until conventional methods are exhausted. Another basic self-limitation within civil disobedience is the commitment (at least tactical) to nonviolence which virtually all sympathetic commentators agree is essential. Recognizing the inflammatory quality in civil disobedience, its practitioners try through this restraint to prevent, or at least to inhibit, the outbreak of serious disorder. Violence initiated by demonstrators would destroy the moral impact of civil disobedience, permitting opponents to avoid the (at times) rather painful confrontation of just claims with their own not completely easy consciences, and to respond in a way—angry violence—which will blot out that ambivalence.

Nonviolence also seeks to avoid creating disrespect for law by demonstrating the moral seriousness and commitment of the civil disobedients. They do *not* lightly and *without grave risks to themselves* undertake to break the law. This is closely related to the idea of accepting arrest without resistance, with the concomitant risk of legal punishment. This acceptance, even when coupled with a determination not to facilitate the work of the police, reinforces the seriousness of the civil disobedient. His actions also indicate that he is not attacking the whole structure of law; he realizes its importance to society and does not seek to avoid its processes.

The suggestion that civil disobedience is destructive of law and order appears to be unfounded. It is clear that its intent and content are not repugnant to preservation of a durable system of law. Although many persons may fail to perceive the "message," the available empirical evidence does not support the conclusion that civil disobedience has weakened the framework of law and order. My conclusion is not changed by the ghetto riots of 1967; at most, one could say that the civil rights movement played a part in changing black attitudes and that civil disobedience was often used by that movement. However, any causal inference about the role of civil disobedience in those riots seems impossible to make. Nor is my conclusion changed by the campus protests since 1968 (which have included much direct action that is not civil disobedience). Here the civil disobedience of the civil rights and antiwar movements was a true direct inspiration to the students who led and supported these campus protests. Many of them perhaps had first become politically conscious as those movements peaked and declined; they had seen civil disobedience used to advance equality and to mobilize sentiment against the war in Viet Nam. Civil disobedients had often bravely borne the violence of opponents and police. These students were prone to accept civil disobedience as a legitimate tactic; but it was not this belief which led them, at times, to employ more militant tactics, tactics which eschewed some of the self-restraints of civil disobedience. It was the belief that civil disobedience had failed to move the "power structure," had failed to alleviate the conditions of most blacks, had failed to stop our participation in the war. The results which such movements produced did not convince these students that the institutions of this society were responsive to what they thought were just claims. If more recent tactics are alleged to be signs of lawlessness, it is at least as plausible to argue that it is the failure of protest, not the practice of civil disobedience, which is responsible. Paul Goodman argues that theoretical considerations would lead to the conclusion that specific direct action, especially if it achieved some success, would

tend to increase civil order since it revives the belief that the community is ours, whereas inhibition of direct action against an intolerable situation inevitably increases anomie and, therefore, general lawlessness. . . .

The conventional argument that general lawlessness is increased by specific disobedience for political purposes depends on the social proposition that law and order are by and large maintained by deterrence and penalties. But in normal civil societies, this is not the case.[50]

In sum, linking defiance of a specific law with the ultimate destruction of our system oversimplifies the relation between disobedience and the maintenance of a democratic system of law. What empirical evidence we have will not support a conclusion that disobedience must preclude a functioning system of law. Obviously, even considerable lawbreaking is not incompatible with law and order and the provision of security for the large majority of society's members.

Another major criticism of civil disobedience is that it cannot be morally justified by the tests generally used to determine whether an act is ethical. One such test is whether the premise of an act can be generalized without producing a rationally untenable result. According to some critics, civil disobedience fails this test. For example, they argue that breaking the law cannot be a (moral) right because if everyone had this right and exercised it, the result would be chaos. No one could rationally desire this result. Therefore, no one has the right to break the law. A similar test is the following: Can the act be performed by others without causing consequences which the first person would not accept, or which would make the first person's act impossible? The critics contend that disobedience to law cannot be made a generalizable principle of conduct because, if universalized, it would negate the conditions under which it is possible, i.e., the existence of law. If we accept the validity of such ethical tests, then an adequate reponse to these arguments is that they phrase the premise of civil disobedience too broadly. Civil disobedients do not claim an absolute right to disobey; disobedience is permissible, they claim, only under narrowly defined conditions. If everyone were to practice civil disobedience with these limitations, chaos would not be the result. Thus, the argument of logical consistency can be utilized only to require of the civil disobedient that he allow others to use the same general principle of conduct, even though they might arrive at very different positions—for example, even though they might use civil disobedience in the service of antithetical causes.

Some critics make similar arguments using the same test of whether the premise of the act is generalizable. They assert that the civil disobedient is acting upon the principle that it is permissible to disobey the law in any way one's conscience dictates, or that the individual is ethically justified in disobeying the law whenever it is expedient for him. Both arguments mistake the premise of civil disobedience. The civil disobedient asserts the moral legitimacy *only* of practicing civil disobedience after an appeal to conscience, and *only* when more than expediency motivates him. He is not claiming that one may follow conscience to any conclusion whatever.

Another test of ethical behavior sometimes applied to civil disobedience is whether it is consistent with certain widely accepted principles. Many persons argue that the obligation to obey the law in a democracy is absolute. They do not foresee any circumstances in a democracy when the obligation to obey would not be paramount. In other words, morally legitimate disobedience is not conceived as a possibility. While the view that the obligation to obey is always paramount may be popular, it is not one supported by liberal-democratic theorists. A more limited form of this argument is that there is *prima facie* obligation to obey the law. Apparently, the presumption is based on the existence of a number of "self-evident" arguments in favor of obedience. For example, one is a variant of the "indivisibility of order" argument: Without obedience to law, no social peace and security would exist; since these are prerequisites for enjoying any rights at all, anyone who wishes to enjoy rights is obliged to obey the law. Another is quite similar to the arguments which contend that the premise of civil disobedience cannot be generalized: It offends our basic notions of fairness to expect others to obey the law if we do not intend to obey. Since their being law-abiding is important for our security and freedom, it is equitable that we also obey. It is not necessary to repeat the comments which I made previously about such arguments; moreover, even if one assumes that a *prima facie* obligation exists, it does not necessarily preclude civil disobedience. It merely requires that some overriding consideration be put in evidence. Of course, *what* will override that obligation is open to question. Most proponents of civil disobedience have not shied away from accepting the burden of formulating a reasonable justification of their act. It is compatible with their notion that civil disobedience is not intended to subvert the system of law and order.

A variant of the *prima facie* obligation argument is the contention that there is a special obligation to obey the law in a democracy because society has conferred on citizens the right to participate in making the laws. Stated somewhat differently, the argument goes thus: By accepting the right to participate, or by having the opportunities which the right to participate confers, the citizen has committed himself to obey. This argument is really a toning down of the argument that consent implies obligation. Since it is difficult to see in the average citizen's relation to the political system anything resembling consent, participation (or the opportunity to participate) is substituted. The idea is to evoke connotations of voluntary action and free choice because there seems to be a common-sense relationship between voluntary agreement and obligation (many of the mundane acts we feel we should do originate in our voluntarily agreeing to do them at some time in the future). While this form of the argument may be more descriptive of what the citizen actually does than is the "consent" version, it is no more cogent as to the implications of "participation." Unless the would-be participant is aware of what having the opportunity to participate implies in terms of obligation, it is rather far-fetched to say that he has bound himself. In any case, the argument does not rule out civil disobedience completely. Advocates of civil disobedience probably are willing to admit that the obligation to obey the law is different in a democracy from political obligation in other political systems, but they are unlikely to take the additional step of admitting that participation in democratic processes implies an obligation to obey the law in all instances.

A more sophisticated variant of this argument is that, theoretically, some disobedience to law can be ethically justified; but if a distinction between legitimate and illegitimate disobedience were applied in practice, it would have deleterious consequences because the public could not readily see the difference. As a result, they might get the impression that law breaking per se was acceptable conduct. This argument assumes, in effect, that moral questions are to be decided by the public's ability (or lack of it) to make ethical distinctions. As I have already pointed out, public misinterpretation is a definite risk for civil disobedience, but it is not a fatal objection. Civil disobedients should consider whether their act is likely to convey fairly accurately their objectives and principles. However, even the danger of distortion does not obviate the possibility that important information will be communicated to the public. Thus, none of the conventional objections to civil disobedience appear to rule it out absolutely from being morally legitimate conduct. It is neither inherently repugnant to the maintenance of law and order, nor does it fail the tests often applied to determine what is an ethical act.

IV

We have just considered a number of objections to civil disobedience per se. Now we will consider some arguments which find civil disobedience objectionable *under certain conditions*. Some people argue that, while civil disobedience may be legitimate in principle, it tends to be abused in practice. For example, some reject the legitimacy of civil disobedience when it involves violating laws that are not themselves considered unjust. Thus, Abe Fortas said in his work on civil disobedience:

Law violation directed not to the laws or practices that are the subject of dissent, but to unrelated laws which are disobeyed merely to dramatize dissent, may be morally as well as politically unacceptable. . . .

It is only in respect of such laws—laws that are basically offensive to fundamental values of life or the Constitution—that a moral (although not a legal)
defense of law violation can possibly be urged. Anyone assuming to make
the judgment that a law is in this category assumes a terrible burden. He has
undertaken a fearful moral as well as a legal responsibility.[51]

Apparently the fear underlying this objection is that civil disobedience
could become very widespread if it were considered acceptable to violate
virtually any law in a civil disobedience protest. Perhaps critics who
make this argument think that disobeying laws that are unobjectionable
themselves (even in the demonstrators' eyes) might convey the notion
that any law, good or bad, may be disobeyed. The rejoinder is that
there is no evidence which demonstrates that these fears are justified.
The key to civil disobedience is its self-limitations, and these seem to
operate just as meaningfully when the disobedience is indirect. To some
extent, rejection of this form of civil disobedience apparently rests on
the view that the framework of law and order is inherently fragile and
that, although civil disobedience may be, at times, morally legitimate,
its occurrence must be minimized. Moreover, the argument may be
assuming that the need for civilly disobedient tactics is rather small. I
hope to show that situations in which nonviolent direct action is
necessary (though not necessarily sufficient) are common. In addition,
indirect civil disobedience may be the only feasible way to use this
tactic against certain laws or policies; at times, it is not possible directly
to disobey an objectionable law or non-cooperate with an objectionable
policy.

Another argument focuses on the claim of civil disobedience advocates that it must be practiced in a conscientious manner. The contention is made that civil disobedients cannot achieve real moral seriousness unless they are themselves the victims of the injustice they are
protesting. Only direct experience of the injustice can produce an
attitude sufficiently serious to prevent irresponsible use of civil disobedience. Otherwise, dissenters may resort to this tactic too lightly. This
argument was originally raised in the context of civil rights demonstrations on behalf of Negro equality, but the same point has been made
against other causes employing civil disobedience, such as antiwar
protests. It is quite likely that the protester would respond in terms of
a sense of brotherhood with the actual victims, and perhaps also stress
the desire to disassociate himself from an unjust policy. Passivity is
apt to be interpreted as neutrality, if not assent, but the protester does
not think anyone can really be neutral. One might try to persuade him

that he really is not responsible for the objectionable policy—for example, to persuade the civil rights demonstrator that he is not responsible for the acts of a particular southern community—but in much the same way that the civil disobedient is seeking to make bystanders feel responsible for injustices in their society, he already feels this responsibility and the need to show that he is trying to end any complicity on his part.

These feelings may be psychologically satisfying for the protester, but the critic may not find them sufficiently persuasive to put an end to his qualms about the possibility of irresponsible behavior. However, the argument may be turned around. The inability to empathize may force the protester to take a leap into moral certainty—a leap which may always be partly incomprehensible to reason. Yet the fact that he is willing to bear the risks and inconveniences of civil disobedience, *even though he is not a victim of injustice*, may be evidence of a high order of altruism and moral seriousness. Perhaps some white students who went to Mississippi had a martyr complex, wanting to expiate the sins of the white community against the Negro; perhaps their need to suffer punishment drove them to rash acts, which, if they had been more dispassionate, they would have decided were irresponsible. On the other hand, it would seem that we have, in the last few years, built up a sufficiently impressive list of violent incidents involving civil disobedients and civil rights workers to deter most persons who are not morally serious from participating. For example, most of the northern students recruited for the 1964 Mississippi (civil rights) Project were at orientation sessions outside Mississippi when news came that Michael Schwerner, James Chaney, and Andrew Goodman were missing. By all accounts, this news deeply impressed upon them the risks they were about to run.

There are some pragmatic reasons for not insisting that only victims be allowed to use civil disobedience. Frequently, the real victims of injustice have been so beaten down that they are not capable of even less controversial forms of protest. Submissiveness may have been internalized or fear become so great as to incapacitate the victim. He may not be physically present to plead his case. The militant Buddhists were able to embarrass the United States government, as well as the Saigon regime, but they were not in a good position to reach the American public. Also, the victim may be much more vulnerable to various forms of pressure if he should publicly protest.

Some critics have condemned civil disobedience when it has

"provoked" hostile reactions which led to disruption. For example, some persons considered civil rights demonstrators responsible for the violence inflicted upon them when they chose to make their protests in communities in which racial sensitivities were keen and tempers already heated. This criticism raises an important question of responsibility: What responsibility does the civil disobedient bear for disturbances caused by spectators who have been "provoked"? One can argue that civil disobedients have at least been one of the precipitating causes of violence, for had they not demonstrated, social peace would not have been disrupted. Some practitioners of civil disobedience might see some value in their being subjected to violence. But even if there were unanimous agreement among all civil disobedients that violent disturbances are to be avoided as a general rule, most would certainly not also accept the view that the likelihood of some disorder is sufficient reason for abandoning civil disobedience. Take a situation where a person knows his action will very probably engender an undesirable counteraction, not because his action almost invariably elicits such a response from other persons, but because of attitudes largely peculiar to his adversary. How much concession to those attitudes *should* he make? As I have noted, the civil disobedient takes steps to limit the implications of his disobedience and to increase the likelihood of his protest "provoking" his opponent to thought rather than to violence. In addition, he may be asked to weigh the possible positive consequences of his actions against the negative. Admittedly, this subjective balance probably would be struck differently by his opponents; nonetheless, he should be able to make a reasoned and reasonable—to the uninvolved— defense of his decision. If more is demanded, he might then be justified in turning the argument around and contending that it is his adversaries' injustice and intransigence that has forced him to civil disobedience. His case is strengthened by his willingness to bear the risks and pains which his opponents frequently are spared by his nonviolence or by the corruption of law enforcement and judicial processes. Civil disobedients might argue that the responsibility (imputed to them) for setting a bad example is not really theirs. They may have created a situation psychologically threatening to the adversary, for example, to the rabid segregationist. But it was the latter's weakly internalized sense of respect for law that permitted his hostility and rage to be acted out.

There appear to be at least two positions which practitioners of civil disobedience have taken toward the violence of opponents. Those who follow Gandhi's philosophy of nonviolent direct action recognize that violence may well occur, but they see it as an important opportunity to exhibit their nonviolence. In the event that violence is inflicted upon the civil disobedient, his non-resistant response may create second thoughts in his adversary's mind, because most men find it distasteful to beat an unresisting person. The Gandhian emphasizes the civil disobedients' offering an example of self-suffering, not the opponent's using violence. In contrast, other practitioners of civil disobedience apparently believe that violence can serve functions other than providing an opportunity to offer non-resistance.

A study of a 1961 civil rights sit-in movement in Maryland indicated that "the primary element in achieving success was the exploitation of elite fear of violence and civil disorder."[52] The demonstrators had not won their goal—a public policy of equal access in public accommodations—by appealing to common values and converting opponents to the ideals of their movement. Some critics of the civil rights movement made similar observations, suggesting that the movement provoked violence because it brought national sympathy and federal intervention in its train.

Does "exploiting" fear of disorder and violence (assuming it is consciously done) contaminate the moral integrity of civil disobedience? It might be argued that such exploitation is incompatible with the high ideals of the civil rights movement or of civil disobedience in general. While there is no easy answer to this problem, the circumstances in which violence generally occurs—that is, as a response to civil disobedience[53]—may partially reduce the responsibility of demonstrators, even when they have chosen their "spots" by the likelihood of violent opposition. But the possibility of violence and disturbance is an important reason for insisting that civil disobedience be used as a last resort. Its use in circumstances likely to produce violence probably should be considered another last resort; that is, it should be used only when nothing else will move the authorities, and even then the extent of the expected disturbance should be weighed against the likely benefits. The justification probably offered by demonstrators in cases where they know protest probably will lead to disruption is that moratoriums on direct action intended to encourage a negotiated settlement lead only to delays and stalling. The protesters' perception of the situation—whether it is a conflict based on opposed interests or a misunderstanding based on ignorance or failure to see the relevance of mutually espoused ideals—no doubt influences the choice of tactics. While such perceptions may be unwarranted preconceptions, a period of unsuccessful attempts at negotiation without the threat of direct action could provide substantial evidence that only the threat of disruption will be efficacious in producing change. The nonviolence which I consider essential to civil disobedience does not preclude a pragmatic attitude toward the violence of opponents. Certainly civil disobedients should not encourage violent reactions where they can be avoided without sacrificing their own objectives—thus the restrictions; but eschewing the benefits to be derived from opponents' violence should not be made an absolute requirement.

In addition to questions about the morality of "exploiting" opponents' violence and about the responsibility of civil disobedients for resulting disturbances, queries have been raised concerning their obligation not to harm those who are not responsible for the conditions against which their protest is directed. One example, already cited, is that of putting inordinate strains on law enforcement and adjudicatory agencies, thereby denying or limiting others' basic rights and protections. Another is that of inconveniencing persons who live or travel in the area chosen by the demonstrators, as illustrated by the stall-in and sit-ins at the New York World's Fair in 1964, and the human chain blocking the Triborough Bridge. Critics of such tactics have suggested that out-of-towners who could not be held responsible for New York City housing conditions were being unfairly bothered and annoyed. At least in this particular case, the inconvenience was not serious. In *any* case, direct infliction of physical harm is ruled out by the self-limitations of civil disobedience. But assuming more than slight inconvenience to others results, one might respond to this objection by questioning whether such "bystanders" are not, in some sense, responsible for the injustices which the demonstrators are protesting. Are not citizens responsible for the acts of officials who are directly and indirectly accountable to the electorate, despite the fact that they have not really participated in the decisions made by such officials? Furthermore, are they not responsible for the effects of their society's institutions, despite the fact that they have inherited these institutions? Many might reject a positive answer to these questions as patently illogical in terms of our usual notions of personal responsibility. However, when the educational possibilities of civil disobedience are recognized, the argument for responsibility is not without meaning. For the civil disobedients are saying: If enough people feel as strongly as we do about this matter, these injustices will not continue. None of the aggrieved bystanders may have participated in making and implementing the decisions under attack, but they might have influenced those actions *had they been willing to take unaccustomed stances.* As Henry David Thoreau suggested in his famous essay, had enough persons refused to pay their taxes to a government which permitted one-sixth of its people to be slaves, that government might have moved itself into accord with the moral notions of its citizens.[54] The intention of such civil disobedience is to bring home to the bystander that, in standing by, he has made a choice—to ignore a grave injustice, which he might help to remedy. Another response is also based on the notion that civil disobedience can be a pedagogic device: Civil disobedience which ends in disruption of some sort has the effect of symbolically spreading the burdens of the inequities in our society. It discloses in a dramatic way the harsh fact that many of our institutions and social practices have high social costs, borne disproportionately by certain identifiable groups within our society.

Nevertheless there do not seem to be any completely satisfactory answers to the question of responsibility for the spectator's suffering. What the attempt to evaluate claims about the moral responsibility of civil disobedients for the consequences of their acts brings out is that civil disobedients must sometimes choose between values which cannot always be maximized simultaneously. The discipline of non-violent civil disobedience is based on the principles of non-cooperation with injustice and minimization of suffering. But these two values are not always wholly reconcilable. At times the public has suffered from the disruption which has occasionally attended civil disobedience demonstrations. Often the civil disobedient causes the spectator some pain, usually psychological, and discomfort. A choice must sometimes be made between non-cooperating and minimizing suffering. Gandhi was willing to recommend non-cooperation with the colonial government of India, even though people might suffer as a result, because in such a situation the obligation not to participate in the commission of evil was paramount for him. He recognized that one could not act in this world without causing some suffering. There were costs to actions, perhaps especially to highly moral actions—from which he concluded, not that he should not act, but rather that he should act by seeking to bear the greatest part of the suffering. He did not approve of a tit-for-tat attitude; in other words, the civil disobedient could not properly "say" to his adversary, "You have imposed such and such a burden upon me and my fellows; therefore, we will make you bear one, too." The civil disobedient had to be willing to suffer without any such feeling of hostility or revenge. Contrary to Gandhi, some dissenters might decide that in some situations minimizing suffering might be more moral than non-cooperating with evil. The choice and its justification may not be convincing to others, but the civil disobedient must at least confront the very real conflict of values. Moreover, civil disobedients have tried and should try to impose a number of self-restraints on their protest: nonviolence, self-suffering, avoidance of impure motives like hatred and vengeance, awareness and evaluation of the gains and costs which are likely, and resort to civil disobedience only after real efforts have been made to succeed with more publicly acceptable methods. But submission to such restraints does not permit ready deductions that the civil disobedient is (or is not) responsible for pains caused, or is justified in any case. What the restraints do is to indicate that he sees the relevance of such considerations and has attempted to minimize detrimental consequences without at the same time yielding up his freedom of action.[55]

Some commentators insist that civil disobedience is legitimate only when it is used as a means of rational and moral persuasion. In a sense, this argument is a complement to those criticisms which object to civil disobedience when it capitalizes upon disruption and imposes penalties on bystanders. May dissenters act to produce change by other processes than persuasion, in the sense of converting opponents to their cause? Must civil disobedients act only where there is a real chance of changing the opinions as to the merits of their objectives held by those who are directly responsible for or support the policies or laws they oppose? To say they may not act to produce change by other processes than conversion is to demand more of dissenters than of other participants in the political system. We do not necessarily object when those directly responsible for legislating and making policy decisions act on claims which they are not convinced have intrinsic merit (for example, by log-rolling) and when those who seek to influence them do not eschew "exploiting" other motivations for action. In the political arena, conversion of opponents is not too common, especially when sensitive issues are the focus of controversy. However much we like to think that conversion characterizes the process of majority rule—the notion that the minority has the opportunity to convince enough persons to accept its views so that it can become the majority—many political settlements which are considered legitimate occur for other reasons. Moreover, legislators can pass a law even though their constituents may not see its merits. Public officials can, in the short run at least, impose constraints and offer inducements to obtain compliance with a decision whether or not those being influenced agree with it. Why should civil disobedients be held to a more rigorous standard than are conventional political activists?

One retort might be that civil disobedients, because they lack the *prima facie* legitimacy of those who are *officially* representing constituents, must do more than would be expected of the latter. The implication of this position is that the *status quo* has presumptive validity and that proponents of any change must bear the burden of proving to the public that the change will be, on balance, an improvement. The social costs of this value-position seem too high for me to accept it. Major changes are necessary to secure social peace and social justice in this society. The obstacles to effective dissent (that is, dissent which has a chance of achieving reform) are very serious. Most persons who are engaged in trying to change the system begin with relatively few resources, and the process of acquiring sufficient resources to reach a bargaining position is a time- and energy-consuming one. Moreover, where public attitudes are not receptive to change or are hostile to dissent, the public may be most insensitive to the grievances and suffering of those who have the biggest stake in reform. In such situations, to insist that dissenters' resources can be used *only* to "convert"— rationally and morally—the public and public officials may be to stifle the impetus for reform.

Earlier, I suggested that certain limitations on direct action—such as admission of legal guilt and acceptance of punishment without legal defense—should not be considered part of the definition of civil disobedience. They were not necessary to distinguish it from other forms of direct action. However, some commentators apparently feel that civil disobedience is *unjustifiable* without them. Now I want to argue that they are not necessary to a justification of civil disobedience. Moreover, these limitations are too stringent from the point of view of viability. They make it too unlikely that civil disobedience can be successfully practiced in the American political context.

What I call "pure" civil disobedience requires absolute non-violence, admission of legal guilt, and acceptance of punishment without question. The reason given for these requirements is that they make every act of civil disobedience a "hard case." I agree that civil disobedience must be a conscientious act. Breaking the law can be morally justified only under exceptional conditions, of which exceptional scruples is one. However, even without the consequences of being absolutely nonviolent and admitting legal guilt, in most cases the possible penalties (both legal and extra-legal) are weighty for most, though not all, people. Even if they are prepared to act in self-defense and to make a constitutional (or merely legal) defense, they may face public obloquy, arrest, physical harm from spectators and/or police, detention, financial sacrifice (due to bail, legal fees, court costs), and in the end, conviction and punishment. This should be adequate, for the majority of people, to inhibit resort to civil disobedience without some serious conviction and thought. For those who take these risks lightly, the requirements of "pure" civil disobedience would probably not act as much of a deterrent.

In addition, requiring that penalties be accepted puts the demonstrator in a particularly vulnerable position. It commits him to accepting punishment regardless of the severity. Such a requirement may also commit him to accepting punishment even when his behavior is legal. Demonstrators may commit acts, knowing that police or local officials probably consider them illegal, which may be considered legal by, for example, the federal courts. One might argue that if they wish to commit civil disobedience, they should commit an explicit violation. However, in cases such as trespass, illegal assembly, and breach of the peace, arrest usually follows an on-the-spot determination (by local officials or police) that a violation has occurred. Or police may decide that a violation is about to occur and order people to leave or be arrested. It is quite possible that the authorities' judgment is legally incorrect or deliberately biased against the demonstrators. Thus, even if demonstrators intend to accept the consequences for civil disobedience, it is legitimate to ask why they should suffer for such acts as the courts decide are legal.

In actual cases of civil disobedience, there are often a number of alternatives open to the police, the prosecuting attorneys, and the judges. First, there is the choice open to police and local officials between arrest and nonarrest. Nonarrest may mean either tolerating what they may consider a law violation or dispersing the demonstrators with violent methods. Secondly, if the demonstrators are arrested, they often can be charged with one of a number of offenses such as trespassing, illegal assembly, disturbing the peace, or with multiple offenses. Sometimes, charges of resisting arrest (if demonstrators "go limp") or aggravated assault (if demonstrators resist the use of police violence) are added. The maximum penalties for such violations are high in some jurisdictions. The prosecution has the options of trying the demonstrators on several counts for the same act (in effect), dismissing all but one of the charges, or not prosecuting at all. The judge can hand out maximum or lenient sentences.

A lawyer is in a position to protect (or attempt to protect) his client from treatment after arrest that violates constitutional standards, and from undue harshness at the trial or sentencing. To suggest that the demonstrator must put himself in the hands of the law and not defend himself legally is probably to subject the civil disobedient, in many cases, to more severe penalties than the average lawbreaker would receive. Anyone familiar with legal proceedings in local and state courts might think twice about the notion of making no legal defense at all. Local authorities have often demonstrated their lack of tolerance for civilly disobedient protest.

I do not believe that it is necessary to pay so high a price to justify civil disobedience. Although it involves violation of a public norm, civil disobedience does not imply a refusal to accept *some* penalties, assuming that they are legal. Because police and judges have often been quick to use the cover of the law against protesters, acceptance without question of local officials' views of their legal authority may mean that protesters' rights will be abused. It is not part of the democratic process that violations of its rules must be accepted merely because committed by officials. The right to contest the judgment of such persons is part of this process—it does not violate the spirit of liberal democracy because it is not a rejection of the exercise of political authority altogether.

The real question is whether law-breaking under *certain* self-imposed constraints can be morally legitimate in a liberal democracy. Those who advocate "pure" civil disobedience say that civil disobedience can be justified only when those restrictions are very stringent. The validity of their argument seems independent of the nature of the political system in which civil disobedience occurs; moreover, they do not seem especially concerned with the viability of the tactic, only its moral legitimacy.

Pure civil disobedience might be feasible under a system of law which worked with nearly perfect impartiality, but ours does not. Civil disobedience must be viable or justification is merely an exercise in theoretical ethics. The question of its legitimacy has to be considered in relation to actual political systems, the realities of their institutions and processes, and the ideals of their ideologies.

The institutional mechanisms of a liberal-democratic polity were conceived as a means of excluding the resort to violence from politics. These mechanisms were supposed to facilitate the making of collective decisions in which all can acquiesce, if not approve, because all have had an opportunity to make their own opinion the prevailing one, and/or because certain kinds of decisions are not permissible under any circumstances. Yet recurrent in our democracy are cases of men who found themselves in a cruel dilemma: They have been caught between their political allegiance and their private convictions, because there was no real possibility of achieving their goals—which they considered of great import—by the conventional methods available. In this situation, the choice seemed to be between acquiescence and resistance, between suppressing one's conscience and risking violent suppression oneself. In other words, liberal democracies have not always produced collective decisions in which all could acquiesce without feeling morally compromised. Yet commitment to the underlying values of liberal-democratic politics has encouraged dissenters to look for alternatives other than violence.

Civil disobedience is an attempt to find a middle way between the horns of that dilemma; those who suggest that there is no middle way which is both justifiable and feasible make it more likely that the dissenter will choose resistance and violence. They make it less likely that liberal-democratic values can be realized for all citizens, that all can at least acquiesce in, if not positively affirm, the decisions made and implemented in the name of the polity. The criterion of what is morally legitimate in political tactics cannot be framed in absolute terms. If liberal-democratic values are considered the ideals of our political system, then they justify unconventional tactics as long as two conditions are met: (1) the tactics are reasonably well adapted to realizing liberal-democratic values; and (2) the tactics are not likely to destroy other means of seeking these values. In other words, if civil disobedience can be shown to foster liberal-democratic values and to be compatible with the maintenance of stable liberal-democratic institutions, then it is legitimate.

In this section, I have concentrated on rebutting various arguments which, in effect, deny that civil disobedience can be morally justified either at all or under certain conditions. Some of these arguments were couched in universal terms; they did not suggest that civil disobedience in a liberal democracy might be a special case. Others attempted to use liberal democracy against a possible justification of civil disobedience. In the rebuttals, especially of the latter arguments, I have hinted at a positive justification of civil disobedience. In later chapters, I shall spell out this argument in a number of variants. For example, I contend that certain groups cannot begin to participate effectively in American politics unless they use civil disobedience and other nonviolent direct action tactics. Unless these alternatives are open to them, they cannot hope to share equally in the material and spiritual goods this society provides to the great majority of its members. They will not experience much equality of opportunity, security, or autonomy. For some dissenting groups, the value of political freedom cannot be kept meaningful without such unconventional tactics. They will be denied a real possibility of achieving extensive social reform. Yet liberal democracy is not intended as a buttress for any particular, static vision of the good society. It is antithetical to viewing any concrete society as the ultimate value. In addition, a liberal democracy, more than other polities, should be able to tolerate civil disobedience and other forms of nonviolent direct action because these tactics do not contradict its ideological underpinnings. These tactics do not appear to threaten the stability of liberal-democratic institutions *as long as the institutions remain true to the purposes for which they were established.*

Notes for Chapter IV

1. Morris L. Ernst, "Free Speech and Civil Disobedience," 3 *American Criminal Law Quarterly* 15 (Fall, 1964).

2. Morris I. Leibman, "Civil Disobedience—A Threat to Our Law Society," 3 *American Criminal Law Quarterly* 21 (Fall, 1964).

3. *Ibid.*, p. 24.

4. *Ibid.*, p. 25.

5. *Forman v. City of Montgomery*, 245 F. Supp. 17 (1965), pp. 24–25.

6. Charles E. Whittaker, "The Dangers of Mass Disobedience," *Reader's Digest*, 87 (December, 1965), p. 122 (emphasis added).

7. *Ibid.*, p 121.

8. *Ibid.*, pp. 122, 123.

9. *Ibid.*, p. 122.

10. *Ibid.*, p. 123.

11. A number of complex questions can be raised about the definition of a political concept. For example, to what extent is definition a political, as

well as an epistemological, matter? I have decided not to deal with such issues. For a discussion of political definition, see Peter Euben's Introduction, *Civil Disobedience*, Harper & Row, N.Y., 1971.

12. Hugo A. Bedau, "On Civil Disobedience," *Journal of Philosophy*, 58 (October 12, 1961), 653–665. The following articles, which I consulted, are not cited below: Darnell Rucker, "The Moral Grounds of Civil Disobedience," *Ethics*, 76 (January, 1966), 142–145; Harris Wofford, "A Lawyer's Case for Civil Disobedience," *Liberation* (January, 1961), reprint, 4 pp.; and John Rawls, "Justification of Civil Disobedience," paper prepared for the Annual Meeting of the American Political Science Association, New York City, September 6–10, 1966.

13. Christian Bay, "Civil Disobedience: Prerequisite for Democracy in Mass Society," paper prepared for the Annual Meeting of the American Political Science Association, New York City, September 6–10, 1966.

14. Richard Wasserstrom, untitled article in *Civil Disobedience*, an occasional paper published by the Center for the Study of Democratic Institutions (Santa Barbara, California, 1966), p. 18.

15. Carl Cohen, "Essence and Ethics of Civil Disobedience," *The Nation*, 198 (March 16, 1964), p. 260.

16. *Ibid.*, p. 261.

17. Wasserstrom, p. 18.

18. *Ibid.*, pp. 18–19.

19. Stuart M. Brown, "Civil Disobedience," *Journal of Philosophy*, 58 (October 26, 1961), pp. 669–681.

20. Even if public officials forego or fail to make arrests.

21. Cohen, p. 258. It should be noted that some of these commentators do not think a nonviolent revolution by civil disobedience is totally excluded by this view. Bedau indicates that civil disobedience with intent to bring down a government would be a borderline case. This would involve disloyalty and unwillingness to acknowledge allegiance to government, but Bedau says peaceful revolution is not logically inconsistent with civil disobedience. Cohen says that "civil disobedience may lead up to a revolutionary conspiracy," but he implies that it would no longer be civil disobedience when it becomes revolutionary in intent. Sharp also envisions the possibility of bringing down a government by civil disobedience (and other forms of nonviolent direct action) but argues that it must have majority support to make the achievement stable and to forestall the need to use violence against opponents of the change. Under some conditions, one could argue, using civil disobedience to change governments might be more consistent with democratic ideals and processes than the actions of the government which was opposed. It may be that violent revolution would also be justified in such circumstances.

22. In Chapter VIII, I will discuss the differences in the way different kinds of regimes respond to civil disobedience and, more generally, to dissent.

23. Cohen, p. 258.

24. Bay, p. 9.

25. Cohen, pp. 261–262.

26. Bay, p. 10.

27. *Ibid.*, p. 8.

28. *Ibid.*, p. 10.

29. *Ibid.*, p. 9.

30. Norman Jacobson, "Civil Disobedience: Philosophy and Tactics," paper presented at the Conference on Law Enforcement and Racial and Cultural Tensions, Berkeley, California, October 9, 1964, p. 5.

31. *Ibid.*

32. *Ibid.*, p. 8. The same kind of description can be found in Rawls, Wofford, Freeman, Frankel, and Hook (see below).

33. Alexander M. Bickel, "Civil Rights and Civil Disobedience," *in* his *Politics and the Warren Court* (New York: Harper and Row, 1965), p. 79.

34. Bedau defines civil disobedience as a nonviolent violation of a positive law. In addition, the dissenter views the act as belonging to the "public life of the community." The act is generally designed and intended to frustrate some objectionable law or policy.

35. Harrop A. Freeman, untitled article in *Civil Disobedience* (Santa Barbara, California: Center for the Study of Democratic Institutions, 1966), p. 3.

36. *Ibid.*

37. Gene Sharp, "Civil Disobedience in a Democracy," *Peace News* (February 22, 1963), pp. 7–10.

38. *Ibid.*, p. 8.

39. *Ibid.*, p. 9.

40. Charles Frankel, "Is It Ever Right to Break the Law?" *New York Times Magazine* (January 12, 1964), p. 41.

41. Sidney Hook, *The Paradoxes of Freedom* (Berkeley: University of California Press, 1962), p. 124.

42. Harry Prosch, "Limits to the Moral Claim in Civil Disobedience," *Ethics*, 75 (January, 1965), p. 104.

43. *Ibid.*, p. 105.

44. The argument has more force in a situation where the police refuse to evict a trespassing sitter-in because they realize that it might constitute state action in violation of the equal protection clause of the Fourteenth Amendment. Here the opponent might feel he must act himself, but even so, civil disobedients might not resist being removed from the premises.

45. To employ William A. Gamson's terms in his book *Power and Discontent* (Homewood, Illinois: Dorsey Press, 1968).

46. Bickel, pp. 80–82.

47. Sidney Hook, "Neither Blind Obedience Nor Uncivil Disobedience," *New York Times Magazine* (June 5, 1966), p. 52.

48. Michael Walzer, "The Obligation to Disobey," paper prepared for the Annual Meeting of the American Political Science Association, New York City, September 6–10, 1966, p. 12. Walzer says that he has never seen it "argued with careful attention to some particular body of evidence" that "disobedience even of bad laws undermines the habit of law-obedience and so endangers that fundamental order upon which civilized life depends." He tends to concur with David Spitz that some laws can be disobeyed without disrupting social order and that "there are many laws which can be disobeyed by *some men*, without prejudice to social order." Caleb Foote, in his address to the Conference on Civil Disobedience and the Democratic Tradition, University of California, Berkeley, California, November 4, 1965, argued that only a portion of offenders must be convicted to communicate to the public

that criminals would be held accountable. Above a certain percentage of convictions, there were diminishing returns in terms of social order. He did not consider the costs of foregoing conviction in doubtful cases to be high.

49. In certain cases, however, the use of civil disobedience may actually be necessary *before* the conventional method of litigation can be utilized—for example, as in attempts to test the constitutionality of the Viet Nam War by refusing induction.

50. Paul Goodman, "Civil Disobedience Decreases Lawlessness," *Daily Californian*, April 13, 1966, p. 13.

51. Abe Fortas, *Concerning Dissent and Civil Disobedience* (New York: Signet Books, 1968), p. 63.

52. Don Von Eschen, Jerome Kirk, and Maurice Pinard, "The Conditions of Direct Action in a Democratic Society," paper prepared for the Annual Meeting of the American Political Science Association, New York City, September 6–10, 1966, p. 13.

53. This was written with civil rights demonstrations of the early 1960s primarily in mind. Lately, demonstrations have often been more "provocative" but it should be remembered that I am speaking of *nonviolent* direct action.

54. Henry David Thoreau, "Civil Disobedience," *in* Milton Meltzer, ed., *Thoreau: People, Principles, and Politics* (New York: Hill and Wang, 1963), pp. 46–47.

55. See, for example Martin Oppenheimer and George Lakey, *A Manual for Direct Action* (Chicago: Quadrangle Books, 1964), p. 83.

V

Civil Disobedience in Action—I: Gandhi and the American Experience

IF ANY ONE MAN can be pointed to as a source of inspiration for the contemporary practice of nonviolence and civil disobedience in this country, it is Mohandas Gandhi. Americans have often emulated the discipline and tactics he developed for himself and his followers. This imitation is particularly clear in the work of Martin Luther King's Southern Christian Leadership Conference (SCLC) and the early activities of the Congress of Racial Equality (CORE). However, it appears that the very stern rigor of the Gandhian discipline has been attenuated and that the philosophy which underlay it has had less appeal for Americans than it did for Indians. Contrasting Gandhi's philosophy and use of nonviolent direct action with the recent American experience is instructive; it will help us to see more clearly how nonviolent direct action has been conceived here.

Gandhi coined the term *satyagraha* to describe the form of action

Notes to this chapter will be found on pages 191-194.

149

he was developing: "holding on to truth" is its root meaning. He also called it "truth-force." In its broadest sense, *satyagraha* is a life-encompassing search for truth. That is man's true purpose in life. There is a state of truth in man's affairs, a true state of relations among men, which, in light of the goals Gandhi pursued in his *satyagraha* campaigns, subsumes a notion of justice, of just relationships. The *satyagrahi* (the practitioner of *satyagraha*) selflessly seeks this state. By the practice of the *satyagraha* discipline, the individual, in a sense, validates the truth of the concrete goals he has set for himself. This is not to imply that their truth *arises* from his practice, but rather that the *satyagrahi's* selfless action persuades the public and his adversary of their truth. Thus, the discipline plays a central role.

Another major concept in *satyagraha* is *ahimsa*; this has been defined (e.g., in a glossary) as "love" or "nonviolence" (as it is generally employed to mean "avoidance of physical violence and non-resistance"), but neither definition does justice to its full meaning. As truth is man's goal, *ahimsa* is the means. *Ahimsa* seems to mean the complete avoidance of any evil in thought and in action; however, it is not merely a negative idea. It requires more than to endure evil at the hands of others. Gandhi says the individual who would live by *ahimsa* should bear with the evildoer but not with the evil. He has the duty to make the evildoer realize their kinship as brothers, "to take pains to devise ways and means of winning [him] over."[1] Gandhi also suggests that an appreciation of *ahimsa* emerges from a recognition that, in this mortal, imperfect world, man cannot attain absolute truth. While the many facets of truth are ultimately reconciled in a unity, truth will appear different to different men according to their lights. Faith in the ultimate unity of truth reassures the honest seeker, but he cannot be certain that he is completely right and others completely wrong. When men come into direct conflict, there is no absolute basis for rejecting the claims of the opponent. There can be no justification for destroying the opponent or even for inflicting evil upon him, even though one's intent is to make him depart from evil ways. The only way of giving due recognition to the fact that man's apprehension of truth is imperfect is *ahimsa*, persuading the opponent by enduring him and somehow reaching his moral consciousness. The relation of nonviolence to *ahimsa* is evident.

Gandhi says that all the aspects of the *satyagraha* discipline "are deducible from Truth, and are meant to subserve it."[2] This is clear with respect to *ahimsa* and with respect to the other requirements, such as chastity and nonpossession. Truth can be sought only by *ahimsa*, by total selflessness. All the aspects of the *satyagraha* discipline are meant to foster the search for truth. Thus, chastity and nonpossession are required because any attachment to the pleasures of this world will distract the seeker.

It is obvious that not all men who participated in the various *satyagraha* campaigns could even approximate the ideal *satyagrahi*; but an ideal is something to strive for, and Gandhi sought to impress its meaning and discipline upon his mass following. For example, participants in a civil disobedience campaign were required to take a *satyagraha* pledge which affirmed their willingness to follow truth faithfully and to refrain from any violence. Meetings were held to discuss the meaning of *satyagraha* and the issues involved in the campaign. Sometimes a day of purification was set aside for fasting; only those who signed the pledge and fasted for 24 hours were allowed to engage in civil disobedience. During a campaign, the *satyagrahi* was expected to engage in continued self-examination of his motives to be sure that they were not tainted by the kinds of evils he was opposing. Self-suffering, another basic aspect of the discipline, was not only a means of breaking through the opponent's prejudices so that his reason could be reached but also a guarantee of the *satyagrahi's* sincerity.

Closely related to the necessity of preparation for nonviolence was Gandhi's insistence that nonviolence be accepted as a creed, not as a policy. The person who adopted nonviolence as a policy, as one among several alternatives, would be tempted to use violence when the circumstances which prompted the original decision changed. The true believer in nonviolence would not admit that there was any choice but to persevere in its use. In addition, Gandhi recognized the importance of having civil disobedience campaigns initiated and controlled by persons who had accepted nonviolence as a creed. By this means, the likelihood of a resort to violence in the face of repression was minimized.

Gandhi refused to continue nonviolent direct action when participants reacted violently because he felt that violence undermined the spirit of *satyagraha*. During the Rowlatt *Satyagraha*, the police responded violently to the *hartal*[3] and the demonstrations, with the result that nonviolence broke down in many places. Gandhi suspended the campaign, began fasting as penitence, and urged others to fast as well.

While preparation is necessary for offering *satyagraha*, it is not sufficient. A series of steps must be followed. Before noncooperation and nonviolent action are offered, more conventional methods must be employed: negotiation, petition, publicity, and so forth. Joan V. Bondurant lists the steps in such a campaign:

1. Negotiation and arbitration. Every effort to resolve the conflict or redress the grievance through established channels must be exhausted before the further steps are undertaken.

2. Preparation of the group for direct action.

3. Agitation. This step includes an active propaganda campaign together with such demonstrations as mass-meetings, parades, slogan-shouting.

4. Issuing of an ultimatum. A final strong appeal to the opponent should be made explaining what further steps will be taken if no agreement can be reached. The wording and the manner of the presentation of the ultimatum should offer the widest scope for agreement, allowing for face-saving on the part of the opponent, and should present a constructive solution to the problem.[4]

Not until the ultimatum has been issued is direct action employed. Even here more conventional methods are used first—economic boycott and forms of strike, picketing, and the like. Then may come noncooperation with the government, such as nonpayment of taxes, boycott of public institutions, and voluntary emigration. Finally, civil disobedience is offered, and if no settlement is reached, *satyagrahis* will go even beyond this technique, taking over governmental functions and establishing parallel institutions. To qualify as true *satyagraha*, a campaign must be carefully graduated, permitting the opponent to change his mind before the next action is taken.

Implicit in Gandhi's conception of *satyagraha* is the idea of moral suasion. In a letter to the British Viceroy of India before he began the civil disobedience campaign of 1930, Gandhi indicated what he hoped to accomplish by nonviolence: "I have deliberately used the word conversion. For my ambition is no less than to convert the British people through non-violence, and thus make them see the wrong they have done to India."[5]

Thus, the early steps in a *satyagraha* campaign are intended to persuade. First, there is an attempt to persuade through reason, for example, through petition and negotiation; then through self-suffering which dramatizes the issues involved; finally, influence is exerted through the coercive element in noncooperation and civil disobedience. The nonviolence of these methods, Bondurant says, "draws the sting" from the element of coercion. Two other elements manifest the basic commitment to persuasion: demands are to be reduced to the minimum consistent with adherence to truth, and continued efforts must be made to find ways to cooperate honorably with the opponent.

Gandhi's tactics encompassed far more than civil disobedience; however, it was probably the most distinctive form of nonviolent direct action he employed. Because it constituted a greater deviation from conventional political practice than most of the other forms, Gandhi felt a special need to justify it. The implicit justification for civil disobedience found in his writings is the conflict between unjust laws and rules and man's nature as a moral being. He suggests that civil disobedience is "the inherent right of a citizen"[6] because without it, he is less than a man. Unless a man insists that he has the moral right to say "no" to a government—to non-cooperate—when it acts unjustly, his moral nature is degraded. In Gandhi's view, men lend their support to evil when they cooperate with an unjust policy or law. The *satyagraha* must maintain his dedication to truth by refusing to be implicated in evils perpetrated by governments.

This is not to say that civil disobedience is morally right under all conditions. It must be scrupulously "civil", which means that the civil disobedient must accept the sanction for breaking the law.

Breach of the laws to be civil assumes the strictest and willing obedience to gaol discipline because disobedience of a particular rule assumes a willing acceptance of the sanction provided for its breach. And immediately a person quarrels both with the rule and the sanction for its breach, he ceases to be civil and lends himself to the precipitation of chaos and anarchy.[7]

On the whole, it would be proper to say that a *Satyagrahi* cannot possibly quarrel with any punishment that might be meted out to an offender.[8]

Gandhi clearly indicated that civil disobedience could not be undertaken lightly; not only did the *satyagraha* have to prepare himself through rigorous discipline, he had to be a truly law-abiding citizen.

Before one can be fit for the practice of civil disobedience one must have rendered a willing and respectful obedience to the State laws. For the most part we obey such laws for fear of the penalty of their breach, and this holds good particularly in respect to such laws as do not involve a moral principle.... Such compliance is not, however, the willing and spontaneous obedience that is required of a *Satyagrahi*. A *Satyagrahi* obeys the laws of society intelligently and of his own free will, because he considers it his sacred duty to do so. It is only when a person has thus obeyed the laws of society scrupulously that he is in a position to judge as to which particular rules are good and just and which unjust and iniquitous. Only then does the right accrue to him of the civil disobedience of certain laws in well-defined circumstances.[9]

Although Gandhi says that acceptance of the sanction for breach of the law is a necessary part of civil disobedience, leaders apparently sought remission of penalties as part of a final settlement in two of his campaigns. In one, the Salt *Satyagraha*, the Government agreed to an "amnesty of persons convicted of nonviolent offense in connection with civil disobedience."[10] In the other, Bardoli, amnesty was an explicit demand of the leader who negotiated the settlement. While this might seem to violate the spirit of civil disobedience, sanctions had already been applied—that is, the *satyagrahis* had been arrested and were being held—so that insistence on carrying out the sentences might have been more unjust, in light of final agreement on the basic issues of the controversy. On the other hand, it does not appear that Gandhi's *satyagrahis* contested their arrests in court. According to Gandhi, civil disobedience is effective precisely because of the injustice of arresting the participants. To contest arrest might destroy the impact.

Gandhi makes a distinction between defensive and aggressive civil disobedience. The former involves reluctant or involuntary[11] disobedience only to "such laws as are in themselves bad and obedience to which would be inconsistent with one's self-respect or human dignity."[12] Aggressive civil disobedience is "nonviolent, wilful disobedience of laws of the State whose breach does not involve moral turpitude and which is undertaken as a symbol of revolt against the State."[13] Violating laws which "in themselves inflict no hardship and do not require to be altered"[14] would fall in this category. Aggressive civil disobedience implies an active rejection, even if symbolic, of the legitimacy of the State. Gandhi employed both forms; presumably the aggressive variety was justified by the fact that Gandhi's movement did not consider British authority in India legitimate. Nonetheless, Gandhi placed considerable emphasis on the need to exhaust constitutional channels before resorting to civil disobedience. He wanted to establish a democratic goverment in India after independence, and he recognized the importance of using methods which would instill in the Indian people attitudes supportive of democracy.

There is some ambivalence in Gandhi's treatment of the problem of coercion and pressure. Before the Hunter Committee,[15] he claimed that the intent of *satyagraha* was not to embarrass the government; neither did the practitioner rely upon numbers but rather upon his capacity to suffer for truth. On the other hand, Gandhi recognized the importance of favorable public opinion, which could intimidate potential opposition. He rejected the boycott of British Empire goods as sheer retaliation and, as such, contrary to nonviolent noncooperation. He could say social ostracism was justified in the case of a person who supports a social evil when the public unanimously opposes it. It is a form of noncooperation with the offender, whose deliberate flouting of social opinion negates his right to be served by society. Yet Gandhi opposed the use of social boycott to deny others subsistence.

Surely, non-cooperators have acquired no right to use that extreme pressure against those who do not see eye to eye with them. . . . We may not make people pure by compulsion. Much less may we compel them by violence to respect our opinion. It is utterly against the spirit of democracy we want to cultivate.[16]

In extreme cases, social boycott against a minority who will not join a nonviolence campaign is conceivable, but it is properly applied and effective "when it is not felt as a punishment and accepted by the object of the boycott as a measure of discipline."

When opinion is divided . . . on the merits of non-cooperation, when its new application is having a trial, a summary use of social boycott in order to bend a minority to the will of the majority is a species of unpardonable violence.[17]

Gandhi was not a systematic thinker and his writings are responses to specific situations; thus, he appears to contradict himself. Yet through his utterances runs a strong commitment (though not an absolute one) to changing the opponents' views through persuasion, instead of being satisfied to gain compliance without agreement. Despite the stress on moral suasion in *satyagraha*, Bondurant argues that some coercion is involved. However, she says that "the difference between violent coercion in which deliberate injury is inflicted upon the opponent and nonviolent coercion in which injury indirectly results is a difference of such great degree that it is almost a difference in kind."[18]

Consistent with Gandhi's view of nonviolent direct action as a means of conversion is his attitude toward the violence of opponents. It presented the *satyagrahi* with the opportunity to offer self-suffering. Self-suffering was an integral part of *satyagraha*; not only did it help the *satyagrahi* perfect himself in nonviolence, it was also the means by which injustices would be remedied. While Gandhi had implicit faith in the efficacy of nonviolence—so that failure in its use was imputed to the practitioner's failing, not to the technique and philosophy—he never denied that great sacrifices might be necessary. He was well aware of the risks involved and made it clear that civil resisters might have to lay down their lives for the cause.

Gandhi did not always spell out the ways in which suffering effected its ends; one important way, of course, was its impact on the persons inflicting the suffering. Seeing their victims gladly suffer without resisting could disconcert even the most ruthless and brutal persons. The emphasis here is on the efficacy of nonviolence. To achieve this effect, *satyagrahis* had to be prepared to risk violence.

Not all of Gandhi's supporters were convinced believers in nonviolence. Sometimes they favored other tactics. Gandhi's way of handling the problem was to teach nonviolence as a quasi-religious doctrine to the masses who participated in his campaigns. In convincing the Indian people to practice nonviolence, Gandhi not only persuaded them that nonviolence was the moral way to deal with opponents, he also induced them to believe that their suffering would achieve their goals. Certain values (see below) in the Indian culture supported this orientation.

Nonviolence, as practiced by Gandhi, was clearly not a way of sparing the civil resisters, even if it could be argued that in the long run nonviolence would entail less suffering than would violence. In four of the five Indian nonviolent direct action campaigns analyzed by Bondurant in *Conquest of Violence*, the participants met with violence, often from the authorities. In the *satyagrahas* against the Rowlatt Bills and the Salt Tax, it seems quite possible that movement leaders expected violence. During the campaign against the Salt Tax, volunteers attempted to occupy the salt depots nonviolently. As they were struck down by the police, others took their places. First-aid units had been organized to revive the injured. *Satyagrahis* did not even attempt to shield themselves from the blows; many were seriously and very painfully injured. Clearly violence and suffering were expected, as the first-aid units indicate, but its repeated occurrence did not prevent the *satyagrahis* from continuing to approach their objective because they viewed their suffering as playing a crucial part in the struggle.

It seems particularly clear from the Salt *Satyagrahas* that situations in which the authorities were likely to use violence were not avoided by the resisters. During one of these campaigns Gandhi seemed to be court-
˹ his belief in the efficacy of suffering. In a letter
ʼe of his arrest, he says, after referring to certain
en by the Viceroy:

> bolder step, and if possible divert your wrath in a
> ːhannel. [paragraph omitted here.] For, according
> *ιha*, the greater the repression and lawlessness on the
> ːater should be the suffering courted by the victims.
> ιlt of suffering of the extremest character, voluntarily

ː, Gandhi did not believe in suffering without
ːely for its own sake. In a statement made after
ttlement with British authorities concluding the
ιce campaign, he said:

> ːfined limits. Suffering can be both wise and unwise
> reached, to prolong it would not be unwise but the
> ι be folly to go on suffering when the opponent makes

it easy for you to enter into a discussion with him upon your longings. If a real opening is made, it is one's duty to take advantage of it.[20]

Nonetheless, settlement came after approximately 100,000 persons had been jailed at some time during the campaign; police firings on unarmed crowds had killed hundreds and wounded thousands. *Lathi* charges (by mounted police armed with metal-capped rods) numbered several hundred and probably injured many thousands of unresisting followers of the movement.

Despite his basic emphasis on the efficacy of suffering violence, Gandhi sometimes seems to suggest that the opponent's violence will also help achieve certain ends. In the same letter to the Viceroy quoted above, he wrote:

It would be cowardly on my part not to invite you *to disclose to the full the leonine paws of authority* so that the people who are suffering tortures and destruction of their property may not feel that I, who had perhaps been the chief party inspiring them to action that has brought to right light the Government in its true colours, had left any stone unturned to work out the *Satyagraha* program as fully as it was possible under given circumstances.[21]

Gandhi realized that British repression would be an object lesson to the Indian people; it would highlight the fact that British rule was not based on the Indians' consent but was imposed against their wills, ultimately by force. This was at least one of the motivations behind the very aggressive campaigns of nonviolent direct action waged by Gandhi against the British government.

In his description of nonviolent direct action in India, Krishnalal J. Shridharani[22] asserts that it was very aggressive at times. He reports cases of "sitting dhurna," where demonstrators lay down in the path of Indian civil servants who refused to respond to calls for noncooperation and then invited the recalcitrants to step on them. There were incidents of persons lying down in front of troop trains and other vehicles. According to Shridharani, this technique had powerful effects in mobilizing public opinion, but it was one that Gandhi disapproved.

Even within the limits of tactics approved by Gandhi, nonviolent direct action was assertive. Although the early steps in a *satyagraha* campaign were designed to maximize persuasion, gradually more extreme measures were introduced if the opponents showed no signs of yielding. The intent seemed to be to maintain the offensive, rather than to respond to the opponents' initiatives. At the point when attempts at negotiation promised no results—and after agitation and public demonstrations had developed "cause-consciousness" among the people—an ultimatum was issued, listing the minimal demands and setting a time limit after which direct action would begin. While the ultimatum, says Bondurant, was supposed to allow the widest scope for settlement without loss of face by the opponent, Shridharani suggests that it aimed to "force the issue,"[23] to make clear to the opponents that the consequences of future actions were serious.

Gandhi's letter to Lord Irwin, Viceroy of India, on the eve of the 1930 civil disobedience campaign illustrates the combination of elements in an ultimatum. After avowing his hope that a way can be found to avoid the necessity of a civil disobedience campaign, Gandhi explains at some length the terrible effects British rule has had upon the Indian people. He expresses the opinion that the British government does not contemplate any change in India's status which will entail giving up the economic benefits of British rule. Then, he announces his plans for initiating a campaign against the Salt Tax, if his appeal has no effect on the Viceroy. His intention, he says, is not to embarrass the Viceroy; he will postpone publication of the letter if the Viceroy is willing to begin serious discussions to deal with the grievances Gandhi has spelled out. The letter is not intended as a threat; Gandhi considers it a duty required of the civil resister to indicate the grave consequences of the action he is prepared to take:

If the (Indian) people join me as I expect they will, the sufferings they will undergo, unless the British nation sooner retraces its steps, will be enough to melt the stoniest hearts. . . .

It is, I know, open to you to frustrate my design by arresting me. I hope that there will be tens of thousands ready, in a disciplined manner, to take up the work after me, and, in the act of disobeying the Salt Act to lay themselves open to the penalties of a law that should never have disfigured the Statute book. [24]

Granting the aggressiveness of the Indian *satyagraha* campaigns, one could argue that it was justified by the fact that this was actually a revolution, rather than a reform movement, and that British rule was not considered legitimate. The Indians sought independence: Their adoption of more limited aims—for example, changes in specific laws or policies—did not signify that anything less than independence was their real goal. This was, in part, a tactical decision. Gandhi realized that Britain could not be moved to take the tremendous step of granting independence at one time. To have insisted on all or nothing would have belied Gandhi's grasp of political realities, but it would also have violated his philosophy of *satyagraha*. The *satyagrahi* was required to do his utmost to persuade the opponent of the justness of his claim; he had, to some degree, to make his actions and demands congruent with the changes his opponent could psychologically, as well as politically and socially, accept. In this early phase, it seems to have been Gandhi's intention to make the British aware of Indian grievances and aspirations. What he wished was for the British to acknowledge their willingness to grant India her independence in the foreseeable future. Gandhi's commitment to *satyagraha* and democratic ideals not only influenced him to set limited goals in the short run, but also to insist on certain self-restraints in the practice of nonviolent direct action despite his attitude toward the British rule. He probably would have practiced such restraint regardless of the kind of regime he was dealing with, though, of course, it was less costly under a regime that was at least partially inhibited by notions of constitutionalism and democracy.

There are a number of important aspects of Gandhi's *satyagraha* which may be compared with the use of nonviolent direct action and civil disobedience in this country: (1) the philosophy and discipline of nonviolent direct action; (2) a nonviolent direct action campaign as an escalation of tactics; (3) the nature and justification of civil disobedience; (4) the effects of nonviolent direct action—conversion versus coercion; (5) the role of the opponent's violence; and (6) the relation of militant tactics and political allegiance.

1. Reading Martin Luther King's descriptions of the campaigns he led in Montgomery in 1956 and in Birmingham in 1963 conveys the impression that he made a very conscious effort to emulate the spirit and practice of Gandhian nonviolent direct action.[25] The philosophy of nonviolence, as he summarizes it, is clearly Gandhi's philosophy: (1) Nonviolence is not truly practised if one employs it because of cowardice or because violence is not feasible. Yet, on the other hand, it is not a passive nonresistance to evil, "for while the non-violent resister is passive in the sense that he is not physically aggressive toward his opponent, his mind and emotions are always active, constantly seeking to persuade his opponent that he is wrong."[26] (2) Nonviolence should not be used to win a victory over the opponent or to humiliate him; instead, the practitioner tries to reach the opponent's conscience and ultimately achieve a reconciliation with him based on moral agreement and understanding. (3) The target of nonviolence is not the evildoer but the evil. (4) Nonviolent resistance implies a willingness to endure suffering without retaliating. (5) Not only is external physical violence eschewed, but violence of the spirit must also be avoided; the nonviolent resister must not hate his opponent or seek revenge. (6) At the heart of nonviolent resistance is the conviction that there is a cosmic force working for justice and harmony.[27]

Some of these aspects are illustrated in King's account of the Montgomery bus boycott. Shortly after the initial decision to boycott the bus company had been taken, King says he found that a local paper was implicitly comparing the tactic to the boycott methods of the White Citizens Councils. This was disturbing to him because the Councils sometimes resorted to means which considerably overstepped the boundaries of the law. He was forced to decide whether or not the boycott was an "ethical course of action." If it were not, moral ends might not justify its use. The boycott could be viewed as a way of putting economic pressure on the bus company, threatening it with bankruptcy. Instead, King chose to see it in Gandhian terms: Not only was it directed to just ends—in contrast to the ends of the White Citizens Councils —it was really a form of noncooperation with an unjust system. Going along with the present system made one a party to its injustice.

King's argument might be viewed as rationalization and justification, not objective evaluation; however, it is clear that the spirit in which action is taken plays a crucial role in Gandhian nonviolent direct action, and King attempted to invest the boycott with the spirit of his interpretation. He urged participants in the boycott not to compel others to avoid riding the buses. Speakers at mass meetings who used inflammatory rhetoric were told that this was out of place. King repeatedly stressed the importance of nonviolence and love of one's enemy.[28]

Other aspects of the campaign manifested the commitment to nonviolence. When a county grand jury indicted over 100 persons for violating a state law against boycotts, no one resisted arrest; many went to the sheriff's office to check whether they were among the indicted. When the federal courts invalidated local and state bus segregation laws, the Montgomery Improvement Association (MIA), the organization directing the boycott, began holding sessions to prepare people for riding integrated buses. Bus boardings were acted out with people playing the role of white and black passengers; nonviolence was stressed. When someone forgot and retaliated to "white" violence or insult, attempts were made to get him to modify his reaction. Blacks were instructed not to go back to the buses and "push people around unnecessarily boasting of our rights."[29] At a meeting on the eve of integration, King said:

This is the time we must evince calm dignity and wise restraint. Emotions must not run wild. Violence must not come from any of us, for if we become victimized with violent intents, we will have walked in vain, and our twelve months of glorious dignity will be transformed into an eve of gloomy catastrophe. As we go back to the buses let us be loving enough to turn an enemy into a friend. We must now move from protest to reconciliation.[30]

The MIA asked ministers to ride the buses during rush hours at the start in order to give blacks confidence and to help maintain nonviolent discipline. Specific instructions were distributed which persons were encouraged to study and memorize; these instructions included admonitions such as:

Do not deliberately sit by a white person, unless there is no other seat.

If cursed, do not curse back. If pushed, do not push back. If struck, do not strike back, but evidence love and goodwill at all times.

For the first few days try to get on the bus with a friend in whose non-violence you have confidence. You can uphold one another by a glance or a prayer.

If another person is being molested, do not arise to go to his defense, but pray for the oppressor and use moral and spiritual force to carry on the struggle for justice.

If you feel you cannot take it, walk for another week or two.[31]

In the Birmingham campaign, when it was decided that direct action had to be used, King and his lieutenants attempted to mobilize and prepare the local black community for participation. Workshops on nonviolence and direct action were set up to indoctrinate volunteers in the philosophy and techniques as preparation for the civil disobedience demonstrations:

We made it clear that we would not send anyone out to demonstrate who had not convinced himself and us that he could accept and endure violence without retaliating.

Not all who volunteered could pass our strict tests for service as demonstrators. . . . Every volunteer was required to sign a Commitment Card that read: I HEREBY PLEDGE MYSELF—MY PERSON AND BODY —TO THE NONVIOLENT MOVEMENT. THEREFORE I WILL KEEP THE FOLLOWING TEN COMMANDMENTS: . . .

2. Remember always that the nonviolent movement in Birmingham seeks justice and reconciliation—not victory.
6. Observe with both friend and foe the ordinary rules of courtesy.
8. Refrain from the violence of fist, tongue, or heart.
10. Follow the direction of the movement and of the captain on a demonstration.[32]

King was the civil rights leader who most closely modeled himself after Gandhi, with his special emphasis on nonviolence as a creed. Other major civil rights organizations began with a similar orientation. CORE was founded in the early 1940's by the pacifist Fellowship of

Reconciliation. James Farmer's original memorandum, in which he formulated the idea of CORE, indicated that nonviolent direct action was to be the basic tactic of the new organization, although Farmer did not think that Gandhi's effort could or should be duplicated.

As listed in a 1963 CORE pamphlet, the basic implications which the organization drew from nonviolence were similar to Gandhi's philosophy:

A CORE member will make a sincere effort to avoid malice and hatred toward any group or individual. . . .

A CORE member will never use malicious slogans or labels to discredit any opponent.[33]

The elaboration of this guideline suggests that, while CORE members should criticize racial discrimination loudly and persistently, they should not direct their criticism against the person engaging in it but rather against the action. This is comparable to Gandhi's injunction that the *satyagrahi* should bear with the evildoer but not with the evil.

A CORE member will be willing to admit mistakes. . . .

A member will meet the anger of any individual or group in the spirit of good will and creative reconciliation: he will submit to assault and will not retaliate in kind either by act or word.[34]

Participants in early CORE projects followed Gandhi in believing that nonviolence could impress even the most hardened opponent. Project participants also followed Gandhian precepts in their refusal to cooperate with what they considered an unjust system. When Freedom Riders were convicted in southern courts, they refused to pay fines and stayed in jail for several weeks, despite mistreatment, before posting appeal bond. Willing acceptance of suffering for the sake of principle was thought by Gandhi to have a positive effect on one's oppressors. Many CORE members were willing to endure suffering because of their faith in the efficacy of nonviolence and their desire not to cooperate in any way with an unjust system.

CORE's rules for action projects were modeled, to some extent, on Gandhian practices. Discipline was stressed. Unauthorized action was not permitted; members were required to follow the orders of the authorized leaders when on a project. Once members accepted the group discipline for a specific project, they were not free to reject it, although those who, under the pressure of the actual situation, felt they could not adhere to the rules were expected to withdraw immediately. Non-retaliation by word or act was the proper response in case of assault. CORE members were warned of the possible consequences of participation, such as physical attack, and were advised not to volunteer unless they were willing to endure them.

The initial statement of purpose drawn up by the Student Nonviolent Coordinating Committee (SNCC) spoke of nonviolence, love, and the appeal to conscience. In his address to the founding SNCC convention, James Lawson, an expelled Vanderbilt divinity student, emphasized Christian nonviolence and the use of radically Christian methods to change evils in society. He asserted that through nonviolence, black students embraced the hardship (violence and jail) of obedience to Christian goals. Nonviolence, he said, took the weapon of manipulation of law and law enforcement away from the power structure, and, at the same time, attracted the support of many whites, southern and nonsouthern. It gave the black a "new sense of his role in molding a redeemed society."[35] As with CORE, the initial impulse to employ nonviolent direct action drew upon a religious, or at least philosophic, commitment to certain ways of responding to evil.

While SCLC attempted to remain committed to nonviolence in the deeply religious and philosophical spirit that King brought to it,[36] other major civil rights organizations eventually adopted a more pragmatic attitude toward nonviolence. Both SNCC and CORE, the most militant of these groups, shifted from their originally less instrumental attitude.[37]

Ingeborg Powell's study of CORE activists in the early 1960s indicated that their commitment to nonviolence was usually not religious or philosophical.[38] The majority apparently accepted it on pragmatic grounds. Some members, especially those from the North, questioned nonviolence and openly recognized the coercive nature of direct action. They even considered the use of violence in the movement, but this referred only to violence in self-defense, where law and order were inoperative. The pragmatic quality of many CORE activists' orientation toward nonviolence was illustrated by the fact that northern members, whose intellectual and emotional commitment to nonviolence seemed weaker than that of the southern members, more consistently maintained the nonviolent discipline both on and off projects.[39]

Powell argues that nonviolence was so bound up with other highly positive features of the civil rights movement, in the minds of southern members particularly, that it was difficult to isolate attitudes toward nonviolence from a generalized positive response to the movement as a whole. The movement provided a new role for the southern Negro, in which nonviolence, courage, militancy, discipline, and direct action were all facets.

Non-violence appears to the members as part of the standard procedure of investigation, negotiation, demonstration and civil disobedience which makes them feel expert and secure in the possession of a standardized and proven method for conducting campaigns. [The various rules of discipline, e.g., against answering back, requiring anyone who loses control to leave the scene of action, etc.] combine to give the demonstrator a sense of having a well defined and firmly structured role in the midst of what is often a dangerous and chaotic social situation.[40]

Powell's observation and participation in a CORE training institute convinced her that CORE staff "did not expect members to take an absolutist or deeply personal commitment to non-violence." At the same time, very high standards of discipline and courtesy were inculcated.

An apparent complement to the pragmatic commitment of CORE activists to nonviolence was a conflict orientation toward black-white relations. That there was some hostility toward white opponents was indicated by the tendency of southern black members to indulge in vicarious violence when in private, lapsing into open hostility and "impolite" behavior patterns. Whether northern black members also felt personal hostility was not evident; they tended to take more radical and alienated positions, but their public and private behavior was more self-controlled.[41] The observation of two other commentators appears to corroborate these findings about CORE activists:

Especially since 1960, CORE has felt what Farmer described as the tension between the "means-oriented idealists," and the "ends-oriented militants," who regarded nonviolent direct action purely as a pragmatic tool for attaining equal rights. In most CORE chapters the latter group has won.[42]

An interview with John Lewis, then SNCC Chairman, in the spring of 1964, showed that SNCC's views were also changing:

The thing we drew up back in 1960 was a type of creed, a philosophic and religious commitment. In SNCC now, there's a growing—and it's growing fast—trend toward "aggressive non-violent action." You no longer walk quietly to paddy wagons and happily and willingly go to jail. There's another type of willingness, and personally, I don't see anything violent about it.[43]

Writing in 1964, the historian, Howard Zinn, said of SNCC:

Today, SNCC's view of nonviolence is more complicated than that simple statement of faith in the power of love ["Love is the central motif of non-violence. . . ."]. Although there are some in the organization who would hold to that original credo without qualification, most SNCC people, in different degree and with a great individuality of response, would probably deny that love, conscience, and morality alone could end segregation. . . .

The recent calls by Malcolm X and others for Negroes to use self-defense, and even retaliation, against acts of violence by whites, have not found approval by the SNCC organization. Yet individual SNCC members have sometimes expressed sympathy for this position. A more moderate attitude was expressed with near-unanimity in an informal discussion among SNCC leaders early in 1964: that they would not stop a Negro farmer in Mississippi from arming himself to defend his home against attack.[44]

After that time, SNCC moved to open acceptance of self-defensive violence and beyond. The same trend occurred within CORE.

Survey data on participants in early civil rights demonstrations corroborates the impression that they generally espoused nonviolence but that their commitment seems to have been pragmatic instead of philosophic or moral. Less than one percent of the black college students interviewed by Ruth Searles and J. Allen Williams accepted the use of violence,[45] and a characteristic feature of the civil rights workers' behavior studied by Jacob R. Fishman and Fredric Solomon was "maintenance of a group ideology and discipline which forbade violent responses of any kind."[46] At the same time, these movement activists' commitment to nonviolence appears to have been based on a pragmatic assessment of the consequences:

Non-violent techniques seem[ed] advisable as good strategy, and their reason for not striking back when being physically abused [was] that it would "hurt the movement." . . . [they felt] that in terms of the political framework and public opinion of the country today, those who become violent are bound to lose in the long run.[47]

The large majority of black leaders interviewed by William Brink and Louis Harris in 1963—many of whom had personally participated in direct action—gave reasons indicating a *rejection* of violence to support their view that blacks would not *have* to resort to violence in order to achieve their aims.[48] At the same time, the little survey data there is available suggests that an attitude toward opponents similar to the Gandhian one often prevailed in the early civil rights demonstrations. Gandhi said that the *satyagrahi* should bear with the evildoer and avoid any hostility toward him. Many of these demonstrators apparently did not view the targets of their protests with any deep hostility or see them as hostile, irreconcilable opponents. Searles and Williams reported that their respondents' attitudes toward whites showed "at least surface willingness to give [them] the benefit of the doubt;" fewer than one-tenth chose hatred of blacks to explain white opposition to the student protest movement.[49] Fishman and Solomon found that the civil rights workers they studied regularly manifested "a show of friendliness toward segregationist opponents."[50] In the authors' opinion, this was a way of "asserting a certain psychological superiority" over them, as well as an attempt to change their attitudes. Donald R. Matthews and James W. Prothro found that "the more active students consistently [were] more tolerant, understanding and optimistic about white people and segregation than [were] the inactive."[51] Only 6 percent of those active in the protests thought all whites were prejudiced, while 22 percent of the completely inactive thought so.[52] However, Everett C. Ladd says that the militants (generally, those black leaders who advocated direct action tactics) in his survey showed little confidence that whites would yield to their demands unless strong pressure was applied. Whites, they believed, are basically hostile to black interests and to blacks as persons.[53]

The early popularity of nonviolence may have been at least partly due to the "feedback" effects of direct action. Powell asserts:

Little tangible bits of utopia were provided in the here and now, not so much by enjoyment of new facilities because these were still regarded as merely symbolic of the eventual goal, but in the sense of strength and exhilaration which a member could draw from participating in a unified, disciplined group effort which confronted the white community with a new image of the militant self-assured Negro.[54]

Don Von Eschen, Jerome Kirk, and Maurice Pinard report that participation in direct action made individuals more optimistic about achieving their goals; this was particularly true among blacks: 79 percent of black respondents reported they were more hopeful about the possibility of desegregation since joining the movement. This is quite similar to Powell's "feedback" effect. Since direct action often produced tangible results quickly, it could attract persons whose initial reaction toward participation was negative—they tended to doubt it would work. One of the major hindrances to mass participation by blacks in the movement, according to the authors, was widespread feelings of alienation and political impotence. Thus, winning concessions in the short run may have been crucial to building a mass base. Movement leaders, they suggest, may have been conscious of how important quick successes were in "breaking down inhibiting images of the political process." Tangible results helped break down a "commitment to routine methods alone." Moreover, the fact that white elites responded only to a prospect of continued demonstrations and the threat of disruption—as well as the very violent reaction of segregationists—probably undermined feelings "that disorderly means were neither necessary nor effective."[55] While tangible results seem to have been an important inducement to participate in nonviolent direct action, it seems reasonable to assume that *continued* results were necessary to make people persist in using it because their attitude toward such tactics was basically a pragmatic one.

2. In *Letter from a Birmingham Jail*, Martin Luther King elaborated on his theory of how nonviolent direct action was to be conducted. A campaign involves four steps: "Collection of the facts to determine whether injustices exist; negotiation; self-purification; and direct action."[56] He suggested that nonviolent direct action is not at odds with conventional methods of settling conflicts, for the object of such action is negotiation. "Nonviolent direct action seeks to create such a crisis and foster such a tension that a community which has constantly refused to negotiate is forced to confront the issue. It seeks so to dramatize the issue that it can no longer be ignored."[57]

The first two major campaigns which King led deviated somewhat from Gandhi's standard operating procedures, but not because King specifically rejected any of them. The campaign in Montgomery was not a full-scale *satyagraha*; it involved only noncooperation, not real civil disobedience, and although there was considerable preparation for nonviolence, the campaign was not a graduated series of actions. The catalyst had been a black woman's refusal to move to the back of a bus when directed by the driver. This spontaneous act presented black leaders in the community with an opportunity and a challenge. How should they respond to the woman's arrest? The idea of a boycott emerged in consultations among a few influential people who learned of the incident. Thus there was no preliminary campaign of publicity and protest (as was the Gandhian practice) against the local policy of segregated seating. Gandhi's campaigns usually began with an investigation of the issues in the controversy, but in this case there was a long history of discriminatory—and worse—treatment of Montgomery blacks on the buses. In contrast to the bus boycott, the Birmingham campaign was consciously worked out in advance. While the plan called for *beginning* with a series of sit-ins at lunch-counters in downtown department stories—which seems a departure from the requirements of *satyagraha*—there had been prior attempts to use more conventional channels of redress. The Alabama Christian Movement for Human Rights (ACHR), a local group first organized in 1956 which later affiliated with King's Southern Christian Leadership Council (SCLC), had instituted a suit to make Birmingham open its public recreation facilities to all residents. The plaintiffs won, but the city chose to close the parks. In 1962, students from a local black college began a series of boycotts against downtown stores, and they were supported by the ACHR. The targets of these boycotts were such practices as the display of jim-crow signs, refusal to employ blacks in any but menial jobs, refusal to promote black employees, and refusal to serve blacks at department store lunch-counters. Shortly before the 1963 SCLC convention, scheduled for Birmingham, local businessmen became upset at rumors that SCLC planned a campaign to coincide with its convention, and they began negotiating with the ACHR. A group of them reached several agreements with black leaders: They would remove the jim-crow signs and jointly initiate with ACHR a suit to overturn city ordinances prohibiting integration of lunch-counters. In the interim, the ACHR agreed to suspend demonstrations and boycotts, but Fred Shuttlesworth, leader of the ACHR, indicated that SCLC would be asked to aid the ACHR in a campaign if the agreements were not kept. After the convention, the signs went back up, and Shuttlesworth and King decided a joint campaign of direct action was necessary. The first two required steps preceding direct action—collection of the facts of injustice and negotiation—had been taken; there was no doubt that racial injustices existed in Birmingham; local businessmen had broken their agreements; city authorities would not negotiate in good faith. The third step before direct action could properly be initiated was "self-purification": participants were indoctrinated in the philosophy and techniques of nonviolence as preparation for the initial demonstrations.

Following the initial sit-ins and arrests, there was a march on City Hall:

Carefully selected and screened, the first waves of demonstrators conducted themselves as they had been trained to do. They marched in orderly files of two, without banners or band or singing. When they reached a point, three blocks from their goal, where Bull Connor's officers loomed in their path, they stood silently by as their leaders politely but firmly refused to obey Connor's orders to disperse. Thereupon forty-two were arrested for "parading without a permit." They were escorted with amazing politeness into the paddy wagons, and they, in turn, allowed themselves to be led without resisting, singing freedom songs on the way to jail.[58]

While the Birmingham campaign, SCLC's first large-scale, planned nonviolent direct action effort, did not strictly follow Gandhi's order of tactics it did include the basic components: negotiation, mobilization and preparation for nonviolent direct action, and a gradual escalation of direct action.

Early CORE projects to integrate restaurants and department store lunch-counters followed a set of steps similar to Gandhian campaigns. First, CORE members would test the facilities in question to determine whether blacks would be served. Once it was clear that they would not be, CORE committees attempted to negotiate with managers or owners.

CORE believes in being practical. Once segregation has been shown to exist, CORE does not immediately stage a sit-in or a stand-in, form a picket line or pass out leaflets. It first tries to meet with someone in authority, if possible the manager or owner of the establishment, to discuss the problem with him. Discussion is sometimes all that is needed. If segregation conflicts with a state or federal civil rights law, a readiness to press charges may suffice.[59]

If negotiation failed, small integrated groups of CORE members would make further attempts to gain service. They would also hand out leaflets informing patrons of the discriminatory policy. More detailed information might also be disseminated to community groups. Finally, CORE would conduct a sit-in; an integrated group would wait to be seated, and if seated, would stay as long as was necessary to obtain service.

The southern student sit-ins of the early 1960s were largely spontaneous, not part of planned nonviolent direct action campaigns. The first occurred in 1960 in Greensboro, North Carolina, when four freshmen at A & T College decided, after a week of talking about integration, to sit-in at Woolworth's lunch-counter. Within about two weeks, there were sit-ins in 15 southern cities.[60] However, this spontaneity did not mean that preparation of demonstrators for nonviolent tactics was ignored. Zinn reports that CORE conducted several days of classes in nonviolence for black students at Claflin College and South Carolina State in Orangeburg, South Carolina, before sit-ins were begun there. By April of the same year a conference of students from many southern communities was convened in Raleigh, North Carolina, to begin coordination of the sit-in efforts; out of this came SNCC. But even after SNCC began to function later in the year, it was not in a position to coordinate the movement; contacts with indigenous groups were too intermittent. Since the sit-ins were locally planned and implemented, it is difficult to determine how much of the nonviolent philosophy and discipline of Gandhi was communicated to participants.

Civil disobedience and nonviolent direct action has been used extensively in campus protests and in the antiwar movement. Like the early student sit-in in the South, this use of direct action has tended to be local and spontaneous. Many participants were directly involved or influenced by the civil rights movement's use of direct action tactics, but it seems doubtful that a great deal of preparation in nonviolence occurred because of the amorphous nature of these movements. The Sproul Hall sit-in on the Berkeley campus of the University of California in December, 1964, the first mass civil disobedience demonstration on a major university campus, does not appear to have been preceded by intensive preparation for nonviolent direct action. Only in a rather general way did the course of the Free Speech Movement follow the series of steps which characterized the Gandhian campaigns. After initial demonstrations which erupted spontaneously when the university administration attempted to enforce restrictions against on-campus student political activity, the movement utilized conventional channels to press its claims. But the conflict was not settled; the administration remained generally unresponsive; and direct action tactics were gradually escalated, culminating in the mass sit-in. Before the

Governor ordered the demonstrators' arrest, they were informed by the Chancellor of the University at Berkeley that they were engaged in an "unlawful assembly" and urged to leave the building. Only those who insisted on remaining in Sproul Hall were arrested. In this sense, the disobedience which occurred was a knowing violation of the law, but it seems doubtful that many of the participants expected to commit civil disobedience before the sit-in began. Most students went limp when arrested, and they were charged with resisting arrest; however, physical resistance apparently was not offered. If the Free Speech Movement was at all typical of other campus movements, then it is unlikely that the Gandhian strategy for nonviolent direct action campaigns was very closely approximated in the campus protest movement.

3. Generally, the justifications given for civil disobedience in this country have been similar to the ones Gandhi provided. For example, King asserted that there is a moral obligation to disobey unjust laws. He implied that one can determine when a law is "out of harmony with the moral law," that is, unjust, without great difficulty.[61] This confidence seemed to stem from his religious principles. At the same time, King suggested a rather different definition of an unjust law—one that is imposed on a minority which was denied the right to vote and thus had no part in legislating the law. A more specific illustration of King's attitude toward civil disobedience is revealed in his account of the SCLC campaign in Birmingham. Shortly after SCLC began its direct action tactics, the city obtained an injunction prohibiting further demonstrations until the court had determined whether the defendants had a right to demonstrate. King indicates that the decision to violate the injunction was not lightly or quickly made. Apparently he considered this a more serious matter than sit-ins and marches because SCLC had never disobeyed a court order in any of its campaigns. According to King, the question of "planned, deliberate civil disobedience" had already been pondered when the campaign was in the planning stage. It had then been agreed that the demonstrators would violate an injunction if one were issued. There is an implicit contrast in King's remarks between deliberately violating a court order specifically aimed at the demonstrators and violations which occurred because local officials on the scene decided that certain behavior was illegal, although perhaps no law specifically prohibited it. While demonstrators apparently expected to be arrested in the latter case, King did not consider this a

planned violation; it was not clear that the laws proscribed their behavior, only that local officials were likely to arrest them for it. King justified his decision to violate the injunction on the grounds that the injunction was being used to thwart direct action for civil rights, and to deny black citizens and white supporters the right of peaceful assembly. An injunction could take years to litigate; in the meantime, the movement would be denied an important weapon. The leaders attempted to minimize the disobedience involved in violating the injunction by announcing publicly the intention to violate it, and King presented a defense: He contended that this was not a lawless act because the State was misusing the judicial process to prevent integration.

King asserted that civil disobedients had to be willing to accept the penalty, but this did not mean that no legal defense was offered when demonstrators were arrested. For example, when the first arrests were made in Birmingham, lawyers working on behalf of SCLC filed a petition in federal district court to have the cases removed from the state courts. When King was convicted for violating the court order, his sentence was appealed.[62]

Although I have not found any detailed justification of civil disobedience in literature on CORE and SNCC, it appears that participants in their direct action projects and demonstrations tended to believe that they were morally justified in violating local regulations and state laws that denied them rights other Americans enjoyed. Fishman and Solomon's study of 19 experienced civil rights workers found a recurring conviction that desegregation was not only morally right but inevitable. The authors assert that "many who participate in sit-ins, boycotts and Freedom Rides view their actions as an outgrowth of their religious and moral principles and as a refusal to cooperate with an evil system;" the demonstrator feels justified "in breaking local laws with which he may be in disagreement" at least partly because of his sense of moral superiority and belief in the inevitability of desegregation.[63] Those CORE members who followed Gandhi's principles probably felt civil disobedience was justified by the moral duty not to cooperate with an evil system. As the civil rights movement developed, the two organizations apparently viewed civil disobedience as a necessary tactic for achieving their goals; that is, conventional channels for pursuing political aims, for example, racial equality, were not very promising.

It does not appear that CORE and SNCC participants in direct action attempted to avoid penalties legally imposed, but generally they retained legal counsel to defend them in court. Sometimes they willingly remained in jail awaiting trial instead of being bailed out; at other times, bail funds were not available and they were compelled to remain in jail. Occasionally, arrested demonstrators pleaded *nolo contendere* or failed to appeal convictions, but this may have been a result of insufficient funds for court costs and legal aid rather than a principled decision to accept penalties without contest. It is also possible that *nolo* pleas were arranged with court officials in return for light sentences.

Southern justice frequently placed difficult handicaps upon the legal defense of civil rights activists; their responses to arrest seem to have been a pragmatic reaction to this situation. To have acquiesced in the decisions of southern judges and prosecuters would have crippled their ability to continue working for racial equality. For example, local judges sometimes prevented out-of-state lawyers from defending civil rights demonstrators; frequently, they set high bail. In the first county court trial of the freedom riders in Mississippi, the prosecutor and the judge insisted that all defendants on bail return to the state, even though under Mississippi law, a lawyer could plead "not guilty" for a person accused of committing a misdemeanor.[64] Gradually, civil rights lawyers developed a legal basis for having such cases transferred into federal courts, where their clients had a better chance for a fair hearing. Quite often, civil rights lawyers contended that no illegal behavior had occurred, for example, as in the case of breach of the peace charges against Freedom Riders, or that no violation of a *valid* law had been committed. In many cases, the Supreme Court ultimately upheld the claims of the demonstrators.

In the campus demonstration cases, it appears that students have generally retained counsel and pleaded not guilty. This was true in the case of the Sproul Hall sit-in defendants. Their lawyers, in demurring to the charges against the defendants, contended that:

[The] free speech, due process, and equal protection provisions of the federal and state constitutions specifically protect these defendants from state court prosecutions for exercising their liberties to speak, to sit-in [which the attorneys considered civil disobedience], to assemble in order to petition for a redress of grievances. This protection is not limited to speech, sit-ins or assembly to petition for the redress of valid grievances only. This state and nation are committed under the Constitutions to protect advocacy of error as well as truth precisely because the framers of the Constitutions had observed that yesterday's error often proved to be today's truth.[65]

Gandhi considered civil disobedience justifiable after more conventional means of redress had been exhausted. It is impossible to determine whether the American practice has conformed to this standard without a very extensive and intensive examination of civilly disobedient acts. The following is only a very impressionistic summary. In what is perhaps the most notable civil disobedience campaign in American history, the southern sit-ins of the early 1960s, resort to this tactic was preceded by a long history of largely unsuccessful use of other available means, such as verbal protest, negotiation, petition, and supplication. For many decades, legal avenues were closed to blacks by *Plessy v. Furguson,* and virtually total disenfranchisement precluded real representation and foreclosed the possibility of change through legislation. As the literature on SCLC and CORE indicates, civil disobedience was not supposed to be employed until more conventional means of achieving movement goals were tried. The readily available evidence suggests that these organizations generally did proceed in this fashion. While it *may* be possible to criticize many of the campus and antiwar protests for "escalating" to civil disobedience rather rapidly, petitions and negotiations have usually preceded such demonstrations. While outside observers probably have thought that movement activists should have given conventional methods more intensive use and more time to have an effect, their evaluation of the target's response—i.e., willingness to negotiate in good faith and to introduce reforms or a concealed desire to prevent change by stalling tactics—probably has differed from that of the protesters.

4. While American practitioners of civil disobedience and nonviolent direct action have recognized that these tactics can work through persuasion, they do not seem to have been as committed to converting opponents as Gandhi apparently was. Even Martin Luther King, who followed Gandhi's views closely, indicated his recognition that nonviolent direct action can put pressure on opponents to accept outcomes they do not prefer. Gandhi also recognized this, but he always stressed the intent to convert the opponent. King maintained that direct action is a means of opening a dialogue and that its ultimate goal is reconciliation with the adversary, yet he did not contend that it works solely or primarily by moral suasion. For instance, in the *Letter,* referring to the new mayor of Birmingham, Albert Boutwell, he says:

I have hope that Mr. Boutwell will be reasonable enough to see the futility of massive resistance to desegregation. But he will not see this without pressure from devotees of civil rights. My friends, I must say to you that we have not made a single gain in civil rights without determined legal and nonviolent pressure. Lamentably, it is an historical fact that privileged groups seldom give up their privileges voluntarily. Individuals may see the moral light and voluntarily give up their unjust posture; but, as Reinhold Niebuhr has reminded us, groups tend to be more immoral than individuals. We know through painful experience that freedom is never voluntarily given by the oppressor; it must be demanded by the oppressed.[66]

Clearly, King recognized the pressure involved in direct action. The ACHR-SCLC leaders decided to launch the Birmingham campaign during the Easter buying season. Expecting a boycott as the "by-product" of the demonstrations, they decided that an Easter season campaign "would be the best time to bring pressure to bear on the merchants," the time when black buying power would be most effective.[67] King contended that Birmingham leaders were influenced by the adverse publicity the city received, the black boycott, and the concomitant decline in white buying.

The shift in CORE and SNCC toward a more pragmatic view of nonviolence was paralleled by open acceptance of nonviolent direct action primarily as a means of applying pressure, instead of an appeal to the consciences of their opponents. The activities of CORE indicate that members recognized that direct action can cause inconvenience for the white community, even if it is nonviolent. Disruption—actual and potential—creates pressure to make concessions in order to avoid further disturbance. In a study of black leadership in New Orleans, Daniel C. Thompson describes the local CORE organization's use of direct action as a means of pressuring state and city officials to abandon jim-crow laws.[68] This approach appears to have been characteristic of CORE. According to Ingeborg Powell, most of the training at an annual CORE institute was devoted to the "study and application of practical techniques of direct action. ... [Its import] was one of learning a strategy to maximize coercion short of physical violence or verbal abuse."[69] The operating assumption appeared to be that results could be obtained only through efficient organization designed to maximize pressure.

SNCC took the same position; the realities of the struggle for civil rights in the Deep South made SNCC activists less sanguine about the efficacy of nonviolence as opposed to direct action. What they realized was that nonviolent direct action worked not merely or mainly by conversion; they recognized that "economic and other pressures may be more decisive than moral suasion to bring about social change."

It should be recalled that the Raleigh statement of SNCC was made on the basis of experience in Nashville, Atlanta, and other border and upper-South areas. The plunge into Alabama, Mississippi, and Southwest Georgia, first in the Freedom Rides and then in the prolonged voter registration campaign, disclosed a different kind of situation, where the usual techniques of nonviolent direct action were simply crushed by police power. The devices that had proved effective elsewhere met with a variety of reprisals from brutal beatings to murder. These experiences have led SNCC to ask the national government to intervene in the Deep South, using not love but the power of arrest and imprisonment to stop brutality and violence against civil rights workers by police and private persons [to clear the way for nonviolent demonstrative activity there].[70]

Survey data on other direct action participants indicates that there was a divergence of views about the way these tactics operate. The respondents in these surveys tended to view direct action as a means of persuading opponents, while SNCC and CORE activists tended to see it as a means of applying pressure or as a form of coercion. The former tended to stress "educational" effects; the latter focused on economic loss, notoriety, and disruption. Both recognized that direct action gains widespread publicity and, to some degree, they realized that this could have effects of both kinds—for example, making the target aware of their grievances and pressuring the target with the possibility of federal intervention or a loss of business.

The civil rights workers interviewed by Fishman and Solomon showed "awareness of the potential for national and international publicity and possible federal intervention on their behalf."[71] Matthews and Prothro report that the students in their survey were aware that direct action would get widespread publicity; they wanted white southerners to recognize their dissatisfaction and the intensity of their demands. The fact that the most active students were the most optimistic (and unrealistic in their perceptions) about white attitudes toward segregation may be indirect evidence that they believed southern whites could be *persuaded* to change prevailing practices.[72] To the militants described by Everett C. Ladd, direct action appeared to have several effects: It had the capacity to "prick the conscience" of whites and to dramatize the plight of the blacks; it increased consensus in the black community and helped mobilize blacks by sharply revealing the existence of racial conflict. In addition, there was an indication that some recognized that the symbolic expression of such protest was heightened because direct action imposed some constraints on the white community. This was brought out by Ladd's description of a controversy among black leaders in the Greenville, South Carolina, NAACP chapter over the continued use of sit-ins. One faction viewed such demonstrations as good because they bothered white consciences. "The greater the number arrested, the more the plight of the Negro was dramatized and *the more whites* were inconvenienced."[73] The other faction contended that black opposition to the segregation of lunch counters had been clearly demonstrated; black discontent was apparent. This faction saw no reason to put more people in jail, especially when bail funds were exhausted and the safety and security of blacks were threatened. The other faction apparently was willing to run these risks in order to drive their point home.

Both parties to this controversy had a "pedagogic" or an "educational" orientation toward direct action—their intent was to communicate to the white community that blacks were intensely dissatisfied with existing conditions and that they no longer would accept the *status quo*. Within this orientation, two tendencies were discernible: some activists seemed to think that direct action achieved its purpose by making protest visible; others recognized that it was difficult to impress the point of these protests upon the white community and that the white community had to be "compelled," in a sense, to see something it preferred not to see. Exhibition of the real sacrifices blacks were willing to make for their demands emphasized their determination, as well as unsettled white consciences.

There is some other scattered evidence that participants perceive direct action as having "pedagogic" publicity effects. A study of leaders and activists in the 1964 civil rights demonstration in San Francisco indicate that 65 percent of them believed—six months after the events—that the demonstrations had helped publicize the problem; i.e., discrimination in hiring practices.[74] The William Brink-Louis Harris survey found that 63 percent of the black leaders in their national sample of 100 thought demonstrations made the public aware of the black's condition. A majority of the sample had personally participated in civil rights demonstrations or other forms of direct action.[75] To some extent, this divergence in orientation toward direct action may be due to a time factor: The attitudes of SNCC and CORE members apparently changed due to their experiences in the Deep South; the early civil rights demonstrations, in which some of the survey respondents participated, were in the upper South.

5. The civil rights movement was never united, and this is evidenced in the different orientations toward nonviolent direct action. Members of SCLC and early CORE activists tended to believe, like Gandhi, that a nonviolent response to the opponents' violence has a softening effect on their hostility. SNCC and later CORE workers seem to have become skeptical of this. Here there seems to be a deviation from the Gandhian position. Civil rights activists apparently have often perceived that opponents' violence, perhaps more than their own nonviolence, could play a positive role in achieving demonstrators' goals.

One observer of the southern civil rights movement, Jan Howard, suggested that "the provocation of violence [was] often used as a latent tactic."

When is the provocation of violence more than a calculated risk of the movement? . . . when the movement adopts a goal which it believes can be fulfilled only through violence. It is then, in effect, relying on violence to achieve some end . . . the instrumental value of violence is built-in impetus for action that will provide it.[76]

It seems clear that violence on the part of opponents often helped the cause of the civil rights movement. For example, a study of a direct action campaign in Maryland (the events described occurred in 1961) suggests that an effective tactic employed to win equal access to public accommodations was choosing as targets for demonstrations localities where strong segregationists lived.[77] These residents were likely to respond violently to the demonstrations. When they did, their violence had several effects: Immediately it made the movement appear more legitimate than the opposition, and it gained widespread attention. The resultant disorder (or threat of it) put pressure on those in positions of power to alleviate the problem. It is not clear whether this tactic was consciously chosen. Yet Howard thought there *had* been conscious reliance on violence to achieve movement goals; she quoted Martin Luther King:

Long years of experience indicate to us that Negroes can achieve this goal [justice] when four things occur: (1) Nonviolent demonstrators go into the streets to exercise their constitutional rights. (2) Racists resist by unleashing violence against them. (3) Americans of conscience in the name of decency demand federal intervention and legislation. (4) The Administration, under mass pressure, initiates measures of immediate intervention and remedial legislation.[78]

Violence (on the part of opponents), Howard claimed, had an attraction —conscious or unconscious—for movement participants because it could arouse public opinion; it could galvanize the passive black to struggle for his rights; it legitimated nonviolent direct action by starkly juxtaposing these antithetical forms of behavior. "The philosophy of nonviolent struggle seems in part to be predicated on the idea that there will be violence against the movement. The success of nonviolent struggle may require that this prophecy be fulfilled."[79]

If Howard's assessment was right, then there were subtle but important differences between Gandhi's view of the role played by the opponents' violence in nonviolent direct action and the view commonly held in the civil rights movement. In other words, it was the violence of opponents, more than the self-suffering offered by participants in nonviolent direct action, that was perceived as impressing the public. The demonstrators' nonviolence was, of course, important because it made the violence of opponents all the more stark. Yet there seems to be a shift in emphasis.

Howard asserted that those in the movement who did not subscribe to nonviolence and those who accepted it only as a tactic were "constantly pressuring the committed to prove that nonviolence works."

Sometimes this pressure forces the committed to exploit violence as a means of gaining symbolic victories for nonviolence. They may hastily involve the movement in a dramatic protest because they know drama has a quick payoff. Or they may try other means of winning laurels for nonviolence even if they have to throw caution and some principles to the winds. As they are forced to take more and more chances, violence as risk becomes violence as certainty.[80]

Howard realized that violence was not always helpful. Moreover, she feared that provoking the violence of opponents would have diminishing returns; eventually, violence would lose its impact even when unprovoked. Since many persons in the civil rights movement were not philosophically committed to nonviolence, it is quite possible that there was pressure on those who were committed. Yet it seems unlikely that the tactic of provoking opponents—if it was actually used—was responsible for the abandonment of tactics which emphasized the non-violence of their practitioners. Americans may have become jaded to the impact of violence perpetrated on civil rights activists, but some movement workers may also have decided that the gains won when the public was aroused by such violence were not worth the personal risks and suffering. The very persons Howard suggests were pressuring those committed to nonviolence probably desired to avoid violence and suffering if possible. Presumably they did not share the Gandhian view that nonviolence means *active* seeking and acceptance of suffering; to them, nonviolence probably meant nonresistance when attacked. On the other hand, those who were philosophically or religiously committed to nonviolence probably believed that their own suffering was efficacious. Yet even Martin Luther King intimated that nonviolent direct action worked because people were shocked by the segregationists' violence, not because the self-suffering of demonstrators was saliently impressive.

King's tactics on the Selma-to-Montgomery March are revealing in this regard. Apparently King and his associates were surprised when state troopers brutally attacked the first march; they had expected, after Governor Wallace's ban, to be arrested. King's explanation of the course of action he chose for the second march indicates this assessment of the attitude of members of the civil rights movement and the public toward nonviolence and self-suffering. He said that he expected terrible violence if the marchers attempted to pass through the police lines. To have gone ahead, he asserted, might have caused friends and supporters to lose confidence in the movement leadership—they might have begun to suspect irresponsibility. On the other hand, King felt that a confrontation of some sort was necessary to reveal the injustice of the state of Alabama to millions of Americans watching on TV. So a decision was made to stop at the police lines and stay until it was clear they would use force. King hoped this course would still shock Americans and that the federal government would respond to such public reactions. He says that he could not, as a nonviolent leader, recommend "breaking through" a wall of policemen[81]. It seems as if King sought to gain federal intervention while minimizing the suffering of the demonstrators. One gets the impression that he thought public reaction would be negative towards a march which ended in violence.

In contrast, certain of Gandhi's demonstrations were designed to emphasize the willingness of *satyagrahis* to suffer and to bring out their deep commitment to nonviolence. Apparently Gandhi not only hoped to shake the British by heightening their brutality, he also wanted to awaken their sympathy and admiration for a people who would, out of conviction, willingly bear such violence without resistance. He probably expected to unify the Indian people, many of whom held self-suffering in high regard, by strengthening their opposition to a government revealed in its most inhumane aspects.

6. Sometimes Gandhi's practice of nonviolent direct action is used to criticize the use of such tactics by civil rights, student power, and anti-war activists in this country. One reason Gandhi is held up as a model is his insistence that *satyagrahis* pay the penalty for their violations of the law. Presumably this makes it clear that no one is "trying to get away with something," that one is protesting in a responsible fashion. Yet for Gandhi, such scrupulousness was compatible with massive and aggressive noncooperation campaigns in which expectations of violence did not deter his *satyagrahis*. It is possible to justify this in terms of Gandhi's objectives and the nature of British rule in India. However, the argument is made that although civil disobedience may sometimes be morally legitimate in a democratic state, it should be conducted so as to minimize law violation, violence, and disruption. Some of Gandhi's more militant measures might not seem equally justifiable in a country where the government is considered legitimate because it is democratic. An American dissenter who thought the government legitimate and democratic probably would not attempt to "disclose to the full the leonine paws of authority" by offering civil disobedience under circumstances that were likely to "provoke" the authorities to severe repression. Nonetheless, the relation between the protester's view of the government's legitimacy and his choice of tactics is complex. For example, the multiplicity of governments in this country creates the possibility that civil disobedients might sometimes find themselves opposing authorities whom they do *not* consider legitimate; for example, civil rights workers *vis-à-vis* certain southern state governments. Decades of virtually total disenfranchisement gave credence to the view that in the Deep South, blacks were more subjects than citizens. They were not part of the constituency to which southern officials considered themselves responsible. At times, civil rights workers apparently

attempted to show the national public that local and state government officials in the South were acting in ways which violated the spirit and often the letter of the federal Constitution. Making this a public spectacle may be shocking and shake confidence in ostensibly democratic government but it does not seem disloyal or revolutionary from the perspective of the federal system, for the civil rights movement sought to have implemented widely professed democratic ideals.

Civil disobedients may view the government and the laws as legitimate, but not the manner in which certain officials are using laws, or the "color of law," to carry out certain policies. Here, exposure of official repression through "provocation" may serve to demonstrate that a democratic government can act *undemocratically* and go to illiberal extremes in defense of a questionable policy. This could act as a catalyst for disaffection from that government, but it may also be a warning to loyal citizens that democracy is not something one can take for granted and that vigilance over the acts of one's governors is always necessary. Furthermore, when those who react repressively are *private* citizens, for example, some southern segregationists, protesters may use nonviolent direct action when violence is known to be likely without feeling the inhibitions which belief in a government's legitimacy might create. The public may not be aware of the incivility of the opposition and of the extremes to which some citizens will go in order to defend their undemocratic practices. In this situation, using nonviolent direct action and the resultant violence to "teach a lesson" may be more justifiable. It is understandable that practitioners of nonviolent direct action may wish to be more aggressive against an undemocratic state; on the other hand, whether or not the resisters consider the government legitimate does not necessarily determine what degree of "aggressiveness" is morally justifiable. In other words, the fact that a government is both democratic and legitimate does not necessarily imply that nonviolent resisters should not be aggressive *vis-à-vis* that government.

Since Gandhi is often held up as a model for emulation, an examination of the reasons for his success will help dispel illusions about the transferability of his methods. Comparison with the southern civil rights movement—perhaps the most successful nonviolent direct action movement in this country—reveals significant differences which help account for the fact that Gandhi succeeded with a "purer" form of nonviolent direct action.

An important factor in Gandhi's ability to use nonviolent direct action militantly and effectively was the Indian people's willingness to accept suffering for the cause. Shridharani suggests a number of reasons "why . . . the Indian people respond[ed] to Gandhi's call for *Satyagraha* so readily." One is "the fact that the Indian people were completely disarmed at the time."[82] Thus, the means for armed resistance were not at hand, and due to close control of the Indian border, not readily imported. However, Shridharani recognizes that this would not by itself account for the Indians' acceptance of nonviolence, for other disarmed people have resorted to violence against their oppressors. He then cites the Indians' "long religious tradition of nonviolence;" the "non-killing of any living thing" had become a "dominant culture-trait," which influenced the Indians' daily activities.[83] Furthermore, during the period when the Indians were disarmed, this tradition "became more embedded in the Indian culture," so that on the one hand most Indians developed "a genuine disgust of violence and bloodshed" and, on the other, there grew a "sort of faith in nonviolence as a means to an end."[84] The civilian population disdained military pursuits, and the British use of "the so-called 'martial races'" as soldiers reinforced the separation between civilians and the military caste. In the Hindu doctrine of sacrifice Shridharani sees another source of the acceptance of *satyagraha*; the Indians have traditionally viewed sacrifice as a "potential means to achieve objectives, and activities undertaken in the spirit of sacrifice, consequently, result in a veritable spiritual force."[85]

The same culture which predisposed the Indians to accept *satyagraha* was the source, in large part, of Gandhi's doctrines. Shridharani traces their roots into Vedic, Upanishadic, and Jain concepts. Beneath the Vedic belief in the efficacy of sacrifice was this idea:

By relinquishing to God the persons, animals, or things that are dear to himself, the votary undergoes suffering and, thereby, gains God's favor. . . . The far-reaching assumption involved here, is that suffering self-imposed and borne in the spirit of sacrifice, is the most potent of appeals. . . . Down under all the complex and refined modern manifestations of the doctrine of nonviolent direct action is the faith that desired ends may be attained through suffering, when it is voluntary and undertaken in the spirit of sacrifice.[86]

Subsequently, the Upanishadic seers purified the Vedic doctrine of sacrifice, in which formalistic ritual had, over time, displaced the element of personal pain. "Suffering, willed and sacrificial" gradually replaced the original practice of sacrifice as the primary force. Later, the development of Jainism introduced the notion of *ahimsa*, which "was invoked in order to raise a lasting barrier against slaughter in the name of sacrifice."[87] As Bondurant says, "The essential elements of *satyagraha*—truth, nonviolence, and self-suffering—had, for the Hindu, roots in their corresponding traditional precepts."[88]

In addition to Gandhi's adaptation and transformation of traditional concepts in his doctrine of *satyagraha*, which found a congenial audience, several other factors may be adduced to explain the success of nonviolence in India: the minority position of the British there, the salience of the cause—independence—for the Indian people, the nationwide grassroots organization provided by the Congress party, and Gandhi's charisma.

In contrast to blacks in the American South, the oppressed in India constituted the overwhelming majority of the population. While the British had a tight monopoly of the means of violence, their administration in its mundane aspects, as well as military and internal security, depended in large part upon Indians for civil servants, police, and soldiers. Gandhi recognized how crucial the "services" were which Indians performed for their rulers; withdrawal, if massive enough, could bring the administration to a virtual halt. Noncooperation, a master stroke of strategy, depended for its effect largely on the extent of British dependence. The type of services also played a role. The contrast can be seen in South Africa, where withdrawal of African labor power could have severe effects on the economy, but since Africans are not used to fill administrative positions, as so many Indians were, the impact of noncooperation is reduced. Not only were the British a small minority, there apparently was little sympathy for British rule; thus, gaining support for noncooperation was largely a matter of convincing Indians to sacrifice the advantages of government employ. Not all did so, but even here, the dependence of the recalcitrants upon their fellow Indians—even merely in terms of social relations—could be turned to the noncooperators' advantage. Not only did the British minority position facilitate the success of noncooperation, it also contributed to the problems of coping with resistance in general. The size of the disaffected population, relative to the British administration, made "policing" a tremendous task in sheer physical terms.

While Gandhi deserves considerable credit for dramatizing the cause of independence so that even the average illiterate Indian could grasp the implications of the freedom struggle, the cause was one with which all Indians could identify and unite despite great social, economic, religious, and language differences. The postindependence divisions which have caused India so many problems suggest the unique ability of this cause to unite India.

The National Congress, the strongest and best organized Indian political party, played an important role under Gandhi's direction in preparing the people for civil disobedience campaigns. While there was a great deal of spontaneity about the participation, over the long period during which Indians struggled actively for *swaraj* (independence), the Congress was organizing and indoctrinating the Indian masses. "To [Gandhi], Congress was not merely an organization but also a convenient vehicle for his prized experiment in *Satyagraha*."[89] Shridharani says that it is difficult to estimate the exact number of villages which the Congress organized, but Gandhi's call for civil resistance in 1930 elicited a tremendous response, which he claims "indicated that one hamlet out of three was thoroughly indoctrinated in the credo of Satyagraha and had a Congress office of its own by the time of the second nationwide Satyagraha."[90]

Another factor which cannot be slighted is Gandhi's charisma. According to Shridharani, Indians virtually deified him; for the masses, he was an *Avatara*, an incarnation of God. The tradition of the *Avatara,* which resembles the idea of the Messiah, had deep roots in Indian culture. "It was Gandhi's behavior patterns that inspired the masses to endow him, as it were, with a halo. Gandhi became a god to them precisely because he reminded them of God-like personalities from India's past."[91] His pure, ascetic life, his dress and sitting posture, his language, evoked revered traditions and called forth an amazing adoration from the Indian masses. When Gandhi traveled, tremendous crowds gathered to catch a glimpse of him, and "mothers brought their ailing babies to be touched by [him]"[92] because he was reputed to have healing powers. His picture was put up in villagers' huts throughout the country. "[The] faith in Gandhi's divine mission was so deeply imbedded in the psychology of the man in the street that to him truth and 'Gandhi says so' came to be synonymous."[93] In the mind of villagers, "there were only two camps in India: Gandhiwallahs and Sirkar (the government)."[94] There was no question where their sympathies lay. The magnitude of Gandhi's influence is evidenced by his ability to persuade Indians to sacrifice even their lives without resisting the violence inflicted upon them. Other peoples have been willing to lay down their lives for independence but few, if any, have eschewed the use of force. In addition to winning the masses, Gandhi was able to attract a number of very capable lieutenants, who helped bear the burdens of campaigns spread throughout the country and who could assume leadership when Gandhi was arrested.

The differences from the American civil rights movement in the South are apparent. First, blacks have been, in most areas of the South, a clear minority, and they have been excluded from even the lowest levels of government administration. Thus, noncooperation with local government could not threaten the standstill it could produce in India. Although cheap black labor is a conspicuous part of the southern economy, it has not been crucial to economic prosperity because of increasing mechanization and the availability of cheap white labor. As a result, southern blacks could not put much pressure on the white power structure by denying white employers their labor. Indeed, the southern black was rather vulnerable if he openly displayed opposition. Loss of a job could mean virtual loss of the means of subsistence; there was no majority community on which large numbers could fall back for material support. Economic boycotts did produce some effects on the white community, but again the southern black could not isolate white segregationists as Indians could the British administrators.

The goal of the civil rights movement—the right to share equally in the rights white Americans enjoyed—certainly was one with which all southern blacks could identify. Yet it was difficult for many older blacks to begin asserting these rights, even to feel that they were entitled to exercise them. An important factor was the fear of retaliation —a thoroughly justified fear; the black community was rarely in a position to defend those members who defied whites. The British also were able to do more or less what they wished with recalcitrant Indians, but as the Indian independence movement gathered momentum, British officials faced the very real possibility of producing more opposition when they dealt violently with Indian protesters. Over a long period, the fear of retaliation apparently contributed to the black's resignation and accommodation to a system of exclusion and exploitation. Another related factor which may have favored the Indian movement was the unity of the oppressor in India. There, attacking various laws and policies meant attacking British rule, whereas in the South, in many instances, local civil rights campaigns were virtually separate and insulated from one another. True, the civil rights organizations sent their field secretaries across the South, but in each community, a different opponent had to be faced. Different targets were chosen, different compromises were reached. Thus, although the movement had a cause which could appeal to all southern blacks, it was not quite the unifying force which *swaraj* was in India.

The movement in India was led by a unified organization, the Congress Party, which monopolized the position of legitimate opposition to British rule. In contrast, the civil rights movement was composed of several organizations which frequently were in conflict; and even when cooperating, they had no master strategy for directing the movement. The Congress Party spread its organization throughout the grass roots of India, something no civil rights organization approximated. SCLC's projects tended to be led from the top, and short-term campaigns did not produce durable local organizations. Other civil rights organizations may have been more successful in their community organizing efforts, but the movement was frequently divided as to goals and tactics. The Congress Party, while encompassing many points of view, managed to maintain a united front and strategy because of Gandhi's skillful leadership and ability to keep his lieutenants working together.

Several other factors probably contributed to making the southern civil rights movement relatively less aggressive and to reducing involvement. Southern blacks were inhibited in developing militant, skilled leadership for a number of reasons. One was the very limited access of blacks to education in the South; another was the dependence of the most educated, most well-to-do segment of the black community, (teachers, businessmen, ministers) upon the white power structure, from which most of their economic support came. Blacks were virtually excluded from politics and thus prevented from developing political skills. In addition, the civil rights movement gained a great deal of financial support and leadership from whites outside the South; while this help cannot be gainsaid, it probably slowed the emergence of black leadership and the development of support within the black community.

The cultural aspect deserves inclusion in any attempt to explain why the two movements differed in accepting nonviolence. Southern blacks were no strangers to hardship and violence and had often accepted oppression without open resistance; their religious leaders had preached that their suffering would be rewarded in the world to come. However, their culture apparently did not include anything comparable to the Hindu beliefs which prepared Indians to accept the *efficacy* of nonviolence and sacrifice as *means of accomplishing worldly ends.* Moreover, no leader with the charismatic appeal of a Gandhi had come to them preaching nonviolence. Until Martin Luther King emerged as a prominent figure in the civil rights movement, no well-known black leader had espoused nonviolent direct action as a way of life and a way of freeing his people. Booker T. Washington had preached acceptance of a subordinate status while the black worked to improve himself; he stressed development of agricultural and manual skills as a means of making the black indispensable to the white man's economy. W. E. B. Dubois rejected such accommodation, arguing for verbal protest and proposing remedial legislation, increased higher education, and economic cooperation among blacks. Marcus Garvey espoused economic self-help and cultural nationalism as the basis of a black independence movement, culminating in the establishment of a separate nation in Africa. The NAACP has always emphasized the demand for civil and legal rights, employing publicity, lobbying, and legal defense work as its primary tactics. A. Philip Randolph wanted black and white workers to ally against capitalist exploitation; radical labor organization with socialism as its goal was the strategy he prescribed. While James Farmer had seen Gandhi's relevance in the early 1940s, King was the first black spokesman who unequivocally endorsed the precepts of nonviolence to develop mass appeal. These different currents continued to run as the civil rights movement developed. Several of these different approaches helped the movement make progress, but they may have worked against the development of a unified movement.

Two other considerations must be emphasized: one is Gandhi, the other is the time perspective. While King played a role similar to Gandhi's, it was on a lesser scale. A very large percentage of blacks identified positively with him, but he does not seem to have been able to draw out the tremendous mass effort that Gandhi elicited. This may be explained partly by the traditional status of the saint in Indian society. King's appeal was a religious one, but his audience probably was more secular in its thinking than Gandhi's. Gandhi attained a position of sainthood among his people, who looked upon him with religious reverence. No doubt some blacks view King in a similar light, especially now after his assassination, but many of his supporters, warm and lukewarm, could not see him in the same way. Their commitment was more diluted because it lacked religious fervor.

Finally, it is worth noting that the Indian independence movement took nearly a generation to achieve its goal, if one dates it from the beginning of the Congress campaign for *swaraj*. World War II also had a major role. In less than one decade, from Montgomery to the emergence of Black Power, the civil rights movement managed to galvanize the black population in an unprecedented way; in terms of legislation, its accomplishments were considerable. Whether one looks at the Black Power movement sanguinely or pessimistically, it is undeniable that the civil rights movement is in large part responsible for the black's growing sense of self-respect and his increasingly militant demands for real equality now, equality in material goods, in political power, in opportunity. Perhaps the black's aspirations have run beyond the willingness of white society to satisfy them; this may be one reason why many blacks seem impatient with nonviolence. They are impatient to share in what American ideals promise and they fail to see why they must make great sacrifices—in life and limb—to achieve what seem small advances toward meaningful equality. The success of the civil rights movement in mobilizing the American black may be partly responsible for growing disenchantment with the methods that characterized that movement. In contrast, Indians, while attracted by the dream of independence, were not accustomed to being told that their birthright was a birthright of equality and freedom. In a sense, Gandhi wanted them to earn their freedom, but black Americans have wondered why they are often expected to prove their right to enjoy the advantages other Americans enjoy by right of birth.

The differences between Gandhi's views and practices and those of the major civil rights organizations using nonviolent direct action and other recent practitioners of these tactics become evident upon comparison. In general, the American practice has been less rigorous. American civil disobedients have often committed knowing but unplanned violations of local regulations which were interpreted and enforced by local officials; the activists have contested their arrests in legal proceedings (and their convictions by lower courts in higher ones), arguing that local regulations were unconstitutional either inherently or as applied to their acts. Most of the activists in the civil rights movement maintained a strict nonviolent discipline while demonstrating, but they generally rejected nonviolence as an absolute commitment. The civil rights organizations were well trained in nonviolent techniques, but the anti-war and student protesters were often less organized and less prepared for responding nonviolently to violence. They did not initiate violence, but on infrequent occasions they apparently were less than passive in protecting themselves from the violence of police and spectators. Furthermore, these practitioners of nonviolent direct action have often seen themselves as engaged in a process of applying pressure to opponents. Therefore, the definition of civil disobedience and the description of how these tactics work which I developed in Chapter IV are more useful in studying the American experience than those of the academic commentators who more closely follow Gandhi.

In this country, practitioners of nonviolent direct action have faced a government different from the one Gandhi's movement confronted. This raises the question whether the need for and effectiveness of nonviolent direct action is significantly influenced by the type of regime. Does the existence of democratic political institutions make nonviolent direct action unnecessary? Do democratic regimes respond differently from other types of regimes to civil disobedience and nonviolent direct action? What are the limits of effectiveness of such tactics within the American political system? At what point do direct action tactics become revolutionary within a democratic polity? Before considering these problems, let us examine some more information about the way in which nonviolent direct action operates: the views of several observers of black political action, primarily in the South, and the perceptions of direct action recorded in public opinion polls. The latter are particularly important because tolerant popular reactions to nonviolent direct action would seem to be a key element if these tactics are to operate primarily as an appeal to the public.

Notes for Chapter V

1. Mohandas K. Gandhi, *Non-Violent Resistance,* compiled and edited by Bharatan Kumarappa (New York: Schocken Books, 1961), p. 41.

2. *Ibid.,* pp. 42–43.

3. A *hartal* is a voluntary closing of shops and businesses, usually for a 24-hour period.

4. Joan V. Bondurant, *Conquest of Violence* (Rev. ed.; Berkeley: University of California Press, 1965), p. 40.

5. Quoted in Gene Sharp, *Gandhi Wields the Weapon of Moral Power* (Ahmedabad: Navajivan Publishing House, 1960), p. 65.

6. Gandhi, p. 174.

7. *Ibid.*, p. 60.

8. *Ibid.*, p. 28.

9. *Ibid.*, p. 75.

10. Bondurant, p. 99.

11. By reluctant or involuntary disobedience, Gandhi seems to mean violations which occur when *satyagrahis* continue to perform normally legal actions which the government has prohibited; for example, such things as publishing non-inflammatory writings, holding public meetings, and picketing.

12. Gandhi, p. 175.

13. *Ibid.*

14. *Ibid.*

15. The Hunter Committee was appointed by the Government of India to conduct an inquiry into the first nationwide satygraha (1929).

16. Gandhi, p. 149.

17. *Ibid.*, p. 148.

18. Bondurant, p. 9.

19. Gandhi, pp. 274–275.

20. Quoted in Sharp, p. 220.

21. Gandhi, p. 275 (emphasis added).

22. Shridharani was a participant in Gandhi's work and a student and observer of it. *War Without Violence* (Bombay: Bharatiya Vidya Bhavan, 1962), pp. 28–29.

23. *Ibid.*, p. 21.

24. Quoted in Sharp, pp. 65–66.

25. King, in the chapter "Pilgrimage to Nonviolence," pp. 71–86 in his *Stride Toward Freedom* (New York: Ballantine Books, 1958), describes his introduction to Gandhi. While a theology student, he heard a sermon by Dr. Mordecai Johnson, President of Howard University, on Gandhi's life and teaching. Its impact stimulated him to delve into Gandhi's life and ideas.

26. *Ibid.*, p. 82.

27. *Ibid.*, pp. 81–86.

28. In refusing to suspend the boycott without a definite agreement, King can be said to have followed the Gandhian principle of not compromising the minimal demands of a just settlement. At the same time, the suggested terms of a satisfactory settlement seem to have been quite moderate and not excessive in terms of Gandhi's injunction to seek the minimal terms compatible with justice. They included: "1) a guarantee of courteous treatment; 2) passengers to be seated on a first-come first-served basis, the Negroes seating from the back; and 3) employment of Negro bus operators on predominantly Negro routes." *Ibid.*, p. 87.

29. *Ibid.*, p. 133.

30. *Ibid.*, p. 138.

31. *Ibid.*, p. 135.

32. Martin Luther King, *Why We Can't Wait* (New York: Signet Books 1964), pp. 61–64.

33. "All about CORE," pamphlet, Congress of Racial Equality, 1963, reprinted in Francis L. Broderick and August Meier, eds., *Negro Protest Thought in the Twentieth Century* (Indianapolis: Bobbs-Merrill, 1965), p. 300.

34. *Ibid.*, p. 301.

35. James M. Lawson, "From a Lunch-Counter Stool," address at SNCC Conference, Raleigh, N. C., April, 1960, reprinted in Broderick and Meier, p. 280.

36. A leaflet, "This is SCLC," which sets forth the objectives, philosophy, and activities of the Southern Christian Leadership Conference (King's organization) indicates that it adhered (in theory at least) to his position. This leaflet was reprinted apparently as late as 1964. Since King's assassination, the SCLC leadership has affirmed his commitment to nonviolence. See Broderick and Meier, pp. 269–273, for the SCLC statement.

37. Even the NAACP, one of the moderate civil rights organizations, reflects this pragmatic attitude. In an address to the NAACP's 57th Annual Convention on July 5, 1966, Roy Wilkins, NAACP Executive Secretary, said: "The NAACP has subscribed to nonviolence as a humane as well as a practical necessity in the realities of the American scene, but we have never regarded this as a deep personal commitment of our members." Reported in the *New York Times*, July 6, 1966.

38. Ingeborg Powell, "Ideology and Strategy of Direct Action: A Study of the Congress of Racial Equality," unpublished Ph.D. dissertation, University of California (Berkeley), 1965, pp. 230–234. Subsequently published as Inge Powell Bell, *CORE and the Strategy of Nonviolence* (New York: Random House, 1968).

39. *Ibid.*, p. 361.

40. *Ibid.*, p. 239.

41. *Ibid.*, pp. 232ff.

42. Broderick and Meier, p. 296.

43. Quoted in Broderick and Meier, p. 317.

44. Howard Zinn, *SNCC: The New*

Abolitionists (Boston: Beacon Press, 1965), pp. 221, 222.

45. Ruth Searles and J. Allen Williams, Jr., "Negro College Students' Participation in Sit-Ins," *Social Forces*, 40 (March, 1962), 218.

46. Jacob R. Fishman and Fredric Solomon, "The Psychosocial Meaning of Nonviolence in Student Civil Rights Activities," *Psychiatry*, 27 (May, 1964), p. 93.

47. *Ibid.*, p. 94.

48. William Brink and Louis Harris, *The Negro Revolution in America* (New York: Simon and Schuster, 1964), p. 206. The study was originally done for *Newsweek* magazine.

49. Searles and Williams, p. 218.

50. Fishman and Solomon, p. 93.

51. Donald R. Matthews and James W. Prothro, *Negroes and the New Southern Politics* (New York: Harcourt, Brace and World, 1966), p. 422.

52. *Ibid.*, p. 421. This was the most pronounced difference between these two groups on the questions tapping such attitudes.

53. Everett C. Ladd, *Negro Political Leadership in the South* (Ithaca, N.Y.: Cornell University Press, 1966), p. 188.

54. Powell, p. 338.

55. Don Von Eschen, Jerome Kirk, and Maurice Pinard, "The Conditions of Direct Action in a Democratic Society," paper presented at the Annual Meeting of the American Political Science Association, New York City, September 6–10, 1966, pp. 12–13. Subsequently published in *The Western Political Quarterly*, 22 (June, 1969), pp. 309–325.

56. King, *Why We Can't Wait,* p. 78.

57. *Ibid.*, p. 79.

58. *Ibid.*, pp. 68–69.

59. "All About CORE," in Broderick and Meier, p. 300.

60. Zinn, p. 16.

61. King, *Why We Can't Wait,* p. 82.

62. Ultimately, the appeal reached the Supreme Court, which refused to overturn the conviction, and King eventually served a short sentence.

63. Fishman and Solomon, pp. 94–98. The authors' explanation seems plausible since the students apparently envinced such attitudes, but it is not clear whether the students themselves offered such beliefs as justification for their acts.

64. William M. Kunstler, *Deep in My Heart* (New York: William Morrow, 1966), p. 45.

65. Memorandum in Support of Demurrer Submitted for Defendants in *The People of the State of California v. Mario Savio, et al.*, Municipal Court for the Berkeley-Albany Judicial District, County of Alameda, State of California.

66. King, *Why We Can't Wait*, p. 80.

67. *Ibid.*, p. 79.

68. Daniel C. Thompson, *The Negro Leadership Class* (Englewood Cliffs, N.J.: Prentice-Hall, 1963), p. 116.

69. Powell, pp. 102–106.

70. Zinn, pp. 222–223.

71. Fishman and Solomon, p. 93.

72. Matthews and Prothro, p. 422.

73. Ladd, p. 263 (emphasis added).

74. Edward Tufte, "The Civil Rights Movement and Its Opposition," unpublished Ph.D. dissertation, Yale University, 1966.

75. Brink and Harris, p. 67.

76. Jan Howard, "The Provocation of Violence: A Civil Rights Tactic?" *Dissent*, 13 (January-February, 1966), pp. 94–95.

77. Von Eschen, Kirk, and Pinard, *passim.*

78. Martin Luther King, "Behind the Selma March," *Saturday Review*, 48 (April 3, 1965), pp. 16–17+.

79. Howard, p. 98.

80. *Ibid.*, p. 97.

81. King, "Behind the Selma March," pp. 16–17+.

82. Shridharani, p. 182.

83. *Ibid.*, p. 187.

84. *Ibid.*, p. 188.

85. *Ibid.*, p. 192. But Shridharani also cites the case of the warlike Pathans, who were converted to non-violence and practiced it more faithfully than the Hindus, as evidence that the latter's tradition was not a *necessary* condition for acceptance of nonviolence.

86. *Ibid.*, p. 165.

87. *Ibid.*, p. 169.

88. Bondurant, p. 107.

89. Shridharani, p. 145.

90. *Ibid.*, p. 146. Shridharani says that Sir Samuel Hoare asserted in the House of Commons that only one-tenth of the villages offered civil disobedience. Since two-thirds of the 700,000-plus villages were then supposedly directly under British rule, this would mean about 50,000 villages.

91. *Ibid.*, p. 207.

92. *Ibid.*, p. 204.

93. *Ibid.*, p. 206.

94. *Ibid.*, p. 207.

VI

Civil Disobedience in Action—II: Observers and Audiences

IT IS EVIDENT that participants in nonviolent direct action have often viewed these techniques as means of applying pressure to recalcitrant opponents. Their perceptions are corroborated by the observations of a number of social scientists, who suggest that direct action has effects both as a method of applying pressure and as a means of communication and that these aspects are often interrelated.

Jacob R. Fishman and Fredric Solomon view the early student protest activities as an attempt to change white attitudes in the South. It is their impression that nonviolence, by projecting the anger and violence onto the white extremist, "help[ed] win the sympathy of the observing public and reduce[d] fears of whites that Negroes intend to retaliate violently for past suppression."[1] They doubt that many strong segregationists were persuaded by such actions; the assertive, yet seemingly passive, public display of discontent by blacks was a real

Notes to this chapter will be found on pages 223–228.

shock to many southerners, and the violent reactions to some sit-ins indicated that some whites found these confrontations very threatening. At the same time, however, the authors believe that moderates were impressed.

Ingeborg Powell argues that nonviolent direct action generates change more quickly than the accepted institutional channels of politics, which are dependent upon the evolution of a new consensus in race relations. Direct action avoids the task of changing white attitudes; it involves only an attempt to build "consensus within one's own constituency which will maximize the coercive pressure which can be brought to bear against the opposition."[2]

The decision to negotiate the desegregation of lunch-counters did not stem from any liberalization of white public opinion or any change in policy by white leaders. It was the direct result of economic losses and bad publicity, whose effect was greatest on large nationwide chain-stores which took the initiative in bringing about negotiations.[3]

The immediate effect of direct action was to shock and alienate the local white community and the specific "targets," but, Powell contends, it also created some responses in the white community which prevented a complete breakdown in consensus between the black and white constituencies. Moderates and liberals emerged to try to win concessions from the white community, so that changes in race relations could occur. Within the black community, established leaders were encouraged by the appearance of liberal whites and pushed by militants to make stronger attempts to convince the white community to change its attitudes. The "radical extremism" of direct action made dealing with the white liberals and black moderates more acceptable to the white community.

From her observations of CORE, Powell concluded that the organization was not primarily concerned with changing white opinion, and the powerful educational impact that direct action had upon whites—generally those more removed from the struggle—was a by-product. Outside the South, the media gave a fairly favorable interpretation of direct action campaigns. To attain this effect, CORE activists did not need to seek alliances with white moderates and liberals. Nonetheless, she suggests that the support of those not directly involved may be essential in the long run for direct action campaigns. The strategy is dependent upon the tolerance of the wider majority, which permits it to function, and on the success of a liberal national leadership in winning acceptance of civil rights reforms from the white community.

According to Don Von Eschen, Jerome Kirk, and Maurice Pinard, there are two requisites for the success of a direct action movement: (1) there must be a blatant conflict between widely professed values and actual conditions; for example, between the American ideal of full equality and the existence of public facilities which refuse to serve blacks; and (2) to convince "elites" who are not sympathetic to the movement's objectives, there must be an additional impetus: the creation of disorder. The authors explain the efficacy of this "lever":

One of the primary operational objectives of elites, and particularly of governments, is the maintenance of civil order and consensus. Failure to do so is likely to provoke retaliation by colleagues and customers, as well as constituents. An excluded group can thus gain attention to its grievances from even unsympathetic elites by interrupting the smooth functioning of the system. . . . These two prerequisites of dilemma and disorder interact in an important way. Although many powerful people in the society may feel the dilemma, under normal circumstances they do not actively work to resolve it. They have other goals that consume their time and energies. In addition, many are dependent for their goals on others who are unsympathetic to the plight of the unincorporated group. . . . At the same time, the dilemma is necessary for the realization of the potential inherent in disorder. Disorder . . . forces even unsympathetic elites to resolve the position of the unincorporated group. But disorder alone is not sufficient. Elites have many alternatives in the face of disorder, one of which is suppression. This alternative will be particularly easy if, as is often the case, the large mass of people too are unsympathetic to the cause of the unincorporated group. . . . Elements among the elites and the attentive public responsive to the dilemma can prevent repressive moves. A dilemma can thus reduce the feasible responses of elites to two: (1) ignore the demands and the activities of the protesters, and essentially tolerate whatever degree of civil disorder they are able to bring about, or (2) grant their essential demand of a *quid pro quo* for ceasing their activity.[4]

Daniel C. Thompson suggests that the nonviolent direct action strategy, more than any other, put segregated southern blacks into communication with people in other parts of the country. It generated more publicity and received extensive coverage (including photographs) from the national mass media. In this way, Americans all over the country became acquainted with the black's situation in the South. The publicity resulting from direct action sometimes drew a response from officials because of the embarrassment it caused them. Publicity generated fear that business would suffer and that industry would hesitate to locate in areas beset by racial conflict. Demonstrations raised the possibility that riots would break out; "ocasionally [such] fears are so obviously well founded that public officials are moved to action."[5] However, their responses were not necessarily conciliatory. Rather, the initial reaction was to pass new legislation or reinterpret old statutes in order to stifle public protest. From his description, it is doubtful that Thompson expected direct action to persuade southern whites to abandon their segregationist practices as unjust. The widespread publicity resulting from direct action apparently could have two effects: It might win support outside the South, which could help in obtaining federal intervention in various forms; it might embarrass and threaten southern officials, forcing them to respond—although, as indicated, repressive measures were the likely response.

Everett C. Ladd's few comments on the effects of direct action indicate that he thinks it puts pressure on the southern white community and that white Americans, who dislike demonstrations, are often willing to pay a price to avert them. He does not suggest that direct action is a suasive technique in the sense of changing attitudes.[6] Similarly, James Q. Wilson suggests that—at least in some cases—mass protest action may be an effective strategy because it can put a deprived group into a position of being able to offer their bargaining opponents a compensation—the compensation of ending the mass protest campaign—in return for concessions.[7] This implies that changing the opponents' attitudes toward the issues involved is not a major factor in obtaining results. It is a question of convincing opponents that the costs of concessions are smaller than the costs of enduring the protest campaign.

Howard Zinn, who personally observed members of SNCC in action, sees nonviolent direct action in similar terms; he says the "sit-ins represented an intricate union of economic and moral power."[8] Elements of pressure and persuasion were combined: On the one hand, the disruption of normal business by a sit-in put pressure on a storeowner or manager to change his policy of segregation; on the other, the sit-ins brought home to moderates and liberals in the immediate vicinity and elsewhere that rights they took for granted were being denied to blacks. Moreover, the sit-ins showed many southerners that desegregation of public facilities would not lead to violence and white withdrawal. Zinn also thinks the sit-ins represented an attempt to work outside normal political channels, to apply the "pressure of masses of aggrieved people" directly to the opposition. The sit-ins suggested that "the power of the popular demonstration [was] superior to that of the parliamentary process."[9]

These studies provide further support for my contention that it is a mistake to overemphasize the notion that civil disobedience (and nonviolent direct action[10] generally) is a method of persuasion and a means of converting the public to a minority's viewpoint. The view that civil disobedience is basically an appeal to the majority is open to a number of objections. As I have already suggested, this description of civil disobedience seemingly makes a good basis for justifying it, but it also restricts the manner in which the tactic is properly employed. In addition, analysis of actual cases of civil disobedience indicates that it has often been effective for other reasons. Other objections can be made. For instance, one can object that this view of civil disobedience uses a simplistic conception of the democratic process: The idea that the minority has the right and opportunity to make itself the majority by winning over citizens to its views; it can then implement these views as public policy. This assumes that the majority, through its representatives, makes policy decisions in accord with its political will, and so if a group wants to change a law or policy, it can do so by converting itself into a majority (In Chapter VII, I will analyze the inadequacies of this view as a description of the American political process). In this conception, civil disobedience can play a role in winning majority support for a minority position. Mass demonstrations—for example, the 1963 March on Washington (no civil disobedience), and the 1968 march on the Pentagon (some civil disobedience)—may approximate the minority appeal to the majority. They dramatize the grievances and demands of the minority before a national audience; the participants hope to sway people to their view by the intensity of their convictions. Such demonstrations may have an impact, but this is hard to measure. Nevertheless, even if they produced the results which this model suggests they can, the model has limited applicability since few nonviolent direct action campaigns have been conducted as direct efforts to convert a hostile or neutral national public.

A more sophisticated view of the way civil disobedience can work in American politics is that a national majority may sympathize with one minority group in conflict with another minority which politically dominates a local area. The first group uses civil disobedience in an attempt to mobilize that latent national majority, to widen the scope of conflict (to use E. E. Schattschneider's expression) so that the national majority becomes involved and thereby becomes the *effective* majority. A variation of this model is that civil disobedience is an appeal to the *representatives* of the national majority to act on behalf of a particular minority against another, locally dominant, minority. These national officials respond because they identify with the first minority's goals and/or fear that their national constituency may become aroused if they do not intervene.

The latter two models may be relatively adequate descriptions of some major civil rights demonstrations and civil disobedience campaigns. The Freedom Rides (1961), the SCLC campaign in Birmingham (1963), and the Selma-to-Montgomery March (1965) did capitalize on the reaction of the national public and national representatives, who were shocked by the violence which southern citizens and police used against civil rights participants. In these cases, federal officials reacted to their perceptions of public attitudes and intervened to aid the demonstrators. Nonetheless, it is not clear that a national majority actually supported the demonstrators' actions. According to Gallup polls, of those who had heard of the Freedom Ride of May, 1961, only a relatively small minority approved.[11] More respondents to a Minnesota poll thought the Selma march "helpful to the Negro cause" than thought it harmful, but the persons who approved were less than a majority.[12]

The key factors in whatever success these demonstrations had seem to have been (1) a dramatic event unsettling to a broad public and (2) federal officials sensitive to such constituency reactions. In some cases, the events necessary to disturb a national public and convince federal officials that intervention was politic did not occur, and local elites held out against protest campaigns. For example, in Albany, Georgia, a long protest campaign, beginning in November, 1961, and continuing into the summer of 1962, resulted only in small gains: desegregation of bus terminals and public libraries. Here the federal government refused to protect the constitutional rights of black demonstrators and civil rights workers. More recently (in 1968), the strike of black sanitation workers in Memphis was not having much impact before the assassination of Martin Luther King. According to a *New York Times* report of April 17, 1968, union officials were not optimistic about a settlement even after his death, but President

Johnson sent Undersecretary of Labor James Reynolds to aid in working out a settlement. Apparently, he got the mayor's agreement to the negotiated terms. In the spring of 1969, SCLC supported a strike of black hospital workers in Charleston, South Carolina, with similar objectives—union representation, higher pay scales, and elimination of discrimination. State law prohibits a state institution from negotiating with a union (one of the struck hospitals was state-run), and the governor refused to try to have the law changed. City officials, fearful of racial violence and perhaps feeling pressure from local merchants whose businesses were being boycotted, were more willing to see the dispute settled. SCLC apparently agreed to drop its demand for union recognition in order to get talks under way with the struck hospitals. However, at the end of May, the strike appeared stymied with no immediate hope of success. President Nixon refused to respond to Ralph Abernathy's appeal for him to intervene. Officials of the Department of Health, Education and Welfare, however, apparently were urging one of the hospitals to rehire the workers whose dismissal had originally set off the strike. A threat to cut off federal funds totalling at least $12 million was made in early June. Possibly federal intervention had something to do with the partial settlement which was negotiated late in June; it was agreed that some of the workers would be rehired. Finally in mid-July, a settlement ending the strike was reached.

At least among the more conspicuous civil rights protest campaigns, there are few examples of success through the conversion of opponents. The Montgomery bus boycott has perhaps been viewed as one such success, but what is often forgotten is that the boycott did not by itself convince the city that it should end bus segregation; a federal court order was necessary. The southern sit-ins of 1960–61 might be viewed as an appeal by a local minority to the local majority, but it does not appear that southern cities and businesses desegregated their facilities because they were converted to the cause of equality. In fact, many southerners may have embraced segregation and white supremacy more firmly because of these demonstrations. Public facilities generally were desegregated because officials and businessmen wanted to avoid economic losses and/or racial disorders. They also realized, perhaps for the first time, that southern blacks were discontented with segregation and were no longer willing to accept it passively, and that desegregation was inevitable in the long run. It is worth noting that the early sit-ins had little effect in the Deep South and that the Federal government played no public role in the desegregation that occurred.[13] More recently, the campaign for community control of the Ocean Hill-Brownsville school district in New York City seems to have been predicated on the notion that pressure, not persuasion, was necessary to achieve this goal. Any attempt to sway the majority or its representatives had to overcome the influence exerted by the powerful teachers' union, the general alienation of white liberals (caused at least in part by black activists' rejection of liberal goals, e.g. integration), and the hostility of whites who felt threatened by the proximity of an increasingly militant black population. Rather than attempt to win popular support for their concept of community control within the city as a whole, black activists tried to use direct action—most of it appears to have been basically nonviolent—to convince city school officials that granting local school administrators the autonomy they wanted would be more conducive to running the public schools in the district than insisting on compliance with existing procedures. Sometimes, they closed schools; generally they prevented unwanted union teachers from working.

Moreover, the political conditions facing blacks in the North and the South do not seem likely to make conversion of the majority through nonviolent direct action more frequent in the future. Northern liberals, a key public for the southern civil rights campaigns, lost some of their ardor when militant protests occurred in northern cities. Ghetto riots have frightened many whites. Lower middle-class whites are deeply resentful of the attention black demands have received. In the South, the shift in black aims from what were often symbolic achievements to improvements in working conditions and living standards seems to have encountered stiff resistance. In the north, opposition to black goals is also likely to be adamant because the aims strike close to home: *de facto* residential and school segregation and white control of public services in virtually all-black neighborhoods.

The "appeal to the majority" view of civil disobedience does not really speak to these kinds of situations; it assumes that the majority—national or local—can be persuaded to accept the protesting minority's point of view. This seems a questionable assumption. Examination of the numerous public opinion polls on civil rights demonstrations, other forms of direct action, riots, and black-white relations will give us a clearer understanding of the role the public is likely to play in the process of working change through nonviolent direct action.

In a sense, these polls provide a test of the view that civil disobedience and nonviolent direct action generally can be used to effect political change by appealing to the majority for support. Few, if any, ask respondents whether their views were changed by demonstrations and other protests. However, responses to other kinds of questions provide an indirect answer. Thus, some polls ask respondents whether they think a particular action was helpful or harmful to the cause of civil rights. If they give the latter response, one might infer that their own attitude toward civil rights probably was not made more positive by the action. Moreover, if they disapprove of nonviolent direct action tactics in the abstract, as well as to specific instances of their use, this would seem to indicate that they are not likely to be favorably disposed to grievances and demands which are pressed in this fashion. If nonviolent direct action proves to be ineffectual in converting the public to the views of the protesters, this does not mean that it communicates no important information which may be crucial to its effectiveness as a form of pressure. For example, nonviolent direct action may be able to communicate the existence and intensity of grievances, as well as a determination on the part of protesters to effect change regardless of risk. Furthermore, through media coverage, such protests become known to the public, discouraging some individuals from frequenting the scene of the conflict. In this way, the local business climate may be harmed.

Much change comes about through accommodation to changed circumstances. In other words, opponents may still disagree, but they yield because the balance of potential costs and benefits from a particular course of action is altered.[14] Not compromising or not making concessions may now appear too costly in relation to the expected benefits from pursuing present policies. Politically relevant circumstances can be changed by mobilizing constituencies which were previously inactive and unorganized for political action (of the conventional variety). This form of amassing resources can be crucial for the effective use of conventional political channels. Communication is directly relevant to mobilizing potentially supportive constituencies, as well as providing other publics with information that may convince them that their position on the issues involved should be reevaluated.

Because nonviolent direct action can communicate different messages to different publics, it is important to distinguish several audiences among the public reactions to these tactics. The survey data allow several to be examined: (1) the "immediate"—this audience consists of white residents in the vicinity of the direct action activity;[15] (2) the "distant"—this group includes persons distributed throughout the country (that is, respondents from samples chosen to be representative of the nation as a whole), not including the South, or from a particular area far removed from the scene of the particular demonstrations about which they were questioned; and (3) "vicarious participants"—this audience consists of blacks from all parts of the nation. Responses from blacks reveal that direct action in the civil rights movement has had quite an impact on them. Since they are a major constituency from which participants in direct action are likely to be drawn, their perceptions and reactions are an important factor in the future course of direct action in this country.

In the South—where civil rights demonstrations and sit-ins have been most prevalent—Donald R. Matthews and James W. Prothro report that only 7 percent of their white sample approved of the sit-ins which had been occurring;[16] 76 percent of the white respondents disapproved, including more than one-half of the moderates and over three-fourths of the segregationists. Even among those who approved of the goals of the sit-ins—the integrationists—only 34 percent approved the method, but only 32 percent disapproved, and none strongly. Matthews and Prothro also asked white respondents about their perceptions of the causes of the sit-ins and of the motivations of participants. One-half said that the sit-ins were due to outside agitation while only 15 percent saw them as spontaneous. Hardly more than one-fourth saw the participants as motivated by a desire for social equality or legal rights; however, nearly two-thirds of those favoring integration perceived this. Apparently, the latter received the "message," but they constituted less than 5 percent of the total sample. Another study of southern white attitudes indicated that more than three-fourths of the respondents disapproved of the actions taken by blacks to obtain civil rights, and 60 percent thought the demonstrations had hurt, rather than helped, the blacks' cause. Slightly more than one-half said that "others are really behind the Negro protest movement."[17]

The high degree of disapproval of civilly disobedient tactics is not surprising, particularly since most of the respondents who disapproved favored segregation. Such responses may be a manifestation of the "powerful psychological defenses" southern whites have erected around their racial practices. Matthews and Prothro doubt that the sit-ins converted many southern whites to the justice of the blacks' cause, but they think that the "frightening ignorance" most whites had of black discontent "probably would have been even greater had it not been for the protests."[18] These data suggest that certain significant obstacles impede effective communication by direct action: (1) where the "targets" of protest embody basic values embraced by the immediate public, the reaction is likely to be very hostile, blocking perception; (2) even those who favor the general objectives of the demonstrators may be reluctant to approve such unconventional methods as direct action, and this may be translated into hostility toward the demonstrators' goals. The available data do not provide a test of this. Obviously, direct action has not wrought any miracles in persuading southern whites that segregation is wrong. It is possible that direct action aggravates the negative effect that any attack on segregation is likely to have on southern whites, but other means of combating the problem do not seem to have been more successful. The Matthews and Prothro survey did reveal that direct action has the capacity to reach the public's consciousness, however negative its reaction. Only 4 percent of the white respondents had not heard of the sit-ins.

A survey of a selected group of Young Republicans and of home-owner association and realty association officials in San Francisco after mass civil rights demonstrations (about 500 were arrested for sitting-in) in 1964 provides some more data on "immediate" audiences.[19] By their own designation, most of the respondents were moderates (52 of 85); only 11 classified themselves as liberals. Despite the small number of "liberals," the survey revealed a significant minority who seemed to approve one form of direct action in support of civil rights aims, at least in a hypothetical case: 43 percent said they agreed "with the use of a boycott against firms who discriminate along racial, ethnic, or religious lines in their employment practices." Since 80 percent of the sample thought civil rights groups were "pushing too hard" or "should not be pressing at all," and only 22 percent believed that discrimination played some part in high unemployment rates among blacks, it seems likely that most respondents thought these demonstrations to protest discriminatory hiring practices were unwarranted. Only one respondent said that the community reaction to the demonstration was "favorable and supportive," while 72 percent thought the community reacted unfavorably, withdrawing its support. Nonetheless, 25 percent recognized that education of the public was one of the aims of the demonstrators. Forty-seven percent of the respondents listed pressure as one of the aims (either alone or in combination with other aims); 32 percent said the demonstrations were effective in achieving these various aims. It is not clear whether these respondents meant only that the demonstrations had been effective in achieving whatever aims they themselves had designated, or whether this was a reflection of the fact that the civil rights groups had won agreements with the employers. In any case, only 21 percent said the demonstrations had been ineffective *with negative effects*. Thirty-one percent thought CORE picketing of the Bank of America on the same issue (an agreement was also reached in in this case) had been effective.

The study reveals that preexisting attitudes and perceptions apparently play a significant role in predisposing a respondent favorably toward the tactics (and goals and organizations) of the civil rights movement. Of the 19 respondents who thought discrimination played some role in the high rate of black unemployment, only 5 disapproved the use of the boycott; 40 of the 66 "non-perceivers" of discrimination disapproved. Of the 11 liberals, only 2 disapproved, while 12 of the 22 conservatives did so. Four of the liberals thought education was the sole aim of the demonstrators; only 2 of the 22 conservatives thought so. About one-third of the "perceivers" listed education alone; less than one-twelfth of the "non-perceivers" did this. Four of the 11 liberals thought the CORE picketing of the Bank of America was effective; only 3 of the 22 conservatives thought so. Just over one-half of the "perceivers" thought it effective, while less than one-fourth of the "non-perceivers" thought so. The ratio of conservatives' rating the community reaction to the demonstrations as unfavorable compared to those rating it mixed was more than 5 to 1; the comparable ratio for liberals was slightly less than 3 to 1. The ratio for "perceivers" was 2 to 1 and for "non-perceivers" about 4 to 1. While this study does not provide support for the thesis that direct action can change attitudes, it does not contradict it, either; it does suggest that "messages" communicated by direct action can reach a sizable minority of the public (or more accurately, the educated public—87 percent of these respondents had attended college), even a public that is not highly disposed to view the civil rights movement using these tactics with a great deal of favor. It also suggests that a sizable percentage of this public may consider direct action a form of pressure.

Although these studies of immediate audiences reveal considerable rejection of nonviolent direct action,[20] some respondents grasped the intent of the demonstrators. One might expect distant audiences to be more tolerant of direct action because they are likely to be less involved in the practices which are the demonstrators' targets. Residents are apt to view demonstrations and sit-ins as an "indictment" of their own community. It is difficult to test this hypothesis with the available poll data because it is not clear what attitudinal variables are being tapped when respondents are asked questions about their reactions to demonstrations. Polls have revealed significant regional differences in reactions to demonstrations, but these differences probably are explained by the national distribution of attitudes toward civil rights, not by relative distance from the demonstrations in question. Thus, for example, Sheatsley reported the following comparisons: Of northern white respondents, 43 percent said that demonstrations hurt the blacks' cause; 60 percent of the southern white respondents thought so; 59 percent of the northern whites disapproved of the actions blacks had taken to obtain civil rights, while 78 percent of the southern whites disapproved.[21] In the same study, Sheatsley found a connection between pro-civil rights attitudes and approval for movement tactics. Respondents scoring high on a pro-integration scale were much more likely to approve of the civil rights movement than were low scorers. Twenty-four percent of the high scorers thought demonstrations had hurt the blacks' cause, compared to 71 percent of the low scorers; and 33 percent of the high scorers generally disapproved of the actions blacks have taken to obtain civil rights, compared with 80 percent of the low scorers.

Two smaller studies suggest that "distant" audiences may be more tolerant of direct action than "immediate" publics; however, it is again not possible to say how much of the difference can be attributed to the distance factor. In the San Francisco study previously cited, only 15 percent of the respondents said that Martin Luther King had *not* helped blacks in the South. Since a large majority of them thought civil rights groups were pushing too hard and that their local community had disapproved of demonstrations in the immediate vicinity, and only a sizable minority of them seemed to be supportive of civil rights goals in California, it may be that they reacted less negatively to demonstrations which were not on their doorstep. This result might be better explained by the perception that civil rights activity was clearly necessary in the South. It appeared that these respondents did not perceive much of a problem in their own area; only 22 percent thought that discrimination played some part in high rates of black unemployment and more than two-thirds were satisfied with the racial distribution in San Francisco public schools.[22] Nevertheless, there was some discrimination in their own area, so it is conceivable that distance (geographical and psychological) permits the individual to recognize the facts of discrimination more readily; thus, he may be less likely to condemn the use of direct action to remedy it. It may also be that direct action itself seems less threatening from a distance. A survey of Berkeley residents done in November, 1960, revealed that less than one-third disapproved of sit-ins at lunch counters in the South.[23]

Conceivably, greater tolerance for such tactics among "distant" audiences could produce outside support for demonstrators who encountered hostile local audiences. Indeed, some southern civil rights campaigns did mobilize support from the national public by demonstrations before hostile local residents. Nonetheless, regardless of distance, there seems to be a fairly high degree of rejection of direct action tactics among white Americans. The Brink-Harris survey showed that over 90 percent disapproved of lying down in front of trucks at construction sites to protest discriminatory hiring, two-thirds opposed lunch-counter sit-ins, approximately 60 percent were against picketing stores, slightly less but still more than one-half disapproved black willingness to go to jail voluntarily for the civil rights cause.[24] At the same time, slightly more than one-half accepted the general idea of demonstrating and thought the March on Washington justified. Other polls of the period (1963–65) indicate that majorities generally disapproved of direct action tactics used in the civil rights movement.[25] Apparently, popular attitudes have not became more favorable since that time.

A study commissioned by the President's Advisory Commission on Civil Disorders reported that "more than a quarter of the white sample . . . believe Negroes are not justified in using '*orderly marches* to protest against racial discrimination' and more than two-thirds believe that 'sit-in' protests are unjustified."[26] It is possible that these attitudes are related to beliefs that direct action is unnecessary and breaking the law never permissible. If so, direct action probably is not an effective means of increasing public support for the goals of the movement, but there is evidence that direct action does reach the public, which is an achievement in view of the public's high level of political ignorance.[27] For example, Gallup reports that 69 percent of a national sample had heard of the March on Washington when interviewed just before it took place. Similarly, 63 percent of a national sample had heard of the

Freedom Ride of May, 1961; while 69 percent of the respondents disapproved, about one-half mentioned that the Freedom Rides had something to do with the integration controversy.[28]

While the public seems generally negative toward direct action, some poll data indicates that it will support federal intervention when civil rights activists are attacked. A 1961 Gallup poll found that 70 percent of a national sample approved President Kennedy's sending U.S. marshals to Montgomery, Alabama, after Freedom Riders had been attacked.[29] In response to a 1964 Harris poll, 71 percent of a national sample said that President Johnson should send federal troops into Mississippi if shootings and killings broke out in the state (this was the summer of the Mississippi COFO project). The same survey revealed that 55 percent of the respondents said they would think more of Johnson if he did send in troops to enforce the school desegregation order or to end bloodshed.[30] These responses give some credence to the idea that nonviolent direct action, if it leads to disruption, may be able to gain its objectives through federal pressure on local officials and citizens.

The possibility of winning public support for the goals of non-violent demonstrators is reduced by the fact that the public does not seem to consider the use of demonstrations less detrimental to the black's cause than it does riots. One might think that whites would be much more apt to disapprove of riots than of demonstrations, but the poll results suggest that most Americans do not think there is a significant difference between blacks' using direct action to further the civil rights cause and their engaging in riots to protest their conditions. Substantial majorities apparently disapprove of both.[31] A re-run of the *Newsweek* survey in 1966 found that 75 percent of the white sample thought riots harmful to the blacks' cause; 63 percent thought demonstrations harmful.[32] Two Harris polls in 1967 reported large majorities unfavorable toward demonstrations (82 percent) and riots (88 percent).[33] A survey done for the President's Advisory Commission on Civil Disorders found that 64 percent of white respondents thought the riots had hurt the cause of civil rights.[34] Although these polls do not attempt to measure intensity of opinion, it does not appear that whites found civil rights demonstrations much less disturbing than they did ghetto riots. This may be one reason why the riots did not increase white support for nonviolent direct action. The Los Angeles survey found that the extremity of the black response to existing conditions apparently did not convince many whites that unconventional—though nonviolent—methods might be necessary to produce change. More than two-thirds of the white respondents said that blacks should use accepted political and legal channels, while another one-tenth felt there was no need for a civil rights movement. Only 17 percent endorsed the use of nonviolent tactics as a means of achieving black demands.[35]

What is most disquieting is the evidence which suggests that the public generally does not perceive a difference between nonviolent direct action and violence. From a survey conducted in December, 1963, Sheatsley reports that 47 percent of northern white respondents and 63 percent of southern said that the civil rights movement has generally been violent rather than peaceful.[36] Respondents to a poll in the fall of 1964 indicated, by a margin of more than 2 to 1, that they thought most of the actions blacks had taken to get things they wanted had been violent.[37] It appears that many persons confuse protest demonstrations with the large-scale ghetto riots which began in 1964. A survey conducted in the Los Angeles area indicated that some white respondents may have attributed the Watts riot to the civil rights movement. When they were asked whether there had been any change in their own attitudes due to the riot, significant change occurred on only two items and one of these was a more negative attitude toward the civil rights movement.[38] Whether this resulted from an inability to distinguish the Watts riot from the activities of civil rights groups cannot be determined from the data. However, a supplemental study for the President's Advisory Commission on Civil Disorders reported that a sizeable segment (35 percent) of the white population did not distinguish between nonviolent demonstrations and riots.[39] This failure to perceive a difference may partially explain the fact that white disapproval of demonstrations and similar tactics has not been much lower than white disapproval of riots.

Perhaps the merging of nonviolent direct action with violence in the public mind is being translated into rejection of the movement's objectives and less support for strong enforcement of civil rights legislation by the national government. Sheatsley's data suggest that inability to distinguish the nonviolence of the civil rights movement from violence[40] is linked in some way to one's attitude toward the movement's goals. But it is not apparent which variable—attitudes toward civil rights or perceptions of the movement—has more influence upon the other. Since demonstrations might be of rather low salience to "distant" audiences, it is possible that their attitudes toward civil rights, which probably are more stable and central in their belief-systems, would have more effect on their perceptions than *vice versa*. For "immediate" audiences, the situation might be somewhat reversed. The problem is complex because the two variables cannot be isolated from each other, and the complexity is increased by the fact that the perceptions of both audiences are usually mediated through news-reporting agencies. Since many whites now seem to confuse riots with demonstrations, the reactions of white residents of Los Angeles to the Watts riot are interesting. They provide a clue to the impact of riots as a form of political communication.

The riot was unmistakably violent. It might be easy, then, for a white audience, particularly one in the immediate vicinity of the riot, to condemn the violence and ignore the conditions which apparently were a major factor in producing the riot. Nonetheless, 79 percent of these white respondents said they were more aware of black problems afterwards, and 54 percent said that the riot was a protest; only 33 percent, however, thought it had a purpose, but this does not seem surprising—only slightly more than one-half of the black respondents thought the riot had a meaningful purpose. Even an action as provocative as the Watts riot seems to have conveyed a relatively accurate "message" to the local white population—that is, that conditions in the ghetto were very bad and that blacks were intensely dissatisfied. However, the means *apparently* negated much of the impact of that message, for 75 percent of the white respondents thought Watts would hurt the blacks' cause (only 19 percent thought it would help), and 37 percent thought whites were now more unsympathetic to black problems (32 percent thought whites were now more sympathetic). Seventy-one percent thought the gap between the races had increased, while only 13 percent thought it had decreased.[41] Interestingly enough, responses on a social distance dimension did not reveal a widening of the gap between the races.[42] The effects of the Watts riot on white respondents in the Los Angeles area appear to have been similar to the effects of civil rights demonstrations on other "immediate" audiences. The riot, like the demonstrations, was able to convey a message to the white audience—it changed cognitions. Indeed, the riot may have been a more effective way of communicating to whites the feelings of the deprived black minority about their living conditions. Moreover, while the riot apparently was no more effective in changing white attitudes toward the blacks' problems, it was not as alienating as might be expected.

A third major audience—"vicarious participants"—consists of the

American black population. Surveys show that civil rights demonstrations apparently have had a tremendous impact upon this audience. Until at least 1966, there was among blacks widespread approval of demonstrations, willingness to participate, optimism that change will come, and recognition that the civil rights movement is their struggle. In one national survey of black attitudes, 56 percent of the respondents thought that civil rights demonstrations over the last few years (the interviewing was done in October, 1964) had helped a great deal, and another 31 percent said they had helped a little. Only 8 percent thought demonstrations had hurt.[43] The Brink-Harris survey also reported widespread belief in the effectiveness of the demonstrations. Eighty percent evinced a positive attitude toward them, and mentions of positive characteristics outnumbered mentions of negative ones by over 10 to 1. The rerun of this survey in 1966 found 73 percent of black respondents thinking demonstrations helpful.[44] A survey of blacks in the Watts area (interviewing was done after the 1965 riot) reported that approximately three-fourths of the respondents thought civil rights demonstrations had helped.[45] Matthews and Prothro's study of southern blacks revealed that 52 percent of the adults approved the student sit-ins, while 22 percent disapproved. Only 14 percent had not heard of them. The authors say that many black adults realized that "the 'revolt' was almost as much against them and their leadership as against the dominant whites;" yet three-fifths of the adults who had heard about the sit-ins approved.[46]

Another indication of black approval for direct action in the civil rights movement were reports of willingness to participate and of actual participation. The Brink-Harris survey found that a considerable number of blacks claimed to have participated:[47]

	RANK AND FILE	LEADERS
In a march	12%	62%
In a picket	9	54
In a sit-in	8	39
In a boycott	33	69
Had gone to jail	4	21

A much larger number claimed they would be willing to participate:

	RANK AND FILE	LEADERS
In a march	51%	57%
In a picket	46	55
In a sit-in	49	57
In a boycott	62	—[48]
Would go to jail	47	58

Another national survey (conducted in the fall of 1964) reported similar responses: Only 26 percent said they would be afraid to take part in civil rights demonstrations.[49] Respondents in the Brink-Harris survey were asked whether they personally felt different lately about getting involved in direct action (in light of the recently increased activity of other blacks in such action). In addition, they were asked in what ways they felt differently. In response to the second question, 46 percent gave responses such as "It is my duty to help; we should all be in it;" 23 percent indicated that they were more conscious of the need and desire for improvement; 9 percent said they had joined an organization to work with other blacks; and 8 percent said they wanted to fight for equal rights.[50] The Los Angeles Riot Survey (Watts area sample) reported that 37 percent of the black respondents said they were now willing to participate. About two-fifths of the 1969 *Newsweek* survey respondents remained willing to engage in demonstrating, picketing and marching.[51] While there is a big gap between expressed willingness and actual participation (except among leaders), these responses seem to be reflections of relatively intense concern and identification with the civil rights movement. Sometimes, at least, these attitudes have been translated into action; Matthews and Prothro found that 24 percent of their sample of southern black college students had participated in the movement in some way or other.[52] As a contrast to this high willingness to participate in direct action, only one-tenth of a national sample of Americans said they had "ever felt the urge to organize or join a public demonstration about something."[53]

The extent of the "mobilizing" effects of direct action upon blacks is apparent. Suzanne H. Rudolph has likened the psychological effects which the southern sit-ins had upon their participants' self-esteem and sense of efficacy to the effects which Gandhi's nonviolence campaigns had upon the Indian people. Gandhi, she says, knew the Indians' doubts about their ability to gain independence from England and their deep-seated fear that the English might be right in their judgment that Indians lacked fundamental qualities of moral worth, such as courage. He created "opportunities for Indians to act in ways which would repair the wounds in the nation's self-esteem inflicted by 150 years of imperialized existence."[54] The civil rights movement, through its direct and vicarious involvement of large numbers of blacks, seems to have played a rather similar role for them. Not only did the movement break down some barriers to their social and political participation in the greater society, it appears to have given many of them some of the psychological resources (for example, greater self-esteem, a sense of efficacy, higher aspirations, greater sense of group cohesion, stronger motivation to self-improvement) necessary to make use of what opportunities have been won. As a rough indicator of the gap that had to be made up, Angus Campbell's data on political efficacy compiled in 1952 and 1956 show roughly the same percentage of blacks and whites in the high efficacy category (about 13 %), but approximately 17 percent of the white respondents were in the low category, compared to 60 percent of the black sample.[55] Data from the American sample of the study reported in *The Civic Culture* reveal, for 100 matched pairs of blacks and whites, that only 49 percent of the blacks expected government officials would give them equal treatment (in matters such as housing regulations or taxes), while 90 percent of the whites expected equal treatment.[56] Eighty-five percent of the blacks, compared to 73 percent of the whites, said they had never tried to influence a local policy decision.[57]

Since blacks are a major constituency for direct action campaigns, their perceptions of direct action and its relation to nonviolence are important. The original Brink-Harris survey (1963) revealed a difference between "elite" and "mass" perceptions of the way direct action operated. The rank-and-file respondent was more apt to think that demonstrations got results (33 %) than was the leadership sample (15%), while the leaders were much more apt (63 %) to think that demonstrations made the nation aware of the black's situation than was the

rank-and-file (18 %).[58] The reasons for these differences are not self-evident. They conceivably could be due to the rank-and-file's being more
militant than the leadership sample; but a much higher percentage of
the latter had participated in direct action, and they were also slightly
more likely to indicate willingness to participate. Leaders probably had
a greater sensitivity to the publicity effects of direct action, but it is not
apparent that their understanding of what direct action accomplishes
was more realistic.

When attitudes toward whites are examined, the reasons for
"elite-mass" differences become somewhat clearer. Fifty-two percent
of the rank-and-file and 89 percent of the leaders said that white
attitudes toward rights for blacks had improved since five years before.
Respondents were then asked the reasons for the improvement. More
often than any other response (12 % of the whole sample), the rank-and-
file cited black pressure; 9 percent said that more whites were aware, or
cited public attention; and 4 percent said that more whites realize that
blacks deserve equal rights. While 24 percent of the leaders cited
pressure, 37 percent mentioned greater white awareness, and 12 percent
referred to greater white recognition that blacks deserved equal rights.
Thus, leaders were more apt to cite changes in attitudes and perceptions
than the rank-and-file; again, this might be attributed to greater sophistication. However, leaders were also more optimistic about white attitudes
toward blacks. Forty-two percent of the rank-and-file thought whites
wanted to keep blacks down, while only 9 percent of the leaders
thought so; 25 percent of the rank-and-file thought most whites wanted
a better break for blacks; 52 percent of the leaders thought so.[59] The
leaders' belief in white sympathy fits well with their view of direct action
and of the reasons for improvement in white attitudes; likewise, the
rank-and-file's suspicion of whites was congruent with its responses in
these two areas. The latter's tendency to cite pressure as the main
reason for improvement does not necessarily mean that they perceived
direct action as the sole, or main, source of this pressure. Nonetheless,
direct action probably is an important part of what they meant by
pressure.

This difference between the rank-and-file and the leaders is also
reflected in their attitudes toward nonviolence. For example, the
Brink-Harris report found that 93 percent of the leader sample
believed that the civil rights struggle could be won without violence, but
only 63 percent of the rank-and-file thought so.[60] Another early

(1964) national survey confirmed the finding that a substantial majority of blacks rejected violence: 62 percent of the respondents agreed that violence would never help blacks get equal rights; 32 percent disagreed.[61] More recent surveys appear to indicate that many black respondents are now willing to entertain the possibility that violence may be useful. In the 1966 *Newsweek* survey, 51 percent of the respondents thought blacks could prevail by reason; 24 percent disagreed. In 1969, the comparable figures were 46 percent and 34 percent. Although the 1969 *Newsweek* national survey found the same percentage of respondents as before (63 percent in 1963) thinking that blacks can win their rights without violence, 52 percent thought Martin Luther King's nonviolent strategy was losing its hold on black people. One-fourth of the respondents in 1969 said that blacks should arm themselves.[62] A study done for the "Riot Commission" reported that 15 percent of its urban black respondents said that the best way for blacks to gain their rights was to be ready to use violence.[63] Polls in three cities between 1966 and 1968 revealed that many blacks condoned violence in self-defense: Houston (N = 572): 24 percent; Watts (N = 187): 44 percent; Oakland (N = 426): 47 percent. Moreover, sizeable minorities justified violence for other reasons: Houston: 26 percent; Watts: 13 percent; Oakland: 29 percent.[64] There seems to be growing acceptance among the black population of the need to go beyond nonviolent methods in order to achieve their demands. Perhaps the recent increase in acceptance of violence was foreshadowed by early black reactions to riots. Although black respondents apparently distinguished nonviolent demonstrations from violent actions like riots and many disapproved of violence, many also saw the riots in a positive light.

In the national survey reported by Gary Marx (1964), only 45 percent of the respondents were willing to say that no good can ever come from riots such as those which occurred in Harlem in 1964: 48 percent said they thought riots do some good in that they cause whites to pay attention to black problems.[65] Surveys in the Los Angeles area after the Watts riot revealed similar attitudes. Joseph Kraft reported that almost one-half of his respondents thought the riot had helped blacks' chances of equality in jobs, schools, and housing; only one-fourth thought the riot had hurt these chances.[66] Another study found that 38 percent of the black respondents from the immediate area thought the riots helped; 24 percent thought they had hurt. A percentage of

51 thought whites would be more sympathetic afterwards; only 12 percent thought they would be less so.[67]

More recent surveys indicate that a sizeable segment of the black community continues to evaluate riots positively. The Brink-Harris re-run in 1966 reported that 34 percent of the black respondents thought riots had helped their cause more than they had hurt it. A study done in early 1968 for the President's Advisory Commission on Civil Disorders reported that 58 percent of its urban black respondents (N = 2814) said that the riots were "mainly a protest by Negroes against unfair conditions." One-third thought the riots had helped the blacks' cause; only one-fourth considered them mainly harmful. Moreover, only 18 percent expected anti-black sentiment to increase among whites as a result of the riots.[68] An even more recent survey, conducted for *Newsweek* in late spring, 1969, found 31 percent of a national black sample (N = 977) saying that riots are justified.[69] A small minority of blacks would even admit that they are willing to join a riot.[70] An intensive study of Watts-area blacks after the 1965 riot provides a look at the attitudes which seem to lead blacks to condone violence. Relatively few (12 percent of the Watts-area respondents thought violent protest was the most effective method for the black to use; 33 percent chose negotiations and 43 percent nonviolent protest. Only 3 percent said blacks *must* use violent action to get what they want. Twice as many respondents disapproved as approved of the riot. Nonetheless, a majority saw the riot as a protest and as having a meaningful goal. Thirty-eight percent named specific grievances as the problem which caused the riot.[71] There was evidence of a sense of heightened militancy in the Watts area, which was being reflected in the widespread support for "conventional" civil rights activity *and* for more extreme action. For example, it was found that approximately 30 percent of the respondents thought "the Muslims were doing 'well' or 'fairly well.'"[72] The author of this study says that he suspects:

The reason for [the high level of this percentage] has not much to do with Muslims themselves but . . . a generally militant pro-Negro attitude toward civil rights and civil rights methods, so that what one is getting is not necessarily approval of the Muslims *per se*, but simply approval of a militantly deviant position which is designed to put whites in their place.[73]

Interpreting—*ex post facto*, of course—the riot in terms comparable to civil rights activity (as many respondents did) is perhaps an indication of the high militancy of these blacks and the salience of racial issues to them.

The connection between militancy and willingness to condone violence is more effectively demonstrated by comparing the responses of militants and non-militants among the Watts-area residents. Blacks in Watts who were more militant on civil rights apparently were more likely to have participated in and condoned the riots. In the Watts area sample, 38 percent of the respondents who reported they had participated in civil rights activity also reported riot activity, as compared to 22 percent of those who did not report previous civil rights participation. On three of the four measures of exposure to riot activity, the same pattern appeared.[74] A similar pattern appeared in the correlations of willingness to participate in demonstrations and riot activity. A special study of Black Muslim sympathizers (the author calls them militants) among the Watts-area respondents revealed that they were somewhat more likely to have engaged in political activity beyond voting, to have been approached by political and civil rights organizations, to have a history of civil rights participation, and to express willingness to demonstrate after the riots, than were respondents who fell into two other categories—those hostile to the Muslims and those uncommitted either way. At the same time, the Muslim sympathizers (militants) more often felt the riot had helped, and reported personal riot activity or exposure to riot activity. When asked (forced) to choose between negotiation, non-violence, and violence as modes of effective protest, 30 percent of the militants chose violence compared to 9 percent of the non-militants.[75] The author of this study, T. M. Tomlinson, suggests several explanations for the apparent relation betwen civil rights activity and support for the riot: (1) "dissonance reduction . . . The more deviant the particular political activity or civil rights activity is, the more this activity is likely to touch the 'middle class morality' that we all possess and as a product of that touching, require a good deal of justification to account for the violence;" (2) an alienated orientation toward the system which leads people to feel that they have nothing to lose by this kind of action—such types would be revolutionary in their approach; and (3) "those who have engaged in prior civil rights activity are in a frame of mind which permits them to view the riot as simply a somewhat extreme extension of their own activity and therefore, it is easy for them to include riots and riot kinds of behavior as legitimate models of protest."[76] It may be, as Tomlinson suggests, that for some civil rights activists a riot is not beyond what they consider permissible and it is, therefore, not too difficult for them to bring one within their frame of reference and view it positively. A national survey seems to corroborate the connection between militancy and condonation of violence. Marx reports that 40 percent of the "militants" in his survey disagreed with the statement that "violence would never help Negroes;" in contrast, only 24 percent of the "conservatives" disagreed. Twenty-four percent of the militants ranked high on acceptance of violence compared with 16 percent of the conservatives.[77] The militants were most apt to think demonstrations did some good, to be able to identify civil rights leaders, and to be members of civil rights organizations. Both studies reveal that a substantial minority of civil rights militants are willing to condone violence. A riot like Watts greatly increases the salience of racial conflict, and may force the civil rights militant to choose between alternatives which are not framed the way he would prefer; in other words, if he condemns the violence, he may sound as if he is espousing the white point of view, particularly at a time when anti-black sentiment may be high. If he condones the riot, he justifies a method of action that he probably would not premeditatedly choose. There is also some evidence that civil rights militants are more likely to perceive discrimination than other blacks;[78] thus, it may be easier for them to believe an outbreak of violence is justified. Those who are less aware of such grievances probably will find the riot less explicable and may be more prone to ascribe the violence to "deviants."

The fact that many civil rights militants do not reject violence totally is further evidence that nonviolence, in this country, is pragmatically espoused. Instead of an abrupt break in the spectrum of direct action tactics between nonviolence and violence, there seems to be a continuum. Apparently, belief in the efficacy of nonviolence is not incompatible with condoning violence in certain circumstances. In such a climate of opinion, resort to violence may be more likely. Though few would initiate it, many have attitudes which probably would not altogether inhibit them from taking part. The frequent response by blacks that riots do some good may constitute a rationalization for "deviant" behavior by members of their ethnic group, but it may also indicate a loss of confidence in conventional political channels. In the Watts area survey, almost as many respondents manifested negative attitudes as manifested positive ones in response to questions about the way they were being represented by public officials. Interviewers received a similar response when they asked the respondents whether elected officials could be trusted. Negative evaluations of Los Angeles Mayor Sam Yorty's performance outnumbered positive ones better than two to one.[79] The militants in the sample were more deeply dissatified with elected officials than the non-militants.[80] Since the militants tended to be more active in civil rights and in the riots, there may be a connection between negative evaluation of local representatives and positive evaluation of both militancy and violence.

Most of the political figures whom the Watts area respondents were asked to evaluate (for example, President Johnson, Governor Brown, local legislators and officials—black and white—and government agencies) received many more positive assessments than negative ones; but it is difficult to believe that such evaluations were usually based on direct experience of the political figures' responsiveness, in light of the fact that most Americans are fairly ignorant of political matters and many have difficulty relating them to the concerns of their everyday lives. But it may not be necessary for people to have experienced a governmental responsiveness in order to have confidence in conventional political channels; if people do not personally (in the sense of feeling involved in an action, even if taken by others) press claims upon their governors, either because they do not feel the need or because they do not understand the relevance of politics, then their confidence in conventional channels may remain untested and intact. It may be that lack of confidence is more apt to be based on a realistic perception of responsiveness than is confidence. The responses which manifest loss of confidence probably reflect more deeply rooted feelings and experiences—of disillusionment and dissatisfaction—which apparently can give rise to defiant and violent behavior. The surveys seem to indicate that civil rights militancy can shade over into acceptance and even advocacy of violence. Nonviolent direct action is an alternative to violence, but for a good number of civil rights activists, the two are not mutually exclusive. If political protest is not to move across the spectrum of tactics toward the extreme of violence, nonviolent direct action must achieve a measure of success. This places a great burden on the ability of nonviolent tactics to produce favorable results. In some political situations, nonviolent direct action may not succeed, particularly if participants are not properly trained and not willing to make great sacrifices. There is some evidence that direct action by blacks in Los Angeles did not have much impact upon the agencies and officials of

Los Angeles government.[81] When direct action fails—and possibly failure here is apt to induce a more intense loss of confidence in public officials than failure in the use of conventional methods—it is difficult for civil rights militants to convince themselves, and others who are less committed than they to nonviolent direct action, that violence is not necessary.

The surveys indicate that direct action has had considerable effect upon the "vicarious participants" among blacks; there has been an increased sense of pride, and of involvement in and commitment to the civil rights struggle. These psychological gains may stem primarily from a perception that members of their race are acting courageously, and are openly refusing to accept existing conditions any longer. The fact that direct action seems to have achieved some gains for at least some blacks may also be a source of the increased confidence and commitment. The high level of approval for direct action would seem to be at least in part a product of the feeling that direct action has been effective. What few studies there are of the effects of direct action upon the actual participants suggest a similar result.

Since the earlier surveys were completed, there have been important changes in attitudes toward violence and tactics among some of the major civil rights groups. In addition, new and more militant leaders have emerged in the black community. The later surveys indicate that the greater emphasis of these leaders on the necessity and legitimacy of violence, especially in self-defense, is reflected in "mass" attitudes. The slogan "Black Power" has called forth widespread enthusiasm, but blacks commonly interpret it in many ways. Black leaders give it varied emphases, some quite compatible with conventional political tactics; others hint at or even flaunt rejection of conventional political practices and institutions. This shift in rhetoric and tactics can be interpreted in more than one way. Some persons contend that Black Power indicates that the tactics of the civil rights movement —civil disobedience and nonviolent direct action—were a failure. Black leaders, it is alleged, now recognize that their people cannot be liberated by reforming American political and social institutions. These institutions are so deeply racist and exploitive that the only changes they can feasibly encompass will not substantially change the position of the black community. Nonviolent direct action is suitable only for obtaining largely token concessions which tend to benefit only the upper strata of the black population. Another view is that the civil rights movement created a "revolution of rising expectations" which is outrunning the capacity of the political system to respond. In a sense, the movement was too successful, and its quick successes made would-be supporters too impatient to persevere with nonviolent direct action when progress became more difficult to achieve. They were not prepared for the more persistent, more energy-consuming, more costly campaigns of action that are necessitated by the deep-seated problems of the urban ghetto. In either case—whether because of "proven" failure or the civil rights movement's inadequate preparedness and understanding of the problems—nonviolent direct action has been downgraded by Black Power advocates. Even those black leaders who clearly eschew violence are proposing changes in the system which they apparently do not think can be brought about by nonviolent direct action campaigns. This is not to say that such tactics are no longer being used, although they are being supplanted. Nonviolence is less often considered appropriate, even when judged on a strictly pragmatic basis.

Parts of the antiwar movement have undergone a similar shift in rhetoric and tactics—an example is the New Left slogan, "From Protest to Resistance"—probably due to frustration and impatience. Teach-ins, mass marches, and demonstrations attracted considerable publicity for antiwar sentiment when the movement began on various campuses, and by raising it to national visibility, these tactics may have catalyzed more widespread dissatisfaction with the War. However, they failed to affect the course of the war in any direct way.[82] In the New Left, many think that our involvement in Viet Nam is a part of American imperialism. Even if protest action could speed the war's end, this would not prevent future United States involvement in similar campaigns. Like some Black Power advocates, these persons favor basic changes in American society, not more reforms. Exactly how these changes will be achieved is not clear. The kind of nonviolent direct action employed by the civil rights movement probably has at most a limited role to play in this revolution.

Since the public has been exposed for some time now[83] to protests often accompanied by violence of some kind (by police, protesters, spectators—hostile and sympathetic—and counter-protesters), it is unlikely that the public today more clearly differentiates nonviolent protest demonstrations (when they occur) from violence. The rash of ghetto riots occurring in the same period probably has not helped in this respect. Thus, popular tolerance for unconventional political action may be declining at the very time would-be participants are moving toward more extreme forms of protest. While unconventional political tactics still can gain considerable publicity, these circumstances do not appear to facilitate its use as a pedagogic tool.

The tactics of the contemporary protest movements have clearly moved beyond the civil disobedience which academic commentators described as an appeal to conscience and as a pedagogic device in the early 1960s. But even when they were writing, their conception of civil disobedience was not adequate to the real phenomenon. What they may have thought they gained in justification, they lost in relevance. Conceivably, they might respond that the use of democratic principles like majority rule strengthens the case for civil disobedience, though not for the more militant tactics which are superseding it. But the appeal to majority rule may actually weaken their position because many persons still interpret majority rule to mean that once the majority has spoken, the minority must go along even if it does not like the majority's decision. If one responds that the minority has a right to attempt to influence the majority and that conventional political methods often do not provide the minority with a real opportunity to do that, then one has essentially moved to the argument that institutional channels are not really available to certain groups of protesters. This argument seems a more solid grounding for the justification of civil disobedience and nonviolent direct action. Furthermore, it is the beginning of an explanation of the apparent decline of such political tactics on the American scene.

Notes for Chapter VI

1. Jacob R. Fishman and Fredric Solomon, "Youth and Social Action, I: Perspectiv eson the Student Sit-In Movement," *American Journal of Orthopsychiatry*, 33 (October, 1963), 879.

2. Ingeborg Powell, "Ideology and Strategy of Direct Action: A Study of the Congress of Racial Equality," Ph.D. dissertation, University of California (Berkeley), 1965, p. 143. Subsequently published as Inge Powell Bell, *CORE and the Strategy of Nonviolence* (New York: Random House, 1968).

3. *Ibid.*, pp. 178–179.

4. Don Von Eschen, Jerome Kirk, and Maurice Pinard, "The Conditions of Direct Action in a Democratic Society," paper presented at the Annual Meeting of the American Political Science Association, New York City, September 6–10, 1966, pp. 16–17. Revised and published in

The Western Political Quarterly, 22 (June, 1969), 309–325.

5. Daniel C. Thompson, *The Negro Leadership Class* (Englewood Cliffs, N.J.: Prentice-Hall, 1963), p. 134.

6. Everett C. Ladd, *Negro Political Leadership in the South* (Ithaca, N.Y.: Cornell University Press, 1966), p. 272.

7. James Q. Wilson, "The Strategy of Protest: Problems of Negro Civic Action," *Journal of Conflict Resolution*, 5 (September, 1961), pp. 291–303. See also Michael Lipsky, "Protest as a Political Resource," *American Political Science Review*, 62 (December, 1968), 1144–1158. Lipsky attempts to develop a theoretical perspective for analyzing the effects of protest actions, based on Wilson's original insight. I had already formulated my own views on the way direct action operates when I came across this article.

8. Howard Zinn, *SNCC: The New Abolitionists* (Boston: Beacon Press, 1965), p. 28.

9. *Ibid.*, p. 29.

10. Nonviolent direct action is a broader category than civil disobedience which subsumes tactics that might be viewed as both greater and lesser departures from conventional techniques; for example, a peaceful legal march, an illegal sit-in, a physical blockage of construction equipment (probably illegal). My immediate concern here is civil disobedience, but there are good reasons for considering them together (as I shall): (1) They are both viewed by many Americans as illegitimate because other, conventional channels allegedly are available; and (2) civil disobedience usually occurs in conjunction with other forms of direct action—sometimes an act of civil disobedience develops from what was initially a legal form of direct action.

11. AIPO release, June 21, 1961.

12. Minnesota Poll, April, 1965, *in* Hazel Erskine, "The Polls: Demonstrations and Race Riots," *Public Opinion Quarterly*, 31 (Winter, 1967–1968), p. 661.

13. Attorney General Rogers apparently, however, worked behind the scenes with some national chain department stores to help them desegregate their southern stores.

14. William A. Gamson, *Power and Discontent* (Homewood, Illinois: Dorsey Press, 1968), suggests a typology of means of influence which distinguishes persuasion from the kind of situation where the balance of benefits and costs is changed by action of the party seeking to exert influence. "Persuasion involves some change in the minds of the authorities [i.e., those whose decision is binding in the particular situation] without adding anything new to their situation" (p. 79). "Constraints are the addition of new disadvantages to the situation or the threat to do so" (p. 75). "Inducements are the addition of new advantages to the situation or the promise to do so" (p. 77). Gamson considers it persuasion to make the person to be influenced aware of already existing circumstances. He says, "Persuasion influence is not always distinguished from constraint and inducement influence by the degree of coerciveness involved. . . . There is no implicit hierarchy of morality involved in the classification of means of influence" (p. 81).

15. Respondents from samples drawn to be representative of the South as a whole will be included here because civil rights demonstrations were widespread in that region and the institutions attacked were representative of southern racial practices.

16. Donald R. Matthews and James W. Prothro, *Negroes and the New Southern Politics* (New York: Harcourt, Brace and World, 1966), p. 434. The interviews for this study were carried out in the first half of 1961. The survey did not include border states. The very large majority of this 7 percent indicated that they favored integration.

17. Paul B. Sheatsley, "White Attitudes Toward the Negro," *in* Talcott Parsons and Kenneth B. Clark, eds., *The Negro American* (Boston: Houghton Mifflin, 1966), p. 317. This survey included border states; the interviews were done in December, 1963.

18. Matthews and Prothro, p. 438.

19. Edward Tufte, "The Civil Rights Movement and Its Opposition," unpublished Ph.D. dissertation, Yale University, 1966.

20. The survey data does not reveal whether respondents perceived the direct action to be nonviolent, but the actions the interviewers referred to were typical forms of nonviolent direct action.

21. Sheatsley, p. 317. Other studies reveal relatively greater objection to civil rights activity among southern white respondents. See Harris Poll, May 17, 1965, in Erskine, p. 658. A later poll by Harris in the same year revealed somewhat smaller regional differences; see Erskine, p. 659.

22. Tufte, "The Civil Rights Movement and its Opposition." There was no data on respondents' perceptions of discrimination in the South.

23. Fredric Templeton, "Alienation and Political Participation: Some Research Findings," *Public Opinion Quarterly*, 30 (Summer, 1966), pp. 249–261. This finding is not reported in the article. I computed it from data collected in this study.

24. William Brink and Louis Harris, *The Negro Revolution in America* (New York: Simon and Schuster, 1964), p. 145.

25. See Harris Poll, July 20, 1964, and September 27, 1965; Minnesota Poll, April, 1965; NORC Poll, December, 1963. These polls are reprinted in Erskine, pp. 656–657 and 661. Also see AIPO release, November 17, 1965, and Gallup Poll Index, AIPO Report No. 1, June, 1965.

26. Angus Campbell and Howard Schuman, "Racial Attitudes in Fifteen American Cities," in *Supplemental Studies for The National Advisory Commission on Civil Disorders* (Washington, D.C.: G.P.O., 1968), p. 51.

27. This is not to suggest that any publicity is better than none. However, the ability to gain visibility is important, especially to a group with few political resources. Unless a cause is visible, politicians are not compelled to take action with respect to it. The unfavorable popular reactions to causes pursued by direct action methods might suggest that political representatives would have similarly unfavorable opinions. This is not necessarily the case.

28. AIPO releases, June 21, 1961, and August 27, 1963.

29. Gallup Poll, June 18, 1961, in Erskine, p. 672.

30. Harris Poll, July 6, 1964, in Erskine, p. 673.

31. See Gallup Poll, June 28, 1961; June 7, 1964; and November 13, 1964; in Erskine, pp. 657, 659, and 660.

32. "Crisis in Color, 1966," *Newsweek*, 68 (August 22, 1966), 57.

33. Harris Poll, June 5, 1967, and August 9, 1967, in Erskine, pp. 659 and 662.

34. Campbell and Schuman, p. 48.

35. Richard T. Morris and Vincent Jeffries, "The White Reaction Study," *Los Angeles Riot Study* (Los Angeles: Institute of Government and Public Affairs, University of California, 1967), p. 34.

36. Sheatsley, p. 317.

37. SRC, September-October, 1964, in Erskine, p. 676.

38. Morris and Jeffries, p. 11.

39. Campbell and Schuman, p. 51.

40. Prior to 1964, the violence of ghetto riots could not have been misperceived as civil rights activity because the first big riots of the decade occurred in 1964. However, the subsequent rash of riots may have increased confusion between nonviolent protest activity and violence.

41. D. O. Sears and T. M. Tomlinson, "Riot Ideology in Los Angeles: A Study of Negro Attitudes," *Social Science Quarterly*, 49 (December, 1968), 484–503. See Tables 2, 3, and 10.

42. *Ibid.*, p. 500.

43. Gary T. Marx, "Protest and Prejudice: A Study of Belief in the Black Community," Ph.D. dissertation, University of California (Berkeley), 1966, p. 32. Revised and published under the same title (New York: Harper and Row, 1967).

44. "Crisis in Color, 1966", p. 57.

45. Survey conducted by Joseph Kraft and reported as "The Attitudes of Negroes in Various Cities," in *Federal Role in Urban-Affairs*, Hearings, Part 6, August 31-September 1, 1966, U.S. Senate Subcommittee on Executive Reorganization, Committee on Government Operations, 89th Cong., 2d Sess. (Washington, D.C.: G.P.O., 1966), p. 1400.

46. Matthews and Prothro, p. 438.

47. Brink and Harris, pp. 203-204.

48. No figure listed.

49. Marx, p. 33.

50. Brink and Harris, p. 202. The reported data do not indicate whether and how much overlap there was in these responses.

51. "Report from Black America," *Newsweek*, 73 (June 30, 1969), 22.

52. Matthews and Prothro, p. 412.

53. AIPO release, November 17, 1965.

54. Suzanne H. Rudolph "The New Courage—An Essay on Gandhi's Psychology," *World Politics*, 16 (October, 1963), 99.

55. Angus Campbell, Philip E. Converse, Warren E. Miller, and Donald E. Stokes, *The American Voter* (New York: John Wiley and Sons, 1960), pp. 105, 453. I recomputed these figures from Campbell's data.

56. Dwaine Marvick, "The Political Socialization of the American Negro," *The Annals of the American Academy of Political and Social Science*, 361 (September, 1965), Table 2, p. 119.

57. *Ibid.*, Table 3, p. 120. Actually, percentages for northern whites and blacks were the same, but in the South 95 percent of the blacks said they had never tried, while only 71 percent of the whites said this.

58. Brink and Harris, p. 202. Here, "leaders" does not necessarily mean civil rights leaders; many were notables in other fields of endeavor.

59. *Ibid.*, pp. 130, 231.

60. *Ibid.*, pp. 73, 206–207.

61. Marx, p. 51.

62. "Report from Black America," p. 23.

63. Campbell and Schuman, p. 52.

64. William McCord and John Howard, "Negro Opinions," *in* William McCord, John Howard, Bernard Friedberg, and Edwin Harwood, *Life Styles in the Black Ghetto* (New York: W. W. Norton, 1969), p. 84.

65. Marx, p. 51.

66. Kraft, p. 1387. The area surveyed by Kraft may have included more than Watts itself.

67. Sears and Tomlinson, Tables 3 and 10.

68. Campbell and Schuman, pp. 47–49.

69. "Report from Black America," p. 23.

70. In the survey done for the "Riot Commission," 8 percent of the black respondents said they would join a riot. The 1966 *Newsweek* survey reported 15 percent of its respondents willing to join a riot; in 1969, the figure had dropped to 11 percent; but support for joiners was high: 54 percent of those who would not join said they would be sympathetic to joiners; only 24 percent said they would be unsympathetic. About one-sixth of a subsample of young (under 30) blacks in Northern cities claimed they were ready to join a riot the next time one occurred.

71. Sears and Tomlinson, pp. 500–501, and Tables 1, 2, and 7. A few of the figures cited here are from the original study by Sears and Tomlinson, entitled "Riot Activity and Evaluation: An Overview of the Negro Survey," unpublished working paper, Department of Psychology, University of California (Los Angeles), August, 1966, but they were not reprinted in this article. Tomlinson plans to incorporate this material into a paper on the political attitudes of militants and non-militants after the Los Angeles riots, to be published as "Contributing Factors in Black Politics," in the May, 1970, issue of *Psychiatry.*

72. T. M. Tomlinson, "Ideological Foundations for Negro Action: A Comparative Analysis of Militant and Non-militant Views of the Los Angeles Riot," p. 4 (to be published in the *Journal of Social Issues*). Also Sears and Tomlinson, "Riot Activity and Evaluation: An Overview of the Negro Survey," Table 12.

73. Personal communication from T. M. Tomlinson.

74. Sears and Tomlinson, "Riot Activity and Evaluation: An Overview of the Negro Survey," Table 12.

75. Tomlinson, pp. 41, 44–45, 58, and 65. Some of the findings are from the original paper, "Negro Nationalism and the August Revolt," presented at a closed symposium organized by the Society for the Psychological Study of Social Issues, at the American Psychological Association Convention, New York City,

September, 1966. Tomlinson points out that his respondents probably would have ranked the Muslims last among the black organizations and that higher support for Muslims in his sample (relative to Marx's) might have been due to the fact that he asked for opinion of the Muslims without relative evaluation.

76. Personal communication from T. M. Tomlinson.

77. The biggest differences were between the relatively few Black Nationalist sympathizers and these other two groups. Seventy-two percent of the former thought riots did some good and 49 percent disagreed that "violence would never help Negroes;" 39 percent were high on acceptance of violence. Marx, p. 188.

78. Marx, p. 80.

79. D. O. Sears, "Attitudes toward Political Officials, Groups, and Institutions," unpublished working paper, Department of Psychology, University of California (Los Angeles), August, 1966, Table 6–5. This paper has been revised for publication in the *Midwest Journal of Political Science* under the title, "Black Attitudes toward the Political System

in the Aftermath of the Watts Insurrection" (forthcoming).

80. Tomlinson, "Ideological Foundations for Negro Action: A Comparative Analysis of Militant and Non-militant Views of the Los Angeles Riot," p. 33.

81. Harry Scoble, "Negro Leadership Study: Tentative Findings," unpublished working paper, Department of Political Science, University of California (Los Angeles), August, 1966, p. 9, says that black protest demonstrations in the Los Angeles area since approximately May, 1963, "accomplished very, very little." His major conclusion is "the lack of public policy impact from such demonstrations."

82. The antiwar protest movement may have been responsible for mobilizing some of the support for Senator McCarthy; the response he received may have been one important consideration in President Johnson's partial suspension of U.S. bombing in order to get talks with Hanoi started in the spring of 1968.

83. Since the disruptions which occurred when black students first entered desegregated schools in the South.

VII

Conventional Channels, Political Opposition, and Nonviolent Direct Action

ATTEMPTS TO RECONCILE the concept of civil disobedience with political obligation in a democracy have postulated that civil disobedience must be a tactic of last resort. Therefore, it should be employed only when political and legal channels prove unavailing or when there is a high probability—based on past experience in similar situations—that resort to such means can produce no even moderately satisfactory results.

Critics of civil disobedience may grant that the southern sit-ins were justified precisely because the polls and the courts were not really open to blacks. But, they often contend, the availability of the ballot and the courts as means of rectification and redress is grounds for denying the legitimacy of civil disobedience. This argument subsumes a number of unexamined premises about democratic politics which condition the meaning and implications of "availability." One such premise seems to be that these channels are available in more or

Notes to this chapter will be found on pages 261–266

less the same way to all and can produce more or less the same results for all, as long as their use is not subject to legal or egregious extra-legal restrictions. A corollary assumption may be that use of the electoral and judicial processes will produce roughly similar levels of satisfaction for all citizens. Of course, this assumption does not imply that there is any *guarantee* of satisfaction, but no student of democratic politics would contend that every individual (or group) who enters the political arena to press some claim can expect to be fully or even partially satisfied every (or any particular) time. No democratic theorist—even one who recognizes that "availability" is not the same for all citizens— would argue that anyone is entitled to expect such satisfaction. Perhaps the most that the individual can reasonably expect is consideration by political and legal authorities, and an occasional result that goes some way toward meeting his demands. This may well be sufficient for most citizens, especially if they do not have any very intense preferences (of political relevance), and/or if they have a variety of political interests, all of relatively equal importance (or unimportance) to them. Satisfaction of one interest will compensate for lack of results elsewhere, and they will be amenable to compromise on one demand in order to gain another. But when individuals or groups have one intense preference on an issue which takes priority over their preferences on all other issues, then concessions from the political system to their other preferences cannot play the same role in creating for them a general level of moderate satisfaction. Because people have a plurality of wants, needs, and interests, it is unusual for them to give a single one of them precedence to the point of sacrificing considerable satisfaction of the others. Yet such instances do occur; to use a very current example, some antiwar protesters have taken the position that the war in Viet Nam is the most important issue of the day, and they refuse to support representatives who are "wrong" on that issue, whatever their position on other matters.

Another situation which deviates from the model of moderate general satisfaction is that of deprived minority groups, in this country most notably the black population. Here there is a whole range of related desires and needs which are frustrated to varying degrees. Even if no one of them were considerably more intense than the others, the general level of satisfaction is so low that any particular one may become the focus of claims that will not readily be yielded up. Appeals for compromise cannot be based soundly on the existence of other countervailing satisfactions; defeat on one issue is not likely to be mitigated by enjoyment of a general level of moderate satisfaction. Thus, a situation is created where exhaustion of "legitimate" remedies will not necessarily terminate a demand. In contrast, for the moderately satisfied or even moderately dissatisfied, the costs of continuing to press claims outside accepted channels (for example, discomfort, insecurity, or alienation of a political representative who may be acceptable on other issues) may be considered greater than the potential gains.[1]

To say that democracy does not guarantee any right to electoral or legal victory is not to say that the citizen whose resort to conventional political methods fails to produce satisfactory results is precluded by his commitment to democracy from employing "extra-channel" methods as well. But this is implicit in the argument that conventional political and legal means are the only proper remedies in a democracy. It presumes that the dissident's task is to persuade the majority of the electorate (or the judges) of the validity of his claim. If he fails to convince them, nothing in our system of government entitles him to press his claim by other, unconventional means. What lies behind the "availability argument" is the notion that democracy is majority rule. The conventional channels provide opportunities to persuade the majority (or its agents) to adopt one's own position. To assume, however, that effective persuasion leads to effective action is simplistic, because there is no unidirectional progression from majority opinion to majority vote to action by the majority's representatives. Actual political practice in our system belies any such assumption.

As has been pointed out in elementary texts on American politics,[2] candidates in Presidential elections do not run on one issue, and the views of the winner's electoral majority may not actually contain majorities preferring the same issue outcomes as he does. The issue most important to some supporters of the winning candidate may not be salient to others. Because of this, he may have gained support from persons who disagreed with him on some issues. Thus theoretically a candidate could take the minority position on each of a number of major issues and yet win a majority of the votes.[3] Even where constituencies are more homogeneous socially and politically (for example, in Congressional districts), this situation could occur. The result could be that some majority viewpoints might not find representation in the policy positions of the winning candidate. Thus, persuading a majority to espouse a certain view on a particular issue provides no assurance that this majority will eventually constitute an electoral majority. It may not really even make sense to speak about *the* political majority. The electoral method, as we know it, does not give us warrant for assuming that the winner necessarily represents the majority preference on all issues. In the courts, persuading the judges (particularly the judges of the court of ultimate appeal) to accept a particular view will probably lead to a clear-cut result—a decision in favor of the petitioners. Nevertheless, the problem of implementing a court decree remains, and where significant social change is involved, there may be even greater obstacles to effective implementation than in the case of legislation. Implementation may depend largely on political agencies, so petitioners still face the difficulties of political persuasion.

On some issues, the established channels may be ill-adapted to allow the expression of disagreement. Voting against a candidate or party at the polls probably is not, in most cases, an adequate way of registering a "no" vote against a particular policy to which the candidate or party is committed. The other candidate's position may not be sufficiently different for the electoral outcome to be unambiguous; other issues of policy may also be salient to the electorate, so that it is hard to say whether voters are deciding on the basis of any one issue. The ballot also seems to be an ineffective means of registering a protest because some issues may not lend themselves to a decision at the polls: They are not clearly identified with any candidates competing for office, or they are difficult to formulate in terms of two alternatives. Of course, there are other conventional methods of expressing political dissent which permit more complex content, but these may lack even the sanction that a negative vote potentially can inflict (in conjunction with a sufficient number of other negative votes). In addition, as I have already suggested, dissident minorities are likely to have intense feelings about the issues that concern them. The "rules" of American politics indicate some concern that the majority should not quickly or without very compelling reasons—made clear to the minority—override the preferences of an intense minority.[4] Yet procedures for mass consultation such as the vote generally allow little opportunity for registering the intensity of one's preferences.

All this is to suggest that the mere opportunity to employ conventional channels for redress is not apt to satisfy some dissident individuals and groups in a democracy. This is not because they unrealistically assume they have a right to prevail. Regardless of their ability to influence public opinion on a particular issue, the conventional channels may simply not be suitable for introducing their specific, intense preferences into government decision-making.

Additional reasons for questioning the availability argument arise from related difficulties: The low salience of politics for the average citizen, and the apparently tenuous relationship between constituents and representatives. Both create obstacles to changing public policy by means of the electoral process. The generally low salience of political matters means that many voters have few, if any, clearcut preferences on the issue of the day. In addition, constituents frequently do not associate their representatives with particular policy stances. A study by Donald E. Stokes and Warren E. Miller revealed that when respondents were asked the reasons for their vote for House representatives (in 1958), few of the responses had any connection with issues. The salience of the party legislative record was no higher for those who deviated from their party preference in voting than for those who were "consistent." The deviaters were no more likely to give issue reasons for their vote, or to indicate awareness of which party controlled the 85th Congress. What the study revealed was rather extensive ignorance about both the incumbent representative and his opponent. More than half of the sample asserted that they had neither read nor heard anything about either one, and less than one-fifth thought they possessed some knowledge about both. The authors concluded that only a very small proportion of the deviating votes in a mid-term election could be attributed to national policy issues. They also thought that "many factors increasing the saliency of candidates are unlikely to enhance what the public knows about their stands on issues."[5]

Not only are political issues not salient to most Americans, it may also be that they do not view the electoral process as a particularly desirable way of dealing with politically-relevant problems. William Buchanan's study of a county seat community in Mississippi revealed "no evidence that the franchise is seen as a means of remedying political conditions."[6] The author found that those with a purposive orientation toward voting did not necessarily consider the political process a preferable way of influencing policy. Such findings are not surprising in light of considerable evidence from all parts of the nation that politics is not salient to most people, and that they do not perceive politics as being closely related to their personal concerns and needs.

While Buchanan's study provides no basis for extrapolation to American citizens in general, *The Civic Culture's*[7] data on American respondents does permit some tentative generalization. When respondents were asked how they would go about influencing their local government, Americans were much more likely to mention organizing a local group to petition officials (via written communication) than working through a political party or voting against an offending official in an election. In other words, the most common form of political activity, voting, may not be perceived by Americans as an effective means of changing an objectionable policy. On the other hand, it is possible that most Americans feel the use of methods other than petition is unnecessary, because they expect elected officials to be responsive to local appeals.[8] Petition is well within the range of techniques acceptable in a democracy. Its use is not to be ruled out as a possible tactic for a dissident minority group, but when it does not work (and in certain situations, it has not been effective), other tactics must be employed. Those who propose to dissenters that they appeal to the public and stake their case on the ballot are proposing a very formidable operation: convincing large numbers of people to deviate from their accustomed—that is, rather uninvolved—attitude toward political candidates and policy issues, and to follow a route which they apparently do not generally associate with influencing government officials.

The model of political responsiveness underlying the availability argument seems to postulate a unidirectional movement of influence from constituency to representative, but studies of the constituent-representative relationship indicate that the actual process is considerably more complex. The authors of *American Business and Public Policy*[9] suggest that a Congressman's own decisions have a great deal of influence on what he hears from his constituents; in other words, their image of him determines to a large extent whether and what they will communicate to him (and that image is created by his own attitudes and actions). Lewis A. Dexter suspects that most political communication is directed to representatives believed to be sympathetic.[10] Messages apparently do more to change the *salience* of an issue for a representative than to change his opinion. He must have relationships with some important groups in his constituency, but even when a particular group has an established relationship with their representative—which may increase the likelihood of their contacting him—this will not necessarily make him more responsive to their views on a specific issue. Often he influences them to accept his views. A key factor found affecting the communication flow was the sheer busyness of the Congressman. More demands are made upon him than he can fulfill and thus he must be selective; it is here, the authors of *American Business and Public Policy* believe, that a Congressman's freedom of decision lies. Dexter also points out that on many issues there is no distinct constituency viewpoint; most citizens are either unaware and/or unconcerned. Generally a Congressman has to anticipate the reactions of his constituents, because their opinions are often ambiguous or unformulated at the time he must decide. In addition, there is the selectivity involved in merely deciding to communicate with him. Thus, when a representative chooses between the interests of competing constituency groups, he is often responding to a part of his constituency as if it were the totality.

The complexity of the relationship makes potential constituent influence difficult to assess. As a result, a dissident minority bent on swaying an elected representative can draw only ambiguous conclusions from these findings. On the one hand, the fact that constituents have no clear-cut preferences on many issues presumably allows a representative to respond to intense pressures from a minority group. He is more likely to take advantage of this situation if the group can convince him that his action on a particular issue will largely determine their support for or opposition to him. On the other hand, it seems to have been the case that the issues pressed on Congressmen by dissident minorities have been relatively salient for the general public—for example, civil rights, the poverty program, the war in Viet Nam, and HUAC. In these cases the public is more apt to have preferences, and representatives are more apt to feel constrained by actual or potential constituency reaction.[11]

In his study of representatives and constituencies, Lewis A. Froman argues that on certain matters, representatives do feel so constrained.[12] He asserts that bills which entail large expenditures and federal intervention affecting a whole range of people throughout the country demand close attention to pressures from Congressmen's constituencies. Such legislation—usually high on the President's schedule of priorities—receives national coverage in the media and is likely to activate individuals and groups in the constituency. Thus, it is important for the Congressman to know how various groups in his district will react. Heightened activation, Froman suggests, probably will increase conflict because the various groups for whom the issue has become salient are likely to take different positions. Conceivably, increased conflict might enable a dissident minority group to gain more of a hearing than would normally be accorded to it, but heightened activation may reduce the representative's flexibility in meeting the group's demands. Similar conclusions could be "deduced" about the chances of a dissident group in a relatively competitive district; close competition makes each voting group more important, but simultaneously reduces either contender's ability to meet the demands of any one group, if they conflict with other group pressures. Froman notes that because competitive districts tend to be more heterogeneous, Congressmen are less apt to take extreme positions. Thus, Democrats from competitive districts are less liberal than Democrats from safe districts, and Republicans from competitive districts are less conservative than Republicans from safe districts. Thus, it might be concluded that greater competitiveness will not increase the potential effectiveness of dissident minorities, because the more competitive the district, the more likely it is to be heterogeneous—and in this environment, representatives tend to feel constrained to avoid extreme positions. On the other hand, in recent years at least, dissident groups employing direct action tactics have often "represented" (if not actually included as participants) nonwhite, relatively low socio-economic status (SES), and urban minorities; and safe Democratic districts tend to have a higher incidence of such groups.[13] Since Democrats from these districts generally take more liberal positions, there is a possibility that such dissident groups will receive more of a hearing than they could elsewhere. Nonetheless, on specific issues of importance to these groups, Froman's findings provide no real guide to the representative's probable response.

Another study of the constituent-representative relationship provides more evidence of its tenuous nature. Miller and Stokes found that the Congressman "has very imperfect information about issue preferences of his constituents."[14] However, he does appear to know more about them on civil rights than on issues of social and economic welfare and of foreign policy. The correlation between the representative's roll-call votes and the majority constituency opinions was highest in the civil rights area, although the divergence between his own attitude and the majority attitude apparently was greatest here.[15] This suggests that awareness of constituency preference may not change a representative's views, but it may well influence his voting. Presumably this is related to the salience of civil rights issues to the general population.

While this result is an apparent contradiction to the usual weak constituency-representative links, it does not invalidate the cautious generalization (based on this literature) that representatives seem to have relatively incomplete knowledge of constituency preferences. This generalization suggests the hypothesis that reaching the representative's threshold of visibility may frequently be difficult for a group within his constituency.

The studies of the constituent-representative relationship reveal how difficult it is to estimate the responsiveness of representatives to constituents. As should be evident by now, these studies do not provide any firm guidance in assessing the opportunities for a dissident minority to influence a representative, or to defeat him if he refuses to be swayed by their arguments. Nonetheless, they do permit a few tentative generalizations. First, a great deal of ignorance and lack of interest has to be overcome to make the general public aware of the Congressman's stand on the particular issue. Success in this regard will not, of course, entail automatic support for the dissidents from the public; it is quite possible that many voters will agree with the representative and not with the dissidents. Secondly, as Stokes and Miller suggest, the representative may be aware that the public is not evaluating him on a particular issue or policy stand:[16] thus he may be able to discount heavily the claims of a dissident group that he is likely to lose votes by not changing his present position. Thus, a minority which sets out to change the position of a representative by mobilizing constituency opinion may frequently encounter real obstacles due to the low salience of politics and the tenuous nature of constituent-representative relationships.

Furthermore, there are other structural and socio-economic factors which handicap minorities that try to use conventional political methods. For example, in homogeneous constituencies, political candidates may feel little impetus to meet the claims of a minority whose preferences are clearly in conflict with those of the majority. Such appears to be the problem of disadvantaged ethnic minority groups, particularly in urban areas. Here vigorous attempts to satisfy the minority would be costly in terms of majority support, and thus officials tend to respond to the preferences of a majority which is homogeneous, at least vis-à-vis the minority group. For example, in Chicago[17] political conditions do not impel the mayor to wage an energetic fight to improve the condition of black people, despite the fact that blacks make up almost one-fifth of the population. He can improve his political position to a limited extent by supporting modest improvements in the black's welfare and status, but any failure to make spectacular efforts will not threaten his position. James Q. Wilson suggests that "when the Negro population is large, as in Chicago, Detroit, and New York, it seems much more difficult to create a situation in which liberal measures be-become good politics."[18] The minority-versus-majority-constituceny problem is obvious in the South where there are few areas in which blacks have an actual or potential majority of the electorate, and where salient preferences are clearly in conflict.[19] In such situations, even very cohesive bloc voting may be unavailing unless the majority is fragmented; then the possibility of holding a balance of power comes into existence.

Even to exert the limited influence which this structural situation may permit, the minority group must first organize its members for conventional political action. However, the available evidence suggests that such minorities are rather difficult to organize. In recent years, there has been considerable study of the relationship between SES and political participation. The results are well known; those with fewer "resources" tend to vote less frequently. Seymour Martin Lipset found that lower turnout is associated with lower education, lower income, and less skilled occupations.[20] As for other forms of participation, such as communicating with government officials, Robert E. Lane has hypothesized from the available data that: (1) petitioning in person is related to possession of social skills and some awareness of politics; (2) lower SES persons are more likely to contact only local officials; (3) "those of lower socio-economic status require greater organization and effort for an audience with an official or to secure an equivalent effect upon that official than those of higher status;"[21] (4) "letter writing is related to verbal skills and personal familiarity with writing expres-sion, a capacity to crystallize the desire to write into a decision to write, upper occupational and educational status,"[22] among other factors. The implications of these phenomena for some assumptions of the avail-ability argument are clear. There are great differences in the degree to which people can and do make use of conventional political channels, and the greater incidence of political participation and effectiveness among upper SES persons cannot be explained merely as a manifesta-tion of generally prevailing levels of moderate satisfaction among lower SES persons, or as an indication of their lack of need and desire.

Political scientists have also been studying the relation between attitudes toward politics and political activity. To some extent, these may be intervening variables between SES characteristics and political behavior. The most unambiguous findings seem to be that there is a definite relationship between level of education and a sense of political efficacy, and that there is a carry-over from sense of efficacy to political activity. Angus Campbell and his associates found a strong relationship between education and sense of efficacy in a national sampling of the population;[23] voting turnout (in the 1956 Presidential election) increased uniformly with increases in the sense of political efficacy—the percentage difference in turnout between high and low efficacy respondents was almost 40 points.[24] In a cross-national study of political attitudes and behavior, *The Civic Culture*, a definite relationship was evident between education and greater incidence of local competence, that is, the belief that one could influence local government.[25] Furthermore, a substantially larger proportion of "local competents" than "non-competents" reported actual attempts to influence local government.[26] In the United States sample, those who thought they could influence local government were at least three times as likely to have made such attempts. A study of two major Oregon cities revealed a "strong relationship between feelings of political potency and educational level, with potency increasing sharply with education."[27] Edgar Litt also found that education and sense of efficacy were strongly related characteristics of respondents in a middle-class Boston ward.[28] It is apparent that the distribution of different amounts of education in our society affects the frequency with which different groups feel they can and actually do make use of conventional political channels.

Since level of education is one of the major determinants of SES, this evidence suggests that some feelings which inhibit political participation[29] are disproportionately manifested by low SES persons. As already mentioned, the findings on political participation related *directly* to SES characteristics indicate more clearly that low SES persons participate less frequently. From this evidence, it appears that they cannot be easily mobilized for political activity of the customary variety, and the difficulty is increased by the lack of political resources (e.g., money, organizational skills, access to the mass media, etc.) that characterizes such groups.

The situation suggests a possible resort to direct action as an alternative to conventional methods.[30] Dissenters must often find ways to influence officials that do not rely directly on mass popular support for their effectiveness. The dramatic effect of direct action and the publicity which often results from its use help to explain its popularity. However, resorting to extra-channel tactics may be, not an *alternative* to conventional methods, but the only means available for organizing effectively to use them. Civil rights demonstrations—one specific example being the use of marches to publicize voter registration drives —apparently have made a very significant contribution to mobilizing American blacks, making them more conscious of their situation and more confident of their efficacy. One result has been increased registration and voting. In other words, extra-channel tactics can help increase political resources and make the use of conventional political methods more effective.[31]

However, the need for unconventional action does not end when such minorities have been politically organized. I have already discussed how the indeterminate and complex relationships between public opinion, political issues, electoral candidates, and official actions hinder the use of conventional methods to redress grievances on relatively specific issues. Other obstacles may be even more intractable. The recent incidence of localized protest demonstrations in northern metropolitan areas has emphasized the fact that the governmental agencies which have been the targets of protest are often not directly accountable to the people. So far, the protests have tended to focus on school boards, urban redevelopment agencies, and welfare departments. Officials of many such agencies are appointed by elected officials. The latter may be considered responsible for the actions of their appointees, but they cannot necessarily influence them easily. Elected officials may have less freedom in *relieving* appointees of their duties than in selecting them for the job, because tenure is sometimes protected by leagl restrictions. Appointed officials may also develop constituencies that can counteract the appointing officials' influence. Thus, even if the latter want to hold their appointees responsible, there are obstacles. If they are *not* inclined to modify their appointees' treatment of dissatisfied groups, the electoral process does not promise to be an effective way of persuading them to do so. For the aggrieved groups must constitute a majority of the elected official's constituency or at least hold a balance of power in the election. Expanding the focus of a protest from the nonelective official to his elected appointer usually means an expansion of the constituency involved—and possibly the reappearance of the deviant-minority-versus-majority-constituency problem. For example, black parents who predominate in a particular school district may be unhappy with the condition of their children's schools. If the local (nonelective) school board proves intractable to petitions and verbal attacks, they can appeal to the mayor; but the latter's constituency may well be predominantly white, and refusal to grant the black parents' demands is not likely to cost him many votes in his white majority constituency. Thus, even if the mayor is not unfavorably disposed toward the parents' claim, there is no great impetus for him to act.[32]

On a more general level, Arthur W. Bromage points out that "of the great metropolitan districts in the United States that operate independently without being subordinate to state or local governments, no more than one-fifth have boards [of various urban governmental authorities] that are entirely elective."[33] Compared to the use of direct election in the constituting of councils in large cities, its use in the constitution of such boards is minor. As a result, there is little direct representation of, or accountability to, the jurisdictional areas of the boards. While appointers of such boards (for example, governors, mayors, and county officials) are elective and thus may indirectly give boards a representative character, board members "may be endowed with powers, terms, overlapping tenures and legal stipulations as to their removal which wall them off substantially from answerability to the metropolitan area."[34]

Since there has been research on representatives' perceptions of their constituents, one can assert with some confidence that there is imperfect communication of opinions and preferences, but in the case of nonelective officials—while such an inference seems even more warranted—there is less direct evidence. One recent study of a planning committee selected by a nonpartisan elective school board throws a little light on the subject. The committee's task was to draw up a blueprint for a new high school designed to "meet the social, educational, and economic needs of the people served by the high school."[35] Its members (30 in number) apparently had considerable contact with the community; some were residents and some were local leaders. The authors found that the committee members quite substantially misperceived the intensity and magnitude of public preferences. Only slightly more than one-half accurately perceived the direction of community preferences. Misperception was most frequent where leaders' preferences diverged significantly from those of the public.[36] Of course, generalization is not possible from one case study, but it might be hypothesized that convergence between appointed officials' perceptions of their constituents' preferences and the latter's actual preferences will not automatically arise from informal contact. Without some formal consultation and some means of ensuring a modicum of responsiveness, it is quite possible that nonelective officials will find constituents dissatisfied with their decisions. Without community support, the effectiveness of well-intentioned improvement programs may be impaired.

In his study of Boston politics, Murray B. Levin uncovered another potential obstacle to effecting political change through the electoral process: The "political choices available to administrators of a city government are severely circumscribed by economic realities and state law,"[37] and thus the choices which *can* be made available to the public through the electoral process are quite limited. "The minimal facilities a city must provide to maintain its viability tend to be not much less than the maximum facilities it can achieve with available funds."[38] Since few real policy alternatives can be presented to the voters, electoral campaigns tend to focus on corruption or inefficiency. But it is difficult for the voters to evaluate the honesty of the candidates. As a result, they lack confidence in their decision at the polls, and the elections themselves may begin to seem meaningless. Whether or not there is increased nonvoting in this situation, policy choices by the electorate—always a difficult matter to effectuate—are virtually ruled out. Moreover, a dissident minority is likely to find injecting real issues into such a context difficult, even though the public conceivably would prefer more reliable bases on which to judge the candidates.

So far, the discussion has focused mainly on potential obstacles to effective use of political channels; however, it is not necessary to rely solely on inference in attacking the availability argument. Several relatively recent studies of urban renewal in northern cities provide detailed descriptions of the obstacles actually encountered by "grassroots" citizen groups when they sought to influence the renewal process. Harold Kaplan's study of urban renewal in Newark indicated that the local opposition group, the Save Our Homes Council (SOHC), suffered from numerous weaknesses, chiefly "those of a sporadic political participant, one who intervenes only in response to a specific, adverse public decision and then only to delay, block, or divert the impact of action."[39] The SOHC lacked funds, information, and skills; having come on the scene rather suddenly, it also lacked stable relationships with the housing authority and the other major participants in the urban renewal process. By the time of its birth—when the decision to renew was announced—the major commitments of support for the project had already been obtained; the mayor had been asked and had given his support before the public was informed, so he could not accurately estimate the magnitude of opposition. Moreover, political leaders from the renewal area had few contacts with him, and he was under no compulsion to help them out. Lack of information and the fact that the mayor had a much wider constituency[40] also proved to be handicaps. The Newark Housing Authority (NHA) staff apparently did not welcome participation by residents from the area or their spokesmen. They told black leaders who tried to intervene that they should help win acceptance of the project from residents of the affected area, since the project would benefit the black community. It was not the NHA's function, they claimed, to consult extensively with those affected by projects (for example, those forced to move), because such consultation, and concessions to local demands which might stem from it, would seriously impede the progress of the projects.

In a study of the failure of local opposition to a renewal project in Boston's West End, some of the same factors appeared. The local politicians all apposed the project but key business and political leaders in the city unanimously favored it. "Election of city councilors at large rather than by wards since 1951 reduced the influence of individual districts. Smaller areas, with few voters, were especially hard hit; and the West End, which was losing population at this time, was virtually disenfranchised."[41] The leaders of the opposition were hampered by insufficient information, which lack was at least partly attributable to the failure of redevelopment officials to inform local politicians of important developments. Even more of a handicap was the inability of local politicians and leaders to make good use of the information they did receive. The author found that most residents were not able to understand the complex series of preliminary and final approvals in the renewal process: They did not believe that redevelopment would actually take place until they received letters announcing the taking of private landholdings in the area. For years there had been talk of redevelopment and occasional announcements of decisions, but nothing had tangibly affected the area's residents. Most of them thought the mayor had complete control over the project and if he were persuaded to stop it, that would be sufficient. Even some of the leaders subscribed to this belief.

In the author's opinion, the most important factor in the West

Enders' failure to take effective action was their "inability . . . to organize in their own behalf."[42] Their experience had not prepared them to join together for community action; they thought local politicians were the ones to fight city hall. The residents were not very receptive when nonviolent tactics were proposed as a means of persuading the mayor to reverse the decision. Many distrusted the mayor and expressed a desire to use violence. Many of the local families were of Italian descent and the Italian men objected to their wives' taking part in a march. The residents' short time-perspective helped conceal the difficulties which redevelopment would cause them. Public announcements, such as notice of the taking of private land, aroused anger, but it subsided too quickly to become a stimulus to action. Resort to legal channels also failed; the committee formed to organize the protest sought a temporary injunction to have further action by redevelopment officials stopped, but was denied. "By the time the case was heard and its appeal defeated, the West End was almost totally cleared."[43] In addition, the author asserts that redevelopment officials failed to recognize the extent of and reasons for hostility, because West Enders did not organize to protest as middle-class citizens would have done. Thus, they were under no pressure to plan for the needs of the residents affected by the project.

A study of urban renewal in Chicago provides some indication that local citizen groups can play a more positive role in the renewal process, but this role turns out to be a predominantly passive one. The authors' case studies of particular localities revealed that citizens were not playing a "crucial part" in "influencing the specific details of the [renewal] plan."[44] Efforts to make agency planners and staff responsive to the needs and desires of local residents encountered numerous difficulties. In one area, the Community Conference, an intergroup relations organization with representatives from block groups, attempted to win broad support for the renewal project in the affected neighborhood and, at the same time, bring the plan into closer congruity with local needs and wants. In the authors' view, the Conference could not have played a more militant role, maintaining "greater distance between itself and the planning process, making stronger stands on policy issues through public attacks on the plan and political pressure on public officials,"[45] without risking serious costs: loss of broad support, decrease in the pace of planning, loss of foundation and business support, and possible competition from a rival organization. Nevertheless, they say, a more militant stand might have made planners more attentive to housing for local residents (one of the Conference's demands) and won a plan whose general features were more acceptable to the public.[46]

The authors sought the factors which facilitated effective citizen action and the techniques which achieved it. In apparent contrast to the Boston study, there were—in the specific area where the Conference was active—individuals who could provide experienced leadership. One particularly effective leader was described in some detail: a resident who was "willing to agitate and negotiate endlessly to accommodate the wishes of other interests . . . insofar as they impinge[d] on his block's claims in the community."[47] He sought to formulate a position acceptable to the large majority of his block neighbors; this objective was facilitated by the saliency and clarity of the issues for these people. He made use of virtually all of the political channels open to citizens: "He contacted his alderman, testified at hearings, conferred privately and publicly with planners and with Conference and Commission officials, and formed *ad hoc* committees of citizens to make representations before boards to meet with landlords and with the perpetrators of neighborhood nuisances."[48] The authors suggest that such methods were efficacious, but it should be noted that the demands made in this case were not nearly so basic as those in the West End episode, which involved stopping the whole project. Moreover, in the "only major controversy in the entire process"—where residents favored public use of a particular site and the planners wished to sell the land to a private social welfare agency—the citizens "in large part" were the losers.[49]

Organizations with a metropolitan constituency were not given an opportunity to make public their appraisals of the Final Plan until the City Council had reviewed it. This was a definite handicap:

By that stage too much had been invested in the specific proposals by planners and the local community for much serious consideration to be given to metropolitan criticisms. Furthermore, the City Council was not empowered to do more than give blanket endorsement or rejection of the Plan, and the latter appeared to all as too drastic a step to be seriously considered.[50]

Although the Chicago case differs from the two previous ones in that considerable attempts apparently were made during the planning process to involve and win the support of local residents, the cumulative impact of a series of decisions and, with them, commitments to the renewal process, seems to have had similar effects on opposition groups in all three cases.

These case studies illustrate the various types of handicaps already discussed—for example, lack of certain resources, difficulty of mobilizing low SES constituencies, "deviant" minority status within a large constituent unit, and tenuous constituency-representative relationships. These studies illustrate particularly effectively how the distance between the individual affected by government action and the official decision-maker—already great because of weak linkages between constituency opinion, representatives' behavior, and the implementation of policy decisions—is increased by the delegation of authority to various governmental agencies. Although such agencies are usually responsible to the elected official who appoints their chiefs, much autonomy in decision-making is actually granted. The apparent reluctance of agency officials to provide for meaningful consultation with groups affected by their decisions, but to whom they are not directly responsible, raises serious questions about the quality of our democracy. Obviously, meaningful grassroots participation in decision-making by governmental agencies is difficult to institutionalize while retaining the benefits of specialization and delegation (such as speed, adequate consideration of technical aspects, and so forth). Discouraging and even denying the legitimacy of participation by the publics whom the decisions most affect may be an "efficient" practice for an agency, but in the process, real costs are imposed upon the affected individuals.

Another serious problem arises from the fact that politics and political decision-making are continuous processes, in which relatively stable working relationships are established between various participants. As a result, anyone who intervenes sporadically into these processes probably is at a disadvantage because he lacks such relationships. To suggest that this is one cost of allowing others to do the political work of society—a cost which all citizens bear whose participation is minimal or nonexistent—does not negate the fact that this cost may be much heavier for certain groups than for others. Low politicization may be functional for a democratic society, as some political scientists contend, but one cannot ignore the fact that it has costs which are not equally distributed among the public.

More specifically, the recurrent obstacles revealed in these case studies clearly indicate that grassroots political groups from low SES constituencies are not in a position to bargain effectively with public officials. Their lack of resources becomes all the more critical *vis-à-vis* renewal agencies in view of the finding that, at least in the past, plans have not included extensive consultation with residents; the latter must be organized and vocal merely to make renewal officials aware of their needs and wants. Since renewal officials and staff have not expected residents to play a formative role in the renewal process, the residents' making themselves heard will not necessarily make officials responsive. Residents must have resources to bargain with as well, but such resources as contact with important politicians and community leaders, political allies in other sections of the city, and organized electoral constituencies are not easily obtained. As Wilson points out, "the problem of many excluded groups is to create or assemble the resources for bargaining."[51] In order for negotiation—a conventional form of political action—to take place, the "target" of the protesting group must be induced to sit down at the bargaining table. One way of creating inducements, in this case negative ones, is through mass protest action." The response to the protest can be conceived as weighing the probable costs of enduring the protest against the probable costs of making concessions."[52] Previously, the target's calculations included only the prospective costs of making concessions to the excluded group; demonstrations introduce a new consideration, making the ability to end them a bargaining resource.

In outlining the requirements for a successful protest strategy, Wilson points out yet another problem: Not only must there be a specific target, it must be capable of granting the demands made. Under pervasive conditions of discrimination, it may be difficult to determine exactly at whom to point the finger. For example, Wilson cites discrimination in housing: "[It] is not the product of public or private decisions by some identifiable decision-maker. It is the result of an infinite number of social choices by tens of thousands of home owners, landlords, realtors, bankers, insurance officers, community groups."[53] The deprived group cannot reach the real cause of its problem; none of the individuals or groups who maintain the pattern of discrimination are in a position to end it by their own efforts. In effect, the target is too diffuse —involving members of the general public, the business community, and so forth—to be a focal point for pressure. Moreover, the protesting minority must have sufficient resources to pressure the target. If the federal government is the target, it is too powerful to be influenced by the resources available to the group alone. If no members of the deprived group are included in the target's constituency (for example as in the case of large home-financing institutions), the group lacks even the bargaining power which resides in the threat to withhold its support or resources. The target must be approached indirectly. Such circumstances require a strategy which can gain the attention of the general public, officials at high levels of government, and high-ranking executives within the relevant business institutions; but a strategy like this involves a great deal of resources and promises to be a long-term campaign—as was, for example, the struggle for federal fair housing legislation. This situation also points toward a strategy of seeking allies; this is facilitated, as was the case in the civil rights movement, when sympathetic attitudes toward the group's goals already exist. However, when attitudes are negative or do not extend as far as the group's range of objectives,[54] the group must have resources to form alliances. In order to gain support, it will have to be able to offer some *quid pro quo*. Such requirements make the obstacles to successful protest action formidable, especially for groups with relatively few resources. The necessity for turning to unconventional tactics becomes all the more apparent.

If a long-range protest strategy is required by the situation, the problem of time limitations appears. Sometimes the protested injustice is a matter of long standing, not likely to change for better or worse, and time is not a major factor in the success or failure of a protest strategy. At other times, as the urban renewal studies indicate, time is important. After a certain date, it is too late to take action. On the other hand, it appears that, in these cases, there more often is a determinate target, and this means that it should be easier to focus protest and that the range of support probably need be less broad. Usually some specific action is being undertaken at a specific time ordered by a specific set of officials. Reversing their decision may be very costly to these officials, but, presumably, they can be pressured to do so, if the costs of inaction are higher. In contrast, in the case where time is not an important factor, the problem faced by the dissidents is often the maintenance of a *pattern* of unjust practices.

A case study of the opposition to New York City Parks Commissioner Robert Moses's decision to permit construction of a Central Park restaurant parking lot is instructive because it illustrates many of the points just made.[55] When mothers and other residents of the neighborhood near the proposed parking lot discovered that Park Department action was imminent, they began organizing and sent petitions with several thousand signatures to both the Commissioner and the Mayor. Moses was unmoved. Stopping the Department from clearing the area required a sit-in by mothers and children in front of a bulldozer. As the protest campaign developed, the support of two city councilmen was obtained, and there were delegations to city officials. Nonetheless, requests for a halt pending further study were rejected. Construction equipment was blocked a second time by two mothers and a child. Subsequently, work was renewed under police guard. Finally, a preliminary injunction was granted by a New York Supreme Court Justice, pending hearings for an injunction the following day. Ultimately, the City decided not to appeal the injunction and the project was dropped.

By itself, the "direct action," that is, the blocking of construction would not have been sufficient to obtain a reversal of Moses's decision. Customary political and legal methods—statements of support from elected officials (the city councilmen), and the court injunction—were instrumental in the local opposition's ultimate success, but the original blocking of construction workers (and the resultant need to use police to "guard" them) played a crucial part. The mothers' sit-in prevented work from going ahead sufficiently far to make the issue moot, and it apparently helped gain wide and sympathetic newspaper coverage. The protests and resolutions of the councilmen were ineffective until the dispute developed much broader implications. Neighborhood residents could not easily move the Park Commissioner despite their organizing and petitioning. The local group lacked adequate resources; a few thousand signatures on a petition and the support of two councilmen made no significant impact on Moses.[56] The size of the opposition was too small to threaten the Mayor politically, so there was no immediate reason why he should try to overrule his Commissioner. Partly through the use of unconventional tactics, the protest gained visibility and support, and this ultimately proved a valuable resource when the the City considered further legal action. Corporation Counsel advised against appealing the injunction because he believed public sentiment would cause the courts to rule against the City, despite its apparently sound legal position.

To recap the argument so far: Certain kinds of political relationships and situations present potential and actual obstacles to effective grassroots political action; certain distinctive groups face serious handicaps when they take action through conventional political channels; unconventional tactics can be a way of at least partially overcoming these obstacles and compensating for these handicaps. Moreover, such tactics may be necessary at times. Social scientists have delineated several important situations in which "extra-channel" political activity may be the only effective way of obtaining concessions from the targets of protest.

A study of school desegregation in northern cities by Robert Dentler indicates that this is one area where conventional techniques, by themselves, are proving inadequate to produce real change.[57] The costs of desegregation may be lower in smaller cities, because more technical solutions involving few community-wide effects are available, but in the great cities, there are few such solutions and their impact on the constituencies involved would be considerable.[58] The result of this situation has been very little progress in most of the largest and most segregated (educationally) cities, despite "ten years of talk and five years of visible struggle." Dentler sees several reasons for this: (1) there are no rewards from the majority (white) community for making changes; (2) superintendents and boards may be limited in their initiative by the political risks which the mayor, who appoints them, is willing to take; (3) there are too many competing groups and thus too great a potential for counterprotest to emerge in response to campaigns of civil rights and black activist groups—this considerably reduces the latters' effectiveness; (4) school desegregation is not a top priority concern of many citizens, black or white—housing, crime, and employment take precedence. It is Dentler's contention that northern big city superintendents possess the resources to run the risks involved and to make change take place, although as yet none has made a devoted commitment to school desegregation. But he does not expect them to take action without prodding. Even in the smaller cities, where solutions are more readily available, Dentler insists that "Negroes must protest in a visible, unequivocal manner." In addition, there must be a sympathetic element in the white community with access to school officials and boards, and an intense stimulus for change from authorities at higher levels of government.

Examination of much of the material on black leadership and black political activity in the last decade reveals that exclusive use of "acceptable" methods, such as negotiation, petition, and voting, has not and will not produce meaningful gains for blacks in many parts of the South. Extra-channel tactics appear to be necessary. For example,

Lewis Killian and Charles Grigg found, in their study of biracial committees in southern communities, that the second most frequent reason given for establishing such committees was "the occurrence or threat of sit-ins."

This fact, plus the time during which most of the committees were appointed (a period during which the sit-ins were the most prominent manifestation of the Negro protest movement) supports the theme that the fear of public disorder stemming out of minority demonstrations is one of the most important stimuli for the creation of the biracial committee.[59]

The authors indicate that direct action tactics which merely seek to publicize a problem and arouse sympathy will not be sufficient.

Appeals to the moral sensibilities of the white community through demonstrations are not likely to be effective unless used in combination with these other sources of power [i.e., economic and political sanctions and federal intervention]. Demands on the white community, unsupported by power, result only in the display of force to show the superior power of the white community, whether under the guise of law or not.[60]

On the issue of most interest to the southern black community, segregation, there is no consensus with the white community. It is difficult to work out a mutually acceptable solution of the conflict because most southern whites think blacks have nothing positive to offer them in return for desegregation. Blacks can agree to accept less than they desire, but obviously they want a certain amount of change, which whites are reluctant to grant. The costs of desegregation are high for whites, especially the psychological costs; but they (in particular, white businessmen) are also interested in a good economic environment.[61] Here blacks have resources which can affect white calculations. They can create negative inducements for the white community by withdrawing their buying power from white merchants and by threatening to disrupt the placidity of commercial district activity with mass demonstrations and sit-ins.

The biracial committee, on its face, appears to be a peaceful and efficient way of settling racial conflicts which obviates the necessity for direct action. However, Killian and Grigg contend that these committees seem to create more problems for black leaders than they solve. Based on the findings of their case study, they assert that black leaders who accept membership on such committees will generally find themselves trying to work with white moderate segregationists, who "have never initiated action to bring any desegregation except in response to pressure from the Negro community."[62] Membership inhibits black leaders from effectively exercising the power of their community. As members, they are more than representatives of a subcommunity in conflict with the dominant white community; they become part of a team which is supposed to represent the entire community. Since the black and white subcommunities have conflicting goals and their representatives have very different and conflicting definitions of the problem of black-white relations, solution of the basic issue separating them cannot really serve as the overriding objective of the committee. By serving on the committee, black leaders evince their "hope that change may come about in the community without the ordeal of nonviolent resistance and demonstrations, with all the risks they entail." As a result:

> The preservation of racial peace becomes the superordinate goal for which both white and Negro members can work. . . . But this creates a serious dilemma for the Negro leader, particularly the militant leader who, if forced to, would choose progress over peace. This dilemma arises from the fact that peace does not serve as an effective, superordinate goal *unless there is some threat to this peace.*[63]

Daniel C. Thompson's conclusions—from his study of black leadership in New Orleans—reinforce those of Killian and Grigg:

> Up until now [1963] New Orleans' officials have made no voluntary effort to bring about positive changes in race relations. White authorities do not effect positive changes in the status of the Negro in any area of community life until professional Negro leaders have voiced long, loud, and concerted protest.[64]

> Over the last twenty years, Negro leaders in New Orleans have accomplished little in advancement of colored people through negotiations.[65]

> Every strategy and technique employed by the "new" Negro leadership is met with stern, often violent resistance from segregationist leaders.[66]

At the time, blacks had obtained only two definite gains—access to the municipal auditorium and desegregation of public libraries—through the use of "genuine negotiation (without threat of legal or direct action)."[67] Though black leaders had petitioned mayors repeatedly for the appointment of biracial committees, only two attempts had been made and in neither case were blacks satisfied with their representation.[68]

Most of the political activities engaged in by Negro political factions have been designed to get some white segregationist elected to public office.[69]

It is only when Negro "action" leaders use direct action techniques such as a boycott, or the threat of it, that white officials actually attempt to meet any of their demands for equal employment opportunities.[70]

Thompson makes it clear that negotiation by itself is insufficient; pressure, including direct action and federal intervention (for example, federal court orders), is also required.

Further support for the general proposition—that is, that accepted methods of political action are inadequate by themselves in much of the South—is provided by Everett C. Ladd's study of black leaders in Winston-Salem, North Carolina, and Greenville, South Carolina. His general view is that "southern whites cannot be expected to give any more than they consider in their interests to give."[71] He found "conservative style" black leaders prone to criticize direct action, but many were well aware that the threat of racial conflict was one of the strongest arguments they could make for programs to improve black conditions. Conservative leadership, Ladd concluded, had a greater potential for effective action in those southern cities where there recently had been large-scale direct action demonstrations, or where they were highly likely to occur.[72] It is difficult, Ladd suggests, to evaluate the effectiveness of militant leaders because many of the changes made by whites are due to fear that militants will take action if no change occurs. While recognizing that the major weapon of the protest organizations—the direct action demonstration—may sometimes "jeopardize other race values" because it "cannot be finely regulated," Ladd asserts that "the protest organizations [have] provided a prod without which little would have been accomplished in many areas."[73]

Ladd sees increasing permissiveness in interracial relations in the urban South allowing a moderate style of black leadership to emerge. The moderates, he says, stress goals that do not maximize race consciousness—as do the goals of militants—but they are more visible and race-related than those of conservatives. Instead of direct action, espoused by militants, and supplication and negotiation from a subordinate position, which characterize conservative methods, moderates attempt to apply pressure through political and legal channels. The preconditions for successful use of these methods—"a certain integration of Negroes into regular political institutions" and "sustained political involvement by large numbers of people at a fairly high level of political sophistication"[74]—are beginning to develop in the South, but Ladd does not think there are yet sufficient bases for effective moderate leadership in much of the rural South and parts of the urban deep South. Ladd's assessment of the decade following the Supreme Court's school desegregation decision is that "direct action literally was the only means available for effectively proomting Negro intersets."[75]

Past disenfranchisement of the southern black population has provided a justification for direct action. However, the recent large increases in black voter registration and voting in the South have given rise to optimistic expectations that black ballots will produce significant changes in their conditions of life, presumably undermining the legitimacy of employing extra-channel tactics. Donald R. Matthews and James W. Prothro's extensive study of southern black politics provides evidence that such optimism is premature. Matthews and Prothro think that blacks will be able to use their votes to alter segregationist practices under certain conditions: when the costs of desegregation for whites are relatively low, when the issue has low visibility in the white community, when the issue is perceived by whites as one of fairness and impartiality, and only when it relates to public, not private, aspects of community relations.[76] But their conclusions about the general effectiveness of black votes as a political resource are quite sobering and deserve to be quoted at length:

Southern Negroes have but one political resource in abundance—votes. Southern whites, most of whom still oppose the Negro's political objectives, tend to have the lion's share of all political resources, including votes. The competition between the two groups for control over public policy will tend to be very uneven unless southern whites fail to use their overwhelmingly superior resources for political ends . . . the more threatened they feel by evidence of rising Negro political power in the future, the more their disproportionate resources will be invested in politics. . . . Racial inequalities in political resources other than the vote, then, probably will result in southern Negroes' receiving less influence over policy than their proportionate share of the electorate would seem to dictate.

Even the vote itself has limitations as a political resource for southern Negroes. They are in a minority almost everywhere in the South. (In the relatively few communities where Negroes are potentially a clear majority of the electorate, white resistance to Negro voting tends to be most vehement, and the barriers to the effective use of the ballot, once achieved, are likely to be greatest.) In order to win, southern Negroes generally have to enter into coalitions with at least some white politicians and voters. In situations characterized by an overwhelming white consensus in favor of segregation biracial coalition-building is almost impossible. A good many Negroes in the South may finally win the right to vote only to find themselves in a more or less permanent political minority.

Where a significant minority of moderate and integrationist whites is in being . . . Negro-white political coalitions are easier to arrange. But opponents of biracial coalitions need merely to take steps to increase the salience of the racial issue to the electorate at large, and the Negro-white coalition usually dissolves. In view of the corrosive effects of the racial issue and the lack of other stable political structures in one-party systems, Negroes in the South may have to rely primarily on joining *ad hoc* coalitions on an issue-by-issue basis. . . .

Such a complex and fluid political situation . . . places heavy demands on political leaders. For one thing, bargaining and negotiations between white and Negro leaders must be almost continuous and call for highly developed political skills. In the second place, followers may become confused by rapidly shifting strategies and alliances. They must be given clear cues and consistent guidance lest they inadvertently throw their votes away. All these things southern Negro leaders must be able to do, and do well, before the Negro vote can have a major impact on public policy, *even in areas where biracial coalitons are formed.*[77]

Among the empirical data on which Matthews and Prothro relied in forming these conclusions was a study by William R. Keech of the black vote as a political resource in Durham, North Carolina. Based on his research in Durham and Tuskeegee, Keech suggests:

The prospects that votes will help eliminate basic inequalities in the life chances of Negroes are contingent on the degree to which appropriate programs fit within the value structure of elites and voting majorities.[78]

Thus, where blacks are in the minority, the degree of social change possible through the electoral process is dependent on the attitudes of *white* leaders and *white* voters. Keech says that black voting brought gains in "fair and just administration of existing laws." However:

. . . with few exceptions, the vote has failed Durham and Tuskeegee Negroes when they sought to change the law in order to eliminate existing discrimination. . . . Because of the effects of past discrimination, Negroes do not have equal opportunity for personal, social and economic advancement even when existing discrimination is eliminated. If social justice demands the eradication of the effects of past discrimination, the vote is even less useful.[79]

Matthews and Prothro also found, in their own research, that there was only a very low correlation between percentage of voting-age blacks registered to vote in southern counties and the presence of school desegregation.[80]

Like other authors who saw that conventional methods were inadequate to improve the blacks' condition, Matthews and Prothro recognized the need for direct action. The best strategy for southern blacks, they suggested, would frequently be to raise their struggles from the local and state level to the national level, where there was more support for black demands (particularly in the big, urban states of the North, which play so crucial a role in presidential elections). Matthews and Prothro asserted that "massive, direct action techniques and civil disobedience" had been primarily responsible for winning national support, at least up until the time they were writing, but they cautioned against the possibility of diminishing returns. Southern blacks might "engage in these practices so often that they will lose majority support in the North, at which point the tactic will become self-defeating."[81] Perhaps this point has already been reached, although more because northern blacks have increased their demands than because southern blacks overused the technique. Nonetheless, it is not clear that direct action has thereby lost its *raison d'etre* in the South. For the picture that Matthews and Prothro drew of southern whites' attitudes and perceptions indicated that many whites were neither willing to accord blacks greater equality nor able to see the need for doing so. Their survey, conducted in 1961, revealed a wide gap between white and black attitudes toward segregation and considerable misperception by each race of the other's attitudes:

Although each race in the South is surprisingly ignorant of the other's point of view, the failure of southern whites to realize how discontented their Negro neighbors are is a more serious stumbling block to racial accommodation. Even in the midst of sit-ins, boycotts, and freedom rides, a majority of southern whites did not realize in 1961 that Negroes were bitterly unhappy about segregation.[82]

Making white southerners more aware and more sympathetic seems a formidable task, particularly in light of the evidence that more education and more political information do not correlate with greater awareness of black attitudes.[83] Given this situation what will induce white southerners to make concessions to black demands? By Matthews and Prothro's own estimate, conventional methods are not promising. National support for southern civil rights goals has dwindled, so non-violent direct action can no longer play the role they saw for it. Widespread racial violence would probably end in the repression of blacks, and massive federal intervention seems unlikely at this time. Thus, perhaps the only feasible course at present—however slim its promise—is for blacks to use civil disobedience and nonviolent direct action to pressure southern whites directly.

Other research reinforces the conclusion that conventional political participation will not produce substantial improvement in black citizens' living conditions. It also indicates that the blacks' dilemma is not restricted to the South. A study by William McCord and John Howard compared two sets of cities, one with substantial (though minority) black representation on city councils and one without much, if any, representation. They expected that black council members might be able to exert some influence over a wide range of municipal affairs, e.g., allocation of city resources, city hiring practices, and allocation of contracts. Their comparison revealed no difference between the two sets of cities. Three of the four cities in each set had experienced riots. The authors were doubtful that municipal representation made much difference in the condition of ghetto life. In two cities in each set, nonwhite unemployment had been greater than 10 percent for over 15 years. Welfare rights organizations had conflicted with authorities, and police action had apparently triggered riots in cities from each set.

In other words, it is not at all clear that there is any measurable difference in ghetto conditions between cities in which Negro representation on the city council is roughly proportional to their numbers in the population and those in which they are underrepresented.[84]

McCord and Howard do not feel that past history gives blacks much "reason to expect tangible gains from political participation."[85]

While James Q. Wilson's study of black politics and leadership in Chicago (*Negro Politics,* published in 1960) expresses scepticism about the effectiveness of direct action, the blacks' situation in Chicago is not one in which conventional political methods are likely to be more fruitful. Wilson believes that there are areas of Chicago race relations in which blacks can do *nothing* to remedy their impotence. On issues like integrated public housing, open occupancy in private housing, and school integration, civic leaders and city officials are either "the willing or unwilling agents of their constituents in racially-tense neighborhoods."[86] Attaining these objectives would have great impact upon and entail considerable costs for the white majority, which does not seem inclined to bear them. A white politician who actively espoused such causes would run serious risks. Nonetheless, in areas involving less controversial goals, Wilson thinks that gains can be made by using direct action to create bargaining resources—that is, the negative inducements of offering an end to mass protest activities in return for concessions.

The literature surveyed in this chapter indicates that within our political system situations will recur where officials are unresponsive to a minority because it is submerged in a large political constituency and has limited rosources. Moreover, the growing scale, complexity, and centralization of our governing institutions suggests that grass-roots political action of the conventional variety can be effective only on a very large scale, which, of course, involves considerable resources. Groups less endowed with resources than, for example, those which supported Senator Eugene McCarthy in 1968, are not really in a position to mount effective grassroots action without employing unconventional tactics which often work more by pressure than persuasion to achieve their effect.

It is the existence of such situations as I have just described and illustrated at some length which ultimately provides the basis for legitimating civil disobedience and nonviolent direct action. To those who argue that the only legitimate means for influencing political decisions in a democracy is persuasion, and that necessity is not an acceptable justification for other tactics, I would reply that they misconceive the nature of liberal-democratic politics. As I have indicated before, the techniques actually considered legitimate in democratic politics frequently do not work by persuasion alone (especially not in the sense of conversion to the persuader's point of view). The "inducements" employed in much political bargaining can be of the negative variety—for example, threats to take action detrimental to the other's interest or to withhold benefits unless certain conditions are met. Yet such tactics are not rejected as illegitimate, while nonviolent direct action, which works in much the same way, often is. Although I have already responded to such criticisms, perhaps some additional comment and restatement would be useful.

The charge of coercion is often levelled against nonviolent direct action as a way of distinguishing it from so-called legitimate techniques. Tom Kahn contends that nonviolent direct action is coercive when it imposes on the "target" a choice between two undesirable alternatives (from the targets' point of view), and makes the target's preference for the *status quo* unrealizable.[87] If we use this definition of coercion, then we must recognize that there are coercive aspects to conventional politics. Politicians frequently pose choices between less desirable alternatives for their opponents, foreclosing the latters' first preference. For example, is the threat to filibuster in order to obtain amendments to a piece of legislation or to defeat it altogether not coercive in the same sense? The proponents of the bill may be "forced" to choose between no bill and a drastically watered-down one. Similar instances are readily conceivable. While controversial, such tactics are generally viewed as a legitimate part of political bargaining.

The fact that threats have to be carried out more often in the case of direct action campaigns does not seem reason for differentiating between political bargaining and nonviolent direct action on the basis of coerciveness. Direct action groups often have relatively little to bargain with because their resources are not significant or highly visible. To make their potential power credible, they may often have to take the threatened action. Thus the imbalance of potential power between contending parties may be one factor responsible for the greater frequency of threats being carried out. Another factor relates to the nature of the demands. In direct action campaigns, the opposing parties may be much farther apart in terms of what is considered minimally acceptable. Politicians, on the other hand, have a lot in common despite policy differences. Second, their interaction tends to be continuous, and compromise is encouraged because of the likelihood of future dealings. In direct action campaigns, the interaction between opponents tends to be more discontinuous and short-term. Finally, there may be an imbalance of security: The protesters may be much less apt than politicians to feel that they can accept defeat or a watered-down compromise.

Ultimately the soundest argument for the legitimacy of civil disobedience and nonviolent direct action is a blend of principle and pragmatism. Liberal-democratic institutions are believed to provide the greatest likelihood in a large polity that public policy will satisfy the needs and desires of the citizenry. No claims to perfection are made for such institutions; rather, it is asserted that they do significantly better in this regard than other kinds of political institutions. However, they apparently do not always provide this kind of general satisfaction for all members. Certain minority groups—socio-economic and ideological—are consistently left out of the political payoffs. The result in the long run is alienation and disaffection from the polity. Widespread tolerance for civil disobedience and nonviolent direct action in general might give the system a second chance in the eyes of at least some of these groups. These tactics do not guarantee that such a group will gain sufficient satisfaction from political institutions to keep it allegiant, to keep it from resorting to more extreme methods, but intolerance and proscription of nonviolent tactics would seem likely to guarantee increased alienation and disaffection. Already such feeling is manifesting itself in more militant tactics for disrupting social institutions, and the frequently repressive responses probably harden, if not enlarge, the opposition to the system. Liberal-democratic values are threatened. Constitutional protections for protesters—freedom of speech, petition, and assembly, scrupulous insistence on procedural safeguards for suspected lawbreakers—and public tolerance for dissent are being eroded as attempts are made to suppress extreme dissenters. The distinctive features of the liberal-democratic polity are becoming blurred.

Critics of my argument may respond that even nonviolent direct action as the nation experienced it in the first half of the 1960s is a threat to the political system, and that the more extreme tactics now being employed merely increase the dangers. Nonetheless, supporters of our system are likely to point to its unique treatment of political opposition and dissent. Liberal democracies do appear to react to dissent differently from other kinds of regimes. A comparison of the way some types of political regimes respond to the tactics of dissenters may help us to see whether liberal democracies *can* treat civil disobedience and nonviolent direct action more tolerantly than other regimes. It would appear that nonviolent direct action has different implications for a political regime depending upon its ideological foundations.

Notes for Chapter VII

1. Even among severely disadvantaged groups, the gains to be expected from extra-channel tactics may be outweighed by the costs, and this is a serious problem in attempting to mobilize such a constituency.

2. For example, Nelson W. Polsby and Aaron B. Wildavsky, *Presidential Elections* (New York: Charles Scribner's Sons, 1964), p. 196.

3. Moreover, recent work in rational decision-making theory suggests that it is not always possible to order uniquely the preferences of a population based on the criteria of equal votes and majority rule. The argument is too complex to go into here. It assumes that individuals order their preferences in a particular way, and this may or may not be true in real life. See Robert A. Dahl, *A Preface to Democratic Theory* (Chicago: University of Chicago Press, 1956), pp. 42–43. Dahl cites Kenneth Arrow's *Social Choices and Individual Values.*

4. Dahl, Chapter 4.

5. Donald E. Stokes and Warren E. Miller, "Party Government and the Saliency of Congress," *Public Opinion Quarterly*, 26 (Winter, 1962), 543.

6. William Buchanan, "An Inquiry into Purposive Voting," *Journal of Politics*, 18 (May, 1956), 291.

7. A cross-national survey of political attitudes by Gabriel A. Almond and Sidney Verba (Princeton: Princeton University Press, 1963).

8. It is difficult to say, on the basis of the evidence presented, whether the choice represents a preference based on actual experience or merely reflects the relative salience of the three methods for the respondents.

9. Raymond A. Bauer, Ithiel de Sola Pool, and Lewis A. Dexter (New York: Atherton Press, 1963), Chapter 29.

10. Lewis A. Dexter, "The Representative and His District," reprinted *in* Robert L. Peabody and Nelson W. Polsby, eds., *New Perspectives on the House of Representatives* (Chicago: Rand McNally, 1963), p. 11.

11. The seemingly high visibility of dissident groups on such issues may be partly a result of the possibility that other dissident groups which are concerned with less salient issues are more successful in using conventional methods of exerting political influence. The latter have to resort less frequently to unconventional methods which tend to gain considerable publicity. An example of such a dissident group using conventional lobbying techniques with great effectiveness is the National Rifle Association. While public opinion seems to favor more stringent gun control, legislation, this interest group has been able to prevent it. Gun control, while temporarily a "hot" issue after the assassinations of Martin Luther King and Robert F. Kennedy, is not comparable in salience to the Viet Nam war, civil rights, or related issues such as poverty.

12. Lewis A. Froman, *Congressmen and Their Constituencies* (Chicago: Rand McNally, 1963), p. 10.

13. These districts rank higher than others on three indicators, percent nonwhite, percent urban, and

population density; and lower on one, percent owner-occupied dwelling units (see Froman, p. 120).

14. Warren E. Miller and Donald E. Stokes, "Constituency Influence in Congress," *American Political Science Review*, 57 (March, 1963), 56.

15. The methodology of this study is rather complex because the constituency samples were not originally drawn so as to be representative of the constituency electorates. The study began with a nationally representative sample which was then broken down into Congressional districts. While the districts were weighted to increase the reliability of the constituency estimates, it is not clear how reliable the determinations of constituency majority preference are on any of the particular issues. There is also the possibility that very high correlations on the civil rights issue area in southern districts were responsible for most of the divergence of the results here.

16. Stokes and Miller, "Party Government and the Saliency of Congress." In their other article (footnote 14), however, the authors suggest that even a small minority's awareness of his position can be important, because small changes in his support could affect his political survival. On the other hand, other voting studies indicate that the most informed voters tend to be most partisan and least likely to switch sides. I have not discussed nonconstituency influences on Congressmen, such as interactions with colleagues and party organization in Congress, but these may also be important factors in the stands he takes.

17. As described by James Q. Wilson, *Negro Politics* (Glencoe, Illinois: The Free Press, 1960).

18. *Ibid.*, p. 100.

19. The likely response of critics to this dilemma is that democratic politics means coalition-building; somehow the minority group must find allies within the majority. This depends on the degree of homogeneity within the majority. What Wilson suggests is true in Chicago— "that success in attaining (liberal measures) is closely related to the extent to which there are powerful white liberal groups in the community" (*Ibid.*)—would be even truer in the South except that such "powerful white liberal groups" do not exist. black leaders must try to cooperate with white moderates, who, as Lewis Killian and Charles Grigg emphasize in *Racial Crisis in America* (Englewood Cliffs, N.J.: Prentice-Hall, 1964), are moderate segregationists. The situation of the southern black will be explored more fully below.

20. Seymour Martin Lipset, *Political Man* (Garden City, N.Y.: Doubleday, 1959), p. 184. Formerly, blacks tended to vote less than whites, but this has changed in recent years.

21. Robert E. Lane, *Political Life* (Glencoe, Illinois: The Free Press, 1959), p. 67.

22. *Ibid.*, p. 73.

23. Angus Campbell, Philip E. Converse, Warren E. Miller, and Donald E. Stokes, *The American Voter* (New York: John Wiley and Sons, 1960), p. 479.

24. *Ibid.*, p. 105.

25. The "local competents" were also more likely to be "national

competents." Almond and Verba, pp. 204–208.

26. Almond and Verba say that the same pattern appeared with respect to national competency and the national level of government, but no specific figures are cited. *Ibid.*, p. 187.

27. Robert E. Agger, Marshall N. Goldstein, and Stanley A. Pearl, "Political Cynicism: Measurement and Meaning," *Journal of Politics*, 23 (August, 1961), 494.

28. Edgar Litt, "Political Cynicism and Political Futility," *Journal of Politics*, 25 (May, 1963), 315.

29. The findings concerning other attitudinal variables, as they are linked with SES characteristics and with political activity, are more ambiguous. Angus Campbell, "The Passive Citizen," *Acta Sociologica*, 6, Fasc. 1–2 (1962), 14; Wayne E. Thompson and John E. Horton, "Political Alienation as a Force in Political Action," *Social Forces*, 38 (March, 1960), 195; and Fredric Templeton, "Alienation and Political Participation: Some Research Findings," *Public Opinion Quarterly*, 30 (Summer, 1966), 256.

30. This is not to suggest that low SES persons are more easily mobilized for direct action than they are for conventional participation. Nonetheless, the civil rights movement is dramatic evidence that large numbers of such persons can be involved if there are unusually intense stimuli. Civil disobedience protests by small groups of activists played an important role in creating such stimuli.

31. Some political scientists have stressed the potential dangers in rapid, mass influxes of normally apolitical persons into politics; the fact that the latter have little understanding of and information about politics, combined with low familiarity with and weak adherence to democratic principles, as well as a short-range time perspective and a tendency to view the world in simplified black-and-white terms, makes them susceptible to demagogic and undemocratic appeals. While it may be debated whether the civil rights movement today may be giving rise to such excesses, the movement as a whole would seem to indicate that "masses" can be rapidly mobilized to seek democratic objectives in self-limited and restrained, if uncustomary, ways.

32. It should be pointed out that lack of direct responsibility to the public may be an advantage if the official is willing to take an action unpopular with the majority.

33. Arthur W. Bromage, *Political Representation in Metropolitan Agencies*, Michigan Government Studies, no. 42 (Ann Arbor, Michigan: Institute of Public Administration, University of Michigan, 1962), p. 47.

34. *Ibid.*, p. 97. Direct election is not necessarily the best solution to the problem of responsibility to the public. If there is a proliferation of special service districts in a metropolitan area, the public will be asked to take part in the election of large numbers of officials, increasing what is already considered a large electoral burden. The result will be low turnout and uninformed voting; in these special service district elections, it may prove even harder to mobilize a protest vote. Also, control over the functions of a metropolitan government will be fragmented, preventing the development of unified planning

and programs. Thus the potential gains of direct election may be more than offset by such costs. Giving elected officials greater authority to control their appointees is one way to ensure greater accountability, but centralization is often resisted by politicians.

35. Roberta S. Sigel and H. Paul Friesema, "Urban Community Leaders' Knowledge of Public Opinion," *Western Political Quarterly*, 18 (December, 1965), 882.

36. The authors define a need as referring to a "consequential, long-range requirement which if not met impairs community health"; a desire was more superficial. Thus, for example, "leaders thought parents would give top priority to integrated schools but parents gave star athletes top priority." Such categorizations as the authors engaged in can present problems of "objectivity," but at least in the case of this example, the distinction seems reasonable. The authors suggest that "it is precisely because we have to assume that on most issues the general public may be more desire- than need-oriented that groups of community leaders play a crucial role in decision-making for the general welfare." However, it is fair to ask in what way community leaders are representative of the constituency they presumably speak for; they may be more need-oriented but their way of defining needs may be dictated by their own values, by the conceptions with which they feel comfortable. Thus, some black leaders may believe that integration speaks to their people's need; others may think black control of local schools is more relevant to the average black child's needs.

37. Murray B. Levin, *The Alienated Voter* (New York: Holt, Rinehart and Winston, 1960), p. 63.

38. *Ibid.*

39. Harold Kaplan, *Urban Renewal Politics* (New York: Columbia University Press, 1963), p. 39.

40. Significantly, the area affected failed to gain allies in other parts of Newark.

41. Herbert J. Gans, *The Urban Villagers* (New York: The Free Press, 1962), p. 298.

42. *Ibid.*, p. 296.

43. *Ibid.*, p. 285.

44. Peter H. Rossi and Robert A. Dentler, *The Politics of Urban Renewal: The Chicago Findings* (New York: The Free Press of Glencoe, 1961), p. 285.

45. *Ibid.*, p. 287.

46. Though the authors maintain that the *specific* details would not have been as satisfactory to the public.

47. Rossi and Dentler, p. 212.

48. *Ibid.*

49. *Ibid.*, p. 219.

50. *Ibid.*, pp. 235–236. The importance of established organization and a broad constituency was underscored by the fact that opposition from the Catholic Church Committee on Conservation and Urban Renewal delayed final Council approval for five months, despite the late date of its public criticisms of the Plan. City officials waited until they assured themselves that the Committee did not have the unified support of the Catholic clergy and laity. Roman Catholics are the largest single denomination in Chicago. Many city

officials are Catholics and "all . . . are sensitive to the grass-roots and organizational pressures" that criticisms of the Church Committee might have created (*Ibid.*, p. 225).

51. James Q. Wilson, "The Strategy of Protest: Problems of Negro Civic Action," *Journal of Conflict Resolution*, 5 (September, 1961), 292.

52. *Ibid.*, p. 294.

53. *Ibid.*, p. 296.

54. Again, the civil rights movement is a case in point; support for voting rights bills is considerably greater than for attempts to eliminate *de facto* segregation.

55. John B. Keeley, "Moses on the Green," *in* Edwin A. Bock, ed., *State and Local Government: A Casebook*, published for the Inter-University Case Program (University, Alabama: University of Alabama, 1963), pp. 25–33.

56. However, one of the councilmen helped create additional resources by his calls for a potentially embarrassing investigation. This became a negative inducement to the Mayor and his Commissioner to change their position.

57. Robert A. Dentler, "Barriers to Northern School Desegregation," *in* Talcott Parsons and Kenneth B. Clark, eds., *The Negro American* (Boston: Houghton Mifflin, 1966), pp. 472–490.

58. "Schemes like rezoning, district reorganization, pairing, free transfer, and open enrollment, to have any effect on the problem as a whole, must be applied in system-wide and combined fashion." *Ibid.*, p. 480.

59. Lewis Killian and Charles Grigg, *Racial Crisis in America* (Englewood Cliffs, N.J.: Prentice-Hall, 1964), p. 29.

60. *Ibid.*, p. 136. The authors seemingly ignore the possibility that demonstrations exert influence by the disruption they may entail.

61. Killian and Grigg's detailed study of a biracial committee in one Florida city revealed that white members were concerned with the community's image as it affected local economic interests, not with segregation as a moral issue.

62. Killian and Grigg, p. 139.

63. *Ibid.*, pp. 77–78 (emphasis added). A black leader who continues to participate in militant protest activities cannot function effectively on the committee because white members will reject him. The existence of the committee itself may then be threatened since other black members are forced to take sides. Black leaders on the committee can leave the dynamic leadership role to others, but by doing so, they leave themselves open to challenge from blacks without a similar commitment to racial harmony. When such potential challengers create issues which appear on the committee's agenda, the black leaders whose job is negotiating may appear to be selling out. If they refuse to negotiate, the committee is undermined. Thus it is difficult for black leaders to play both roles—member of a biracial team and activist in the struggle with the white community. Wilson, in "The Strategy of Protest," recommends a division of labor between black protest leaders and bargainers, but he recognizes that cooperation may be difficult, for those filling the two roles must agree on goals and on when to compromise,

although they have different constituencies and compete for the limited resources of the black community.

64. Daniel C. Thompson, *The Negro Leadership Class* (Englewood Cliffs, N.J.: Prentice-Hall, 1963), p. 22.

65. *Ibid.*, p. 106.

66. *Ibid.*, p. 119.

67. *Ibid.*, p. 106.

68. *Ibid.*

69. *Ibid.*, p. 112.

70. *Ibid.*, p. 135.

71. Everett C. Ladd, *Negro Political Leadership in the South* (Ithaca, N.Y.: Cornell University Press, 1966), p. 173.

72. Ladd says that this generalization must be qualified. See *Ibid.*, p. 174.

73. *Ibid.*, p. 272.

74. *Ibid.*, pp. 212, 215.

75. *Ibid.*, p. 95.

76. Donald R. Matthews and James W. Prothro, *Negroes and the New Southern Politics* (New York: Harcourt, Brace and World, 1966), pp. 479–480.

77. *Ibid.*, pp. 478–479 (authors' emphasis).

78. William R. Keech, *The Impact of Negro Voting: The Role of the Vote in the Quest for Equality* (Chicago: Rand McNally, 1968), p. 108.

79. *Ibid.*, p. 107.

80. Donald R. Matthews and James W. Prothro, "Stateways versus Folkways: Critical Factors in Southern Reactions to *Brown v. Board of Education*," in Gottfried Dietze (ed.), *Essays on the American Constitution* (Englewood Cliffs, N.J.; Prentice-Hall, 1964), p. 152.

81. Matthews and Prothro, *Negroes and the New Southern Politics,* p. 477.

82. *Ibid.*, p. 354. For the data, see pp. 332, 337, and 352.

83. *Ibid.*, pp. 354–355. The authors did find that more education, information, and contact with blacks did correlate with more moderate or integrationist sentiment, leading them to suggest that these factors contributed to the formation of such sentiments.

84. William McCord and John Howard, "Collective Styles of Life," *in* William McCord, John Howard, Bernard Friedberg, and Edwin Harwood, *Life Styles in the Black Ghetto* (New York: W. W. Norton, 1969), p. 289.

85. *Ibid.*, p. 287.

86. Wilson, *Negro Politics*, p. 287.

87. Tom Kahn, "Direct Action and Democratic Values," *Dissent*, 13 (January-February, 1966), 25. He also suggests that forms of direct action may be "self-expressive" rather than coercive.

VIII

Regime Response
to Political Dissent
and Civil Disobedience

ONE CHARACTERISTIC OF LIBERAL DEMOCRACY said to distinguish it from
other types of political systems is the wide latitude given to freedom
of expression. Broad guarantees of protection extend to political dissent,
as well as to other expressions of nonconformity. Proponents of liberal
democracy have defended freedom of expression on the grounds that
it is functional for society; it aids the search for truth; it promotes
diversity and prevents social ossification. More specifically, political
dissent—open opposition and political criticism—has been defended
for its contribution to responsible government. Theorists who define
the essence of modern democracy as "free competition for a free
vote" recognize political opposition as a *sine qua non*. Obviously, unless
there is some right to dissent, there can be no viable opposition.
Political opposition creates the possibility of responsiveness; if the
"ins" ignore the people's wishes, they may find themselves replaced
by the "outs." However, the defense of dissent can be extended beyond
the minimum necessary to ensure that a competing political party exists.
The existence of an alternative party implies a choice, but the differences

Notes to this chapter will be found on pages 295–298.

267

between the two parties determine how meaningful the choice actually is. Party opposition is a necessary condition of political responsibility, but it is not a sufficient one. Even when two parties are *close* competitors, one cannot conclude that government necessarily will be more responsive to its constituency than when competition is weak.[1] Dissent—both within and without the circumference of party competition—can contribute directly to the quality of governance. It means criticising what are thought to be mistaken and/or unpopular policies and advocating new and better ones. The possibility of being replaced by the political opposition compels the government of the day to take public reactions into consideration. Thus, public criticism[2] which may sway the voters must be answered; government decisions must be defended with plausible arguments. Certainly, if one believes that liberal democracy should encourage the citizen to do more than carry out his "task" of deciding "who shall decide what government shall do," an enlarged right of dissent seems advisable. Yet despite these salutary effects, defenders of dissent usually have not maintained that this right is entitled to absolute protection: No freedom can be absolute. Freedoms of equal value may come into conflict; in order to give the maximum latitude to each that is compatible with enjoyment of the other, the competing claims must be balanced. Or, it may be security and freedom which conflict. Freedom to dissent can claim no exemption from the necessary process of balancing. In practice, however, political dissent seems to be more vulnerable to suppression because many think it constitutes a greater threat to governmental stability than other expressions of nonconformity or the exercise of other freedoms.

If it is true that *even* liberal-democratic societies are more apt to restrict *political* forms of dissent, then civil disobedience, which constitutes a first step beyond legal methods of protest, seems especially vulnerable. Civil disobedience makes special demands on any political system for the following reason: Although it is a departure from conventional forms of political action, such as legal picketing, lobbying, electioneering, and petitioning, it is consciously self-limited. Its practitioners hope that the regime will distinguish it from revolution and subversion, despite its being extraordinary. The intent is not overthrow, but the regime may fail to see that or willfully ignore it. What kind of regimes can make a distinction between unconventional (sometimes illegal) forms of political protest and revolution and subversion? What regimes feel and in actuality are less threatened by such actions? In theory and practice, are liberal-democratic regimes more capable of tolerating civil disobedience than nondemocratic regimes? If so, what is the explanation?

To answer these questions, it is necessary to examine a more general question: How do liberal-democratic and nondemocratic regimes respond to dissent in general? The following chart presents an impressionistic view of the ways in which certain types of political systems differ with respect to dissent.

| | TYPE OF POLITICAL SYSTEM[3] | | |
Variable	Liberal-Democratic	Modern Autocratic	Quasi-Totalitarian
1. Scope of permissible dissent (legal restrictions and political conventions):			
Content	larger	smaller	smallest
Methods	larger	smaller	smallest
2. Perceived (by rulers) threat from proscribed actions involving dissent.	lesser	greater	greater
3. Severity of sanctions against proscribed dissent.	lesser	greater	greater
4. Difficulty dissenters face in reaching an audience.	least	greater	greater
5. Transition from popular acquiescence to open resistance and violence.	slower	faster	fastest
6. Constraints upon potential dissenters imposed by ideological commitments and material dependence.	moderate	low	high

No attempt will be made here to examine large numbers of cases to test these generalizations about the variables. Instead, I will present some examples of regime responses to the tactics of dissent to illustrate the general propositions and to provide some suggestions, albeit sketchy, for answers to our original questions. First, some discussion of the variables seems warranted.

Some nondemocratic regimes readily equate nonpolitical expressions of nonconformity with political dissent and deviation, thereby widening the range of potentially proscribable behavior. Yet in all systems, democratic or not, there seems to be a point at which political dissent is equated with sedition, subversion, or revolution. At this point, rulers perceive it as a threat either to the legitimacy of their holding power or to the legitimacy of the system of governance.[4] Nonetheless, dissent which is subjectively and objectively threatening to rulers in one system will not (and should not) distress rulers in another. Several factors seem to be at work here: One is the scope of dissent legitimated by the political culture, including general attitudes toward dissent as well as explicit legal restrictions. For example, there may exist a system commitment to protecting a broad range of protest behavior; this would affect the way in which specific legal restrictions are interpreted. The scope of dissent has two components—content and methods; both may independently affect the regime's perception of a threat. For example, unconventional tactics may create considerable consternation; however, if the protest's objective is of little import, the regime may not be especially distressed, whatever methods are employed. If the content controverts a basic principle of the political culture or the "ruling ideology," then even very limited methods of protest may be proscribed. The scope of dissent legitimated by the political culture presumably affects the response of both rulers and ruled. However, the political culture may be bifurcated, and what the rulers and some citizens consider unacceptable may be considered legitimate by others, and vice versa. This can occur where one political culture has been superimposed on another, for example, as in the East European Communist nations, or where regimes of radically different character have succeeded each other and no political consensus has developed, as in Spain.

The scope of permissible dissent seems closely related to the regime's willingness to permit social, economic, and political change which is not planned and directed from the centers of authority.

Conceivably, a regime may want to respond positively to protests and complaints and, simultaneously, retain control of any basic change that occurs in society. This presents a problem: If the regime allows some degree of dissent, it may have difficulty drawing the line against autonomous change. Once people feel they have the right to protest, they may begin to think they also have the right to initiate change. Moreover, those who protest may change the behavior of their audience. To distinguish dissenting from initiating change is not necessarily simple. Therefore, a regime that commits itself to responsiveness limits its control over change. A stable *modus vivendi* being hard to find, regimes which prefer to avoid this problem may prohibit open dissent to begin with. Therefore, one would expect the scope of dissent to be narrow where autonomous change is not considered tolerable.

The distribution and intensity of discontent within the system also seems to influence the regime's perception of dissent. Where intense dissatisfaction is not prevalent or is only found concentrated in circumscribed areas, even very extreme forms of protest may evoke little sympathetic response from the general population. For example, violent direct action in this country seems to attract only those persons who are very alienated from the system. On the other hand, where intense dissatisfaction is widespread, relatively restrained forms of protest may catalyze opposition which previously was latent—as did a student demonstration in Hungary (in October, 1956), public meetings of anti-apartheid organizations in South Africa, petitions and marches in Spain, and peaceful civil rights demonstrations in certain black ghettoes. Assuming that a regime is aware of the discontent, its perception of specific acts of protest (in this context) will be affected. If the people are near their "boiling-point," a regime may find any form of open protest objectionable.

The severity of sanctions a regime imposes is closely connected to the magnitude of the perceived threat. Indeed, it may sometimes be difficult to determine that a particular occurrence of dissent is perceived as threatening except by the fact that sanctions are imposed, and the perceived degree of the threat may be revealed only by the severity of the sanctions. However, a regime's choice of sanctions may be influenced by other considerations as well. For example, different types of regimes may react differently to individual acts of dissent which they do not regard as especially threatening in themselves. The protest act may be illegal, and most regimes publicly proclaim that law violations should be punished. Yet some regimes may not wish to discourage protests of a similar nature that are legal. Thus, they may be lenient. Other regimes may prefer to discourage any protest. This would influence their choice of sanctions. For example, American judges occasionally give a defendant in a civil disobedience case a suspended sentence or a nominal fine. They thereby honor a system commitment to protect (and even encourage) *certain* forms of expression. In contrast, the sentencing of several Soviet writers to substantial prison terms at hard labor for having their critical works of fiction published in the West seems to have been intended to inhibit dissent among Russian intellectuals. It seems doubtful that the Soviet leaders considered these writers' works in themselves a significant threat to the regime's stability.

The scope of permissible dissent has considerable influence on the difficulty which dissenters encounter in reaching the public. The content and the methods which are specifically outlawed or considered illegitimate partly determine who can reach an audience and how this can be done. Some years ago, when the government of Northern Rhodesia wished to repress all propaganda against discriminatory treatment of natives, it required all large-scale meetings to be authorized in advance.[5] By this blanket regulation of "method," the government could, whenever it chose, deny dissenters on this issue the opportunity to reach a large audience. Yet one must look beyond scope to aspects of the political and social environment which inhibit or facilitate dissent. If, for example, virtually all resources necessary to publish or broadcast are inaccessible to unauthorized persons, it may be nearly impossible to reach an audience of any size. If state police surveillance is widespread, individual relationships of trust and confidence, without which organizing dissent on any scale is extremely difficult, are likely to be rare. In other words, a regime may inhibit activities and monopolize resources which are preconditions of dissent. In a country such as ours, a similar phenomenon may occur because the mass media are largely controlled by a small number of persons and organizations. Here the government has had to regulate the use of the media, specifically radio and television, in order to prevent private denials of certain facilities to political opposition.

An environment which inhibits dissent by legal restrictions, monopoly of media resources, police surveillance, and so forth may crucially influence public reaction to open dissent when it occurs. Where virtually no open dissent is permitted and where considerable latent disaffection exists, the sudden public appearance of even limited forms of protest may result in a rapid transition from apparent acquiescence to open and violent resistance. In effect, public protest communicates to a discontented populace that dissatisfaction exists; it tells people that others feel as they do; whereas before they could not be sure of this— now they are no longer isolated. The fact that protest has reached public view, because the authorities either chose not to suppress it, or failed to detect it in time, probably will be interpreted as a sign of regime weakness, not as responsiveness or liberality. In this context, limited forms of dissent may be able to generate widespread resistance. Therefore, *any* dissent may be extremely threatening to a regime which desires to suppress all dissent to the degree it can. Where a wide spectrum of protest is permitted, the transition will probably be more gradual; airing grievances opens the possibility of remedial action by the regime, and, at least, it reduces tension. If a regime *generally* permits certain kinds of dissent, it probably intends to be responsive to some degree. How responsive is something for the protesters to find out; but, having opportunities to express themselves legally, they probably will not feel compelled immediately to go over to open resistance.[6]

Political dissent usually requires persons with literary, organizational, or agitational skills; at least, it usually must be instigated by such persons. Thus, the degree to which such persons—usually intellectuals —are bound to the regime or the political system by material or ideological considerations influences the incidence and course of dissent. Whether or not social pluralism is a necessary concomitant of liberal democracy, there seems to be some evidence that some types of nondemocratic regimes are less tolerant of social pluralism. For example, quasi-totalitarian regimes inculcate a political orthodoxy, restrict associations, and often provide few career opportunities for intellectuals outside regime-controlled activities.

South Africa provides a good illustration of how narrow the scope of dissent can be in a nondemocratic regime. The Afrikaner-dominated regimes consider the doctrines of white supremacy and apartheid to be fundamental principles of South African society. No public disagreement in this area is acceptable; any dissent is viewed as extremely threatening. As a result, virtually no method of protest against these doctrines remains legal. Sanctions have frequently been severe, despite the avowedly reformist nature of much of the protest.

The Suppression of Communism Act, passed in 1950, has been the cornerstone of the government's campaign against anti-apartheid dissenters. In creating the crime of promoting communism, the act very broadly defined the content and methods of proscribed dissent:

The crime of promoting communism not only includes the advocacy or use of unconstitutional techniques for the complete transformation of the social structure; its statutory meaning has been extended in South Africa to cover gradual non-revolutionary change within the constitutional framework if furthered by illegal acts. Communism is defined generally in the act as Marxian socialism and, in particular, as any doctrine or scheme which aims at the dictatorship of the proletariat, or "*which aims at bringing about any political, industrial, social or economic change* within the Union by the promotion of disturbance or disorder, by unlawful acts or omissions or by means which include the promotion of disturbance or disorder, or such acts or omissions or threats."[7]

Although this act was aimed primarily at resistance to apartheid, it gave the regime—particularly in conjunction with other laws making specific acts illegal—the power to reduce drastically both the content and methods of permissible dissent concerned with virtually any form of social change.

The course of the South African regime's increasingly repressive actions against dissenters on apartheid indicates the lengths to which a regime will go that refuses to permit autonomous change, in this instance in a particular social institution. Such a regime has to narrow the scope of permissible protest because legitimate means can be used to organize illegitimate protest. Thus, even hitherto permissible protest may have to be proscribed. In 1950, the campaign of the South African government began, as noted above, by very broadly defining the offense of promoting communism, which involved unlawful acts or acts promoting or threatening disturbance. In response to nonviolent direct action, the regime also subjected civil disobedience to special penalties. At the same time, it placed harsh penalties on acts of *organizing* civil disobedience. It also used provisions of earlier legislation to restrict the activities of the anti-apartheid movement: Meetings were prohibited; other gatherings were roughly dispersed; leaders were prevented from visiting certain areas and/or banished to remote places. Certain organizations were declared unlawful, and the administration was given legal authority to force their members to resign. Although the South African regime's record of progressively restricting more and more limited forms of protest is not chronologically perfect, legislation in the 1960s demonstrates its determination to deny the dissenters even very conventional political means. In 1962, a bill was passed making it an act of sabotage to paint on any building wall "words which call for the grant of increased political rights for the African people."[8] Conviction requires a sentence of not less than five years. A 1963 law allows the Minister of Justice to prohibit a person who, in his estimation, "is likely to address a meeting called for the purpose of protesting against Apartheid" from being absent from his home, or from "communicating with any person, during such period as the Minister may specify."[9] In 1966, the Minister of the Interior introduced a bill in Parliament which "would abolish multiracial political parties and make illegal any mixed groups that propagate, *discuss*, *study* or encourage *political views*."[10] By now, virtually any activity that can even remotely be connected with protest on this particularly sensitive issue has been outlawed.

By refusing to permit any dissent on apartheid, the South African regime has forced dissenters to go outside the range of reformist techniques and resort to means that are more properly called revolutionary. In November, 1961, some members of the African National Congress formed an organization—called Umkonto, or "The Spear of the Nation" —whose purpose was to commit sabotage. One of the founders and active members of Umkonto justified the resort to sabotage on the grounds that there appeared to be no way for the Africans to struggle successfully without violence against the principle of white supremacy. He said, "Fifty years of non-violence had brought the African people nothing but more and more repressive legislation, and fewer and fewer rights."[11] The founders contended that violence was bound to occur in any case, due to the government's policy; they claimed:

Unless responsible leadership was given to channel and control the feelings of our people, there would be outbreaks of terrorism which would produce an intensity of bitterness and hostility between the various races of this country which is not produced even by war.[12]

Perhaps these predictions are unduly pessimistic; they may be only rationalizations for Umkonto's stand, but they are evidence that at least some of the anti-apartheid dissenters no longer think that reformist methods are feasible.[13]

Events in Hungary preceding the Revolution support the same thesis: A regime which is not prepared to be responsive must narrow the scope of dissent and act repressively in the long run. When the Hungarian Communist Party liquidated the New Course (a policy of liberalization) and ousted Imre Nagy from the premiership in 1955, the Party writers initially attempted to make the leadership aware of popular disaffection. However, the leadership responded with repression, seizing an issue of a literary journal and dismissing its editor, as well as several staff members of a Party newspaper. This was the signal for more open opposition. In October, 1955, "the most prominent members of the Writers' Association sent the Central Committee a memorandum [endorsed by the Party cell of the Association] protesting against these and other 'brutal' interventions in cultural life."[14] They asked the Central Committee to "suppress the antidemocratic methods by which organs and functionaries conduct affairs, methods that disfigure the Party's cultural policy, paralyze our intellectual life," and urged it to "reconsider the abusive administrative measures and guarantee the writers, journalists, and other intellectual workers a climate of Communist frankness and honesty."[15] The Party's reaction was harsh:

The Central Committee meeting in December stigmatized the writers' actions as seditious, and the signatories of the memorandum (about sixty in number) were put under the strongest pressure to withdraw their signatures. The majority did, but not so the most prominent ones. . . . In December, the unrepentant writers were called before a plenary session of the Budapest Party "Activists" and were treated to long speeches of vilification amidst the howls of an enraged mob of five thousand. The leaders of the writers' opposition expected arrest. . . . No police measures were taken, however.[16]

The form of protest—an intra-Party communication, strongly worded, no doubt—was limited. But the regime had no desire to be responsive and equated dissent with sedition.

A nonviolent direct action campaign in Northern Rhodesia provides further illustration of the way a consciously unresponsive (to certain grievances) regime seems impelled to increase restrictions upon the methods of protest. In the early 1950s, the Zambian African National Congress (ANC) organized this campaign to protest racial discrimination against natives. More limited forms of protest had not produced any change. When the campaign began, volunteers were sent in groups of 10 to 100 to seek equal treatment at preselected business establishments. These businesses discriminated by imposing restrictions upon native customers which were not applied to whites. Kenneth Kaunda, one of the Congress leaders, says that police arrested and beat thousands during the five years of the campaign. The regime also took action against activities which—in the abstract—were less provocative. Police permission was required in order to hold large-scale meetings; specified procedures had to be followed by the ANC. Many of the ANC leaders were banned from speaking, and were arrested or harassed in other ways. When the ANC initiated a campaign to boycott the Benson Constitution, under which a few Africans had been given the franchise, the Governor, on learning of its success, prohibited all public meetings of the movement. Petitions for removal of the ban were ignored, so the ANC finally notified the Governor of its intent to defy the ban. As the Congress proceeded to act, over 100 leaders "were rounded up and sent into rustication in remote areas." Kaunda and some of his colleagues "were rearrested and charged with 'conspiring to effect an unlawful purpose' and sentenced accordingly."[17] Previously legitimate activities apparently had to be proscribed because they were potential means of organizing illegal (or even legal) activities which were considered extremely threatening.

Contemporary Spain provides a good example of a regime in which the scope of dissent is so limited that practically any form of open protest is illegal. As a result, much of the protest focuses on the right of political opposition and related freedoms. For example, the government has established official organizations in many spheres of activity— in politics, in the economy, in education; any other organizations are illegal. The desire for autonomous organizations has frequently been the source of open protest. The usual regime response seems to be suppression—either directly through police force or indirectly through the threat of imposing legal sanctions; even rather limited methods of dissent have been subjected to sanctions. This is another case of a regime which does not intend to be responsive to proposals for reform which are autonomously initiated. It is clear that General Franco wants to control the direction and pace of any change in Spanish society.

In the spring of 1966, students at the University of Barcelona began to press for recognition of their right to form student organizations free from governmental supervision. According to the *New York Times* there were several weeks of disturbances at the University, culminating in a police raid on campus to break up a student meeting called to protest the expulsion of several students. Many of the students were beaten, while a Jesuit priest, who was also a professor, was severely clubbed. Subsequently, the University chancellor requested the closing of the school. As a result of these events, sixty-seven professors sent a communication to the Minister of Education protesting the government's actions and asking for the chancellor's dismissal, reinstatement of the students, and official recognition of the illegal student organization. Not only did the regime use force to put an end to illegal student activities, but even the petition of the faculty was viewed with suspicion and its signers subjected to the possibility of legal penalty. "The Ministry of Education's response was to send written notification to the 67 signers of the document instructing them to appear before the investigating judge for questioning."[18]

On several other occasions in the last few years, the Franco regime has indicated that it does not consider rather conventional forms of political action legitimate, despite its ostensible intention to democratize Spanish politics. In November, 1966, the Spanish Parliament approved a new constitution designed to implement this intention, but in December, the *New York Times* reported: "The regime's new technique is one of subtle intimidation; of prison terms or fines after scrupulously correct judicial proceedings and of skillful innuendo designed to link the democratic opposition with Communism."[19] Although Franco "acknowledged the need for differences of opinion and for dialogue under the refurbished system," he did not rescind the long-standing ban on political parties. According to the same issue of the *New York Times*, "the regime interpreted [this in action] to mean that the basic national policy was not to be questioned and that to do so indicated a subversive attitude." Apparently, the Franco regime was manifesting the same tendency to equate dissent and subversion that was evident in South Africa. When about 200 opposition leaders sent a petition to the government, requesting a postponement of the national referendum on the new constitution (they wanted time to organize an opposition campaign), the collective petition was returned because it deviated from the prescribed form; only individual petitions were considered legitimate. At the same time, the dissenters and their organizations were vigorously attacked in the government-controlled media, as well as in the privately-owned press. "The signers of the petitions were described as unpatriotic, and comments on them were juxtaposed with the news that exiled Communist leaders also opposed the referendum."[20]

Although relatively limited forms of dissent have been proscribed and force has been employed to suppress demonstrations by students, priests, and workers, the Spanish government apparently has not made strenuous attempts to prevent dissenters from reaching potential supporters among the disaffected population. Illegal organizations, particularly in labor, are rather extensive, and are more powerful than their legal, official counterparts. This may be a reflection of the autocratic, as opposed to quasi-totalitarian, nature of the Franco regime. In other words, while the regime has attempted to restrict participation in the political arena to a limited number of persons, and to suppress debate on certain issues, it has not really attempted to structure the whole society. The regime has not won enough allegiance from key groups in the population—for example, intellectuals, clergy, and labor leaders—to prevent opposition leadership from springing up. In accord with the view that Spain is autocratic, rather than quasi-totalitarian, is the fact that opposition leaders have opportunities to support themselves materially in ways not directly dependent upon the regime. Viewing Spain as an example of a modern autocratic regime suggests that the possibilities for dissent may be somewhat greater there than in a quasi-totalitarian regime. This difference could be at least partly responsible for the fact that no rapid transition from acquiescence to open opposition and resistance has occurred on a mass scale in Spain. In other words, the existence of an infrastructure of illegal opposition organizations may be acting as a restraining factor. At the same time, the signs of a prospective liberalization—though clearly limited in nature—are perhaps communicating to the disaffected that the regime's grasp on power is weakening. The last few years have witnessed a number of demonstrations, sit-down strikes, and other forms of social and political protest. There have been arrests, violent clashes with police, and restrictive measures such as the suspension of civil liberties for limited periods. The repressive responses are an attempt to prevent the existing disaffection from breaking out all over the society, but the regime seems to be finding it difficult to cope with the problem of controlling the democratization of Spanish society. Since Franco apparently does wish to maintain firm control over any liberalization, he may think that any concessions to proposals for change will encourage autonomous changes—there being no clear line of distinction between initiating appeals to the regime for change and initiating change autonomously.

As was already indicated, the events prior to the Hungarian Revolution in 1956 revealed an unresponsive regime repressing very limited forms of dissent. The Revolution itself provides an illustration of a rapid transition from apparent acquiescence to overt resistance in a political system with virtually no channels for public dissent.[21] The events culminating in the Revolution were critically influenced by two "idiosyncratic" factors: The Hungarian Communist Party was in a state of considerable flux, and considerable latent dissatisfaction existed among the Hungarian population. Yet the pattern may not be unique.

The disaffection of the Hungarian masses was catalyzed inadvertently by student protest activities. In the fall of 1956, students at the University of Szeged seceded from the Communist League of Working Youth, their organizational access to the Party apparatus, and formed an independent student organization. Other students followed their lead. The Party did not interfere, although this meant an end to Party tutelage. These independent organizations in Budapest began calling mass meetings to discuss national problems. Committees drafted proposals to be presented at mass meetings. The success of the Polish intra-party opposition's bid for national independence inspired the Hungarian dissidents. The unprecedented turnout which occurred when the regime, after "rather difficult negotiations," allowed a solemn state funeral for the purged Lazlo Rajk and his co-victims, also contributed to the growing confidence of oppositional elements. For the first time in years, great masses of people marched through the streets without police interference, and the honoring of the purge victims cast an invidious shadow on the Party leaders then in power.[22]

Despite the growing disenchantment among intellectuals and writers in the Party, they were not ready to break with the Party or Communism. Their ideological commitments inhibited their bid for mass support.[23] Paul Kecskemeti suggests that the students, to a degree, also were an elite group and inhibited in the same way as the writers.

Like the writers' campaign, the students' action was confined to non-violent, verbal manifestations against the existing order, and restricted itself to using legitimate organizational bases and communication channels. To this extent, the students' initiative was intrinsic to the elite pattern of the revolution: it was an attack from within the Communist power system; and, moreover, one that stopped short of any direct physical clash with the apparatus.[24]

However, it would seem that calling mass meetings to discuss national problems was, at the least, on the verge of taking the conflict outside the Party; even though it may have passively acquiesced, the Party could not have considered this legitimate. As Kecskemeti says,

The students were much further from the center of power than the writers or the bureaucrats who had carried on opposition from the inside.

They did not feel responsible for the regime and were not tormented by the need to redeem themselves before their own consciences, the people, or history.[25]

They did not seem, as did the writers, to be appealing "to a higher Party authority" against those Party members and practices which they considered deviant from the Party's proper course. Like the mass, "they made a sudden jump from seeming discipline and quiescence to overt insubordination."[26]

The specific incident which touched off the October Revolution began with a peaceful expression of dissent but rapidly progressed to overt and violent opposition. A request for a student demonstration was granted—apparently with reluctance—by the regime.

The students' parade on October 23 was peaceful and well-behaved enough, but the crowds it attracted became more and more agitated. The crowd's insistence upon having the students' demands put on the air, and the radio authorities' stubborn refusal to do so, finally led to a violent clash in which a new pattern of revolutionary behavior, the mass pattern, came to the fore.[27]

Kecskemeti described the Hungarian Revolution in these terms:

It was . . . a delayed reaction to all the negative experience of the past, a reaction released when elements of weakness appeared in the image of the regime, and elements of strength bulked larger in one's own self-image. . . . It was the "thaw" originating in the Soviet Union, a loosening in the fabric of dictatorship, that sparked active opposition in the disaffected part of the elite. . . . The mass revolt in Budapest broke out when the crowds saw that the students could demonstrate with impunity, and when numbers and excitement gave them a feeling of strength.[28]

In the absence of conventional channels for public protest, the dammed-up energy of discontent seemingly surged out of control. The crowd's reaction to the students' demonstration went beyond the expectations of both students and officials. The novelty of the situation apparently confounded the regime; it was not accustomed to dealing with autonomous popular participation. The course of the workers' activity also showed a dramatic shift from quiescence to revolution—from "total discipline to total rebellion." As soon as the street fighting broke out in Budapest, workers began organizing: "The first workers' council was set up . . . in Budapest on October 24. From there, the movement spread rapidly; within three days, a network of councils covered the entire country."[29] Manifestos were drawn up; radical demands were articulated. A general strike was called, and "work stopped in all plants."

Kecskemeti's explanation for this rapid transition suggests that some of the very conditions which inhibited dissent in Hungarian society made it uncontrolled when the regime's control weakened. He asserts that many groups in Hungarian society had been intimidated and were reluctant to express criticism of the regime—particularly those groups which did not feel very secure about their position within the system, such as non-Party writers and university students of middle-class origin. Groups under direct control were "atomized"; for example, workers in state enterprises were afraid to communicate with their fellow workers. In a sense, politics was a tabued subject; no habitual or conventional ways of acting politically existed and no political relationships (outside the Party, that is) had been allowed to develop. The students' demonstration was a sign that the regime's control had weakened, and the mass turnout gave would-be opponents assurance that they were not a tiny, isolated minority. Because of the lack of conventional channels for expressing discontent,[30] new forms had to be developed; and they were, of course, not tied into the existing power structure, which had no place for them. Thus the structure of the regime virtually ensured that opposition—when it became overt—would be revolutionary, and this meant a high probability of violence.

While the Hungarian Revolution was a unique event in the Soviet bloc, two other mass disturbances occurred in the same period—the East German uprising of 1953 and the Poznan riot in Poland in 1956. The foregoing explanation of the Hungarian case points to certain factors which may help account for the difference between the outcome in East Germany and that in Poland.[31] The East German revolt was similar to the Hungarian Revolution in its rapid transition from acquiescence to general resistance; violent clashes erupted in many parts of the country after Soviet tanks dispersed the large-scale demonstrations and strikes which occurred in East Berlin. "In both cases, mass revolt was entirely spontaneous and unorganized, the outgrowth of a street demonstration that had attracted large crowds."[32] In contrast, Kecskemeti says that in Poland:

There was no sudden, explosive change from total quiescence to total insubordination. Considerable mass activity had preceded the October climax. Not only did the ferment in public opinion stirred up by intellectuals thus have a longer time in which to act upon the public mind, but the Polish political authorities themselves encouraged the masses to become politically active and express their feelings.[33]

As he suggests, it may have been the masses' belief in Gomulka's ability to meet their demands that made the outcome in Poland different—in Poland, there was no widespread rebellion followed by violent suppression as in Hungary and East Germany. While the Polish people's faith in Gomulka probably was important, it also appears that the Polish regime recognized the safety-valve effect of permitting open dissent. Possibly they structured it sufficiently to prevent the discontent from getting beyond their control. In East Germany and Hungary, the authorities may not have been sufficiently aware of the intensity and extent of discontent to open up safety-valves; thus, the outbreaks were more intense.

As Kecskemeti suggests, open mass protests in quasi-totalitarian societies are not likely to be common; they "seem to be contingent on specific circumstances." Yet when protest does become overt in such societies, their regimes face a real danger that it will not be limited and disciplined; instead, widespread, fairly spontaneous, and possibly violent resistance—for example, mass strikes and clashes with police—may well occur. Perhaps intense popular dissatisfaction is more likely to develop in such regimes because they make greater demands and impose greater restrictions upon the people than do liberal-democratic regimes.

Liberal-democratic regimes are more likely to learn of discontent before it has reached the point of explosion because procedures for consultation and accountability exist and because the right to dissent is given considerable latitude. Nevertheless, the ghetto riots and violent confrontations between police and demonstrators in recent years are evidence that in the United States, at least, procedures for consultation and conventional political channels have not prevented accumulations of deep discontent. Either the available channels have not been sufficient to convey the intensity of felt grievances, or the receivers of the "messages" have not been prepared to make responses which will eliminate the grievances (it is perhaps a combination of both factors). In the former case, improving the means of consultation and widening the "structure" of protest might solve the problem; in the latter, more drastic means of protest may appear—to the discontented—to be the remedy. In the short run, permitting a broad scope of protest probably will inhibit a transition to more extreme expressions of discontent, such as resistance and rebellion. However, if the messages conveyed by permissible protest do not succeed in convincing the regime to act responsively, then the regime will probably respond by narrowing the scope of permissible protest, thereby restricting rights embodied in its ideology. Indeed, this seems to be what is happening now in the United States.

The reaction of two nondemocratic regimes to civil disobedience provides more basis for an answer to our original question: Are liberal-democratic regimes more capable of tolerating civil disobedience and nonviolent direct action? When Gandhi led the second nationwide *satyagraha* against the Salt Tax during 1930–31, the British authorities condemned the campaign as totally illegitimate, although the movement chose limited objectives for its campaign and employed the self-disciplined tactics of nonviolent direct action. In a speech to the Indian Legislative Assembly on July 9, 1930, the Viceroy, Lord Irwin, said:

Those who have identified themselves with this movement would have us regard it as a perfectly legitimate form of political agitation, to which resort it had only under pressure of regrettable necessity. I cannot take that view. In my judgment and in that of my Government it is a *deliberate attempt to coerce established authority by mass action, and for this reason*, as also because of its natural and inevitable developments, *it must be regarded as unconstitutional and dangerously subversive. Mass action, even if it is intended by its promoters to be non-violent, is nothing but the application of force under another form, and, when it has as its avowed object the making of Government impossible, a Government is bound either to resist or abdicate.* The present Movement is exactly analogous to a general strike in an industrial country, which has for its purpose the coercion of Government by mass pressure as opposed to argument, and which a British Government recently found it necessary to mobilize all its resources to resist. Here it has been sought to employ more dangerous weapons even than this, and the recent resolution of the All-India Working Committee of the Congress, insidiously designed to seduce police and troops from their allegiance, leaves no longer room for doubt of the desperate lengths to which the organizers of the Movement are prepared to go, and gave [sic] Government no option but to proclaim the body responsible for such a resolution an unlawful association. He would in truth be a false friend of India who did not do his utmost to protect her from acquiescence *in principles so fundamentally destructive*. . . . Therefore it is that I have felt bound to combat these doctrines and to arm the Government with such powers as seem requisite to deal with the situation. I fully realize that in normal times such frequent resort by the Governor-General to the use of his special powers would seem indefensible. But the times are not normal, and, if the only alternative is acquiescence in the result of efforts openly directed against the constitutional Government of the King-Emperor, I cannot for one moment doubt on which side my duty lies. . . . *So long as the Civil Disobedience Movement persists, we must fight it with all our strength.*[34]

The British authorities undoubtedly perceived that the ultimate goal of the movement was independence, but the immediate objectives of the satyagraha campaign were quite limited. The inference one might draw from Lord Irwin's remarks is that mass nonviolent action threatened the form of rule the British had imposed on India. It would, in effect, begin changes in the Indian people's way of thinking and acting which would ultimately be incompatible with autocratic rule. Gandhi saw this:

A civil resister never uses arms and hence he is harmless to a State that is at all willing to listen to the voice of public opinion. He is dangerous to an autocratic State, for he brings about its fall by engaging public opinion upon the matter which he resists the State.[35]

In the early 1950s, a passive resistance campaign against apartheid in South Africa was launched by the African and Indian Congresses. The movement's practice of civil disobedience appears to have closely approximated the theory behind this method of dissent: The approach was nonrevolutionary; the campaign was dedicated to eliminating certain laws which enforced apartheid and to beginning progress toward equality for African and Indian members of the South African nation. Leo Kuper describes the movement as democratic and reformist in spirit:

No immediate claim is made for direct political representation or for full democratic rights, which are held out as a goal for the future. . . . The resistance acts take the form of deliberate breach of selected pass-laws and apartheid regulations, and express the apparent anomaly of the acceptance of a democratic creed and the rejection of one of its basic tenets, respect for law. The rejection, however, applies to specific laws and not to the legal process as such. Indeed, the resisters court arrest and the attendant penalties, justifying their defiance, at the ideological level, in terms of a higher ethical imperative, the allegiance owed to God over against the duty to

Caesar, and on the grounds that the rejected laws do not rest on the will of the majority of the people and offend against the dignity of man. . . . The defiance acts themselves were so planned, and for the most part so executed, as to give the minimum offence to the sentiments of the whites. The rationale underlying the dignified acceptance of punishment is that the noble sacrifice of self-interest for an ideal would stir the "higher orders" of the mind, the moral conscience of the rulers.[36]

Nonetheless, the regime viewed the movement as revolutionary; its reformist intentions and limited tactics did not prevent it from falling within the very broad definition of subversive behavior. Furthermore, the South African government felt that civil disobedience was a sufficiently threatening method of dissent to require specific legislation proscribing it. Having already outlawed dissent in broad terms, the regime reacted to civil disobedience as an offense of more than ordinary magnitude. In 1953, an act was passed to punish civilly disobedient acts, such as refusal to carry curfew passes and trespass on white-only facilities, which had not been deterred by existing penalties. It read:

Whenever any person convicted of an offense which is proved to have been committed *by way of protest or in support of any campaign* against any law or in support of any campaign for the repeal or modification of any law or the variation or limitation of the application or administration of any law, the court convicting him may, notwithstanding anything to the contrary in any other law contained sentence him to (a) a fine not exceeding three hundred pounds; or (b) imprisonment for a period not exceeding three years; or (c) a whipping not exceeding ten strokes; or (d) both such fine and such imprisonment; or (e) both such fine and such whipping; or (f) both such imprisonment and such whipping.[37]

While acts of civil disobedience were thus subjected to severe legal penalties, even harsher sanctions were directed against the organizing of civil disobedience. Kuper suggests that the regime had reason to consider civil disobedience a worse crime than other forms of dissent:

Since domination rests on legislation, the sanctity of the law is vital to its maintenance. If the laws do not command the voluntary acceptance of the the non-whites—because they are so easily deceived by agitators, communists, Indians, liberals, Anglican pastors, or the United Nations, and thus fail to appreciate the beneficient dispensations of their rulers—then conformity must be compelled. Civil disobedience, no matter how trivial the form in which it is expressed, becomes a major criminal offense, analogous to treasonable activity.[38]

If this was the regime's implicit rationale for the vigorous suppression of civil disobedience, it suggests one reason why civil disobedience may be objectively threatening to a nondemocratic regime. Subjects in a nondemocratic political system may think that their rulers' actions violate the regime's bases of legitimacy, but the theory (i.e., the ideological underpinnings) of such systems does not make the rulers' legitimacy (or the propriety of their laws and actions) rest—ultimately—upon the subjects' views of their fitness. The person who says, in effect: "My personal judgment is so important to me that I cannot obey a particular law," and /or "Whether or not my consent has been formally solicited, I can withdraw it if I wish," is saying something profoundly at odds with the rationale of a nondemocratic political system. Moreover, by being civilly disobedient, he is attempting to say it publicly; he is not addressing himself solely to the regime. Civil disobedients are, in effect, publicly insisting that the disagreement (or agreement) of dissenters (and the population in general)[39] is not irrelevant to their obeying the law. This assertion represents a claim which, if fulfilled, would radically change that system. Even an unsophisticated public may be able to "perceive" that the protesters are asserting that they have a right to break the law if they disagree with it,[40] that their opinion of the law is related to their obeying it. If so, civil disobedience can communicate the idea that laws have no automatic claim to respect; in order to gain obedience, they must be able to elicit the "consent" of those expected to obey. Practiced on a mass scale, civil disobedience might destabilize a nondemocratic regime by broadcasting this message. For if other citizens begin to act similarly (even if not so defiantly), the regime has but two choices in the long run: suppression or responsiveness. If it takes the latter course, the regime will encourage more expression of discontent, and by modifying its policies to ameliorate unsatisfactory conditions, it opens the possibility of real change in the structure of the system.

Is the "message" of civil disobedience as destabilizing in a liberal democracy? Will it undermine the acquiescence which supports a democratic system of law and order? It seems fair to assume that only a relatively small minority would actually change their behavior from acquiescence to open disobedience unless intense discontent was already very extensive. Such disobedience, while creating some disruption, would not necessarily weaken the system; it might well indicate to those in office where intense discontent exists and what policies are failing to elicit "consent" from those affected. A liberal democrat might argue that there are other ways to indicate disagreement that are less disruptive; he might insist that the doctrine of majority rule implies obedience by the minority which lost on a particular issue. Yet if liberal democracy is committed to creating circumstances in which the very large majority of people feel uncoerced in their behavior most of the time—in which they feel able to act freely upon their individual judgments and convictions—then the fact of minority disagreement is not irrelevant, especially if it is intense.

If a large number of citizens disagree enough to break the law, this is significant, even if the disobedience is not motivated by a deep sense of injustice—for example, violators of Prohibition or college students and teenagers smoking marijuana. It indicates that something has gone wrong, that popular morality and legislative intent may be at odds, or that moral standards are changing and the law may be lagging. When a significant number of citizens disagree intensely enough to identify themselves publicly as lawbreakers, with the attendant risks of arrest and punishment, this is even more significant. It is one thing to commit covert violations—they occur all the time and frequently go unpunished—and another to disobey publicly, to say that existing conditions are so unjust that one would rather be a lawbreaker than an obedient citizen. Moreover, the resort to civil disobedience may reveal not only that feelings are intense but also that democratic procedures have broken down or are not available. Thus, it may in effect represent a demand for the reinstatement or creation of procedures for consultation and responsiveness.

While the "message" of civil disobedience is antithetical to the ideological rationale of nondemocratic regimes, it is not incompatible with liberal-democratic ideology. In any political system, a citizen may at times feel himself caught between his belief that a particular law is unjust and his feeling that he should obey the law, but in theory at least, *only* the democratic citizen feels obliged to obey because he has given his "consent" to the system of governance. Thus, to disobey the law appears to violate his self-imposed commitment. In no other system is political obligation thought to be a duty assumed by the individual—a voluntary binding of the self. Even though, as we have already noted, many citizens do not express anything approximating consent, this view of the citizen's relation to his polity seems to be widely held in our society. In practice, the democratic citizen may obey the law because he considers the system legitimate; but this belief is related to his having a say on certain important matters. Government periodically solicits his opinion, and he has the constitutional right to express it even if unsolicited. Unless men can exercise their judgment, employ their reason, and sound their consciences to evaluate the government and laws they obey, they cannot be free, and, at the same time, law-abiding citizens. Only democracy grounds political obligation on this understanding. The legitimacy of that government (and its laws) derives from the fact that it solicits and encourages (for example, by institutionalizing means of expression) the citizen's judgment.

Civil disobedience—that is, an intentional, public, nonviolent violation of a law or public norm as a protest—is possible in any political system which has laws; however, use of this formal definition alone might lead one to ignore the environment in which the actual phenomenon takes place. The variables discussed here have considerable effect on civil disobedience: They determine whether it can be a meaningful—because distinctive and viable—form of political action in a particular system. Civil disobedience is *intended* as a limited, nonrevolutionary form of protest. To be so in fact as well as intent, political authorities must recognize the act as a special case of dissent—not legal necessarily, but also not subversive or revolutionary. If a regime considers civil disobedience akin to treason, this does not negate the intent of the persons who engaged in it, but it obviously will affect the way the regime treats them. If a regime refuses to tolerate virtually any open protest, the distinction between civil disobedience and other forms of dissent becomes almost (but not completely) meaningless, because any open protest, assuming it is intentional, will automatically involve a crime in the regime's eyes. Conceivably, a regime will consider it an even more serious offense to protest by deliberately violating a law which is not *itself* a restriction on free expression, than to engage in a form of proscribed expression. In this sense, civil disobedience can still be distinguished from other forms of protest—the distinction between a situation where the law violation is a means of protest, and one where law violation is a necessary consequence of protest. Thus, for example, South Africa passed laws specifically outlawing civil disobedience, and organizing and supporting activities as well. The smaller the scope of permissible protest, the more civil disobedience loses its significance as a graduated response—one which demonstrates the seriousness of the dissenter's convictions and determination to see justice done, while still expressing a loyalty to the system. In short, if protest is a crime, then civil disobedience is likely to be considered more than a mere crime; if protest is legitimate, civil disobedience may be viewed as no more than a crime and quite possibly less.

When a regime tends to associate public protest with crime and civil disobedience with revolution, it does more than merely rob civil disobedience of significance as a graduated form of protest. In refusing to recognize the intent of the civil disobedients, the regime destroys the viability of their form of protest. If civil disobedients cannot reach a wide audience because of media control, then their act is robbed of most of its impact. The disruptive effects of civil disobedience, unless it is truly massive (and this assumes the opportunity to organize extensively), are limited. A regime which can conceal the act probably can suppress the dissenters without a great deal of difficulty. If the costs of engaging in protest and civil disobedience are made sufficiently high, the calculations of would-be dissenters will be considerably altered. They may well decide that this action is not worth the risks, and choose either begrudging acquiescence or more extreme tactics, such as sabotage and other forms of violent resistance (perhaps guerilla warfare). This seems to have happened in South Africa after civil disobedience was suppressed. While grudging acquiescence does not endanger the stability of a regime in the short run, it may ultimately become a threat. For large numbers of would-be dissenters create a situation where rapid transition to resistance is possible once dissent becomes public.

At the beginning of this discussion, I suggested that the scope of permissible dissent has two components, content and methods, and that each might have an independent effect upon regime perceptions of dissent. However, a crucial factor differentiating regime responses to dissent may be the regime's ability to keep the two components separate in any evaluation of the danger of a particular protest. It may be that liberal-democratic regimes have a greater capacity to separate the two components. In other words, a liberal-democratic regime may be able to tolerate the pursuit of undesirable objectives (or worse from the regime's point of view) as long as the dissenters employ limited methods, whereas a nondemocratic regime may not find it easy to separate the means from the ends. If the ends are objectionable, then virtually any means used to promote them will be considered objectionable. Why? Apparently because such regimes fear public dissemination of ideas antithetical to the prevailing ideology. Even if the goals are not especially objectionable, the means may be considered so because they carry a message of their own. As already suggested, methods which communicate the idea that the public's opinion on matters of concern to the government is relevant and important are not likely to be welcomed. In contrast, it is conceivable that liberal-democratic regimes may be more tolerant of unconventional tactics, especially when the objectives are not repugnant to the regime or when they are praiseworthy.

Nonetheless, it is difficult to make comparisons of the response of liberal-democratic and nondemocratic regimes to movements using unconventional tactics because the circumstances under which various movements have occurred and the nature of the movements themselves have been so different. As a contrast to the South African reaction to the passive resistance movement against apartheid and the British reaction to Gandhi's *satyagraha* campaign, one might point, in this country, to official reactions to the activities of the American Nazi Party and to *some* of the antidraft protests. In the latter cases, the authorities have been more or less tolerant of protest activities whose purposes they found objectionable when the methods of protest have been legal and/or self-restrained. On the other hand, one might argue that the American cases involved smaller numbers or at least had a much smaller potential audience (to support the protests) relative to the size of the audience supporting the regime—or that treatment of some antidraft protests was not especially tolerant precisely because this is an issue on which the regime apparently did not intend to be responsive to protest. As an example of intolerant treatment of conventional forms of political activity by a liberal-democratic polity, one could point to the legal persecution of the Communist Party in this country. On the other hand, one might argue that the suppression of the American Communist Party resulted, at least partly, from the methods imputed to it, that is, recruiting for espionage and organizing for subversion.[41]

We have found cases of nondemocratic regimes proscribing rather innocuous (per se) methods of dissent. In contrast, liberal democracies have not resorted to the same sweeping restrictions on protest. Actions which are suppressed by other types of regimes are permitted. The impression persists that considerably more public protest can occur without the imposition of serious sanctions in such systems. Yet it is difficult to determine how much this is due to a system commitment to free expression, rather than to regime confidence that extreme protest is very isolated and weakly supported. Christian Bay, for example, says:

> If the domestic methods of democratic governments have been less extreme, less brutal than those of most dictator regimes, this probably reflects the usual stability of established democratic regimes, more so than any real appreciation of the value of dissent and dialogue about political funda- mentals.[42]

Some have argued that little extreme dissent occurs because a system such as ours is responsive—responsible criticism has an impact; con- cessions are made. Thus, the very fact that American political leaders have rarely felt threatened by protest is testimony to the regime's willingness to tolerate and respond to public criticism and dissent. It has also been argued that little extreme dissent has occurred in our society because the substantive basis for it has been small. The liber- tarian ideals of our affluent society have infrequently been put to the test by radical protest, and the relative infrequency of such opposition has permitted a tolerant response.

Both of these arguments have an element of plausibility, but stated without qualifications they are vulnerable to adverse evidence; counter-cases can be cited which weaken their force. However, a com- prehensive counter-argument has been launched by Herbert Marcuse. He contends that an advanced industrial society like ours undermines radical protest in subtle ways.

> Universal tolerance is possible only when no real or alleged enemy requires in the national interest the education and training of people in military violence and destruction. As long as these conditions do not prevail, the conditions of tolerance are "loaded": they are determined by the institution- alized inequality (which is certainly compatible with constitutional equality), i.e., by the class structure of society.[43]

> With the concentration of economic and political power and the integration of opposites in a society which uses technology as an instrument of domination, effective dissent is blocked where it could freely emerge: in the formation of opinion, in information and communication, in speech and assembly. Under the rule of monopolistic media—themselves the mere instruments of economic and political power—a mentality is created for which right and wrong, true and false are predefined wherever they affect the vital interests of the society. This is, prior to all expression and communication, a matter of semantics: the blocking of effective dissent, of the recognition of that which is not of the Establishment which begins in the language that is publicized and ad- ministered. The meaning of words is rigidly stabilized. Rational persuasion,

persuasion to the opposite is all but precluded. The avenues of entrance are closed to the meaning of words and ideas other than the established one—established by the publicity of the powers that be, and verified in their practices. Other words can be spoken and heard, other ideas can be expressed but, at the massive scale of the conservative majority (outside such enclaves as the intelligentsia), they are immediately "evaluated" (i.e., automatically understood) in the terms of the public language—a language which determines "*a priori*" the direction in which the thought process moves. Thus the process of reflection ends where it started: in the given conditions and relations.*44*

Nonetheless, Marcuse admits that democratic tolerance "with all its limitations and distortions . . . is under all circumstances more humane than an institutionalized intolerance which sacrifices the rights and liberties of the living generations for the sake of future generations."*45* Without discussing here the implications for radical action which Marcuse draws from the nature of democratic tolerance, one can accept his judgment as the minimal statement of the difference between existing liberal democracies (he calls our system a "totalitarian democracy") and other real political systems.

In light of liberal-democratic ideals, Marcuse's assessment of the performance of the American polity is not especially satisfactory. If our political system, as an exemplar of modern democracy, has not been an exemplar of political tolerance, the impressionistic evidence assembled here suggests that liberal democracies *should* be exemplars of political tolerance; in theory at least, they can best afford to be so.

Why do regimes in general perceive dissent as threatening? The foregoing examples indicate two basic reasons. First, the regime considers certain principles and institutions sacred and unchangeable. These are not considered subject to debate; to engage in political activity in an attempt to exercise political influence over such matters is not considered acceptable. A second reason, which may be related to the first, is a regime's desire to control social change to the greatest degree possible. Some regimes may be inclined to do this because their leaders hold rigidly to an ideology. In both instances, the regime's position means, in effect, that responsiveness to dissident claims, desires, or demands is not possible from the regime's point of view. Concessions will be made only under extreme duress.

If these factors are important causes of negative regime perceptions of dissent, then liberal democracies, in theory at least, should be less likely to perceive dissent as threatening. For such regimes are not supposed to hold rigidly to any particular principle or ideology. Commentators on democracy suggest that a democrat must be loyal only to the principle of democracy itself, i.e., to democratic ways of making political decisions. But even here a democrat should not be rigid. As I see it, commitment to democracy (or better, liberal democracy) means adherence to the general principles which underlie the theory of the liberal-democratic polity; for instance, to the notions that government should be responsive to the governed and that the political community should protect the freedom, especially the individual autonomy, of its members. Thus when procedural rules and institutional frameworks no longer serve these basic purposes as well as they once did, a democrat will be tolerant of experiments with other methods. This does not mean that he must condone the destruction of older democratic institutions and rules, but he should permit and even engage in a process of supplementing and transforming them. Thus, in liberal democracy, there should be few, if any, principles or institutions about which the regime cannot be responsive to desires and demands for change.

Second, liberal democracies, again in theory at least, do not object to privately initiated social change. Indeed, since the protection of individual autonomy is a basic ideal in such systems, a monopoly over efforts to produce social change would be contradictory. We have generally applauded sincere and reasonable private efforts to deal with social problems. It is a legitimate function of liberal-democratic governments to ensure that such private efforts do not infringe on the rights of others, as well as to facilitate them where they do not. In addition, liberal-democratic governments have had to take the responsibility for initiating social change when private efforts are inadequate or not forthcoming. But the liberal-democratic state should not desire to control *all* social change.

Moreover, governmental responsiveness is part of the liberal-democratic ideology. As long as vested interests which are not intrinsically related to liberal-democratic values do not inhibit a liberal-democratic regime, it can be responsive to the needs and desires of a great variety of social groups. For these reasons, such a regime should not perceive dissent as a threat.

The illustrations presented here also suggest that dissent is destabilizing to a political regime only under certain conditions; for example, when there are no existing channels and acceptable methods whereby popular discontent can be expressed and communicated to leaders. In this situation, if there is intense and widespread discontent, it appears that even rather limited forms of dissent can touch off extreme resistance. Liberal democracies, to an extent greater than other regimes, have an "infrastructure" for protest and should recognize that narrowing it is disfunctional for the stability of the system. Narrowing the scope of permissible protest makes sense only if the regime does not want to be responsive. If it does, then maintaining and enlarging this infrastructure will better serve its purposes. Such action will help maintain the allegiance of discontented groups, inhibit the perception that only extreme tactics are effective, and indicate to the regime where and what is the discontent. When alternatives to violence and rebellion are reduced, then dissenters face the difficult choice between acquiescence and open resistance. Suppression of limited forms of protest thus leads either to latent disaffection or to more extreme tactics. Presumably the liberal-democratic regime would desire neither. Dissent, however, need not be destabilizing if citizens are given a broad range of acceptable means by which to influence their government.

The suppression of rights of dissent can create conflict—latent or overt—about the rules of political action themselves; in a liberal-democracy, such action calls into question the regime's commitment to liberal-democratic ideals and can weaken the allegiance of many who see their first loyalty to these principles. These kinds of considerations lead me to conclude that liberal democracies can and should be more tolerant of dissent in general and of civil disobedience and nonviolent direct action in particular than other types of political regimes.

Notes for Chapter VIII

1. William A. Gamson, *Power and Discontent* (Homewood, Illinois: Dorsey Press, 1968), pp. 32, 112, 113. Although responsiveness is a difficult concept to define, it seems possible to distingush it from action taken in response to constituency discontent: the latter is the more inclusive category. Gamson suggests that authorities can handle the discontent of "potential partisans"—"that set of actors who, for a given decision, are affected by the outcome in some 'significant' way"—in two ways: "modification of the content of the decision" and "effort to control the potential partisan." The first probably constitutes being responsive. As Gamson says, "Both aim at removing the pressure that potential partisans are likely to put on authorities, one by yielding ground and the other by directing counterinfluence." Officials often take various measures to avoid constituency dissatisfaction; for example, concealment of actual

behavior, misrepresentation of the decision taken, postponement of decision until a time when constituents are less likely to exert influence, instigation of counterinfluence against the dissatisfied constituents who are attempting to influence them, and the like. Such actions should not be confused with responsiveness.

2. This refers to criticism coming not only from the likely successor to the present majority party, but also from those who are not in a position to compete directly. The existence of party competition may well have the virtue of widening the relevant public to which the government of the day must listen. Yet without broad constitutional protections, party politicos might not themselves tolerate dissenters.

3. By a "quasi-totalitarian" regime, I mean one in which the government (or the political party which controls the government) has established a set of broad institutionalized controls over most forms of political, economic, and social activity. I say "quasi" to suggest that the regime is not necessarily as monolithic and dependent upon terror as was the model totalitarian regime defined by political scientists (e.g., Carl J. Friedrich and Zbigniew K. Brzezinski) in the 1950s. A "modern autocratic" regime is one ruled by a relatively small, self-perpetuating elite. It differs from the quasi-totalitarian regime in that its control over society is not nearly so encompassing; there may be many proscriptions upon certain kinds of behavior but the institutions of control have either not been established or have not been successful in monopolizing activity in their area. By "modern" I mean to distinguish this kind of regime from autocratic regimes in traditional societies where modernization has not occurred.

4. In some systems, there may be a tendency to identify the former with the latter. It should be noted that at times rulers may well be acting cynically when they equate dissent and subversion. To do so is an effective "smear" technique which can be employed even when the dissent is not really considered very threatening. Even if it is used cynically, the tactic still is indicative of a certain orientation to dissent.

5. I am not sure whether this regulation applied only to the African National Congress, the main organization fighting discrimination, or to all groups.

6. This difference is suggested by Kenneth Kaunda's comparison of the situation of a colonial nationalist leader in England and in Portugal:

I find it easy to fly to London at any time to call a press conference, hold public meetings and in other ways embarrass the government which is in power in Britain by organizing public opinion against them. I do not say this is easy. But because the British claim to adhere to political doctrines of equality and democracy and because they operate these within certain limits, it is for me on behalf of the Northern Rhodesia people, to try and challenge them in their consciences. The position of a leader from Angola or Mozambique is very different. If such a person should fly to Lisbon, it is highly unlikely he would be allowed to return to continue his political work. Quoted in Clara Urquhart, ed., *A Matter of Life* (London: J. Cape), 1963, pp. 134-135.

7. Leo Kuper, *Passive Resistance in South Africa* (New Haven: Yale

University Press, 1957), p. 61 (author's emphasis).

8. Leslie Rubin and Neville Rubin, *This is Apartheid* (London: Christian Action, 1965), p. 13.

9. *Ibid.*

10. *New York Times*, September 20, 1966 (emphasis added). The immediate target of the bill was the Progressive Party, which was planned to enter the October elections in which four whites would be chosen to represent one and one-half million persons of mixed race. The Progressives were given a good chance of winning. The act forced them to choose between their multiracial membership and legality.

11. *Student Action on Apartheid*, I (April, 1965).

12. *Ibid.*

13. Leo Kuper, *An African Bourgeoisie: Race, Class, and Politics in South Africa* (New Haven: Yale University Press, 1965), pp. 383–385. In this later book, Kuper expresses similar pessimism about the situation.

14. Paul Kecskemeti, *The Unexpected Revolution* (Stanford, California: Stanford University Press, 1961), p. 68.

15. *Ibid.*

16. *Ibid.*, pp. 68–69.

17. Urquhart, p. 130.

18. *New York Times,* May 5, 1966.

19. *Ibid.*, December 5, 1966.

20. *Ibid.*

21. I consulted Paul E. Zinner, *Revolution in Hungary* (New York: Columbia University Press, 1962) to check Kecskemeti's interpretation of the Hungarian Revolution. The explanation in Zinner's book seems to differ seriously from Kecskemeti'' only in so far as the former stresses the decline of isolation among the people after Stalin's death. For example, Zinner says the "rudiments of an autonomous public opinion's reappeared in the period before the Revolution. Kecskemeti, at the Second Seminar on the Hungarian Revolution (transcript published by Society for the Investigation of Human Ecology, Forest Hills, N.Y., September, 1956), took issue with this assertion. He contended that "open expression of political disgruntlement and disaffection within the mass" did not begin until later (pp. 12, 17). It may be that post-Stalin changes reduced "atomization" in Hungarian society and this opened the communication necessary to generate opposition. In this sense, the transition to open defiance may not have been so rapid. Basically Zinner views the Revolution as the product of a deep discontent pervading Hungarian society, which had no "organized, orderly" way to express it. The regime failed to grasp the depth of this discontent and to respond to it but at the same time, the regime faltered in its control over the manifestations of discontent. This apparently triggered the uncontrollable outburst.

Anatomy of Revolution: A Condensation of the United Nations Report on the Hungarian Uprising (Washington, D.C.: Public Affairs Press, 1957) does not present any evidence confuting Kecskemeti's point that public expression of discontent by the mass began with the Rajk funeral. In this case, as in others, my sources are limited; other interpretations of the events in question may be possible. While these examples illustrate my generalizations, I do not claim they constitute validation.

22. Kecskemeti, p. 77.

23. *Ibid.*, p. 103.

24. *Ibid.*, p. 81.

25. *Ibid.*, pp. 81–82.

26. *Ibid.*

27. *Ibid.*

28. *Ibid.*, p. 82.

29. *Ibid.*, p. 115.

30. *Ibid.*, p. 106. Even the intra-Party opposition lacked legitimacy with many Hungarians, so it could not structure the protest. Nor was it prepared to take the kind of stand that might have gained legitimacy for it. "The opposition . . . had no thought of forcing the hand of those in power. To all Party men, however critical of the regime, a change in leadership not decided upon by the appropriate Party authorities was unthinkable."

31. Kecskemeti, in making the comparisons, admits that it is difficult to generalize about these incidents because the circumstances were different in all three; however, he appears to assume that there were sufficient similarities in the nature of the regimes and in the mass atomization of the societies to permit some generalization.

32. Kecskemeti, p. 130.

33. *Ibid.*, p. 117.

34. Gene Sharp, *Gandhi Wields the Weapon of Moral Power* (Ahmedabad: Navajivan Publishing House, 1960), pp. 168–169 (emphasis added).

35. Mohandas K. Gandhi, *Non-Violent Resistance* (New York: Schocken Books, 1961), p. 174.

36. Kuper, *Passive Resistance in South Africa*, p. 43.

37. *Ibid.*, p. 62 (emphasis added).

38. *Ibid.*, pp. 62–63.

39. In South Africa the white population can vote, so their opinions might be considered relevant; however, virtually no alternative positions on apartheid are advocated by the political parties.

40. They are actually trying to convey a more complex message than this, but this is one component.

41. This is a complex case in which certain recurrent American attitudes seem to have influenced perceptions of the Party and in which the relation of the Party to the Soviet Union during the Cold War had a significant influence on the outcome. These factors seem to have influenced perception of the objectives of the Party's methods, e.g., organizing, indoctrinating, and recruiting for the purpose of overthrowing the Government (it was alleged). In this case, the methods were not separated from the content, in effect.

42. Christian Bay, "Civil Disobedience: Prerequisite for Democracy in Mass Society," paper presented at the Annual Meeting of the American Political Science Association, New York City, September 6–10, 1966, p. 14.

43. Herbert Marcuse, "Repressive Tolerance," *in* Robert Paul Wolff, Barrington Moore, Jr., and Herbert Marcuse, *A Critique of Pure Tolerance* (Boston: Beacon Press, 1965), pp. 84–85.

44. *Ibid.*, pp. 95–96.

45. *Ibid.*, p. 99.

IX

The Role of Civil Disobedience in the Liberal-Democratic Polity: Beyond Civil Disobedience

I

IN THIS WORK, I have argued for a definition of civil disobedience which is, I think, more useful than others found in the contemporary literature. I have not insisted upon an absolute commitment to nonviolence and to acceptance of legal penalties, nor upon the notion that civil disobedience is basically persuasive. My definition encompasses more of the protest actions which have taken place in the last ten years or so than do more restrictive definitions. By attempting to justify a broad conception of civil disobedience, I had hoped to keep the concept relevant to what is going on today in this country. The narrow definition of civil disobedience—involving

Notes to this chapter will be found on pages 346-350.

strict nonviolence, ready acceptance of all penalties, and persuasion of the majority—is easier to justify as compatible with liberal democracy, but it does not describe much of the protest which has occurred, and which is often credited with producing needed reforms. Moreover, the civil disobedience most of the academic commentators have described does not appear to provide a psychologically feasible or highly effective alternative to conventional methods of exercising political influence. Thus, to condemn as illegitimate protest actions which deviate from the narrow definition seems to limit the possibility of producing change through unconventional methods when conventional methods are unlikely to produce the necessary or desirable reforms. This is, to me, a shortsighted view. Moreover, these commentators expect civil disobedience to achieve its goals in a fashion that often seems unrealistic. Surveys of attitudes toward civil disobedience and nonviolent direct action indicate relatively low acceptance and frequent association with violence in the public mind. They also suggest that conversion is not a frequent result. Such tactics have gained widespread attention; however, when public attitudes are not favorably disposed toward the goals of the protest, their effectiveness appears to depend on factors other than winning public support for the protest. It is the targets' fear of unwelcome publicity, and of public avoidance of their facilities due to demonstrations, which apparently motivates them to negotiate and compromise. Those who point to Gandhi as the proper model for civil disobedience seem to lack a full grasp of the kind of civil disobedience movement Gandhi led. This movement was rather aggressive and often used direct action despite expectations of considerable repressive violence. It could and did at times produce what many Americans would consider very unwelcome "disruption."

It is obvious that intense minorities with many claims—often legitimate but not easy to satisfy—have found that conventional political channels do not promise them much hope of satisfying their needs and desires. Therefore, if liberal-democratic values are to remain meaningful for all citizens, public officials and public opinion must accept some unconventional forms of political action. Unless the claims of minority groups can be pressed in ways that are effective and still relatively tolerable, they will be and are being pressed in ways that are less tolerable to the majority. Furthermore, the alternative to tolerance of a fairly generous conception of civil disobedience is repression—to the detriment of liberal-democratic values. If the only permissible alternatives to conventional political activity are "pure" civil disobedience and legal forms of nonviolent direct action, then morally conscientious citizens who intensely dissent face a difficult choice; either they must restrict their protest to tactics which promise limited results at best, or they must go beyond them at the risk of being considered derelict in their obligations as citizens or even disloyal.

I have attempted to provide evidence for the usefulness of civil disobedience and nonviolent direct action within our political system as it now operates. There are certain recurrent obstacles to effective political action at the grass roots, and for groups with few resources, these obstacles are extremely formidable. The low salience of politics to most Americans puts a tremendous burden on any group of dissenters which attempts to win its demands by taking its case to the electorate. Links between electorate and representatives seem tenuous, and the impetus to respond to a dissenting minority within the representative's constituency is usually small, especially when meeting its demands would require sacrifices by the majority. Social science surveys show that persons of lower socio-economic status are less likely to participate politically and that they less often possess the attitudes and skills, as well as the resources (such as money, time, contacts) necessary for effective political action. Civil disobedience and nonviolent direct action have at certain times and places helped dissenting minorities to overcome some of these obstacles. The threat of direct action has given resource-poor groups something to bargain with; marches, sit-ins, and other demonstrations have mobilized previously apathetic persons, thus making their use of conventional channels (e.g., the ballot) potentially more effective. Moreover, by the publicity it has attracted, civil disobedience has won widespread support for certain objectives and has pressured officials and businessmen to negotiate and accept some of the protesters' demands.

Throughout this work, the analysis has proceeded within the framework of liberal democracy. Its values have provided the criteria of judgment and the principles of justification. Of equal significance has been the assumption that the American political system remains a liberal democracy—that its actual practices and institutions approximate liberal-democratic principles sufficiently to make the label reasonably accurate. Despite much current criticism of the state of American democracy, and my own reservations about it, this has been my implicit premise. From this perspective, I have evaluated civil disobedience, asserting its justifiability in terms of liberal-democratic values and its functionality for liberal-democratic politics. At this point, I would like to consider certain fundamental questions which a wide ranging examination of the concept and practice of civil disobedience must confront. In short, civil disobedience demands an evaluation of liberal democracy as we experience it (and attempt to explain it) in contemporary America. What is it which permits us to call our polity a liberal democracy? What role does the average citizen play in it? What role can he reasonably be expected to play? What is the average citizen's obligation to the polity? What kind of allegiance and obedience can reasonably be expected of him? What is the traditional liberal-democratic answer to the problem of political obligation and what relevance does it have for us today? What implications do the answers to these questions have for the conceptions of civil disobedience and liberal democracy presented here? I will not try to answer these questions one by one but will come at them together from a number of perspectives.

When political scientists began to study voting in Presidential and Congressional elections, they found that a large segment of the adult population was only superficially involved in political affairs. Many voters were relatively indifferent about the campaigns, unconcerned about the outcomes, and uninformed about the candidates and issues. Moreover, there were many others who were so uninvolved they failed to vote. This seemed a disappointing finding in light of democratic ideals, which suggest that intelligent, active popular participation plays an important role in the democratic polity. However, the same studies also revealed that the characteristics associated with relatively more involved participation were not such as to give confidence that an electorate composed mainly of involved citizens would necessarily be a good thing for a democratic polity. The most involved, it seemed, were the most partisan, least flexible, and most anxious about the opposition's winning. Thus, since flexibility and low affect appear to be necessary for a democracy—permitting compromise and change in policies and leadership—the presence of uninvolved voters and even non-voters was not to be viewed with alarm. If everyone were intensely involved, leaders would be placed under severe constraints by the inflexible desires and expectations of their supporters, and would find it difficult to engage in the bargaining process which characterizes democratic politics. Moreover, this argument seemed strengthened by other research which indicated that the psychological characteristics required for democratic participation in group activity were very demanding, and that those groups which were relatively uninvolved showed a high incidence of undemocratic attitudes.[1]

Suggestions were made that democratic theory be revised in light of these findings: The citizen of classical democratic theory—deeply involved to the point of keeping well-informed, participating and caring about political outcomes, independent and non-partisan in his attitudes toward the political competitors, and willing to accept the prospect of defeat without resorting to uncivil behavior—was a chimera. Few citizens resembled the model and moreover democracy could function effectively without many such citizens. In other words, popular participation of the kind envisioned in classical democratic theory was not the keystone of democracy.

However, recent events in our political system suggest that this argument focused too much on the benefits of nonparticipation and failed to consider the costs. The "revisionist" theorists[2] were saying that a democratic political system would be quite stable if most citizens were both apolitical and loyal (or at least not disaffected). In other words, they may have been assuming that it is psychologically quite feasible to be nonparticipant and yet allegiant and obedient, but they did not consider whether apolitical and allegiant attitudes are likely to coexist in fact. It may be, instead, that many citizens' lack of involvement[3] is not a result of indifference or satisfaction but of alienation. The "fact" that people live in a democracy does not by itself ensure allegiance and obedience. Many who are politically passive may have no strong sense of the system's being legitimate. Not only may they feel that conventional politics does not seem related to their needs, they may also sense that their participation is not really welcome —for when they do become involved, they are frequently criticized for allegedly being incapable of "realistic" democratic participation. Yet social conditions have often denied such groups the training in democratic procedures necessary for this kind of participation. We are being compelled by the current condition of our society and politics to recognize that there are psychological limits to political allegiance. What I am trying to suggest is that the recent increase in the kind of acts which imply a weakened sense of allegiance or feeling of obligation to obey law is related to the widespread political apathy discussed by political scientists.

There has been a tendency in the last few decades for scholars to view democracy as a body of rules and regulations, as a technique rather than as a substantive definition of the good life. Such phrases as "agreeing to disagree" and "counting heads instead of breaking them" illustrate this view. In other words, democracy eschews any substantive absolute—it demands an absolute commitment only to keeping open the democratic processes of competition and compromise, inquiry and consultation. Democracy represents a procedural consensus. This view has plausibility but its implications must be made explicit. For example, several commentators have noted that the democratic process does not work well when moral issues, issues that are unsuitable for compromise, are the focus of controversy. They point to the Civil War as the clearest example of this. Assuming that there is only a procedural consensus, not a consensus on what constitutes the good life, democratic procedures begin to break down when basic objectives, rather than ways and means, are disputed. Competition over means is politically feasible, but ends are less amenable to this kind of treatment. One could argue that the democratic process will only work under two circumstances: either if political professionals and activists are successful in keeping basic moral issues out of the political arena most of the time, or if there actually is some kind of consensus—perhaps highly nebulous in the popular mind—as to what constitutes the good life and ethical behavior. Viewing democracy as a set of procedures implies either an amoral[4] perspective or a consensual moral perspective. From the first perspective, it appears that men can act in democratic politics without having to deal with the moral nature of man. Their political activities and their private consciences will rarely, if ever, come into conflict, because political issues and political settlements and compromises will rarely impinge directly on basic moral concerns—for example, definitions of self and of desirable human qualities, the ethics of face-to-face relationships, and the nature of human dignity.[5] The alternative perspective recognizes that democratic politics *does* impinge on moral questions, but assumes that the range of differences as to what constitutes integrity and other moral qualities is not great; it assumes that there is rough agreement on what it means to act ethically, on what is so repugnant to conscientious scruples as to be unacceptable, on what treating other human beings decently means. Perhaps our society has been relatively unique in excluding controversy over ultimate moral values from politics; perhaps the politicians have been able to define the issues in other terms, helped by the American penchant for resolving social and moral problems through legal techniques.

It seems now that our democratic system of politics is being strained precisely because basic moral conflicts have entered political controversy, and there is a clearer, if still inarticulate, perception that there is no real consensus on what, in practice, constitutes the good society or decent behavior toward one's fellow citizens. For a long time, our democracy functioned smoothly, partly because of its irrelevance to the immediate concerns of most apolitical citizens. That the apolitical often suffered from discrimination, poverty, poor health, and ignorance was not really an issue within the political system. The political settlements which were effected between the active minorities could be made at the expense of the inactive, especially those who were unlikely even to vote. Even when the intensely deprived were aided by government, those just ahead of them on the socioeconomic ladder bore a disproportionate share of the costs. While these are economic and social problems, they also involve ethical considerations: Will those who actively influence government policy use their influence for egoistic or altruistic ends? What obligations do the more fortunate have to other members of their society? Is greater equality, economic and social, worth a sacrifice of economic freedom and of the personal freedom to associate with whomever one pleases? How should the costs of government, as well as the benefits, be distributed? Since, in the past, the apolitical did not press their claims, these issues could be ignored or given minimal treatment. Perhaps in the end, the failure to treat such matters contributed to the dissolution of the basic conditions which allegedly facilitated democracy: consensus (or belief in it) and the exclusion of moral issues from politics. The myth of consensus can no longer be maintained in the face of the increasing disaffection of the apolitical, and their dissident and alienated behavior is impinging on the political system, pushing controversy over hitherto-excluded ethical matters into the political arena.

Many people today, including some of our best-known politicians, feel that the key issue facing American society is "law and order." They see recent events as signs of growing disrespect for law, of a growing tendency to resort to violence; the rising crime rate, ghetto riots, open looting, the increase in shootings, the Columbia episode, raucous anti-war demonstrations, the recent assassination of two of our leading citizens, the demonstrations at the Chicago Democratic convention, the occupation of university buildings by armed black students, and the rash of bombings and bomb threats—all, they feel, are part of the same general phenomenon. Some persons take a punitive attitude toward these developments: The way to solve the problem is to beef up police forces, put lawless elements on notice that violence and looting will not be tolerated, and hand out stiff prison sentences to those who are caught. The way *not* to handle it is to let rioters know they can loot with impunity, hamstring police and the courts with restrictions so rigorous as to allow guilty men to escape punishment, and give in to the demands of lawbreaking students or rioting ghetto dwellers. Other persons recognize that fear of the authorities is not a durable basis for law and order, especially in a society which prides itself on being democratic. The grievances and frustrations which trigger lawlessness and violence must be eliminated by removing the root conditions; steps must be taken to create an environment in which attitudes of despair, anxiety, hatred, cynicism, alienation, and frustration are not engendered. The relevance of American political institutions to the lives of the disaffected must be made manifest. However, there is no agreement on what is necessary to do this, nor on whether or not Americans will support the proposed correctives. It seems evident that a minimal effort will be doomed to failure. Despite the superficiality and distortion to which the "law and order" issue is vulnerable, there is a sense in which it *is* the most important issue, more important than Viet Nam or poverty, for example. It is most important because it is the most encompassing one. It encompasses basic attitudes towards authority and law, perceptions of the quality of life and of opportunities for its improvement and evaluations of the performance of American institutions.

If it is true, as the advocates of "law and order" imply, that there was a time when serious crime, violence, unconventional political tactics, deliberate law violations, and physical attacks on government officials were infrequent or even rare, then the following conditions probably were present: (1) economic prosperity; (2) relative social mobility; (3) limited government intervention in the daily lives of citizens; (4) a national government relatively much smaller *vis-à-vis* state and local government, so that government was perceived as closer to the individual; (5) the two-party system not quite so entrenched (so third-party movements were not automatically considered unrealistic); (6) discrimination and intolerance toward minorities either decreasing and/or latent (because of geographic isolation, unmobilized passive discontent, and the small size of minority groups); (7) international involvement sufficiently limited not to affect domestic conditions adversely; and (8) the tone of life less impersonal, anonymous, bureaucratic, conformist, and conspicuous-consumption oriented.[6] To argue this way seems to imply that a return to an earlier (and idealized) decade is necessary. This is not possible, obviously. But it is important to recognize that the changes in society may have eroded the psychological bases for the kind of obedience advocates of "law and order" presumably wish to restore.

In this general context, civil disobedience seems more necessary than ever, yet it is being explicitly and implicitly rejected. Too often, Americans have asserted that a member of a democracy must obey the law, without considering the conditions which would make such (virtually absolute) obedience psychologically feasible for the individual. This rigid view of political obligation has prevented civil disobedience from gaining the public acceptance (or, at least, tolerance) which helps to make it politically efficacious as well as psychologically possible for large numbers of people. At the same time, the rewriting of democratic theory in political science threatens to undercut the import of civil disobedience in a totally different fashion. In effect, revisionist theorists have separated democratic theory from the political-philosophical basis which is so crucial for the origins and justification of civil disobedience in modern liberal democracies. These empirically oriented political scientists are suggesting that the "classical democratic" idea of the participant citizen is unrealistic, and in a sense unnecessary—perhaps even harmful if taken to its logical conclusion.

Of a piece with this kind of thinking is the theory that competition between elites—the minority of activists and professional politicians—engenders responsiveness to the relatively apolitical majority. Not only is high involvement on a large scale likely to be detrimental, it also is not even necessary to ensure that the system respond to the needs and desires of its constituents. The *possibility* of participation—that is, participation of minimal involvement such as voting—must be ever present, but this is all that is required. Political allegiance is important as a system input—if the apolitical majority considers the system legitimate, this will contribute to stability. The supportive attitudes of the general population, combined with their low participation, permit the active minorities to cope flexibly with political and social problems as they emerge. Since they are not under pressure from large numbers of intense but unsophisticated supporters, whose political expectations are likely to be exaggerated, they can work out realistic solutions—without fear of disaffecting large portions of the population.

What, then, distinguishes democratic politics from other forms of politics? Two things: (1) the fact that periodic collective decisions by citizens have a large role in determining which of the active minorities shall control the government; and (2) the existence of certain rules which prohibit such things as coercion of citizen-voters or suppression of political opposition. Joseph Schumpeter boils it down to free competition for a free vote.[7] If American democracy and politics are viewed from this perspective, the theory of civil disobedience elaborated here is almost irrelevant. Like predemocratic acts of civil disobedience, it is an extraordinary act, almost a political freak. Some political scientists (of the revisionist persuasion) have recognized that civil disobedience may be, for certain minority groups, a means of making conventional political tactics more useful. However, viewed from the systemic level, civil disobedience (or even the threat of it) is not functional, because the political system operates more or less satisfactorily without this kind of intense involvement. Employed on a large scale, civil disobedience might be detrimental to the functioning of the revisionists' democracy, not so much because it could clog the machinery of government as because its practitioners would limit the necessary flexibility of political elites.

To argue, as I have done, that civil disobedience is well within the corpus of liberal-democratic thought and is an extension of democratic political techniques is not necessarily to suggest that civil disobedience must be epidemic in a healthy liberal democracy; indeed, that might be a sign of political illness. But it is to suggest that civil disobedience must be endemic, latent but always a possibility. It is also to suggest that liberal democracy requires participant citizens if it is to fulfill its ideals—so far as they may be approximated in the world of action. In other words, the revisionists have cut the heart out of liberal democracy—the preservation of individual moral autonomy. This is not really a politically relevent concept for them. They may contend—with some justification—that democracy, as we know it, is significantly different from other political systems, especially one-party states. But when the average citizen's most important contribution to the political system is reduced to his having "supportive attitudes"[8] or idle political resources that can be employed when political actives overstep the bounds of fair play or disregard popular desires—when his basic political function (and a collective one, at that) is thought to be providing "diffuse support"[9] or serving as a potential boundary-maintaining element—we are at a level of analysis where democracy, traditionally understood, begins to seem irrelevant. Propagandists and popularizers of democracy can provide the rhetoric which plays a part in the inculcation of supportive attitudes. No doubt some semblance of democratic practice to give the rhetoric substance is also necessary to create these attitudes—but not a great deal of genuine democracy.

II

Although the basic source of political obligation in liberal-democratic thought is consent, consent in the *concrete* sense of a conscious, individual avowal of allegiance to a polity obviously is not now and probably never was a reality for most citizens of liberal democracies during the last few centuries. The social contract was a hypothetical construct without much historical basis except for rare cases like the Mayflower Compact. The problem Locke faced was to determine what could reasonably be taken for consent so as to bring within the bounds of political obligation all those inhabitants of England who really took no part in their governance. The social contract concept sounded eminently reasonable and just, but Locke had to stretch the meaning of consent rather far to encompass all the "non-members"—those who could not be viewed as giving their consent by their choosing of parliamentary representatives. By making "tacit" consent subsume any landed property-holding and even travelling on the highways of England, Locke in effect implied that there was a second basis for political obligation— acceptance of the protection of a government, of the security which the King's officials provided for the ordinary inhabitant.

Carried forward to modern times, these two sources of political obligation can be rephrased as (1) the legal opportunity to participate in democratic institutions, e.g., to vote, hold office, petition officials; and (2) acceptance of the various benefits liberal-democratic governments[10] provide (or attempt to provide) for their citizens—e.g., security of person and property, opportunities for material well-being, for education, recreation, and so forth. Moreover, participation should serve a purpose beyond making the citizen feel that he has performed his duty or engendering in him a sense of personal satisfaction either because he has proved his loyalty to a particular candidate or party or has vented his antagonism toward political opponents. In other words, political participation should be a means of achieving meaningful political goals. Taking advantage of the legal opportunity to participate in democratic institutions may *not*, in the American political system, be a very meaningful or effective way of gaining political objectives for certain groups in the population, especially for those with relatively few resources. But unless participation has this potential, it does not seem a sound basis for inferring political obligation. This does not mean that any group can legitimately expect relative success in achieving its objective every or any particular time it becomes politically active. But it does mean that a group may not be excluded or denied legitimate expectations from political action time and time again. In some cases, it seems easy enough to determine that a group has been so treated; in others, such an evaluation is more difficult to make. Nonetheless, membership in a liberal-democratic polity cannot automatically be taken as implying consent—and, therefore, political obligation.

Similarly, it seems possible to say that certain groups have been largely denied the benefits which government provides for most citizens. To some extent, this is a matter of relative treatment. Obviously, lower-class blacks have obtained some benefits from government, but relative to many other groups, they have profited but little. Thus, it is possible to argue that the second source of political obligation is not always present, either. Moreover, this basis for obligation seems pragmatic rather than moral—the government expects certain actions in return for its services. Ordinarily citizens do not ask themselves if the exchange is a fair one, but it seems a reasonable question to ask under some circumstances. Thus, if the individual or group feels that conventional political participation has not been meaningful or effective for them, and the government's objectives seem deeply divergent from their own values, needs, and aspirations, the question may legitimately be raised.

In liberal-democratic theory, the reason for the establishment of government is the protection of the members' liberties (broadly conceived); governmental authority is a trust delegated by the people. This cannot mean that individuals or minorities can set their own interests and liberties before those of the others in determining whether or not the government is fulfilling its trust—but if such individuals or minorities begin to think that their interests and liberties are being systematically sacrificed to those of the majority, it is likely that they will lose confidence in the system and become disaffected.

As Hanna Pitkin has pointed out, there are two perspectives to political obligation, the internal and the external: the individual's personal conception of his obligations as a citizen, and the authorities' and other citizens' view of what a particular citizen owes to the polity. This seems another facet of the uneasy tension in liberal-democratic theory between the claims of the majority and of the individual. When the two perspectives are divergent, it may be possible to assess who is more correct—the individual or his fellow citizens (or the government) —about the extent of his obligation. But such judgments do not solve the problem unless the "mistaken" party is persuaded of its error. In order to maintain a stable liberal-democratic polity, the problem seems to be more one of keeping the two perspectives from getting too far apart rather than deciding which is correct. If we think individuals or groups have erred in deciding that they can throw off their obligations to the polity, we may feel justified in dealing with them punitively. But if disaffection is widespread, applying punitive measures will be a short-sighted policy. The disaffected may become more alienated and may begin to mobilize and unite to defend themselves. Thus, out of relatively latent disaffection, the government may create an active opposition movement. Even in cases of *isolated* disaffection, harsh treatment, while more feasible, may belie liberal-democratic values, which imply a commitment to avoid coercion and to preserve the individual's integrity. Civil disobedience can serve as a means of bringing divergent perspectives closer together, but only if it can operate in a climate of regime and public tolerance.

Liberal-democratic theory therefore has no definitive answer to the question of the limits of political obligation because it never definitively determines who is to judge. But if one accepts the ambiguity of the two perspectives, then there does seem to be something more to say—which is that liberal democracy was conceived as a way of achieving a congruence between them. Liberal democracy did not expect that the citizen would always agree that what he was thought obliged by his governors and fellow citizens to do was in his best interest (or even in that of the polity collectively), but that he would never feel that what others considered his political obligation would be repugnant to his own conception of it and to the purposes and values liberal democracy was designed to serve. The hope of liberal democracy was that the two perspectives would never be so divergent that the individual could not accept the external one without feeling he was being denied the right to enjoy the values liberal democracy prized—life, the pursuit of happiness as he defined it, independent judgment, legal equality, freedom of conscience, equal opportunity, and the like. In every age, liberal democracies must strive to bring the two perspectives into congruence.

III

The import of some of the contemporary attempts to define the role which the average citizen can and does and should play in our polity, is to reject civil disobedience as neither functional nor justifiable. This, in itself, does not augur well for the possibility that civil disobedience can help Americans resolve contemporary conflicts and remedy contemporary inequities and injustices. However, some consideration of the conditions under which civil disobedience appears effective is necessary before concluding that civil disobedience can play no useful role. Having argued that there are recurrent situations where civil disobedience and other forms of nonviolent direct action appear necessary, and that in certain significant cases they have produced some change, I now wish to consider more specifically when they have been effectual and when not. What are the limits of civil disobedience? What are the prospects for peaceful revolution? Under what conditions would radical change be possible by nonviolent means in our political system? Under what conditions do people feel the need to go beyond civil disobedience and nonviolent direct action to more drastic means of effecting change? Is there any justification within liberal-democratic theory for going beyond limited, nonviolent methods?

The little evidence there is suggests that civil disobedience and nonviolent direct action are most effective when there is a determinate "target"—that is, a relatively limited, unified set of decision-makers, official and/or unofficial, which directly controls the determinate decisions that the dissenters are seeking to influence. Such tactics have worked where, for example, the target was (1) a business management which could respond by hiring a few minority-group employees or integrating its lunchcounters; (2) municipal or county officials who could respond by desegregating public facilities; (3) a state or city welfare agency which could reallocate some of its funds to meet clients' demands for statutorily-guaranteed goods or services; (4) a university or college administration which could establish joint faculty, student, and administration policy-making bodies or could agree to drop legal charges and academic sanctions against student protesters; and (5) a national legislature which responded to an insistent President and public opinion and could pass legislation providing guarantees to persons exercising federal rights and to civil rights workers. When, however, the target is diffuse, when there is no limited set of decision-makers directly in control of the relevant decisions, civil disobedience seems to be a less effective tactic. It may help mobilize a wider base of supporters, thereby making other political tactics (e.g., electoral opposition) feasible. It may pressure the immediate object of the protest demonstrations to seek to influence other decision-makers who have influence or authority in the sphere of desired action. But unless it is truly mass civil disobedience and threatens widespread disruption, it apparently cannot exert enough influence upon the diffuse network of decision-makers to achieve the desired result. Moreover, mass civil disobedience probably increases the likelihood of a repressive response from the immediate authorities.

Sit-ins worked against lunch-counter segregation in the South, but nonviolent direct action seems to have had little impact on *de facto* segregation. While civil rights demonstrations may have had some role in the passage of the national fair housing bill, real residential integration can come only through a large number of interlocking decisions by a large number of individuals—officials of federal and state agencies concerned with fair housing and public housing, managers of banks and other financial institutions, realtors and realty association leaders, builders and developers, private homeowners and officers of homeowner associations, officials of federal agencies which back mortgages on private homes and deal with financial institutions, Justice Department officials immediately concerned with enforcing the new federal law. For all these individuals and agencies, residential integration relates to only one part of their activity and not necessarily the most important part. Influencing even the key positions in this network requires a tremendous amount of resources, which probably is beyond the capacity of any minority group to amass. Furthermore, civil disobedience may not be the most effective way to employ many of the resources it possesses.

The notion of "institutional racism" gives an indication of some of the difficulties involved when the target is diffuse. As Stokely Carmichael and Charles V. Hamilton describe it, institutional racism depends on widespread racist attitudes and practices, overt and covert.[11] It is difficult to pinpoint the specific decisions and actions which maintain such racism; in many cases, "non-decisions" and inaction probably are sufficient. What is required to change this are widespread changes in basic attitudes (especially of those who control the decisions or nondecisions), and/or significant changes in the distribution of power, i.e., giving the discontented greatly increased control over the decisions in which they are most interested. These are the kinds of changes usually associated with revolution.

Therefore, it appears that civil disobedience is functional only as a means of achieving piecemeal reforms. The southern sit-ins and marches which helped obtain federal civil rights legislation are one important instance. Such reforms could help maintain the long-range stability of our political system, assuming it is still a viable liberal democracy. Without severely disrupting the system's functioning, civil disobedience and other tactics of nonviolent direct action can warn officials that pockets of intense discontent may be building up. Again, assuming that officials are responsive to their constituents and take liberal-democratic principles seriously enough to attempt to alleviate the grievances of even small minorities, civil disobedience can help jog the system to respond before the discontented turn to extreme tactics.

In a viable liberal democracy, civil disobedience need not be more than a latent possibility, occasionally surfacing when the conventional channels are somewhat more clogged than usual. Civil disobedience, as I have described it, has its best chance of achieving results when governors are responsive to constituents' opinions and needs and sensitive to liberal-democratic values. It requires a certain degree of tolerance on the part of governors (and citizens) to differentiate it from extreme resistance, and to permit, even encourage, it to function as an alternative to violent and uncivil tactics. Futhermore, unless civil disobedience can gain visibility, its efficacy is limited, for even when it works more through pressure than conversion, that pressure can be created by changes in public attitudes. Visibility requires opportunities to plan and carry out civil disobedience; nondemocratic regimes which encountered such tactics have tried to prevent dissenters from using them. Visibility also requires mass media which will give civil disobedience demonstrations coverage, especially relatively undistorted coverage.

However, the problems which minority dissenters have tackled in the last few years seem to be characterized by diffuse decision-making—the kind of situation in which nonviolent direct action is least effective. Take, for example, unemployment in the black ghetto. Several years ago, Martin Luther King's SCLC began a campaign to create a sizable number of jobs for blacks in Chicago. Presumably, the main targets were local business management, trade union officials, and city officials. Assuming that this group of decision-makers had the desire to respond positively, their resources were still limited in relation to the problem. A key factor in any attempt to create jobs on a large scale is the local economic climate, which is significantly influenced by the state of the national economy. The latter is, of course, the result of myriad decisions, public and private, made within and without the country. Or take black control of ghetto schools. A campaign with this objective was begun a few years ago in several parts of New York City by local civil rights organizations. To achieve this goal, changes had to be made in school administration for the whole city and the approval of at least one state agency, the Regents, was required. This situation raises the problem of indirect accountability; the immediate decision-makers, the City School Board, are responsible to officials who are publicly accountable to a much larger constituency than the dissenting group. Another tough problem is public school desegregation in the South. The Supreme Court ruled in favor of this policy, but to make it a reality, a whole network of individuals and public agencies must cooperate—federal agencies, federal judges, state and local school boards, state governors and legislators, local community "influentials," and white parents of school children. However, no censensus on the justice or practicability of school integration exists among them. Events of the past fifteen years have shown that states and localities have considerable resources with which to hinder substantially federal efforts to implement school integration.

The frustrations of the antiwar movement have been the result of a situation in which the target is diffuse because it is so huge. The sheer size of the target has made it extremely difficult either to bring pressure at enough points to change the target's decision or to find any one point at which the pressure of nonviolent direct action could make a distinct difference in policy. Antiwar demonstrators have focused on many targets, e.g., university administrators, Dow recruiters, municipal officials, Congressmen, Department of State representatives, draft boards, and even the Pentagon. All of these separate actions have helped make antiwar sentiment more visible. While this has influenced Presidents and other political representatives, it has not resulted in a clearcut decision to withdraw rapidly from the war. It now appears that the rash of campus protests in 1968–1969 caused sufficient dismay in the Administration to alter certain policies related to the war, but not the basic policy itself. For example, reducing draft calls apparently was seen partly as a means of weakening the attractiveness of radical antiwar activity to college students, so that the Administration's basic stand would incur less opposition. Even when it became clear that the American people were rather divided and uncertain about continuing the war, the great volume of antiwar protest, which included many tactics which deviated from the discipline of nonviolent direct action, was not sufficient to alter a major policy commitment of the national government. It is conceivable that great amounts of unconventional protest can alter minor policies. Yet the hope of changing minor policies probably is not enough to win *broad* support for unconventional protest. Paradoxically, the issues likely to attract widespread participation in unconventional protest are the very ones on which it is least likely to have an impact—major ones like the Vietnam war itself. Thus, in somewhat different fashion from the civil rights movement, the antiwar movement has again raised the problem of the scale of the target. When the scale is tremendous, nonviolent direct action does not now appear to be an effective method of producing political and social change.

If even the use of large-scale nonviolent direct action is not enough to change major governmental policies and widespread social practices, what alternative is left? Liberal-democratic ideology (I say "ideology" here because I am not aware that any liberal-democratic *theorist* has articulated this thesis) suggests that a liberal democracy can undergo a revolution peacefully if it is undertaken in accord with liberal-democratic practices, i.e., through the ballot box. Yet it is clear that the attitudes which would make a revolution possible by a peaceful third-party movement do not now exist and can be created only by vast amounts of political action, publicity, propaganda, and, most likely, some kind of social crisis in addition. Perhaps political resources are widely dispersed in our society, as the pluralists content. Nonetheless, there are considerable differentials which create tremendous difficulties for any third-party movement *vis-à-vis* the two major parties, for minority dissenters *vis-à-vis* the influential supporters of the *status quo*—the individuals who control and direct the major institutions of this society and who would find any basic change in the distribution of wealth and power repugnant. These disadvantages are likely to be heightened by the tactics the professional politicians employ. The first thing that major parties do in response to third-party movements or threats of breakaway factions is to stress their unfeasibility. To vote for a third party is to waste your vote, it is argued. A second tactic is to put the third party beyond the democratic pale, to suggest that it is not really consistent with our values and institutions.

How does a third-party movement reach the stage where it can present a "realistic" alternative to the established parties? Liberal-democratic theory assumes a relatively open and permeable political arena, a relatively autonomous public opinion, wide-open political debate, protection of even extreme dissenters as long as their tactics are limited, and widespread attitudes of political and social tolerance. Only under these conditions could radical dissent obtain widespread visibility as a source of meaningful (feasible) alternatives, and only then could political competition among politically-active minorities (of which democratic revisionists make so much) create the possibility that public officials would be responsive to demands for radical change. Merely listing the conditions which seem necessary makes one skeptical that this can occur. The growing centralization of government and its increased influence upon individuals' choices, the increasing size and concentration of industry (including the mass media), the increasing interdependence of government and economy, and the accepted "imperatives" of the struggle with the Communist world all militate against it.

Even a nonviolent direct action movement of truly massive scale—such as we have not yet seen in this country—does not seem to have much greater possibilities of effecting radical change, because its success depends, though perhaps to a lesser extent, on the presence of the same conditions that would facilitate a third-party movement. It would probably require widespread disaffection from the system to organize a nonviolent direct action movement of sufficient scale and intensity to have a chance of bringing about basic changes in the distribution of power. While such a movement might be compatible with a democratic, libertarian orientation—as it was for Gandhi—it might not be psychologically harmonious with a belief in the legitimacy of public officials or contemporary political institutions. Could such a movement succeed without large-scale disruption which would have high costs for all involved? I think not, unless the movement relied primarily on forms of noncooperation which did not create confrontations and on the establishment of parallel institutions. A movement of this sort would put considerable strain upon both sides not to stray beyond the ambit of liberal-democratic values. Even on the optimistic assumption that such a movement could create a majority favorable to its objectives, this would be no guarantee that official decision-makers and influential persons in private institutions would be responsive to such a majority. Initially, change probably would have to be produced outside the established institutions. More important, it is unlikely that a majority favorable to radical change would be allowed to develop. Early in the movement's growth, the regime probably would make strenuous efforts to coopt its leadership (actual and potential). In the long run, would our government and its supporters react with relative tolerance to such a movement? If popular leaders who identify with the system feel that the institutions which give them influence and authority are likely to be changed radically by such a movement, will they defend themselves by liberal-democratic methods alone, or will we witness a rapid erosion of constitutional limitations and guarantees of civil liberties, as well as the use of considerable force? Are they likely to abdicate, as the British did in India, when they must think that very much more is at stake here?[12] It seems more likely that the regime and its supporters would denounce such a movement as revolutionary or subversive and mobilize their propaganda resources to convince the American public that it must be outlawed and crushed. An attempt probably would be made to legitimize repressive tactics.[13] Would movement leaders be able to maintain their followers' determination to continue *nonviolent* direct action despite repeated failures to achieve their objectives? Would they be able to maintain commitment to the self-limitations of civil disobedience, especially in response to regime repression?[14]

Recent events suggest that the answer to these questions is no. At the beginning of the 1960s, the appearance of a civil disobedience movement and a civil disobedience literature seemed to reflect a belief that nonviolent, self-limited tactics could remedy the injustices of American society. Perhaps there was a growing awareness of situations where obedience to law was repugnant to private conscience and personal dignity and integrity. But change was thought possible within the "rules of the game" as long as the rules were flexibly interpreted. Recently, there has been an increase in the number of citizens who explicitly reject the "rules of the game" (at least verbally). This seems to reflect the frustration "movement people" have encountered in their campaigns against the relatively intractable political and social problems discussed above. We hear and see signs that many dissenters have begun to feel that the rules are "stacked" against them, that the rules are inherently biased toward the *status quo*; that they are not neutral between conflicting groups as democratic rhetoric suggests. To conform to these rules seems, to them, to be conceding continued defeat. In other words, the legitimacy of the system of political authority is being called into question.

What seems to characterize the conditions under which people feel the need to go beyond civil disobedience and nonviolent direct action? The felt need seems to arise out of a sense that the system is not really open to radical change or to certain conceptions of the good society. It seems to arise out of a belief that unconventional but nonviolent tactics can effect only limited reform and that the need for radical change is imperative. It emerges from the experience of repeated failure to achieve more than gradual reforms despite an abnormally large amount of unconventional and conventional political action, and despite the expenditure of considerable resources on causes which previously received relatively little attention. Although a revolution based on nonviolent direct action was never mounted and thus not put to the test, movement activists have reacted to the frustrating experiences of the last few years by going beyond such tactics. These changes in the orientation of contemporary radical movements thus make speculation about the revolutionary potential of nonviolent direct action somewhat less relevant than it used to be.

I have argued that it is both pragmatic and principled for a liberal-democratic polity to tolerate unconventional but self-limited tactics such as nonviolent direct action. Assuming that today's militants are correct in their perception that nonviolent direct action alone cannot bring the changes they desire—and I think they are—how ought committed liberal-democrats respond to the tactics and goals which now preoccupy radicals? Let us examine these tactics and goals and consider their implications before coming to a conclusion.

IV

When mass civil disobedience first appeared on the American scene in the early 1960s, a major concern of the academic writers who commented upon it was to state the conditions under which that tactic was legitimate. However, it is possible to interpret some of the early articles on civil disobedience as implicitly recognizing that the civil rights activists were revising or redefining the prevailing concepts of democratic politics and political action. In a few short years, the civil rights movement ran its course, to be replaced by more militant movements. The tactics, attitudes, and goals of the new radicals are different from those of the early civil rights activists; they imply a different conception of politics. The implicit conceptions of politics embodied in these movements are "ideal types;" not all movement participants conformed to these patterns. Yet the idealizations help to draw out the implications of the differences between the early and later movements.

The civil rights activists (and perhaps the commentators) wanted to revitalize contemporary American politics. Yet the conception of politics which the original movement participants and the early commentators developed was not merely a restatement of traditional liberal-democratic norms—e.g., permissible tactics limited to persuasive means —and goals—e.g., legal and political equality. The motives and means of political action were also to be transformed.

If we draw out the implications of the commentators' statements and the participants' actions, what kind of politics do we find? The politics of civil disobedience was to be a politics of (1) conviction—participants would demonstrate their sincerity and conscientiousness by willingly submitting to arrest and even legal punishment; (2) altruism—participants would protest against injustice and stand up for the rights of others, especially the rights of those who could not stand up for their own;[15] and (3) commitment to principles and comrades—agreement with opponents was sought but not at the expense of compromising the cause and its supporters. But this politics implied more than that; opponents would be confronted with good will. Civil disobedients would demonstrate a willingness to give even persons who had clearly manifested ill will the benefit of the doubt; they would assume that their opponents had consciences which could be reached. They would act on the premise that opponents could recognize injustice when confronted and would not wilfully continue to ignore injustice or to act unjustly.

The politics of civil disobedience was to be a face-to-face politics; participants would confront their opponents as individuals without mediating institutions. The rules, the structure, of the politics would emerge at first from a kind of tacit communication between civil disobedients, opponents, and audiences. Civil disobedients would seek to lay down ground rules—limits—through their initiating acts, hoping that opponents would interpret their intentions properly and respond— eventually at least—within the same limits. The act of civil disobedience was intended to initiate dialogue, to open a process in which participants could then use conventional methods of achieving agreement about social change. While civil disobedients tried not to harbor hostile feelings toward opponents, they recognized that change—the elimination of injustice—could not occur without some conflict and that conflict and change impose costs on the persons involved in these processes. To facilitate conciliation in the act of initiating conflict and change, civil disobedients sought to bear most of the initial burdens and to limit the potential costs for all by restricting their tactics. They also recognized the danger that conflict could escalate out of the participants' control, causing both sides to lose. Thus, civil disobedients constrained themselves by the principle of strict nonviolence. This meant more than structuring conflict; it meant attempting to transform it. Participants would not seek victories over opponents. As Gandhi expressed it, injustice, not the unjust, was the opponent. The goal of civil disobedience was change, but the intent was to convince opponents that, in changing themselves or permitting change, they were not losers. Civil disobedients would seek to find a moral basis for that perception; by appealing to the most basic feelings presumably shared by the antagonists—their common humanity, their ability to empathize in the face of human vulnerability to emotional hurt and physical pain, their desire for respect and dignity—civil disobedients hoped to persuade their opponents that change would make everyone a winner. The desired change would enhance the humanity of persons on both sides of the conflict. If injustice was rectified, all men were the beneficiaries, for injustice kept men apart.

Early commentators on the politics of civil disobedience tended to be optimistic about the possibility of mutually satisfactory conflict resolutions because they thought a consensus on liberal-democratic values existed—at least on the "procedural" meaning of democracy.[16] Civil disobedients would try to make the principles of this consensus salient in their demands, while attacking targets which exposed the gap between practice and principle. In this sense, the politics of civil disobedience was not unlike traditional forms of liberal-democratic politics, where agreement on concrete policies was worked out within a context of agreement on basic principles. Nonetheless, the politics of civil disobedience was not a politics of material interest, and the desired result was persuasion, or conversion, in terms of principles, not compromise in the traditional American fashion (i.e., each side agreeing to give up some part of its demands).

The politics of civil disobedience was a politics of mass participation, of mass involvement; it was to be democratic and voluntaristic. Decisions would be made by majority rule, if not consensually, and risks of action would be voluntarily endured. No compulsion would be used to gain support and cooperation. The relevance and purpose of action would have an immediacy lacking in other forms of politics.

While the early uses of civil disobedience in the 1960s can be viewed as an attempt to revise prevailing notions of democratic politics, it cannot be said that the concept of politics just described was adequate to encompass the direction movement (civil rights and antiwar protest) activities took. It was not long before civil rights activists realized that demonstrations were succeeding not merely or even because their opponents took the symbolic message of the protest to heart, but rather because their opponents wished to avoid the costs of the disruption that attends mass demonstrations. While demonstrators continued to stress nonviolence, orderly behavior, and nonresistance to arrest, disruption occurred because (1) the demonstrations involved many participants; (2) large crowds were attracted; (3) local police forces were strained; and (4) violence, usually initiated by police or spectators, often erupted. As a result, the attention of the mass media was attracted, and shoppers avoided business districts because they found the protest frightening or distasteful. Moreover, community leaders feared that the adverse publicity would make outside firms hesitate to move into their area. Thus, the costs of protest—actual and prospective—were largely economic; there were declines in sales, increased expenses for police and judicial services, and possible loss of new investment. Local leaders also feared that the tensions engendered by protest activities would cause racial violence. In other words, demonstrators could make their opponents bear real costs, even though their tactics were not inherently disruptive. The disruption was not so much a direct result of the tactics themselves as of the reactions of the public and the police. Their reactions caused the adverse publicity and the decline in business.

By 1964, some demonstrators were using tactics which directly produced disruption, such as blocking doorways in business establishments, although the discipline of nonviolence still permitted relatively easy control through arrests which demonstrators did not resist or avoid. In the years following, such use of direct action tactics increased. Antiwar demonstrators began interfering with recruitment on campus by representatives of the Dow Chemical Corporation. Students used the sit-in to physically block recruiters from reaching students who wished to be interviewed.[17] Since university administrators generally were reluctant to bring in local police to arrest demonstrators, such protest actions either succeeded in convincing universities to change their policies regarding corporate recruitment or, at the least, they inconvenienced the recruiters themselves.

In 1966, Arthur Waskow[18] proposed a conceptualization of movement activities which was more relevant to what had been happening. He suggested the notion of a "politics of disorder" to contrast with the "politics of order" and the "politics of violence." The politics of disorder seeks to bring about change by using new techniques which look disorderly to those who are inside the system. The outsiders seek admission to the system of political order, but they realize that change is required before they can enter. In some respects, the politics of disorder is similar to the politics of civil disobedience, e.g., deep commitment, mass involvement, and non-revolutionary ends. In other respects, it is not: Activists are often motivated by anger and hatred (though they direct these feelings toward change and not against the opponent); they are not violent in deed but their nonviolence is not the pure Gandhian variety. Thus, we have two conceptualizations of the early protest movements. Are the newer movements[19]—again, perhaps only half-consciously—attempting to recast politics and political action in similar fashion? There are similarities: To some extent, they all share a conflict orientation; they engage in a politics of the deed; and their political action is face-to-face. Yet the newer movements imply a conception of politics rather different from the politics of civil disobedience (there are lesser differences from the politics of disorder) because they have reacted to the frustration of the civil rights movement.

The realities of our political system—entrenched and intransigent elites with vested interests in the *status quo*, the weakness of liberal-democratic values as a motivating influence on such opponents, the frequent resort to violence by opponents—have led to an emphasis on pressure, instead of moral suasion. The newer movements are less moral in orientation; they consider the problem of producing change not a matter of translating existing value consensus into policy agreement,[20] but a matter of redistributing power. The first contemporary civil disobedience movement, the civil rights movement, tended to accept the prevailing view that power was diffuse in America; movement activists saw the problem not as one of power but of values. If the American public would face up to the implications of its democratic principles, the ideals of the system could still be made operative. These activists were well aware of deep-seated prejudice and ignorance of racial injustice, but they did not think that the goals they sought were antithetic to the existing political system. They did not see that racial equality could not be achieved without redistributing power.

At one level, the action of civil disobedience was face-to-face; at another, it relied on modern communications technology to interact with its audience—on the national level, it was a politics of mass communication. As such, it could be what many early commentators called it—an appeal to the majority. The premise of the politics of civil disobedience was that liberal democracy was still viable in America, that an intense minority, through dramatic action and mass media, might sway the apathetic majority and make itself the effective majority. The weight of this new majority would then be felt in the institutions of government and ultimately in government policies and actions. The majority, through its representatives, could make its voice heard, and so it seemed to do when Presidents Kennedy and Johnson responded to civil rights activity with legislative proposals and executive intervention. The difficulty with this view of American politics was that the legitimation of demands by national spokesmen did not amount to implementation, especially in a political system where local opportunities to block federal initiatives are numerous. The national majority appeared to support sporadic federal intervention and federal legislation directed toward the South, but it was never clear that much pressure existed for a vigorous campaign of enforcing laws and court decisions.

The civil rights movement is often said to have caused a revolution; politically, this is not accurate at the national level or, generally speaking, at the local level. Whites may have become more conscious of their attitudes about race, but the attitudes were not radically modified.

The most pronounced changes took place among the black population. Here behavior, as well as attitudes, was changed to some extent; for example, black political participation has increased. However, on the mass level, it is most noticeable in the conventional forms. Thus, although participation in nonviolent direct action was relatively high during the heyjjay of the movement, the long-term changes appear in voting rates. Significant redistributions of power do not seem to have occurred except where strong grassroots organizations were built with indigenous leaders and mass participation *and* where blacks had an opportunity to become the effective electoral majority.

The newer radical movements have generally eschewed the national political arena to act, instead, within smaller political units and smaller institutions like the campus. Activists have not shifted their attention because these smaller spheres are more democratic than the national but because these are the activists' natural communities and are more easily influenced or even controlled.[21] Liberal critics of student radicals have claimed that the campus is virtually the only place in American society where dissent can get a tolerant hearing. They contend that campus demonstrators are hurting their own interests when they resort to disruptive tactics. The university, they say, is a sanctuary which student radicals can ill afford to destroy; by alienating those who administer and teach within those sanctuaries, they alienate the more liberal elements within our society, the would-be supporters of their radical objectives. However, to the radical student, the university or college is a microcosm of the larger society. Despite its claims of adhering to humane values, he sees it serving the corrupted values of the society outside, reflecting in its own policies the social injustices which it ignores outside its walls. Its government is even less democratic than the government of the larger polity. Like the priorities of the larger society, the priorities of the university are distorted; equipping students to struggle for social justice ranks below training personnel for the corporate "technostructure," while the academic's disinterested pursuit of abstract knowlege cloaks an insensitivity to the sufferings of real human beings.

Tactically, it is easy to see why student radicals have chosen the universities and colleges as their targets. Obviously, they are readily accessible and there is a potential constituency within them because many students feel a vague kind of alienation from American society in general and the university in particular. Moreover, the administrators of a university or college seem especially vulnerable to direct action tactics. Many administrators and more faculty members share the liberal's aversion to using violence against demonstrations and other protest tactics, although administrators are now showing much greater readiness to call in municipal police to handle campus disruption. In addition, the campus administration constitutes a cohesive target; i.e., it largely controls the decision-making process which could produce the changes the students demand. While administrators are beholden to trustees or regents, they usually have considerable autonomy in handling the internal affairs of a college or university. Presumably, they have generally had the confidence of the trustees, who would normally be reluctant to substitute their own judgment for the judgment of those immediately responsible for the administration of the college or university. Recent events have, of course, made student activities more salient to trustees and, in the case of state-run universities, to the governors and legislators who control their appropriations. Probably this has considerably reduced the autonomy of administrators on many campuses. Yet in the short run at least, it must have appeared to many student activists that their demands could be substantially met by the resources available to administrators;[22] this, of course, is not to suggest that administrators were willing to incur the costs of meeting such demands.

It is only in the university or college that the radical student can be politically potent. In the larger polity, he is disenfranchised legally until he is 21, but more importantly, the distribution of political resources and the hugeness of the political apparatus pose, at the present time, virtually insuperable obstacles to his political effectiveness. On the campus, he has a chance to effect his will, not easily to be sure and sometimes at great personal cost, but the results of political action can be seen. Effects are visible to him.

Both the early and the more recent movements have, in effect, sought community in the movement; the personal loyalties developed, the intense experiences participants have gone through together, have been a source of appeal, a source of internal strength. Although the civil rights activists developed a community within the movement, they basically sought admission for their constituency into the larger political system;[23] their community was not seen as a substitute for participation in the larger community. Yet the latter was not really a community: Affective ties were diluted; value commitments were weaker and less frequently motivated political action; relations had to be mediated by institutions. In contrast, the newer movements are seeking to build new communities, viable in human terms, within old institutions. These efforts represent a reaction to the non-communitarian nature of contemporary American politics; for some time now, our liberal democracy has not been participatory. The trend of our politics is toward transforming individual participation into a ritualized performance, whose instrumental functions can be perceived only when aggregated at the system level. Popular belief in the legitimacy of the political system and emotional identification with its symbols do not serve to make individual acts of participation more meaningful for the individual. Political action in which commitments, choices, means, and ends are scaled to the individual's understanding and closely related to his daily life experiences, is not available to the average citizen.

The politics of civil disobedience could be conceptualized as a purified version of liberal democracy as we believed we experienced it. The political context—a liberal Supreme Court, a liberal President, a liberal public opinion (in the North at least), even the gap between democratic creed and actual practice which allegedly made Americans feel guilty—made a politics of civil disobedience seem feasible. Because this politics did not question the basic character of the system, its goals, norms, and limits could be extrapolated from liberal-democratic politcis. The politics of civil disobedience sought to extend liberal-democratic values to a part of the population excluded from the body politic; it basically accepted liberal-democratic norms—the one major change in rules was to make law-breaking legitimate *under carefully prescribed conditions*. Apparently, early commentators and practitioners of civil disobedience believed that the American legal system was a relatively neutral mechanism for protecting basic constitutional rights. Their respect for law may well have convinced them to shape civil disobedience so it would be compatible with maintaining the legal system. Not only were civil disobedients to submit to arrest and punishment, breaking the law was to be a last resort. The politics of civil disobedience was avowedly nonrevolutionary. In their own eyes, civil disobedients were not placing themselves outside the existing system of maintaining order; they were submitting to it as an imperfect but legitimate system. The congruence between liberal-democratic ideals and institutional realities was considered close enough for a principled democrat to give the system his allegiance. The civil disobedients questioned only the legitimacy of specific acts of authority. This was the key distinction civil disobedience made. In effect, the theory of civil disobedience implied that it was legitimate for a democratic government to suppress an avowedly revolutionary movement. The civil disobedients' hope for different treatment was predicated on making clear the distinction between civil disobedience and revolution.

Actors in the new politics have often employed revolutionary rhetoric, and they have occasionally had recourse to violence in self-defense. Nonetheless, all but a small minority have shunned the image and tactics of an armed conspiratorial movement—for several reasons, tactical considerations among them. Some activists realize that such a concept of revolution has been antiquated by the American political system. Although there is considerable concentration of power and authority, it is difficult to conceive how control might feasibly be seized by a revolutionary conspiracy and then employed to move the system toward the goals of the revolution. For the traditional pattern of revolution—seizing the institutions of legitimate violence and deposing those who command them—does not seem applicable to a government as powerful as ours. As long as elected representatives in the official chain of national command retain the allegiance of the armed forces, it is unlikely that the physical elimination of top-ranking officials and the seizure of government agencies by a militant elite would be sufficient to make a revolution successful. Revolution must take a form different from seizing power at the top; moreover, it probably cannot be a revolution by an elite alone. There are too many points from which resistance could be mounted by supporters of the *status quo* to permit a small group to win control without mass support. This does not mean that a *majority* must actively or passively support the revolution, but it must have a mass base if it is to successfully resist counter-revolutionary efforts. For these reasons, it would seem that the very small minority of committed and would-be revolutionaries cannot reasonably plan revolution in the old mode.

Moreover, there is still considerable commitment among these activists to democratic and humane values, and these values are a constraint on the means available to the new politics. Many members of the New Left are aware that the means of making revolution significantly determine the character of the revolution and the post-revolutionary society. If the revolutionaries are intolerant, undemocratic, and violent, there is little hope that the revolution will usher in a tolerant, democratic and nonviolent society. Such activists seem committed to a long struggle to weaken the system attachments of groups at the bottom of the socio-economic pyramid and change their orientation toward the institutions and values of American society. They see the need to heighten the consciousness of alienation among students, blacks, poor whites, and the lower classes in general. If the revolution is not to devour its children, it cannot be made in the old way. Furthermore, it does not make much sense to view the new radicals as a revolutionary organization plotting revolutionary strategy and tactics, because the New Left is organizationally and ideologically fragmented. However, these activists have not shunned traditional revolutionary garb because of any strong feelings that the system is legitimate. They want to transform American political and social institutions in a radical way but without betraying their adherence to democracy, equality, and humanism.

The changes radical students have sought reveal their desire to make the universities and colleges models for change in the greater society. Foremost among their demands has been recognition of students as real participants in governing the campus community; power concentrated in the hands of trustees and administrators must be shared with the major internal constituencies of the university—students and faculty. Radical students feel that their education and life on the campus has been determined for them in large part without their having a voice. Their demand reflects—as a negation—the reality of politics in the larger society, where the great majority of the population plays only a superficial role in making the decisions which crucially affect their lives. In addition, radicals have demanded that universities change their policies so that they will actively foster social change. For example, admissions policies have come under attack for excluding members of minority groups. Activists want admissions criteria changed so as to eliminate the differentials in access to higher education caused by socio-economic stratification. In effect, this is a demand that universities and colleges divert some of their resources to rectify the inequities—poverty and prejudice—of the larger society. Black student activists have called for courses which recognize their heritage and contemporary problems. They have demanded resources and opportunities to develop the group consciousness and personal sense of efficacy the larger society denies to black people. In a few instances, they have even tried to compel the university to accept "community control" of the new ethnic studies programs. This is a clear example of the attempt to pressure established institutions into redistributing authority and resources.

In addition, student radicals have demanded that universities disentangle themselves from commitments which support the military establishment, the vast apparatus which gives American leaders the power and inclination to block social revolution around the world. The universities' common practice of permitting campus recruiting by certain government agencies and corporations has been attacked. Students have also objected to research with military applications being done under university auspices. Radical activists believe that these activities represent complicity with the military-industrial complex in the service of life-denying ends.

The university, if so transformed, would constitute virtually a counter-institution within the society. This may seem highly subversive to those who fear for the status quo. However, resocializing the college student would help foster a process whereby society might be changed over time without a violent struggle of major proportions between defenders and opponents of the status quo. Not only would universities and colleges become social laboratories for experimenting with new modes of social organization, they would also become active participants in fostering social change. These institutions would initiate and support research and action programs in which students would be prepared for the task of transforming society.

Some of the recent activity of black power advocates can be viewed in a similar fashion. While radical students have fought for increased self-government and to establish (or perhaps reestablish) the autonomy of the university, some black militants have begun to work for community control over the institutions of the ghetto, in particular, the schools and the police. They want control in order to make these institutions sensitive to the needs and desires of the community. They want to overcome the educational deficiencies which contribute to their difficulties, and they believe that black children must see black people in control and must be given a black heritage if they are to develop a sense of self-respect and a sense of efficacy. They feel that the strictly educational and the social-psychological aspects of the experiments in black community control of public schools are interdependent.

White police in the ghetto represent—literally and figuratively—the repression that white society imposes on the black population. Community control of police would remove this alien and alienating presence and also give residents an opportunity to deal with the problems of local order and social deviance in a fashion which takes into consideration the unique society of the ghetto. It would also enhance the sense of efficacy which comes from control over vital decisions.[24] Because the economic resources of the ghetto community have been drained, community control of schools and police means that the larger white community must be prepared to help support the costs of running these institutions without retaining control as the *quid pro quo*. Thus, the demands imply a redistribution of political power and economic resources.

It is no easy task to develop a politics for achieving these goals which can navigate between the shoals of suppression as a revolutionary-subversive movement and of gradual acquiescence in a reformist approach. It is difficult to specify the appropriate norms and limits of political action for the newer movements. While some underpinnings might be found in a reinterpretation of liberal-democratic theory, our popularized democratic ideology will not serve. Many citizens still believe that our political system represents the most practicable approximation of liberal democracy despite the fact that the reality of our politics is increasingly remote from it. The politics of the newer radical movements contradicts that reality but is all the more incomprehensible to persons socialized to accept the existing politics as politics per se. It does not seem possible for the new politics to develop if its goals, norms, and limits must be validated by comparison with the prevailing ideology of democracy (i.e., popular conceptions of the way our democracy operates),[25] because the latter fails to recognize the existence of serious deviations from liberal-democratic values within our society.

In the period since the civil rights movement began, the institutional biases of the American legal system have been revealed, and the efficacy of legislation and litigation as instruments of social change has been called into question. This explains, at least in part, why the new activists have thrown off the restraints of constitutionalism to some extent. Protecting the institution of law no longer seems so vital in the new politics, because its actors seek changes which legal means cannot readily encompass but which law and legal mechanisms can hinder. Submission to arrest makes less sense because activists are placing themselves outside the existing system of order. Moreover, they often believe that direct physical confrontation with the authorities will reveal more starkly the institutional biases of the legal system. While they may realize that law is necessary for a stable polity, new polities must first emerge; then law and norms can be stabilized again.

Respect for existing law, they feel, should not inhibit experiments with new social and political forms.

The loss of legitimacy which the system has suffered in the eyes of activists is reflected in the frequently heard demand that all participants in a demonstration, e.g., a building seizure, receive a pledge of amnesty before they terminate their demonstration. Apparently amnesty has been sought with less compunction than in the past.[26] Earlier demonstrators more readily accepted the notion that they *should* be willing to pay a price for their disobedience. This was a way of symbolically demonstrating that they were not repudiating all authority. Sometimes student protesters did make demands for amnesty or lenient treatment by the authorities, but they were not comfortable repudiating the authority of *any* body the university might appoint or recognize to sit in judgment upon them. Recently, New Left activists have contended that protest actions on campus do not constitute disobedience because the administrators of the university do not have the authority—in their eyes—to determine what is proper and improper on the campus. They do not accept the rules. These activists claim that they are interfering with an immoral institution; to be penalized for fighting injustice would be unjust. In this sense, their demand for amnesty represents a change from the perspective of civil disobedience. These demonstrators have lost confidence in the authorities' responsiveness and are more certain that there is a basic conflict of interest in their confrontations. They are more likely to believe that campus administrators are primarily concerned with repressing radical protest, not with reforming the university or the larger society.

The newer radical movements have extended direct action beyond the range employed in the politics of civil disobedience. In the last two or three years, there appear to have been more incidents involving inherently disruptive tactics. For example, the administration building sit-in has progressed to occupying campus buildings and preventing entry by those who are not protesting. This tactic has primarily interfered with the holding of classes. Some damage has occurred to buildings during such seizures, and there have been scuffles when students opposed to the demonstrators have tried to enter or to prevent those within the buildings from going and coming. Participants have barricaded themselves against police entry but generally seem to have exited without struggle once police forced their way in and made arrests. In the Columbia University seizures in the spring of 1968, much of the violence seems to have occurred when police forcibly entered the captive buildings. On the outside, sympathizers and faculty massed in front of the buildings in an attempt to prevent police violence against demonstrators and bore the brunt of the police's initial use of force. Whether those outside also caused most of the injuries police suffered is unclear. Demonstrators also were injured when they were dragged from the buildings.

In several protest campaigns, students filed through classroom buildings chanting slogans. Sometimes participants attempted to persuade those inside the classes to join in campus strikes; at other times, the intent seems to have been to disrupt the holding of classes. Physical attempts to block students from entering campus gates or buildings represent an escalation of such tactics. Blocking can take the passive form of student's locking arms in a doorway or the active form of repulsing anyone who tries to break through the chain of demonstrators. Tactics like these were used at San Francisco State and the University of California (Berkeley campus) during the Third World protests in the fall of 1968 and early 1969. Participants dispersed when police appeared on the scene. These activists were not trying to make a point by being arrested.

The limits placed on political action by the civil disobedience paradigm have proved too confining for movements which seek change in the distribution of power and the structure of institutions, rather than equal access to public facilities and exercise of rights on the same basis as other citizens. Civil disobedients' willingness to court arrest and reluctance to use violence under any circumstances permitted officials to end any particular protest action by arresting participants or inflicting violence. Even if the participants defended themselves in court, the cost of mass legal defense usually was high, especially in relation to the movement's resources. Often, repeated mass civil disobedience (subject to diminishing returns in effects) or legal demonstrations which officials considered threatening (often because of the possibility of violence) were required to keep pressure on the target or attract national attention. But mass arrests could immobilize the movement's base: How many people will keep going back to get arrested especially when the penalties are increased and higher bail is set for second and third offenders? Perhaps participants in civil disobedience (and the commentators) were not prepared for these harsh realities because they assumed that the consciences of opponents and audiences would be touched relatively quickly and this would lead to affirmative action.[27] The shock value of an unconventional, unaccustomed but very conscientious act was thought to stimulate reflection, reconsideration, and even revisions of private views *and* public behavior. But even when the audience's sympathies were engaged, translating favorable attitudes into concrete reforms was not easily or quickly achieved.

After a few years of civil rights demonstrations, activists began to realize the necessity of putting pressure on opponents; without at least the fear of disruption, local elites frequently were not inclined to make concessions to civil rights groups. In the last few years, leaders of protest demonstrations have justified disruptive acts as the *only* way to make decision-making elites responsive to their demands. They apparently have decided, based on their own attempts or those of others to proceed through established channels or to use "persuasive" forms of nonviolent direct action, that no meaningful responses will be made to their demands. They believe they will either be offered much less than they desire, or encounter official efforts to stall and postpone action. However much some persons might like to condemn this kind of thinking as cynical rationalization, this perception is common among the New Left activists who have sparked many of the recent antiwar and campus protests. Many black power advocates share this perception; they have lost faith in the tactics of the civil rights movement. Some have become convinced that violence is necessary or even that violence alone will succeed.

As a result of this change, the newer politics relies on a kind of confrontation which is different from a moral confrontation of conscience. Disruptive confrontation must change the opponent's reckoning of the costs of inaction against the costs of change; that is, the costs of maintaining the status quo have to be increased. In contrast, civil disobedients sought, as Gandhi maintained was proper, to bear the major costs of the conflict generated by their demands for change. The theory of the newer politics often consciously recognizes that the conflict initiated by the protesters will not produce the kind of change they hope for unless opponents and established institutions bear real costs. The newer movements have often used direct action tactics which reduce costs to participants—minimizing arrests and injuries—while increasing nuisance value and disruption. The intent is to prolong the staying power of the movement, the ability to mount mass direct action over an extended period of time. For example, the building seizures of recent campus protests, while ultimately leading to arrest and injury in most cases, attempted to combine the shock value which civil disobedience had with staying power and the possibility of partially disrupting the educational process. Campus authorities generally were shocked at the audacity of the students; in addition, certain campus facilities were kept from use for a period of time, and the clear possibility of injury made forcible recapture of the buildings a matter to be carefully considered. Police violence might well increase the activists' support. Although the activists' tactics have often failed to preserve their base of support in the long run, they have not often shared Thoreau's view that putting just men in jail will work a change in the public's attitudes and actions. They recognize the danger that the movement can be suppressed by the jailing of activists for long periods. To some extent, the demand for amnesty in recent campus protests can be explained as a tactic to avoid crippling sanctions. Student radicals have seen the effects of severe university discipline upon their activities. They are in the best position to minimize sanctions while they still control a building.

Within the politics of the newer movements, confrontation and disruption are seen to serve the function of de-legitimizing authority. For example, a building seizure puts university officials in a situation where violence may come to seem the only viable response. When they employ physical violence to coerce protesters, the authority of the institutions is revealed as ultimately resting on coercion. The coercive power behind the facade of authority is bared. Gandhi spoke of wanting the British Government to show the Indian people the "leonine paws" of its authority, and student activists have frequently referred to the "radicalizing" effects of police violence. Some of the inculcated respect for traditionally legitimate institutions is diminished when officials cannot obtain obedience by invoking authority. Such confrontations transform institutions—abstractions symbolized by certain persons playing defined roles—into the bodies of violence wielders, i.e., police who strike, mace, and tear-gas. The latter is a far different social reality from the relatively august image the government of a university or city normally projects. In such confrontations with police, the activists' violence has usually taken the form of throwing various objects (stones, bottles, bags of feces) at police during their attempts to block demonstrators' forward progress, clear areas, and/or arrest demonstrators. One cannot say that all of this violence has been defensive, but much of it has occurred in response to police violence against demonstrators. While police spokesmen and demonstration leaders have usually differed as to what constituted "necessary force," outside observers have sometimes corroborated the participants' claims that police used unnecessary force. Police behavior during the demonstrations at the 1968 Democratic Convention in Chicago is perhaps the most notable example. Police used a great deal of violence against demonstrators (and innocent bystanders) who responded by throwing objects and yelling obscenities. In addition, some demonstrators smashed windows and otherwise damaged police vehicles. At the same time, there were reports of police damaging parked vehicles thought to be owned by demonstrators. In some antiwar protests, participants threw eggs and balloons filled with paint at public officials. More frequently, demonstrators have used obscene language toward police and other authorities. Allegedly, this is a form of "psychological violence" or "psychological warfare" used by radicals;[28] some activists, it is claimed, have attempted to incite police to violence by getting crowds of demonstrators to yell various obscenities at them. The alleged motive is to shock the public and "radicalize" those demonstrators who are still "naive" about the police and public officials. Although it is quite possible that a few demonstrators have had this intent, in general the use of obscene language seems a response to frustration at the police's breaking-up of demonstrations and a symbol of defying the authorities. In confrontations where the only superior resource demonstrators have is numbers and where most of them are inhibited about resorting to physical violence, obscene language may be one of the few outlets for the tensions which develop.

There have been a few scattered incidents of protesters engaging in direct physical combat with students who opposed their efforts. In at least one incident on the Berkeley campus, Third World supporters used sticks to beat students who crossed campus picket lines. It would appear that the protesters initiated violence in some instances. At Columbia, there were brief scuffles between opposing student factions; apparently these fights erupted spontaneously in tense situations.[29] Such physical confrontations—they seem to have been of short duration and to have produced only minor injuries, if any—constitute most of the physical violence used by demonstrators against persons other than police.

In such confrontations, self-defense is defense against a person, not against an abstract institution, and the policeman is a more vulnerable opponent than an institution. In this face-to-face interaction, at least the feeling of personal efficacy is possible, whereas it is usually denied when the institutions must be confronted as abstractions. The interaction of violence and counter-violence is foreign to the interactions by which these institutions normally maintain themselves. At the same time, solidarity is often increased—at least in the short run—among the protesters and their supporters. The polarization which has frequently followed the initial confrontations has a similar effect; the emotional ties, the loyalties of the counter-community are strengthened.[30]

Even when confrontation leads to negotiation and agreement, instead of to violence, the results may be de-legitimizing or destabilizing for the established institution. If departures from rules are necessary to accommodate protesters and de-fuse the confrontation, the necessity of adherence to established rules comes into question. If offers of structural reorganization are necessary to avoid violence, redistribution of power may occur, although it is always possible that activists will find the changes insubstantial after their support has dwindled with the subsiding of conflict.

The ambivalent attitude toward violence in the newer movements does not represent a callousness toward the dangers of escalating violence. Activists generally seem mindful of it; most do not want to see violence employed, especially not greater violence than has already occurred.[31] But they refuse to be hamstrung by an ethic which rules out persistent disruption (except through mass civil disobedience, which is increasingly difficult to mount over time) and active self-defense. In the politics of civil disobedience, violence was thought to block the possibility of dialogue—it was not a means of moral persuasion. Disruption (especially physical violence) caused by demonstrations is easily used by the authorities as a pretext for not negotiating in confrontation situations. Yet disruption is a means of making conflict overt. The new radicals see basic conflicts of interest between certain classes which conventional politics tends to conceal under the umbrella of a vague consensus. The usual strategies of American politics—broad coalitions, compromise of interests, logrolling—have worked to the disadvantage of those groups and classes which have a relatively small share of political resources. The New Left activists seek not aggregation but rather polarization of groups in the political communities they attempt to organize. They seek a mass base, but not by building a broad coalition based on a lowest-common-denominator consensus or mutual adjustment of interests. They want to organize the groups and classes which have the most to gain from a radical restructuring of American society. In order to accomplish this, latent conflicts of interest must be made overt and conscious by disruptive tactics.

At the same time, relatively extreme tactics may have a different effect. In the civil rights movement, the activities of more extreme groups apparently encouraged the movement's opponents to negotiate with the more moderate elements. Such a strategy may be less feasible for the new movements because the moderates and radicals of the civil rights movement probably had more in common than the new radicals and today's counterpart of the civil rights moderates.[32] Nonetheless, there may be at least short-term goals desired by reformers that will also aid radical activists. Radicals run the obvious risk that such reforms will diminish their potential base of support, but they might also make the reformed institutions easier for radicals to work within for radical change. A more probable danger of the politics of confrontation is that radical activists will be repressed and their movements crushed, while less radical elements will be coopted. This is a serious risk for the newer movements, for, in trying to develop a politics that avoids reformism, they may isolate themselves, thereby making repression a more feasible course for the authorities.

Many citizens find these developments threatening; they regard the protest movements of the past few years as regrettable and unnecessary. Such perceptions are unfortunate, because change and pressure to produce it both seem necessary to preserve this society from even worse strife. It is possible that change resulting from student demonstrations in the last three years could have been brought about at less cost to both students and colleges had radical students been more patient and less disruptive in their tactics. But it is not at all clear that administrators would have been nearly so prompt in initiating changes if militant protest had not occurred. The fact that administrators continued to resist student demands, almost always offering less than the protesters want, and this in the face of both pacific and militant protests, makes one wonder how much reform on the campus we would have witnessed in the absence of disruptive tactics.

Where change has come on the campus, it creates the possibility—far from a probability—that the institutions which educate the intellectual elite may be set against the menacing trends of this society: alienation of the have-nots, misallocation of national resources, maldistribution of wealth, corporate manipulation of consumption and work, loss of personal and political autonomy. It provides some little hope that the universities and colleges will not serve merely as a sanctuary from some of the crises of the present but as a citadel from which will come the intelligence, social sensitivity, and militancy and determination to change the course of America's future.

It seems unlikely that black demands for a redistribution of political power and economic resources will be granted without considerable pressure from the black population. Yet expansion of community control would begin a process of redistributing political authority and economic resources which might ultimately overcome the alienation of the blacks and other ethnic minorities. Like the transformation of the universities and colleges, community control suggests the idea of counter-institutions, institutions which reverse the dominant patterns of the society.

V

The changes already suggested by the new radical movements—restructuring of universities and colleges, community control of the ghettoes—are revolutionary in the sense that our society will be radically transformed if these changes are not stunted and suppressed before they generate effects felt in the larger society. Much more than the civil disobedience and nonviolent direct action of the early 1960s, the tactics and emerging ideology of the New Left students and black militants challenge the assumptions of the American polity as to what changes are necessary, how change should come, with what speed, and who shall bear the costs. It is clear that our society is in crisis, and massive efforts to rectify social and economic injustice are necessary. Our society will be changed whether the supporters of the status quo or their opponents prevail. Probably the result of their collision will be a society different from that which either side envisions. Yet it can be a society which will not have to engage in massive internecine warfare to resolve the very real conflicts of values and interests. Moreover, it is possible that many of the practices of liberal democracy can be retained despite radical change.

A precious advantage which supporters of liberal democracy think it has over many other political systems is that physical violence is not necessary as a means of settling intranational political conflicts.

There has been considerable violence which, in a sense, was political in our history, but generally we have avoided the resort to violence in settling the key questions of politics. Perhaps this was at least partly due to the fact that violence was often condoned outside the perimeter of established political institutions. Groups which sought to improve their status or might have, had they been given the opportunity, were kept down partly by violence or the threat of it. On the other hand, liberal-democratic ideology made such practice questionable, so that politics almost had to ignore it—the contradiction might have disturbed the generally tranquil political process. Today, this is no longer possible; what might have been extra-political conflicts in the past have become political and the nature of the political regime has been called into question. The form of our government is no longer considered irrelevant to the nature of the conflicts. In the past, government often did intervene in "extra-political" conflicts and not as a neutral third party, but the substance of the conflicts was not seen as inherent in the structure of the polity. Today, opponents of the status quo see the conflicts and the system as interrelated. Thus, solving these social conflicts means changing the structure of our institutions.

Radical change probably is necessary to prevent the growing aliena-tion of discontented groups from erupting into large-scale conflict. At the same time, the majority of Americans seem to be opposed to such change today. It is difficult to be optimistic about the survival of liberal-democratic values in this confrontation. Those who favor repression of radical dissenters will stress the necessity of limiting our vaunted freedoms in times when the Republic is under attack. Those who are the object of repression may become totally alienated from our liberal-democratic heritage, rejecting the values as well as the institutions which purport to embody them. If radical protest is violently suppressed and radical activists more or less permanently incarcerated, it is very likely that constitutional rights of dissent will be denied and that conditions which belie liberal-democratic values will persist. Either way—repres-sion or radical transformation—there will be disruption; while the costs would be differently distributed in each case, they will be widely dif-fused. Most Americans will be touched one way or another. Yet there is a danger that most Americans will acquiesce in a course of political repression without any sense of what will thereby be lost, concerned only that this "threat" be removed.

Originally I suggested that Americans who are firmly committed to our system in its present form had to realize that our political and social institutions are seriously malfunctioning and that those citizens who are troubled by contemporary trends in our society, but who still retain a sense of allegiance, might find civil disobedience a partial means of eliminating the gaps between our ideals and our practices. Now, however, these Americans are faced with the problem of responding to the tactics and demands of a minority which rejects both the status quo and reformist methods of change. For those allegiant citizens who are sensitive to the needs of the deprived and cognizant of the meaning of liberal democracy, the resolution of this problem will be difficult. Our commitment to freedom is not truly tested except when the use of such freedom is not congenial to our predilections. In a sense, the challenge of the New Left is a challenge to America's commitment to liberal democracy. For the committed liberal-democrat, it is important that he try to meet that challenge without sacrificing his principles.

What I want to suggest is that by viewing the radical student and militant black movements as revolutionary and subversive—and therefore to be repressed—we run the risk of transforming our political regime into a regime where liberal-democratic principles would justify minority revolution. This may sound paradoxical since it is generally thought that liberal democracy contains a justification only for majority revolution.

The ideas of Locke and Jefferson on revolution suggest that two conditions must exist to justify such an extreme act: The rulers (1) *undertake consciously to subvert* the liberties of (2) *the people*, i.e., the clear majority of the members of the body politic.[33] The first condition is met only by evidence of continual "abuses," "prevarications," "usurpations," and the like; presumably such evidence will make the people aware that their governors are working against their welfare. This differs from the justification of civil disobedience in two ways. To justify civil disobedience, it is not necessary that a majority feel aggrieved by the treatment they have received from the political regime. Indeed, civil disobedience is important precisely because it is a way out for the dissenting but allegiant individual and minority. Under conditions where even dissenters who would use civil disobedience still find legitimacy in the political system (and perhaps even in the specific officials exercising authority), it is unlikely that the *majority* will consider their governors to be subverting their liberties. Thus, majority disaffection is almost *a priori* excluded from the circumstances which make disobedience civil. Secondly, the conditions justifying civil disobedience require that the minority be prevented from pressing its claims because conventional channels are unavailable or unlikely to bring success. There is no assumption that blocked channels represent any design on the part of the governors to take away the liberties of the dissenting minority; indeed, belief in the general legitimacy of the authorities might imply the opposite assumption. Civil disobedience assumes that conventional channels are open for other persons and groups, and that such channels can be opened up for the minority by civil disobedience (and other forms of nonviolent direct action) or the threat of it. Making an appeal to the public—by using civil disobedience—is based on the assumption that governors will at least be responsive to a broader constituency than the dissident minority itself, that the channels are open for the demands and opinions of a broader constituency to be heard and made effective. Thus, if a civilly disobedient minority can win the support of a significant part of the public (either in terms of numbers or personages), their demands presumably will be met (to some extent). If a situation of sufficient tension is created by nonviolent tactics, even persons who are not especially sympathetic to the demonstrators may press officials to settle the conflict by making concessions. That civil disobedience is sometimes used to pressure government officials directly does not necessarily imply that officials are seen as unresponsive to public (majority) opinions and demands and that an appeal to the public is unlikely to succeed in its ultimate objective. The protesters may assume that public opinion is not *likely* to be mobilized or swayed, or that to do so would consume more resources than the group can afford. Some officials or agencies, e.g., those of the federal government, may be viewed as responsive if dissent can be made visible to them. This may require that other (less responsive) officials be directly pressured. Once this visibility is achieved, the former officials will act so as to circumvent or counteract the actions of unresponsive officials, e.g., on the local level. In any case, the unresponsiveness of officials which makes civil disobedience seem necessary may be seen as deliberate but, at least at the highest levels of government, not as an intent to repress the dissenting minority.

There is a point, however, at which the justifications for majority revolution and minority civil disobedience merge into a justification for minority revolution. A group of dissenters, having found conventional methods unavailing and having engaged in civil disobedience only to be suppressed, may begin to feel that it is more than a question of clogged channels in a basically liberal-democratic system but rather a (conscious) attempt by governors (with or without the majority's support) to prevent them from enjoying rights others already have or to subvert their existing liberties. In other words, they may have good reason to think that they are being excluded, and the fact that the majority of the members of the body politic can participate and think the system democratic and legitimate is irrelevant.[34]

The case of the anti-apartheid dissenters in South Africa is an illustration of this kind of situation. For the white population in South Africa which does not question apartheid, liberal-democratic institutions still provide some semblance of democracy and protection of private liberties. But for natives, "coloreds," and opponents of apartheid, this is not so. The latter might claim that they have the majority of the people behind them, but even if the natives and coloreds were a minority in South Africa, the situation would seem unchanged. If the dissenting minority would be willing to extend freedom to the majority but not vice versa (perhaps it is the majority's representatives who are not willing to do so and their constituents do not care much either way), then the basis for a liberal-democratic justification of minority revolution would seem to exist.

Liberal-democratic thinkers have often recognized the danger of majority tyranny.[35] If the mechanisms which the Framers installed in the federal system to prevent this—checks and balances, a bill of rights backed by an independent judiciary—are not operative with respect to a particular minority, then we have the possibility of a politically disfranchised (in a broad sense) minority which need feel no political obligation because the traditional liberal-democratic bases of political obligation do not exist for them. It is no response to tell such a minority that they can again enjoy democratic rights if they will drop the demands which were the reason for their suppression in the first place. Unless their demands are clearly repugnant to liberal-democratic values, suppression in defense of the polity subverts the values for which it was established. Sometimes those who dissent from the prevailing version of the "good society" (but who are still allegiant to liberal democracy) are told that their demands would change the face of our society in ways that the majority does not prefer (or which a powerful minority considers threatening) and that, therefore, they are not entitled to enjoy liberal-democratic protections. Especially if they employ methods which are thought illegitimate, they may be denied such protections even when they act in legitimate ways. In this case, the minority may have good grounds to believe that the governors of the body politic have a conscious design to subvert their freedom.

The case of the New Left is more difficult. Not only do government officials and a majority of the people repudiate its goals and tactics, they also question its allegiance to liberal democracy. Indeed, many in the New Left have begun to speak and act as if certain traditional liberal-democratic principles were not of importance to them. The New Left's objectives are considered a subversion of our system; moreover critics contend that if the New Left were to succeed in changing American society according to its designs, it would deny freedom to the majority who opposed it. This is possible but by no means certain. To some extent, it would depend upon which groups within the New Left emerged as dominant. The tactics now being employed more frequently interfere with the rights of others. These tactics go beyond civil disobedience but they generally retain some elements of restraint. Perhaps the explanation is that most radical activists have made a tactical decision not to use more extreme tactics now. Yet it seems that most persons who consider themselves a part of this movement have not, at this time, declared (violent) war on the system. There are some who sound as if they had declared war; their version of a successful revolutionary movement is apocalyptic —a violent struggle between the exploited and the guardians and functionaries of the old order. Yet, I think, many of the current objectives of student activists and black militants would, if implemented, not destroy the freedom enjoyed by the majority; where this freedom conflicts with the welfare of minorities now denied the privileges of the majority, it would probably be restricted. The achievement of at least some of the radicals' objectives might aid in meeting the crises which our society now faces. Moreover, these goals are not repugnant to liberal-democratic ideals, such as autonomy, equality and participation. Nonetheless, the New Left is viewed, increasingly, by public officials, political commentators, and the public as threatening, subversive, violent, and destructive of all we value. The reaction of public authorities has been increasingly repressive; there has been more use of police violence, legal harassment of leaders, denial of rights and privileges which are extended to other groups deemed politically acceptable, and infiltration of organizational activities. If carried to greater extremes, this repression tends to put the New Left in the position of the persecuted minority within a system which purports to guarantee liberal-democratic freedoms to all (but those it deems subversive). We run the risk of creating a regime against which our own liberal-democratic principles would justify revolution. This is not to suggest that all tendencies within the New Left are positive or to be viewed optimistically. But a repressive course seems likely to strengthen those tendencies which are intolerant and violent, to create in the New Left a mirror-image of the intolerant and violent side of our own society.

Some commentators have suggested that the virtue of liberal democracy is that it does not define for all time the good society, the substantive goals which a liberal-democratic political system should seek. Rather, it provides a procedure by which goals can be defined for the time being and modified as circumstances and opinions change. There is no orthodoxy in the area of goals. But we have reached a situation (perhaps the potential for this has long been inherent) in which Americans seem to be saying that we *do* have a fixed conception of the good life, and that liberal democracy can be practiced only within the boundaries of this conception. Liberal-democratic values and this substantive conception of the definitively good life seem not to be intrinsically related (historically related, yes). What does this "good society" look like? Much like our present society: Its distribution of resources and power, its predominant values, the goals for which it presently allocates its tremendous resources, its politically nonparticipant character. Moreover the values which have come to encumber our liberal democracy influence crucially the impact of the political system upon the lives of various group within our society. I would contend that the negative reaction to the New Left is more due to the majority's identification of prevailing social and political arrangements with liberal democracy than to conflicts between New Left goals and liberal-democratic values.

It seems an apt metaphor to describe our present condition as arteriosclerosis of the body politic: The gradual accumulation, within the basic political structure, of vested interests in the status quo and of values extrinsic to liberal democracy, which clog the conventional political channels and prevent the transmission of claims which would alter the status quo but would permit the authorities to be responsive to all members of the body politic. Liberal democracy had to be a reality before civil disobedience could come into existence; now what seems the exhaustion of civil disobedience may be an indication that the reality of liberal democracy is fast disappearing.

Notes for Chapter IX

1. The voting studies and studies of authoritarian attitudes are well-known. For the psychological requisites of democratic participation, see Ralph K. White and Ronald Lippitt, *Autocracy and Democracy: An Experimental Inquiry* (New York: Harper, 1960), Chapter 15.

2. I mean this term to apply to such social scientists as Robert A. Dahl (see *Who Governs?* and *A Preface to Democratic Theory*, Ch. 4–5), Joseph A. Schumpeter (see *Capitalism, Socialism, and Democracy*, Ch. 21–22), Bernard Berelson (see *Voting*, Ch. 14), Giovanni Sartori (*Democratic Theory*). Perhaps persons like William Kornhauser (*The Politics of Mass Society*), Seymour M. Lipset (*Political Man*), and David B. Truman (*The Governmental Process*), should also be included. This list is not intended to be exhaustive. These writers have attempted to reformulate democratic theory based on empirical studies in order to make it more descriptive and explanatory of certain contemporary political systems. This is not to say that they all explicitly make the argument I have outlined in the text. However, their conception of democracy has been criticized for being elitist and for implicitly (at least) rejecting classical liberal-democratic values. See Jack Walker, "A Critique of the Elitist Theory of Democracy," *American Political Science Review*, 60 (June, 1966), 285–295. While Dahl ("Further Reflections on the Elitist Theory of Democracy," *American Political Science Review*, 60 (June, 1966), 298) may have a point when he argues that these writers do not fit into one category—elitist theorists of democracy—I think that their theoretic conclusions are value-laden. By suggesting that the democracy of classical theory is unrealizable and that our modern liberal democracies are viable, successful systems, they appear to imply that classical liberal-democratic values should no longer be the normative basepoint from which to judge actual democracies.

3. In this section, lack of involvement in politics refers to conventional politics. The voting studies which "discovered" the uninvolved very largely based their indices of participation on conventional political activities. Thus the "uninvolved" means not only such groups as blacks, other deprived ethnic minorities, and whites in lower SES brackets, but also radicals and students. One could argue that the latter, while not economically deprived, have been excluded from political participation in ways similar to the exclusion of deprived groups.

4. This does not mean that democracy has no relation to certain moral values.

5. Again, this is not to say that political actions have no impact on these basic moral concerns, but rather that they cannot decide such matters or directly create such feelings.

6. I find myself listing many of the characteristics whose absence is commonly ascribed to "mass society." In effect, the erosion of habitual obedience may be seen as a manifestation of a more diffuse anomie, which critics argue is a product of "mass-ness."

7. Joseph A. Schumpeter, *Capitalism, Socialism, and Democracy* (New

York: Harper and Brothers, 1947), Chapter 22.

8. The term is David Easton's; see *A Systems Analysis of Political Life* (New York: John Wiley and Sons, 1965), p. 273.

9. It is only fair to say that I have not seen any writer say this explicitly. John Wahlke ("Public Policy and Representative Government: The Role of the Representative," a report from the Laboratory of Political Research, Department of Political Science, University of Iowa, September, 1967) comes close, however. See pp. 29, 31.

10. I add "liberal-democratic" because such governments may provide certain unique benefits, but this basis of obligation could exist without the government being liberal-democratic.

11. Stokely Carmichael and Charles V. Hamilton, *Black Power: The Politics of Liberation in America* (New York: Vintage Books, 1967), pp. 4–6, 22.

12. The Cold War has probably conditioned many people to believe that implementing the kinds of changes radicals are suggesting would prevent us from maintaining our superiority over the Soviet Union.

13. Recent treatment of some anti-war protesters gives little encouragement to the view that the government would act more tolerably if the movement had a wider base of support.

14. The turn from nonviolence in both the black power and the anti-war movements makes me skeptical that radical activists would have either the commitment or the patience to stick with nonviolent direct action for very long. I doubt many Americans are prepared to endure suffering comparable to Gandhi's *satyagrahis*, though it is possible "nonconfrontational" forms of noncooperation might have mass appeal and not be as difficult to sustain.

15. Admittedly, some participants were demonstrating for their own rights.

16. In practice, it might have been more accurate to view the early civil disobedients as attempting to build or extend a consensus in liberal-democratic values bacause the conflict focused on an area—political and social relations between the white and the black races—where a national consensus never existed.

17. In the early campus sit-ins, students generally attempted to permit passage for those not involved in their demonstrations. While often refusing to leave unless arrested, they permitted ordinary operations to continue, albeit at a somewhat less efficient pace.

18. In *From Race Riot to Sit-In, 1919 and the 1960's* (Garden City: Doubleday and Co., 1966).

19. The ensuing description and contrast draws more from recent radical student actions than from black power activities in the ghettoes, but some of the black militants' actions and intentions are similar to those of the students. For the material on tactics, I relied heavily on reports in the *New York Times* and on *Rights in Conflict*, a report submitted by Daniel Walker (New York: Signet Books, 1968) and *The Politics of Protest*, a report submitted by Jerome H. Skolnick (New York: Ballantine Books, 1969).

20. Or even a matter of first building or extending a value consensus.

21. This is not to imply that all the organizations within the civil rights movement sought national action as a substitute for building a base in local communities. Some saw the need to do the latter, although at times they may have been compelled to use readily available personnel, e.g., college students, who are usually transient members of a community.

22. In some instances, protesters may well have made demands that required the approval of trustees and elected officials, with the intention of calling the latters' authority on the campus into question.

23. Waskow says the politics of disorder has the same goal.

24. There have also been calls for black control of the economic institutions of the ghetto. This can mean collective enterprises or more black entrepreneurs.

25. Perhaps this partly explains why the models of political action which inspire the new activists sometimes seem so foreign to the American tradition.

26. It is difficult to determine from press reports of campus demonstrations whether the demand for amnesty has been made a *sine qua non* of any negotiated settlement by the new radicals. However, a demand for amnesty in itself does not take an act out of the category of civil disobedience. If the demonstrators can make the demand stick, this implies that they are in a position to avoid or prevent their arrest. If so, they are not really risking the consequences of civil disobedience and their act is not civil disobedience. However, merely trying to reduce or obviate the penalty, when arrest is quite feasible for the authorities, is not reason to exclude the act from the category of civil disobedience. Tying the designation of acts as civil disobedience to the motives of the protesters opens up a whole realm of subjectivity; designation may then turn on whether the observer approves the group or its motives. In extending broad freedoms of dissent, liberal democracy, in theory at least, puts no restrictions on who may use them. The test of the right to dissent should not be what the public thinks of the dissenter's beliefs, goals or sincerity. Similarly, if civil disobedience is to be tolerated, it should be tolerated whoever uses it. Of course, the motives of the civil disobedients are relevant when individuals decide to support or oppose the cause in which civil disobedience is being used.

27. According to Raghavan N. Iyer (in *Civil Disobedience*, an occasional paper published by the Center for the Study of Democratic Institutions [Santa Barbara, California, 1966], p. 24), Gandhi did not expect *satyagraha* movements to achieve their goals quickly; moreover, he thought they would have to endure repression if they were to succeed.

28. On the other hand, on some occasions, police have used violence and the threat of violence in a psychologically intimidating manner. While obscenity is a deviation from the discipline of nonviolence, it is not physical violence and seems a weak psychological "weapon" relative to the ability to threaten physical violence convincingly.

29. Judging from the brief accounts in the *New York Times* and in *Up*

Against The Ivy Wall: A History of the Columbia Crisis, by Jerry Avorn and other members of the Columbia Daily Spectator (New York: Atheneum, 1969), I doubt it is possible to say definitely that one side was responsible for the clash.

30. This is not to suggest that all such interactions work to favor the protesters.

31. Violence by activists which was not clearly self-defensive has been sporadic and limited. For example, student demonstrators have damaged campus facilities in a few seemingly unprovoked outbursts of violence. They have broken windows and furniture in campus buildings. These incidents appear to have been perpetrated by a relatively small minority of demonstrators. There have also been a number of bombings and burnings of campus buildings where protest campaigns were in progress. However, in most cases, the perpetrators have not been apprehended, so it is impossible to say that student protesters have been responsible for more than a few of these crimes. The burning of the main library at Indiana University in May, 1969, was, for example, attributed to student protesters, but the arsonist turned out to be unconnected with the campus protesters.

On northern campuses, the seizure of a building by militant black students at Cornell is perhaps the only case in which student protesters openly displayed arms. They claimed that they were fearful of attacks by white students and police and that their action was self-defensive. There have been other reports of students arming themselves, e.g., the black students who occupied Hamilton Hall

during the Columbia protests; however, if the reports are correct, the arms have not been shown publicly. At a few southern black colleges, there have been armed clashes between snipers and police and national guard forces. These appear to be exceptional incidents and probably indicate as much the fear black students have of violent treatment by police as the militancy of the students involved.

Lately, there have been numerous clashes between police and armed Black Panthers. Most of these occurrences have been surrounded by controversy about their origins. Both sides claim self-defense and it is impossible to evaluate the claims with the information available. The Panthers contend that the police generally are trying to eliminate them from the scene.

32. Liberals to the left of the liberal establishment in the Democratic Party would seem to fit in this category.

33. See Locke's *Second Treatise on Civil Government*, § 255, and the Declaration of Independence. Both Locke and Jefferson speak of "the people," but I think interpreting this to mean the majority is a fair gloss, because both argue that it is majority will which must be followed in the body politic.

34. A. C. Ewing, in *The Individual, the State, and World Government* (New York: Macmillan, 1947), discusses the problem of when rebellion is justifiable. He suggests that because the evil effects of initiating violence are incalculable, there is a general duty not to rebel; however, violence cannot be ruled out *a priori*

in all cases. In a polity where "legal means of effecting peaceful change by turning out the government in the next general election" exist, it is more difficult to justify violent methods, but under certain circumstances revolution can be justified under such a government. He makes the crucial criterion whether or not the rebellion is likely to produce less evil than continuation of the existing circumstances. I have couched the argument for revolution in terms of liberal-democratic principles, ignoring the question of balancing evils. Ewing's criteria are important ones for would-be rebels to consider before employing violence, but they are not specific to liberal democracy. For a fuller explanation of Ewing's position, see his book, especially pp. 74–78.

35. One can conceptualize majority tyranny in different ways. Looking at it as actual domination by the majority, as opposed to the majority's representatives and leaders who may or may not be very responsive to their constituents, is not realistic.

SELECTED BOOKS AND ARTICLES

Barker, Sir Ernest. *Principles of Social and Political Theory*. Oxford: Clarendon Press, 1951. 284 p. This is one of the first modern attempts to reconcile civil disobedience with a theory of political obligation.

Bedau, Hugo A. "On Civil Disobedience." *Journal of Philosophy*, 58 (October 12, 1961), 653–665. This article is probably the best early discussion of the characteristics of civil disobedience.

—————, ed. *Civil Disobedience: Theory and Practice*. New York: Pegasus, 1969. This is an anthology of writings on civil disobedience.

Bell, Inge Powell. *CORE and the Strategy of Nonviolence*. New York: Random House, 1968. 214 p. The author emphasizes the use of nonviolent direct action as a means of putting pressure on opponents in civil rights activity.

Bickel, Alexander M. "Civil Rights and Civil Disobedience." *Politics and the Warren Court*. New York: Harper and Row, 1965. Pp. 77–91.

Black, Charles L., Jr. "The Problems of the Compatibility of Civil Disobedience with American Institutions of Government." 43 *Texas Law Review* 492 (March, 1965). This legal commentator attempts to specify the criteria for justifying civil disobedience. He sees it as a form of moral suasion.

Bondurant, Joan V. *Conquest of Violence: The Gandhian Philosophy of Conflict*. Rev. ed. Berkeley: University of California Press, 1965. 271 p. This work is a valuable analysis of the Gandhian philosophy and use of nonviolent direct action.

Broderick, Francis L., and Meier, August, eds. *Negro Protest Thought in the Twentieth Century*. Indianapolis: Bobbs-Merrill, 1965. 444 p. The anthology includes selections from various civil rights spokesmen relating to the use of nonviolent direct action.

Brown, Stuart M. "Civil Disobedience." *Journal of Philosophy*, 58 (October

26, 1961), 669–681. The author takes the position that civil disobedience cannot be legally justified.

Civil Disobedience. Santa Barbara, California: Center for the Study of Democratic Institutions, 1966. Pp. 2–10. This booklet presents selections on civil disobedience and nonviolence by a number of authors.

Cohen, Carl. "Essence and Ethics of Civil Disobedience." *The Nation,* 198 (March 16, 1964), 257–262. The author attempts to define civil disobedience in terms of criteria of legitimacy.

Ewing, A. C. *The Individual, the State, and World Government.* New York: Macmillan, 1947. 322 p. This work includes a discussion of the conditions under which rebellion is legitimate, particularly in a democratic state.

Fishman, Jacob R., and Solomon, Fredric. "The Psychosocial Meaning of Nonviolence in Student Civil Rights Activities." *Psychiatry,* 27 (May, 1964), 91–99.

————. "Youth and Social Action, I: Perspectives on the Student Sit-In Movement." *American Journal of Orthopsychiatry,* 33 (October, 1963), 872–882. These articles are an early exploration of the motivations of civil rights participants, based on interviews with a number of activists.

Fortas, Abe. *Concerning Dissent and Civil Disobedience.* New York: Signet Books, 1968. 64 p. In his discussion of the conditions under which civil disobedience is legitimate, the author places fairly stringent restrictions on its use.

Frankel, Charles. "Is It Ever Right to Break the Law?" *New York Times Magazine* (January 12, 1964), p. 17+. This legal commentator views civil disobedience as an appeal to the majority.

Freund, Paul. "The Civil Rights Movement and the Frontiers of Law." *The Negro American.* Edited by Talcott Parsons and Kenneth B. Clark. Boston: Houghton Mifflin, 1966. Pp. 363–370. Freund's discussion of civil disobedience recognizes that it can raise discretionary questions for the courts; the issue of illegality and punishment is not automatically settled by the nature of civil disobedience.

Gandhi, Mohandas K. *Non-Violent Resistance.* Compiled and edited by Bharatan Kumarappa. New York: Schocken Books, 1961. 404 p.

Green, Thomas Hill. *Lectures on the Principles of Political Obligation.* Reprinted from *Works of Thomas Hill Green.* Vol. II. London: Longmans, Green, 1941. 252 p. Green raises the question whether there can be a right or a duty to disobey the law in a democratic state.

Hook, Sidney. "Neither Blind Obedience Nor Uncivil Disobedience." *New York Times Magazine* (June 5, 1966), pp. 52–53+. The author fears that civil disobedience will set a bad example and may weaken respect for law unless it is carefully controlled.

Keeton, Morris. "The Morality of Civil Disobedience." 43 *Texas Law Review* 507 (March, 1965). The author offers an intensive discussion of "responsible" civil disobedience.

Killian, Lewis, and Grigg, Charles. *Racial Crisis In America*. Englewood Cliffs, New Jersey: Prentice-Hall, 1964. 144 p. This study of the dynamics of biracial committees in southern cities suggests that white members are reluctant to make concessions unless there is a threat to community harmony.

King, Martin Luther. *Stride Toward Freedom*. New York: Ballantine Books, 1958. 190 p. This is an account of the Montgomery bus boycott.

————. *Why We Can't Wait*. New York: Signet Books, 1964. 159 p. This description of the 1963 SCLC campaign in Birmingham includes King's ideas on nonviolent direct action.

Kuper, Leo. *Passive Resistance in South Africa*. New Haven, Connecticut: Yale University Press, 1957. 256 p. This is a sociologist's account of an unsuccessful civil disobedience campaign against apartheid in South Africa during the early 1950's.

Ladd, Everett C. *Negro Political Leadership in the South*. Ithaca, New York: Cornell University Press, 1966. 348 p. In this study of black political leadership in two southern cities, the author comments on the effects of large-scale direct action (or the threat of it) on the ability of black leaders to work effectively.

Lipsky, Michael. "Protest as a Political Resource." *American Political Science Review*, 62 (December, 1968), 1144–1158.

Lynd, Staughton, ed. *Nonviolence in America*. Indianapolis: Bobbs-Merrill, 1966. 535 p.

Marshall, Burke. "The Protest Movement and the Law." 51 *Virginia Law Review* 785 (June, 1965). The former Assistant Attorney General distinguishes civil disobedience from that direct action which can be viewed as "testing" or is done under under the color of federal law.

Matthews, Donald R., and Prothro, James W. *Negroes and the New Southern Politics*. New York: Harcourt, Brace and World, 1966. 551 p. This comprehensive survey of black and white political attitudes and political participation includes data on perceptions of the student sit-ins. The authors are pessimistic that recent increases in black political resources will dramatically affect southern politics.

Peck, James. *Freedom Ride*. New York: Simon and Schuster, 1962. 160 p. A participant in CORE's early activities gives a personal account.

Pitkin, Hanna. "Obligation and Consent." Part I. *American Political Science Review*, 59 (December, 1965), 990–999.

————. "Obligation and Consent." Part II. *American Political Science Review*, 60 (March, 1966), 39–52. These articles are an insightful discussion of these two concepts in liberal-democratic theory.

Plamenatz, J. P. *Consent, Freedom and Political Obligation*. London: Oxford University Press, 1938. 162 p. The author makes an interesting attempt to relate the concepts of consent, political obligation, and representative government.

Prosch, Harry. "Limits to the Moral Claim in Civil Disobedience." *Ethics*, 75 (January, 1965), 103–111. This critique of civil disobedience is rather polemical.

Searles, Ruth, and Williams, J. Allen, Jr. "Negro College Students' Participation in Sit-Ins." *Social Forces*, 40 (March, 1962), 215–220. This is an early survey of black students who participated in the southern civil rights protests.

Sharp, Gene. "Civil Disobedience in a Democracy." *Peace News* (February 22, 1963), 7–10. The author provides an interesting discussion of some of the problems of reconciling civil disobedience with democracy.

————. *Gandhi Wields the Weapon of Moral Power*. Ahmedabad: Navajivan Publishing House, 1960. 316 p. The author, who is himself a pacifist, gives an account of Gandhi's early civil disobedience campaigns.

Shridharani, Krishnalal J. *War Without Violence*. Bombay: Bharatiya Vidya Bhavan, 1962. 299 p. The author, who accompanied Gandhi on the Salt Satyagraha, describes and briefly analyzes the techniques and actual use of nonviolent direct action.

Spitz, David. "Democracy and the Problem of Civil Disobedience." *American Political Science Review*, 48 (June, 1954), 386–403. This article is an early attempt to reconcile civil disobedience with majority rule in a democracy.

Taylor, William L. "Civil Disobedience: Some Observations on the Strategies of Protest." *Legal Aspects of the Civil Rights Movement*. Edited by Donald B. King and Charles W. Quick. Detroit, Michigan: Wayne State University Press, 1965. Pp. 227–235. The author excludes "testing" from the purview of civil disobedience in this critical analysis of civil disobedience from a legal point of view.

Thoreau, Henry David. "Civil Disobedience." *Thoreau: People, Principles, and Politics*. Edited by Milton Meltzer. New York: Hill and Wang, 1963. Pp. 35–58.

Tussman, Joseph. *Obligation and the Body Politic*. New York: Oxford University Press, 1960. 144 p. The author's insightful discussion explores the implications of membership in a democratic body politic and the dilemmas of reconciling individual autonomy and social coordination.

Von Eschen, Don; Kirk, Jerome; and Pinard, Maurice. "The Conditions of

Direct Action in a Democratic Society." *The Western Political Quarterly*, 22 (June, 1969), 309–325. Using empirical data, the authors attempt to analyze the dynamics of nonviolent direct action.

Walzer, Michael. "The Obligation to Disobey." *Political Theory and Social Change*. Edited by David Spitz. New York: Atherton Press, 1967. Pp. 185–202. The author offers an intriguing argument supporting a duty, rather than a right, to disobey the law. He weighs obligation to certain voluntary associations against obligation to the state.

Waskow, Arthur I. *From Race Riot to Sit-in: 1919 and the 1960's*. Garden City, New York: Doubleday, 1966. 380 p. The author includes an analysis of direct action in the 1960's.

Wasserstrom, Richard. "Disobeying the Law." *Journal of Philosophy*, 58 (October 12, 1961), 641–653. The author discusses the problem of when disobedience to law is justifiable.

Wilson, James Q. "The Strategy of Protest: Problems of Negro Civic Action." *Journal of Conflict Resolution*, 5 (September, 1961), 291–303. This is an interesting discussion of mass protest action as a political resource.

Wyzanski, Charles W., Jr. "On Civil Disobedience." *Atlantic Monthly*, 221 (February, 1968), 58–60. A distinguished jurist makes some unsympathetic comments on civil disobedience.

Zinn, Howard. *Disobedience and Democracy: Nine Fallacies on Law and Order*. New York: Vintage Books, 1968. 124 p. The author offers a point-by-point rebuttal of Fortas's book, taking a much more favorable view of civil disobedience.

INDEX

A

Abernathy, Ralph, 201
Agreement of the People, 13–14
Ahimsa, 150–51
Alabama Christian Movement for
     Human Rights, 169, 176
Allen, John W., 12
*American Business and Public
     Policy* of Bauer, Pool,
     and Dexter, 234–35

B

Barker, Ernest

on political obligation, 77–82
Bay, Christian, 110, 113, 116,
     119, 292
Beckett, Thomas, 7
Bedau, Hugo, 110, 120, 146*n.,*
     147*n.*
Bentham, Jeremy, 24–25, 50
Bickel, Alexander, 119, 125
Black leadership
     attitudes toward protest dem-
     onstrations, 25–54
"Black Power", 221–22
Bodin, Jean, 11
Bondurant, Joan V., 152–53,
     155, 158, 185